Ned Snell
with revisions by Bob Temple

SAMS Teach Yourself the Internet in 24 Hours

2002 EDITION

06723 22145 8227 24

Sams Teach Yourself the Internet in 24 Hours, 2002 Edition

International Standard Book Number: 0-672-32214-5

Library of Congress Catalog Card Number: 2001088016

Printed in the United States of America

First Printing: August 2001

03 02 01 4 3 2 1

Trademarks

All terms mentioned in this book that are known to be trademarks or service marks have been appropriately capitalized. Sams Publishing cannot attest to the accuracy of this information. Use of a term in this book should not be regarded as affecting the validity of any trademark or service mark.

Warning and Disclaimer

Every effort has been made to make this book as complete and as accurate as possible, but no warranty or fitness is implied. The information provided is on an "as is" basis. The author and the publisher shall have neither liability nor responsibility to any person or entity with respect to any loss or damages arising from the information contained in this book.

Acquisitions Editor
Betsy Brown

Development Editor
Heather Goodell

Managing Editor
Charlotte Clapp

Project Editor
Leah Kirkpatrick

Copy Editor
Michael Dietsch

Indexer
Eric Schroeder

Proofreader
Paula Lowell

Technical Editor
Galen Grimes

Team Coordinator
Amy Patton

Interior Designer
Gary Adair

Cover Designer
Aren Howell

Production
Mark Walchle

Contents at a Glance

Table of Contents

PART IV Needles in a VERY Big Haystack 233

About the Authors

Ned Snell has been making technology make sense since 1986, when he began writing beginner's documentation for one of the world's largest software companies. After writing manuals and training materials for several major technology companies, Snell switched sides and became a computer journalist, serving as a writer and editor for two national magazines, *Edge* and *Art & Design News*.

A freelance writer since 1991, Snell has written 12 computer books and hundreds of articles, and is the courseware critic for *Inside Technology Training* magazine. Between books, Snell works as a professional actor in regional theater, commercials, and industrial films.

Bob Temple is the owner and president of Red Line Editorial, Inc., an editorial services and content services provider. He has written five other books on Internet-related topics, including three others for Sams Publishing. In addition, he is the author of 18 children's non-fiction books.

Dedication

For my family.

Acknowledgments

Ned Snell

I sat down and wrote a book very much like this one, but that's not the book you're holding.

The book you're holding is a better book, in which my work has been guided and shaped by the good folks at Sams Publishing.

If you like this book, you owe them thanks, as I do.

Bob Temple

I would like to thank Brenda Haugen for the research assistance she provided on this project, as she has on so many others.

Tell Us What You Think!

As the reader of this book, *you* are our most important critic and commentator. We value your opinion and want to know what we're doing right, what we could do better, what areas you would like to see us publish in, and any other words of wisdom you're willing to pass our way.

You can email or write me directly to let me know what you did or didn't like about this book—as well as what we can do to make our books stronger.

Please note that I cannot help you with technical problems related to the topic of this book, and that due to the high volume of mail I receive, I might not be able to reply to every message.

When you write, please be sure to include this book's title and author as well as your name and phone or fax number. I will carefully review your comments and share them with the author and editors who worked on the book.

E-mail: `consumer@samspublishing.com`

Mail: Mark Taber
Assoicate Publisher
Sams Publishing
201 W. 103rd Street
Indianapolis, IN 46290 USA

Introduction

Hello? *Hellooooo?* Is anybody there? Nobody reads introductions. I don't know why I bother.

Oh well, looks like it's just you and me. So welcome to *Sams Teach Yourself the Internet in 24 Hours*, the book that gets you into and all around the Internet in a single day's worth of easy lessons. Each of the 24 chapters in this book is called an "Hour," and is designed to endow you with new Internet skills in one hour or less. (That means you and I can spend only a few minutes here in the Intro and keep on schedule.)

Before we get started, it has come to my attention that a few among the more than 100,000 readers of previous editions of this book were involved in mysterious accidents. For example, a florist in Weehauken arranged and delivered a bouquet of cellophane wrapped in roses, and a surgeon in Phoenix transplanted an appendix. An investigation revealed that these readers suffered sleep deprivation from taking the book's title too literally; they went cover-to-cover in a single, non-stop, 24-hour period. Please spread your time with this book across multiple sessions *totaling* 24 hours, and keep your arms and legs inside the book at all times. Thank you.

Oops, one more thing. To save time and paper, and to help you begin learning the lingo, I may refer to the Internet here and there as "the Net," with a capital N. You'll know what I mean.

Who I Wrote This Thing For

That settled, let me tell you what you're in for. I've designed this book for people who

- Are absolutely new to the Internet
- Want a quick, easy, commonsense way to learn how to use it
- Don't appreciate being treated like an imbecile

(By the way, being new to the Internet doesn't mean you're an idiot or dummy. You just have other priorities. Good for you.)

This book is *system neutral*, which is another way of saying you can use this book no matter what kind of computer you have. As you'll see, using the Internet is pretty much the same no matter what computer you access it from. Where necessary, such as in discussing the hardware you need to connect to the Internet, I do discuss both PC and Macintosh versions.

You do not need to know a thing about the Internet, computer networks, or any of that stuff to get started with this book. However, you do need to know your way around your own computer. With a basic, everyday ability to operate the type of computer from which you will use the Internet, you're ready to begin. I'll take you the rest of the way.

Don't have a computer yet? In Hour 2, "What Hardware and Software Do You Need?" I'll help you choose one that's properly equipped for the Net.

Overwhelmingly, most people on the Internet use either of two programs for most of their Internet activities: Microsoft's Internet Explorer or Netscape.

So it's just common sense that examples in this book showing step-by-step techniques for some activities show the steps you would use in the latest versions (at this writing) of these "Big Two" programs: Internet Explorer 6 and Netscape Navigator 6.

Note, however, that there's plenty in this book for you even if you don't use one of these programs. Most of the instructions in this book are not specific to one program, but work with most Internet programs. And because both of these Big Two programs are free, you'll also learn in this book how to get one for free, if you want to switch over.

How This Book Is Organized

This book is divided into six Parts, each four "Hours" long:

- **Part I, "Getting Started,"** introduces you to the Net and the many different things you can do there, and shows how to get yourself and your computer set up for it.
- **Part II, "Talking to the World,"** takes you through online communications, including email, chat, instant messages, newsgroups, and mailing lists. It's all the ways you interact with others online.
- **Part III, "Software for Your Journey,"** shows you how to get the latest versions of browsers, and how they work. We also cover America Online, and talk about add-on programs you'll use online.
- **Part IV, "Needles in a VERY Big Haystack,"** is all about finding stuff online. Whether you're looking for programs, people, sites, or other types of data, we cover it here.
- **Part V, "Making the Web Part of Your Life,"** is about how the Web fits in with you, or at least how it can. We include keeping the Web safe for families, buying and selling, creating pages, and using wireless technologies.

- **Part VI, "Integrating the Web into Your Life,"** gives you 10 ideas for how the Web can change your business life, 10 more for your personal life, 10 for your family life, and 10 for your school life.

As you can see, the Parts move logically from setting up for the Net to using it, and from easy stuff to not-so-easy stuff. So no peeking ahead to see how it ends.

After Hour 24, you'll discover an appendix, "Fun Web Sites to Visit," which offers up an easy-to-use directory of Web pages I think you might enjoy visiting. There is also an appendix covering advanced features like FTP, and another on online privacy issues.

Finally, there's a glossary, although I must point out that I use very, very little technical terminology, and I explain it very well when I do. So you'll probably never need the glossary. But just in case you want a glossary, you have one.

Things You Would Probably Figure Out by Yourself

There's a long tradition in computer books of using the introduction to explain the little tip boxes and other page elements that are absolutely self-explanatory to any reader over the age of six. Just call me "Keeper of the Flame."

Instructions, Tips, and Terms

Here and there, I use step-by-step instructions to show you exactly how to do something. I will always explain how to do that thing in the text that precedes the steps, so feel free to skip 'em when you want to. However, anytime you feel like you don't completely understand something, do the steps, and you'll probably get the picture before you're done. Sometimes we learn only by doing.

I call attention to important new terms by tagging them with a New Term icon. It won't happen often, but when it does, it'll help you remember the terms that will help you learn the Internet.

You'll also see three different kinds of handy advice set off in boxes:

A Tip box points out a faster, easier way to do something, or a cooler way. These boxes are completely optional.

A Note box pops out an important consideration or interesting tidbit related to the topic at hand. They're optional, too, but always worth reading. (Otherwise, I wouldn't interrupt.)

A Caution box alerts you to actions and situations where something bad could happen, like accidentally deleting an important file. Beause there's very little you can do on the Net that's in any way dangerous, you'll see very few Cautions. So when you see 'em, take 'em seriously.

Q&A

At the end of every hour, there's a fast, fun Q&A (Question & Answer) session that delves into a few common questions related to the hour you've just read. Again, the Q&A is optional, but it's a great place to learn *just a little more* about the topic at hand before moving on.

One More Thing...

Actually, no more things. Start the clock, and hit Hour 1. Twenty-four working hours from now, you'll know the Net inside out.

Thanks for spending a day with me.

PART I

Getting Started

Hour

Hour 1

What Is the Internet and What Can You Do There?

You probably think you already know what the Internet is. And you're probably 90 percent right, for all practical purposes. But by developing just a little better understanding of what the Net's all about, you'll find learning to use it much easier.

You don't need to know exactly how the Net works to use it, any more than you need to know the mechanics of an engine to drive. This hour is *not* about the tiny, techie details of how the Net works. Rather, this hour is designed to give you some helpful background—and perhaps dispel a few myths and misconceptions—so you can jump confidently into the stuff coming up in later hours.

If some of the information in this chapter seems a little, shall we say, *elementary*, I'm sorry. But it's a good idea to have a basic understanding of the Internet before you jump headlong into it. So if I cover some things that you already know, well, then you're ahead of the game!

At the end of the hour, you'll be able to answer the following questions:

- What *exactly* is the Internet?
- Where did the Internet come from, and where is it going?
- What are clients and servers, and how do they determine what you can do on the Net?
- What types of activities can you perform on the Net, given the right hardware and software?

Understanding the Net (Easy Version)

No doubt you've heard of a *computer network*, a group of computers that are wired together so that they can communicate with one another. When computers are hooked together in a network, users of those computers can send each other messages and share computer files and programs.

Computer networks today can be as small as two PCs hooked together in an office. They can be as big as thousands of computers of all different types spread all over the world and connected to one another not just by wires, but through telephone lines and even through the air via satellite.

To build a really big network, you build lots of little networks and then hook the networks to each other, creating an *internetwork*. That's all the Internet really is: the world's largest internetwork (hence its name). In homes, businesses, schools, and government offices all over the world, millions of computers of all different types—PCs, Macintoshes, big corporate mainframes, and others—are connected together in networks, and those networks are connected to one another to form the Internet. Because everything's connected, any computer on the Internet can communicate with any other computer on the Internet (see Figure 1.1).

A Little History Lesson

The successful launch of Sputnik by the Soviets in 1957 may have triggered the space race, but it also helped bring about the Internet (although somewhat indirectly). In part because of Sputnik, the Advanced Research Projects Agency (ARPA) was formed as part of the U.S. Department of Defense, also in 1957.

Among other things, ARPA created research centers at a number of universities across the country. It soon became clear that these research centers needed to be able to communicate with each other through some type of infrastructure. The first four sites to be connected were at the University of California-Los Angeles (UCLA), the Stanford Research Institute, the University of California-Santa Barbara (UCSB), and the University of Utah.

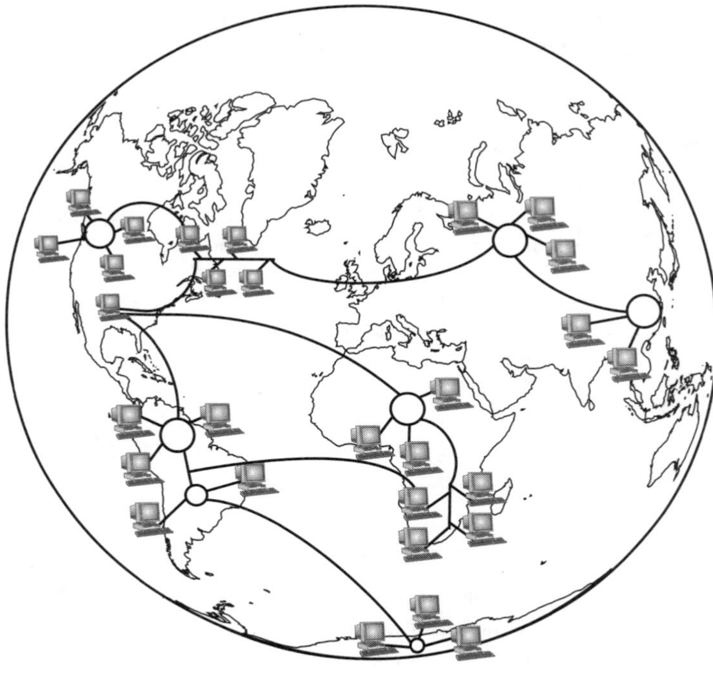

FIGURE 1.1
The Internet is a global internetwork, a huge collection of computers and networks interconnected so they can exchange information.

Because this first network was military-oriented, the distribution of information through it was highly secretive. A system of splitting data into tiny "packets" that took different routes to the same destination was developed to make it more difficult to "eavesdrop" on these transmissions. It is this method of "packet switching" that allows the Internet to function as it does today: Large numbers of computers can go down, and data can still be transferred.

By 1969, new research into networking was being conducted. Standard systems of networking were needed in order for computers to be able to communicate with each other. Over time a system known as TCP/IP was developed; it became the standard protocol for internetworking in 1982.

NEW TERM **TCP/IP.** An abbreviation for the Internet's fundamental communications system. It stands for *Transmission Control Protocol/Internet Protocol*, but you don't need to know that unless you think it will impress your friends. (Pronounce it "tee see pee eye pee," and say it real fast.)

Because all these internetworks communicated in the same way, they could communicate with one another, too. The government, defense contractors, and scientists often needed to communicate with one another and share information, so they hooked all of their computers and networks into one big TCP/IP internetwork. And that fat internetwork was the infant Internet.

When you use a computer that's connected to the Internet, you can communicate with any other computer on the Internet.

But that doesn't mean you can access *everything* that's stored on the other computers. Obviously, the government, university, and corporate computers on the Net have the capability to make certain kinds of information on their computers accessible through the Internet, and to restrict access to other information so that only authorized people can see it.

Similarly, when you're on the Net, any other computer on the Net can communicate with yours. However, that does not mean that someone can reach through the Net into your computer and steal your résumé and recipes.

What It Became

The first great thing about the Internet's design is that it's open to all types of computers. Virtually any computer—from a palmtop PC to a supercomputer—can be equipped with TCP/IP so it can get on the Net. And even when a computer doesn't use TCP/IP, it can access information on the Net using other technologies, "back doors" to the Net, so to speak.

The other important thing about the Net is that it allows the use of a wide range of *communications media*—ways computers can communicate. The "wires" that interconnect the millions of computers on the Internet include the wires that hook together the small networks in offices, private data lines, local telephone lines, national telephone networks (which carry signals via wire, microwave, and satellite), and international telephone carriers.

It is this wide range of hardware and communications options, and the universal availability of TCP/IP, that has enabled the Internet to grow so large so quickly. That's also why you can get online from your home or office, right through the same telephone line you use to call out for pizza. Heck, you can even get online from the neighborhood park using wireless technology. It's a crazy world.

NEW TERM **Online/Offline.** When your computer has a live, open connection to the Internet that you can use to do something, you and your computer are said to be *online*. When the Internet connection is closed, you're *offline*.

Making the Net Work: Clients and Servers

The key to doing anything on the Net is understanding two little words: "client" and "server." Figure 1.2 illustrates the relationship between clients and servers.

Most of the information you will access through the Internet is stored on computers called *servers*. A server can be any type of computer; what makes it a server is the role it plays: It stores information for use by clients.

A client is a computer—or, more accurately, a particular computer program—that knows how to communicate with a particular type of server to use the information stored on that server (or to put information there). For example, when you surf the Web, you use a client program called a Web browser to communicate with a computer where Web pages are stored—a Web server.

NEW TERM **Web browser.** A program that gives a computer the capability to communicate with Web servers and display the information stored there. You'll learn much more about Web browsers and other client programs as your 24 hours tick by.

In general, each type of Internet activity involves a different type of client and server: To use the Web, you need a Web client program to communicate with Web servers. To use email, you need an email client program to communicate with email servers.

This client/server business shows what the Internet really is—just a communications medium, a virtual wire through which computers communicate. It's the different kinds of clients and servers—not the Net itself—that enable you to perform various activities. And because new kinds of clients and servers can be invented, new types of activities can be added to the Internet at any time.

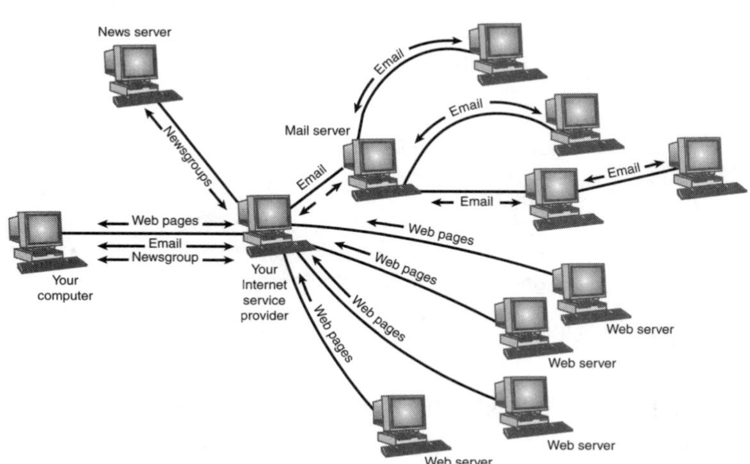

FIGURE 1.2
From your computer, you use a set of client programs, each of which accesses a different type of server computer on the Net.

What Can You Do Through the Net?

I've known people who have gone out and bought a PC, signed up for an Internet account, and then called me to say, "Okay, so I'm on the Internet. Now what am I supposed to do there?"

That's backward. I think the marketers and the press have pushed so hard that some folks simply think they *must* be on the Net, without knowing why, sort of the way everybody thinks they need a cell phone. But unless there's something on the Net you want or need to use, you don't need the Net. You shouldn't buy a rice steamer unless you like rice. You don't need a cell phone if you never leave the house. Don't let Madison Avenue and Microsoft push you around.

So here's a good place to get a feel for what you can actually do on the Net. If nothing here looks like something you want to do, please give this book to a friend or to your local library. You can check out the Net again in a year or two, to see whether it offers anything new.

A great place to try out the Internet without having to spend a bunch of money up front is your local library. Usually, you can get online for free there, and see what's available.

Browse the Web

It's very likely that your interest in the Internet was sparked by the World Wide Web, even if you don't know it. When you see news stories about the Internet showing someone looking at a cool, colorful screen full of things to see and do, that person is looking at the World Wide Web, most commonly referred to as "the Web" or occasionally as "WWW."

The term "the Web" is used so often by the media to describe and illustrate the Internet, many folks think the Web *is* the Internet. But it's not; it's just a part of the Net, or rather one of many Internet-based activities. The Web gets the most attention because it's the fastest-growing, easiest-to-use part of the Net.

All those funky-looking Internet addresses you see in ads today—`www.pepsi.com` and so forth—are the addresses you need to visit those companies on the Web. With an Internet connection and a Web browser on your computer, you can type an address to visit a particular Web site and read the Web pages stored there. (Figure 1.3 shows a Web page, viewed through a Web browser.)

New Term **Web site** and **Web page.** These terms are used flexibly, but, in general, a Web site is a particular Web server, or a part of a Web server, where a collection of Web pages about a particular organization or subject is stored.

When you use your Web browser to contact a Web site, the information on the server is displayed on your computer screen. The particular screenful of information you view is described as one Web page.

For example, the site shown in Figure 1.3 is one Web page from `www.pepsi.com`. All the pages that Pepsi has put up for you to see make up Pepsi's Web site.

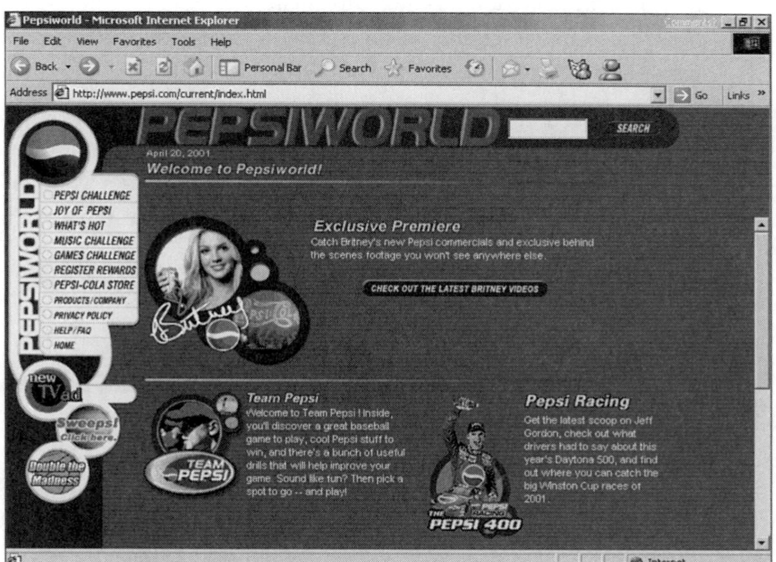

Figure 1.3
Seen through a Web browser, a Web page is a file of information stored on a Web server.

By browsing the Web, you can do a staggering number of different things, including all the activities described in the following sections—and much, much more. The last section of this book, Hours 21–24, outlines a number of ways the Internet can change your life.

Visit Companies, Governments, Museums, Schools...

Just about any large organization has its own Web site these days. Many smaller organizations have their own sites, too, or are covered in pages stored on others' sites. You can visit these sites to learn more about products you want to buy, school or government policies, and much more.

For example, I belong to an HMO for medical coverage. I can visit my HMO's Web site to find and choose a new doctor, review policy restrictions, and much more. I can do this any day, any time, without waiting on hold for the "next available operator."

Just as easily, I can check out tax rules or order forms on the Internal Revenue Service Web site. Or view paintings in museums all over the world. Or find out when the next Parent's Night is at the local elementary school.

Read the News

CNN has its own Web site (see Figure 1.4), as do the *New York Times*, the *Wall Street Journal*, and dozens of other media outlets, ranging from major print magazines and fly-by-night rags spreading rumors, to small sites featuring news about any imaginable topic. You'll also find a number of great news sources that have no print or broadcast counterpart—they're exclusive to the Web.

Whatever kind of news you dig, you can find it on the Web. And often, the news online is more up-to-the-minute than any print counterpart because unlike broadcast news, you can look at it any time you find convenient. Best of all, after you read a news story on the Web, no one ever says, "Thanks for that report, Carla. What a terrible tragedy."

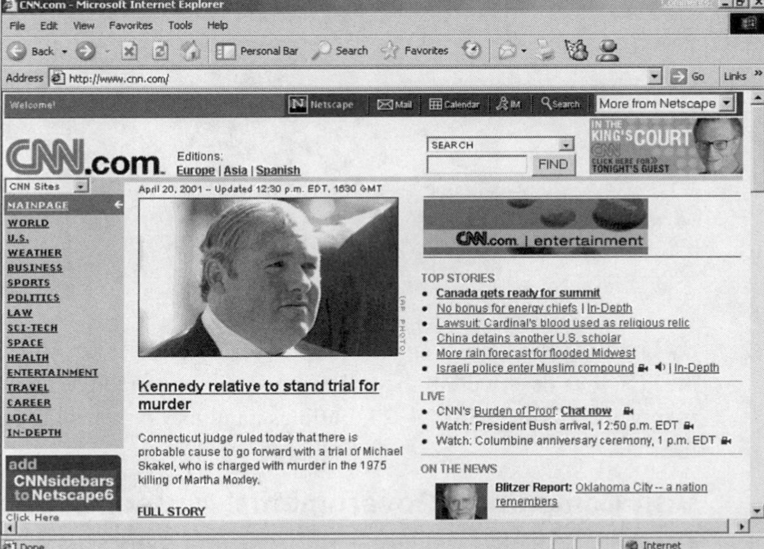

FIGURE 1.4
CNN is among the up-to-the-minute news sources available on the Web.

Explore Libraries

Increasingly, libraries large and small are making their catalogs available online. That means I can find out which of the dozen libraries I use has the book I need, without spending a day driving to each. Some libraries even let you borrow online; you choose a book from the catalog of a library across the state, and in a few days you can pick it up at a library closer to you, or right from your mailbox.

Often, entire collections of works, scholarly papers, entire texts of books, research works, and more are available through libraries online.

Read

Books are published on the Web, including classics (Shakespeare, Dickens) and new works. You can read them right on your screen, or print them out to read later on the bus. (*Please* don't read while you drive. I *hate* that.) The Web has even initiated its own kind of literature, *collaborative fiction*, in which visitors to a Web site can read—and contribute to—a story in progress.

Get Software

Because computer software can travel through the Internet, you can actually get software right through the Web and use it on your PC. Some of the software is free; some isn't. But it's all there, whenever you need it—no box, no disc, no pushy guy at the electronics store saying, "Ya want a cell phone with that? Huh? C'mon!"

Shop

One of the fastest-growing, and perhaps most controversial, Web activities is shopping (see Figure 1.5). Right on the Web, you can browse an online catalog, choose merchandise, type in a credit card number and shipping address, and receive your merchandise in a few days, postage paid. Besides merchandise, you can buy just about anything else on the Web: stocks, legal services, you name it. Everything but surgery, and I'm sure that's only a matter of time. One of the hottest trends in online shopping continues to be the online auction house, a Web site where you can bid on all kinds of items, new and old, from odds and ends to *objets d'art*.

The controversy arises from the fact that sending your credit card number and other private information through the Internet exposes you to abuse of that information by anyone clever enough to cull it from the din of Web traffic. But that risk factor is rapidly shrinking as the Web develops improved security. (For more information about Web security, check out Appendix C, "Protecting Your Privacy (and Other Security Stuff).") And while shopping from your PC, you can't get mugged in the mall parking lot.

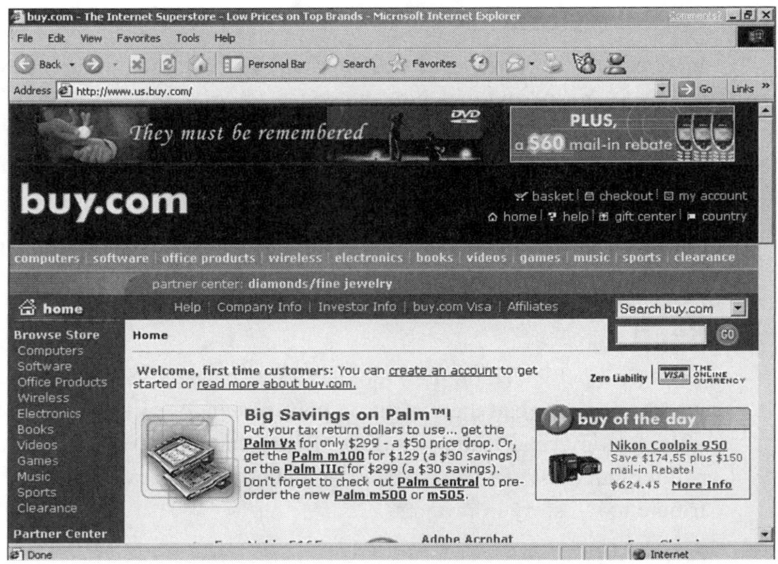

FIGURE 1.5
Shopping may be the fastest-growing online activity.

Watch TV and Listen to CD-Quality Music and Radio Broadcasts

Through your Internet connection, you can actually watch live TV broadcasts and listen to radio programs. The sound and picture quality won't be as good as you get from a real TV or radio (unless you have a "broadband" Internet connection—see Hour 3, "Getting Connected to the Internet"). But the Net gives you access to programs you can't get on your own TV or radio, such as shows not offered in your area or special programs broadcast only to the Internet. With music, however, there's no compromise. Right from the Internet, you can copy high-quality music files that you can listen to anytime, even when you're not on the Internet.

> You can not only listen to CD-quality music online, but also buy it by downloading it to your computer and playing it there, or copying it to a portable player. See Hour 12, "Plug-in and Add-on Programs."

Play Games, Get a College Degree, Waste Time…

Have I left anything out? There's too much on the Web to cover succinctly. But I hope you get the idea. The Web is where it's at. In fact, there are many folks on the Internet who use the Web and nothing else to get and disperse information. But those folks are missing out.… Read on.

1

Oooops. There's one more thing you can do on the Web: *publish*. Just as you can access any Web server, you can publish your own Web pages on a Web server, so that anyone on the Internet with a Web browser can read them.

You can publish Web pages to promote your business or cause, to tell others about a project or hobby that's your passion, or just to let the world know you're you. You'll learn how in Hour 19, "Creating Web Pages and Multimedia Messages."

Exchange Messages

Email, in case you didn't know, is a message sent as an electronic file from one computer to another. Using Internet email, you can type a message on your computer and send it to anyone else on the Internet (see Figure 1.6).

Each user on the Internet has a unique email address; if your email address is `suzyq@netknow.com`, you're the only person in the world with that email address. (Isn't that nice?) So if anyone, anywhere in the world, sends a message to that address, it reaches you and you alone. As mentioned earlier, to use email, you need an email client program, which interacts with the email servers that store and send email around the world.

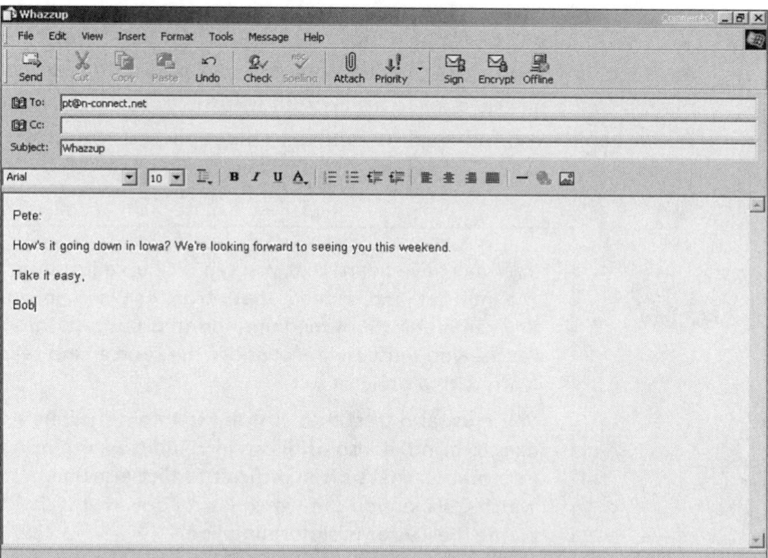

FIGURE 1.6
Email is a great way to keep in contact with people, especially those who live far away.

Email is great for simple messages, but these days, it can do more. You can attach computer files to email messages to send them to others, broadcast a message to two or a hundred recipients at once, and even create cool, colorful messages with graphics and sound.

Most email is sent and received through a program called an email client. But some folks send and receive email directly from a Web page, using their Web browsers. Still others can send and receive Internet email through their digital cell phones, pagers, and palmtop computers. You'll learn how to use all kinds of email in this book.

Have a Discussion

Using your email program, you can join *mailing lists* related to topics that interest you. Members of a mailing list automatically receive news and other information—in the form of email messages—related to the list's topic. Often, members can send their own news and comments to the list, and those messages are passed on to all members.

One of the Internet's principal discussion venues is the *newsgroup*, a sort of public bulletin board. There are thousands of newsgroups, each centering on a particular topic—everything from music to politics, from addiction recovery to TV shows.

Visitors to a newsgroup post messages that any other visitor can read. When reading a message, any visitor can quickly compose and post a reply to that message, to add information to the message, or to argue with it (usually to argue—you know how folks are). As the replies are followed by replies to the replies, a sort of free-form discussion evolves.

You may have heard that you can pick up a lot of unreliable information on the Internet, and, indeed, that's true. As when absorbing information from any communications medium—print, broadcast, Internet, water cooler, back fence—you must always consider the source, and take much of what you learn with a grain of salt.

You must also trust that, just as the Internet offers a forum to nutballs with axes to grind, it also offers an incredible wealth of authoritative, accurate information that's often difficult to find elsewhere. It's just like TV: You can watch CNN, or you can watch *Hard Copy*. If you choose the latter, you can't blame the TV for misinforming you.

Chat

1

Exchanging messages through email and newsgroups is great, but it's not very interactive. You type a message, send it, and wait hours or days for a reply. Sometimes, you want to communicate in a more immediate, interactive, "live" way. That's where *Internet Relay Chat*—a.k.a. "IRC" or just "Chat"—comes in.

Using chat client programs, folks from all over the world contact chat servers and join one another in live discussions. Each discussion takes place in a separate chat "room" or "channel" reserved for discussion of a particular topic. The discussion is carried out through a series of typed messages; each participant types his or her contributions, and anything anyone in the room types shows up on the screen of everyone else in the room.

> In addition to chat, there are other ways to have a live conversation over the Internet. As you'll learn in Hour 12, you can hold voice and video conferences through the Internet, wherein you can see and hear your partners, and they can see and hear you.
>
> You can also have live text and voice chats through any of several different "instant messaging" programs that enable you to not only chat, but also find out which of your friends are currently online and up for a gab session. You'll learn about instant messaging in Hour 6, "Chatting and Instant Messaging."

Run Programs on Other Computers

Not everything on the Internet sits on a Web server, email server, news server, or chat server. There are other kinds of computers and servers connected to the Net—ones you can use, if you know how, through an Internet technology called Telnet. When you use a distant computer through Telnet, you can run programs on it and access its data as if you were there.

There's so much on Web and news servers these days that you may never want or need to journey beyond them. But for the adventurous, Telnet offers access to information you can't get any other way. In Appendix B, "Tools for the Serious User: FTP and Telnet," you'll discover Telnet and FTP, two powerful tools for exploiting the Net beyond the confines of the Web, email, and newsgroups.

Summary

The Internet is a huge, and growing, internetwork that nobody really planned but that happened anyway. Your job is not really to understand it, but to enjoy it and to use it in whatever way you find valuable or entertaining.

The value and entertainment are stored all over the world on a vast array of servers; to tap the benefits of the Net, you deploy a family of client programs that know how to talk to the servers. In a way, most of this book is really about choosing and using client programs to make the most of the Internet's servers.

Q&A

Q If the Net "just happened," who's in charge? What keeps it going?

A That's one of the really neat things about the Internet: Nobody's in charge. (Microsoft, Netscape, and America Online *want* to be in charge, but that's different.) There are volunteer committees that handle such things as making sure every computer gets its own, unique Internet ID (which is essential to the workings of the Net) and approving the *standards* for such things as the way Web browsers communicate with Web servers. But nobody really controls the Internet, and nobody owns it.

It's the standards that keep the Internet going. The Internet is made up of privately owned computers and networking equipment whose owners have put them on the Net for their own reasons. But because that hardware is part of the Net and obeys its standards, you get to use it, too. It's really a big, fat co-op, an amazing example of how independent parties collaborating for their own self-interest can inadvertently create a public good.

As you'll learn in Hour 3, you generally pay a subscription fee to an Internet provider in order to use the Internet, but that fee covers the provider's costs (plus profit) in maintaining its service. You're not paying "The Internet" a dime, because there's no actual organization to collect your money. In principle (if not always in practice), the Internet is free.

Q You just mentioned America Online. Isn't that the same thing as the Internet?

A No and yes. As you'll learn in Hour 3, America Online (AOL) is a commercial online service. It provides its subscribers with a range of information and services that are not on the Internet, and it also provides those subscribers with access to the Internet, just like any other Internet provider. Millions of folks use AOL, but the majority of Internet citizens use other Internet services. If you're one of the many who has signed up for AOL or will be, you'll find lots of useful information in this book.

Q I have this funny rash on my elbow. Is it psoriasis?

A Stick to the subject. Or, better yet, learn to search for information on the Web (as you will in Part IV, "Needles in a VERY Big Haystack"), and you can find out everything you ever wanted to know about rashes.

In the meantime, dab on some cortisone cream, don't walk on it for a few days, and call me if it gets worse.

HOUR 2

What Hardware and Software Do You Need?

Got a computer made within the last 10 years? Then odds are you can get it onto the Internet. The power of your hardware doesn't have that much to do with whether you can get *on* the Net. But it has everything to do with what you can *do* there.

In this hour, you'll discover the hardware required to use the Internet and explore the available options and the pros and cons of each. After you've settled on a computer, you'll need to know which client programs and other software your Net travels will demand.

At the end of the hour, you'll be able to answer the following questions:

- What kinds of computers can I use to surf the Net, and how should they be equipped?
- How fast of a modem do I need?
- What's an Internet appliance, and should I consider one?

- What's "WebTV" and how is it different from surfing the Net through a computer?
- What software do I need to get started, and where can I get it?

Modems—Wherein the *Lack* of Speed Kills

There are ways to connect to the Internet without a modem, which you'll discover more fully in Hour 3, "Getting Connected to the Internet." But odds are that you will start out with a modem and phone line for your Internet connection, so you must consider the capabilities of your modem in choosing or upgrading your computer for Internet access.

NEW TERM **Modem.** A modem is a device that enables two computers to communicate with one another through phone lines. Using a modem (installed inside, or connected to, your computer), you can communicate through a regular phone line with the modem at your Internet provider. That's the main way (although not the only way) you connect to the Net. Other, newer options include cable Internet.

If you will use one of the new, high-speed "broadband" Internet connections, such as DSL or cable Internet, you will not need a traditional modem; each of these technologies requires a special communications interface (see Hour 3). However, nearly all new PCs include a fax/modem, and even if you use broadband for Internet, you may want the modem, too, for such activities as PC faxing.

It doesn't really matter what brand of modem you buy, or whether it's an internal modem (plugged inside your computer's case), an external one (outside the computer, connected to it by a cable), or even one on a PC card inserted in a notebook PC.

What does matter is the modem's rated speed. That speed is usually expressed in *kilobits per second* (kbps, often further abbreviated to simply "K").

The higher the number of kbps (or K), the faster the modem. And the faster your modem is, the more quickly Web pages will appear on your screen, which makes Web surfing more fun and productive. A number of other Internet activities—especially such things that involve audio or video—will also run more quickly and smoothly over a faster modem.

On some modem packages, you may see the speed expressed in bits per second (bps). For example, a 56K modem may also be described as a 56,000 bps modem, though 56K is the more common usage.

Most modems for use with regular telephone lines are rated at one of the following speeds:

- 28,800 bps (28.8K)
- 33,600 bps (33.6K)
- 56,000 bps (56K)

The minimum modem speed for Internet cruising (including Web browsing) is 28.8K, although at that speed, you'll be very frustrated by the length of time it takes pages to appear. Most experts deem a 28.8K connection unacceptably slow. Modems rated at 56K are affordable (almost all new PCs and Macs come pre-equipped with a 56K modem), and almost always your best option.

A 56K modem is capable of sending data at 56K, but almost never does. Noise in the phone line and other limiting factors keep actual speed down to around 53K or even lower. No matter—that's still a whole lot snappier than what you'll see through a 33.6K or 28.8K modem.

And under current telecommunications law, 56K modems can only *send* information to the Internet at 56K; they *receive* information at a maximum rate of 53K, even on the clearest line.

It's important to keep in mind that a faster modem does not always deliver vastly superior performance. A number of factors—such as the reliability and noise level in your phone line, the speed supported by your Internet provider, and the responsiveness of the servers you contact—may cause 33.6K and 56K modems to perform no better than a 28.8K modem much of the time. In some areas, the equipment installed by the local phone company may not even support Internet connections any faster than 28K or so. Using a 33.6K modem or 56K modem through these lines won't hurt anything, but the performance you'll see will not be any better than what you'd get through a 28.8K modem. (Little by little, local phone companies are upgrading their lines to support faster access.)

Finally, although it's the most important factor, connection speed is not the only thing that governs the apparent speed with which things spring onto your screen. If it takes your computer a long time to process and display the information it receives through the Net, you'll see some delays that have nothing to do with the speed of your modem or phone lines or Internet provider. A fast computer is almost as important as a fast modem—it's a team effort.

There's a special consideration you must make when choosing a 56K modem that's not an issue with modems slower than 56K: the communications standard followed by the modem.

All new 56K modems made for PCs and Macs follow a standard called V.90. Older 56K modems may follow either of two other, older standards used before V.90: X2 and Kflex. (The box that any new modem or computer comes in usually states which standards the modem supports.)

The Internet provider you select (see Hour 3) must support the same standard as your modem; for example, if you have a V.90 modem, your Internet provider must support V.90 in order for you to get 56K access. If your modem's standard is different from your provider's, your modem will still function, but will run at a slower speed (28.8K or 33.6K).

Because V.90 has been adopted as the standard for today and tomorrow, most Internet providers who offer 56K access do so through V.90. So when purchasing a 56K modem, make sure it's a V.90 one.

Choosing a Computer

I've told you that almost any computer—even an older one—can be used to get on the Internet, and that's true. But to take full advantage of what the Internet offers, you need a top-of-the-line computer, or pretty close to it.

You see, some Internet tasks, such as email, demand little processing power from a computer and don't require a really fast Internet connection; they're neither *processor-intensive* nor *communications-intensive*. However, the main thing most newcomers to the Net want is access to the Web, and browsing the Web is just about the most processor-intensive, communications-intensive thing a computer can do.

To take full advantage of the Web, a computer must be able to display and play the multimedia content—graphics, animation, video, and sound—that's increasingly built in to Web pages. Such tasks require a fast processor and plenty of memory. In fact, a Web browser capable of supporting this multimedia is about the most demanding application you can put on a PC or Mac, requiring more processing power and memory than any word processor or spreadsheet on the market.

In addition to the multimedia, more and more Web pages feature programs (more about that later) that enable all sorts of advanced Web activities (see Figure 2.1). To run the programs in Web pages, your computer must use a fast 32-bit processor (such as a Pentium or better) and operating system (such as Windows 95, 98/Me, or XP), which have been available in PCs and Macs for only the last few years. As a rule, a PC that cannot run Windows 95 or higher, and a Mac that cannot run System 7.5 or higher, cannot run Java programs or the browsers that support the programs.

NEW TERM **Java.** Java is a programming language specially designed for use in computer networks, such as the Internet. On the Web, programmers add Java programs to Web pages to enable the page to do stuff it couldn't do otherwise, such as collect and process order information for an online store or make images dance around the page. Java makes the Web more powerful and interactive, but also more complex and demanding.

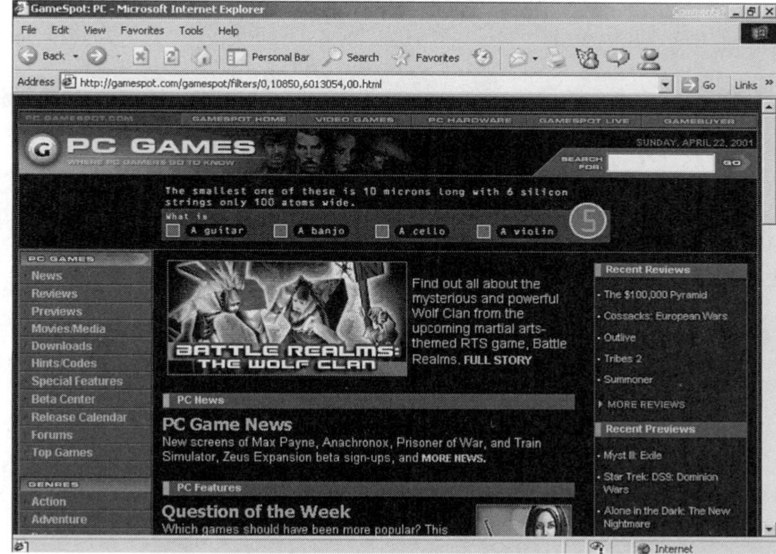

FIGURE 2.1
To enjoy the multimedia and Java content built in to many Web pages today, you need a powerful, well-equipped computer and a fast modem.

What about notebooks and other portable computers? No problem. Notebook PCs, Mac notebooks, and other portables make perfectly good Internet computers, as long as they meet the same general requirements (processor, modem speed, and so on) that a desktop computer must meet, as described later in this hour.

Note, however, that a portable computer always costs much more than a desktop computer with the same specifications. Also, some portables with otherwise acceptable specifications may have screens that are too small for comfortable Web browsing; any screen that measures less than 12 inches diagonally is probably too small, unless you have really, really, really good glasses.

Any size screen is fine, however, for email and other text-based, off-the-Web Internet activities. That's especially handy when you use a handheld PC or "palmtop" computer to access the Net on the go.

Finally, newer, more powerful computers are required to run the newest, most advanced operating systems, such as Windows XP on the PC or OS X on the Macintosh. These operating systems have been designed with the Internet in mind, making setting up your computer for the Net much quicker and easier.

Again, you can get a lot out of the Internet on a less capable computer—you just won't see or hear what your computer can't handle. But the bottom line is this: Most of the exciting innovations on the Internet, now and in the future, are designed for use by the newest, most powerful computers. So if you're shopping, aim high. And if you're standing pat now with an older machine, forge ahead with the understanding that your Internet experience is not going to be all that it might be.

A PC for the Internet

To make the most of today's Internet, the minimum reasonable PC would be equipped as follows:

- **Processor.** A Pentium processor (or Pentium equivalent, such as the Celeron, AMD K6, or Athlon) is recommended for its capability to support the preferred operating systems listed next; look for a Pentium rated at 500MHz or faster (even 1GHz processors are very affordable now). The latest Pentium version is Pentium 4.
- **Operating System.** Windows 95, Windows 98/Me (Millennium Edition), Windows 2000, Windows XP, and Windows NT are all fine choices. On all these Windows versions, except some installations of Windows 95, you'll find a built-in Web browser (Internet Explorer) and an easy-to-use program for setting up your Internet connection.
- **Display.** The ideal display for Web browsing is configured to run at 800×600 resolution and 16,000 colors (also known as *high color*, or *16-bit color*). Higher-color modes, such as 24-bit color (millions of colors; often called *true color*), are fine, but little online requires those modes. Web designers are increasingly moving to a 1024×768 resolution, but most Web pages today are still designed to look their best when displayed at 800×600. If the prices are similar, you might want to look at a 1024×768 display.
- **Memory.** If you're running Windows Me or XP, at least 128MB of RAM is recommended to support Windows and a browser. A reasonable minimum for older versions of Windows, such as Windows 98, would be 64MB. The software package's box may indicate a lower minimun, but experience teaches us that the minimum is almost always insufficient for decent performance and reliability.
- **Hard Disk.** I can't tell you how big your hard disk should be, because I don't know how much other software you have. I can tell you that, after you've set up all

of your Internet software, your hard disk should be at least 50 percent empty. Windows Web browsers need lots of free disk space for temporary data storage; when they don't have enough, performance and reliability suffer.

- **CD-ROM Drive.** A CD-ROM drive is not required for any Internet activity. However, you may need one to install the Internet software you need in order to get started, if you acquire that software on CD. For installing software, the speed of the CD-ROM drive is unimportant; any drive will do. Every new computer comes with a CD-ROM, anyway.
- **Other Peripherals.** There's plenty of fun sound and music online these days, and to hear it you'll need a sound card and speakers (or headphones) installed in your PC and configured in Windows. If you plan to create your own Web pages (see Hour 19, "Creating Web Pages and Multimedia Messages"), a scanner or digital camera is a useful addition.

A Mac for the Internet

To make the most of today's Internet, the minimum reasonable Macintosh system would be equipped as follows:

- **Processor.** A PowerPC-based Mac (such as the iMac) is recommended. Anything older than that won't support today's Web browsing.
- **Operating System.** OS9 or OS X is recommended. They have a built-in, easy-to-use routine for setting up your Internet connection; built-in Java processing; and a complete set of Internet-client programs.
- **Display.** The ideal display for Web browsing is configured to run at 800×600 resolution and 16,000 colors (also known as *high-color* or *16-bit color*). Higher-color modes, such as 24-bit color (millions of colors; often called *true color*), are fine, but little online requires those modes. A resolution of 640×480 is an acceptable alternative, but most Web pages are designed to look their best when displayed at 800×600.
- **Memory.** Consider 64MB the workable minimum for Web browsing on any Mac.
- **Hard Disk.** Should be large enough to leave at least 25 percent free space after you have installed all of your software.
- **CD-ROM Drive.** A CD-ROM drive is not required for any Internet activity. However, you may need one to install the Internet software you need in order to get started, if you acquire that software on CD. For installing software, the speed of the CD-ROM drive is unimportant; any drive will do.

- **Other Peripherals.** If you want to make a long-distance phone call through the Internet or have a voice conference, you'll need a microphone hooked to your Mac, and for videoconferencing, you'll need a Mac-compatible video camera. If you plan to create your own Web pages (see Hour 19), a scanner or digital camera can be handy.

If you're considering a Mac for the Net and have high-speed Internet service available via your cable TV supplier (see Hour 3), I should point out that most new Macs—including that cute little fruit-colored iMac—come pre-equipped with the communications hardware required for using a cable modem. Most PCs do not include this hardware, which you must then purchase (or rent from the cable company). However, more and more PC manufacturers are including Ethernet cards preinstalled, which allow for high-speed Internet access.

Internet Appliances and WebTV

Over the last couple years, a whole new category of computer device has emerged, sometimes called a *Net appliance,* or *Internet appliance*.

Essentially a PC stripped down to the components required for Net surfing, a Net appliance is generally less expensive than a full-blown PC, and smaller and more stylish than most PCs, as well. Most often, Net appliances have flat LCD screens (like those used in notebook PCs), and are designed for those who want to use the Internet but do not need a computer for any other purpose.

Their affordability made them quickly popular. While some models were available for less than $200, others can be had for free at this writing, as long as you agree to a three-year connection package with the Microsoft Network. Like most technologies, this market was quick to develop. Some of the major players, however, have also been quick to pull out.

One of the first companies to offer an Internet appliance, Netpliance, still offers its "i-opener" but has announced a new direction for the company. And 3Com, maker of the popular Palm handheld devices, announced the demise of its Audrey device in the first quarter of 2001.

There are still some good options out there, however, and they are worthy of consideration if you want a computer to use on the Internet, but do not need to use that computer for any other reason, such as word processing. Some folks who have full-blown computers may purchase Net appliances so they can have a second Internet machine in a bedroom or the kitchen. (It's a pretty inexpensive machine for the kids to use for games or homework research while another child can use a "real" computer to write a paper.)

Besides being incapable of taking on non-Internet computer tasks, a Net appliance may prove difficult or impossible to upgrade as Internet technology evolves and may limit the range of client software you may use, as well.

Compaq's iPaqs

Compaq offers two different iPaq models, retailing for around $500 at this writing. Both can be significantly reduced through various rebates, including the aforementioned MSN Internet access agreement.

Both come with a monitor and a wireless keyboard (see Figure 2.2). The more-expensive model offers a space-saving flat-panel monitor, but it is a markedly smaller screen than the cheaper, bulkier unit.

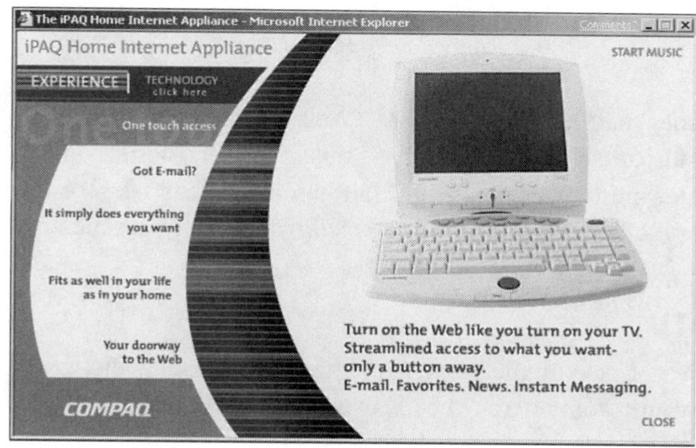

FIGURE 2.2
The iPaq is an attractive alternative to a full-blown PC for some people.

These machines allow you Internet access at the touch of a button, and have enough expandability to include a port for a printer, for example. So it's plenty powerful enough for handling your emailing, shopping, or general surfing needs.

MailStation

If email is your primary reason for wanting connectivity, then MailStation is a good option for you. For $99 (at this writing) plus a $9.95/month connection fee, you get a keyboard attached to a tiny LCD screen (see Figure 2.3). It basically resembles a handheld device, such as a Palm, with a keyboard attached. This is the absolute bare minimum in Internet connectivity, but for many people, it's all they need.

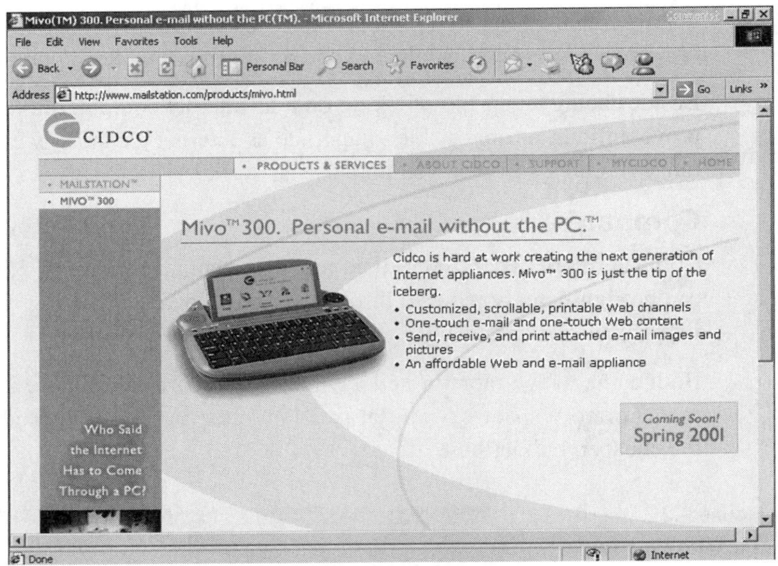

FIGURE 2.3
MailStation allows quick access to email in a tiny package.

Who does the MailStation unit fit? Well, think about Grandma. Maybe she lives on the other side of the country or maybe she winters in Florida. The thought of a full-blown computer intimidates her. With MailStation, she can take the unit with her to her winter home, plug her phone into it and be corresponding with the grandkids before you know it.

WebTV

WebTV is based on the premise that there are people who want to use the Internet but don't want a computer. (WebTV is owned by Microsoft.)

Instead of buying a PC or Mac, all you need for WebTV is a WebTV terminal (a VCR-sized box) and a subscription to the WebTV Internet service. The terminal uses your TV as a display, and you navigate the Internet through the terminal's wireless remote control or an optional wireless keyboard. It uses your telephone line to connect to the Internet, just as a computer would.

You can find WebTV terminals at electronics and appliance stores—anywhere that sells TVs and VCRs. Models are available from Philips/Magnavox and from Sony, so shop around and compare.

The WebTV scenario has a few advantages. It's cheap (less than $100 for the most basic, "classic" model; around $300 for a full-featured unit). WebTV is also comparatively easy to set up and use, if you use the WebTV Network Internet service, which is priced comparably with most other Internet providers.

WebTV enables you not only to browse the Net, but also to jump easily between TV shows and related information. While watching *Survivor*, for example, you can display a *Survivor* Web page in a picture-in-picture window on your screen, or call up an online TV guide. You can also engage in a live chat (via typed messages) with others watching the show at the same time. By touting this capability, the WebTV people have changed their pitch lately. Instead of selling the system as an alternative to a computer, they're pitching it as a way to enhance your TV viewing. It's high-end TV, not low-end Internet.

The system also has some major drawbacks, similar to those of Net appliances. The investment you make in a full computer buys you not only an Internet machine, but also one you can use to write letters, pay bills, do your taxes, play games, listen to CDs, teach your kids Spanish, and much more. A WebTV terminal, while technically a computer on the inside, is a single-purpose machine: You can use it for the Internet and nothing else.

Beyond all of that is the somewhat fuzzy question of whether the Internet is easier and more fun to use from a little screen on a desktop or a big TV in the living room. Some say it's more fun in the living room; some say Web pages and email text are hard to read and navigate from a TV screen.

What You'll Miss with an Internet Appliance

Internet appliances like those previously mentioned are great for people with specific needs: You're on a tight budget; you just want email; you want a cheap second machine; and so on. But there are major drawbacks for people who have other computing needs.

We all know a person or two who had a computer eat a file somewhere along the lines and has decided they have no place in their lives. Then the email arrives with an attached picture of the new niece or nephew. Sure, you can view it on the appliance, and even forward it to other family members. But when you decide you want to put your little one's photo out to friends, well, you're out of luck.

The key factor missing is that you can't manipulate files on an appliance. There's no saving, editing, copying, or anything. You can't install new software and it's difficult to upgrade to the latest technologies. It won't be long and the Internet will outpace your equipment.

They do make a nice second machine, because they are inexpensive and can offload some of the demand for screen time in a one-computer family. But before you buy one as your *only* Internet connectivity, be sure that what you're getting is all you'll need for a while.

Other Internet Options

The overwhelming majority of folks just getting online now are doing so through their own, personal Mac or PC, at home or at work. That's the main scenario, and that's where much of this book's focus will rest.

However, I should point out that there are many, many folks online who are not using PCs or Macs or are not even using their own computers or signing up with an Internet provider. Here are a few ideas for getting online without buying a computer:

- **School or Company Computer.** If the company you work for or school you attend has an Internet account, you may be permitted to use the organization's computers to explore the Net (usually within strict guidelines). Locate and speak to a person called the network administrator or system administrator; he or she holds the keys to the computer system and is responsible for telling you whether you may use the system and how and when you're permitted to use it.
- **Public Library.** Many public libraries have Internet terminals set up for use by patrons. You may use these terminals to do quick research on the Web or newsgroups. As a rule, you cannot use them for email, because you won't have your own email address, and library machines are never equipped for chat. Even if they were, it's not polite to hog a library PC (as many evil people do) for a long, chatty Internet session.
- **Cyber Café.** In all cool cities, you can find *cyber cafés*, coffeehouses equipped with Internet-connected computers so patrons can hang out, eat, drink, and surf (see Figure 2.4). Some cyber cafés will let you have an email address, so you can send and receive email. Still, there might not always be a computer available when you need one, and you could probably afford your own computer with what you'll spend on Hawaiian Mocha and scones.
- **Copy Shop.** Many full-service print/copy shops, such as Kinko's®, also offer Internet terminals for rent at reasonable rates.

In general, the compromises you must make to enjoy these alternatives makes them poor long-term substitutes for having your very own computer and Internet account. However, these are great ways to get a taste of the Net, and reap some of its benefits, if you're still trying to make up your mind about the Internet or are still saving up for that new computer.

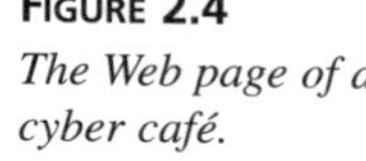

FIGURE 2.4
The Web page of a cyber café.

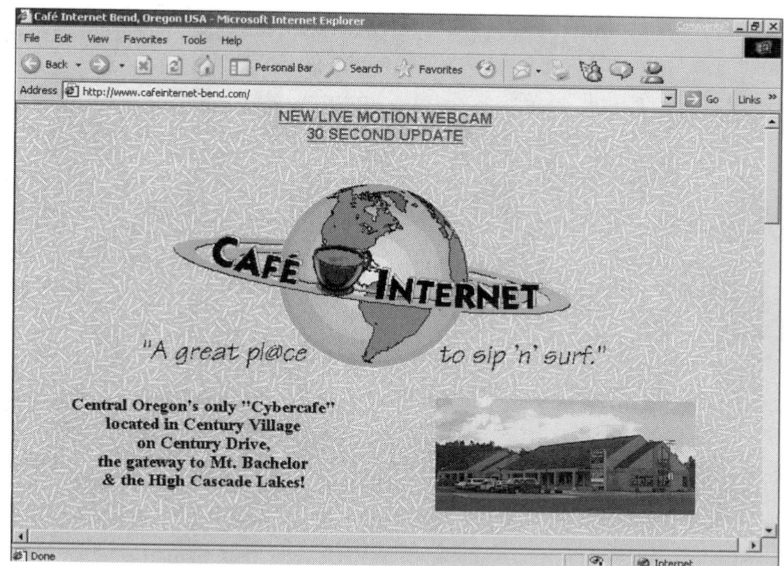

Getting Internet Software

Getting Internet software is like borrowing money: It's only difficult when you really need it. If you already have money (or Internet software), getting more is easy. So the trick is getting started.

You see, once you go online, you can search for, find, and download all the software you want, some of it for free, most at least cheap. You'll learn all about downloading software in Hour 15, "Downloading Programs and Files."

NEW TERM **Download.** To download is to copy a file—through a network—from another computer into your own. When you get software online, you copy that software from a server somewhere, through the Internet, to your computer and store it on your hard disk.

What Do You Need?

To figure out what Internet software you need to get started, you must begin by looking at what your computer already has. Recall from Hour 1, "What Is the Internet and What Can You Do There?", that you need two types of software:

- Communications software, which establishes the connection between your computer and your Internet provider.
- Client programs for the activities you want to perform through the Net: a Web browser for the Web, an email program for email, a newsreader for newsgroups, and so on.

Table 2.1 shows what software each popular operating system (PC and Mac) includes.

TABLE 2.1 Required Internet Software Each System Features or Lacks

Computer Type	*Operating System*	*Internet Software Included*	*You Still Need*
PC	Windows 98/NT/ 2000/ME/XP	Communications software, plus clients for Web browsing, email, newsgroups, and more.	None
	Windows 95	Communications software. (A few clients are included, such as email, Telnet, and FTP. But these are not designed as beginner's clients, and no Web browser is included.)	Client software
Mac	OS8, OS9, OS X	Communications software, plus clients for Web browsing, email, newsgroups, and more.	None

You needn't feel that you have to get all of your client software right away. At first, all you'll really want or need is your Web browser and an email program.

You won't need client software other than your Web browser and an email program until we get into more advanced topics, like creating your own Web pages. If you want to, you can simply set yourself up for Web browsing now, and forget about all the other software until you need it. You'll learn more about each of the other clients—including how to get some of the more popular options—in the hours in which those clients are introduced.

Where Can You Get It?

The best place to get your start-up Internet software is from your Internet provider (which you learn to select in Hour 3).

Why? Well, again, once you're online, you can easily acquire any software you want. All you need from your startup software is a way to begin. Whatever your Internet provider offers is usually given free of charge, and may include an easy-to-use setup routine, specially designed for your Internet provider.

You'll often see "free" Internet software offered as a "bonus" by Internet providers and PC sellers, and bound into the backs of computer books. While this stuff can help you get started, and is therefore worth considering, it's a mistake to think it's as valuable as it's touted to be. Certainly, it's rarely valuable enough to be the main reason you choose a particular provider, PC, or book.

Much of the software you get this way is outdated, or is "trial" software, which you may have to pay for if you use it for longer than a month or two. Often, the trial software has key features removed or disabled, to get you to pay for the full version. And even when the software truly is free, it's almost always stuff you could also download for free, for yourself, from the Web, often in a more up-to-date version.

As an alternative to using the software your provider supplies, you can walk into a software store and buy commercial Internet software right off the shelf. Most prepackaged Internet software is inexpensive ($5 to $50), and often comes with setup programs to conveniently sign you up with one or more Internet providers. Be careful, though, not to pick up a box that is designed to sign you up with one (and only one) Internet provider, unless it happens to be the one you already plan to use.

Both of the two major Internet client suites described next are available on CD-ROM at any software store.

About the Suites: Microsoft Internet Explorer and Netscape

In just the past few years, the two major suppliers of Web browsing software—Microsoft and America Online (Netscape)—have recognized that it's confusing for Internet users to have to go out and pick separate programs for each Internet activity.

Don't confuse America Online, the online service, with America Online, the company that markets the Netscape browser. It's the same company, but two different enterprises.

The first America Online, or AOL, is a commercial online service that offers Internet access among other activities. If you are an AOL subscriber, you can use either browser—Netscape or Internet Explorer—to explore the Web.

A few years ago, America Online, the company, purchased the company named Netscape, and now owns Netscape, the browser. But you can use the Netscape browser with any Internet supplier—you are not restricted to AOL just because America Online owns Netscape.

Confused yet?

So both Microsoft and America Online (Netscape) have developed "Internet suites," bundles that include a whole family of Internet programs that install together and work together well. Within each suite, you can jump from one program to any other simply by clicking a button or choosing from a menu. For example, you can conveniently jump from cruising the Web to checking your email to opening a newsgroup, all with a few clicks.

Both suites include a Web browser, email program, and newsgroup reader. Both also include a Web authoring tool for creating your own Web pages. You can buy either suite on CD at any software store, or order the CD directly from the developer. You may also be able to get a copy from your Internet provider. And, of course, once you're online, you can download the latest version of either program.

In this book, we've devoted an entire hour to each of the browsers, plus another hour devoted solely to the America Online service. You can find these hours in Part III, "Software for Your Journey."

Summary

The window through which you view something frames and colors that thing, affecting your entire perception of it. Look at a landscape through a big, clean window, and then again through a small, dirty, distorted window, and you experience two very different yards.

A person who visits the Net through a slow, tired PC and modem or through inferior software does not perceive the same world that someone else sees through a capable PC and snappy software. When you choose your computer and software, you are defining the character of your Internet experience to come.

Q&A

Q I really don't have a need for a *computer,* but I want email and to view the Net. Is an appliance for me?

A Yes, but not just any old refrigerator will do. You need an Internet appliance, or WebTV. These are designed specifically for people who want to email, shop online, check out entertainment options, read the news, and so on, but have no need to create an Excel spreadsheet or, for example, write a book like this one.

Q What's the quickest, easiest way to make sure I have everything I need without having to get it piece by piece?

A Buy a new computer. Just about any computer, be it from an electronics superstore or a catalog company like Gateway or Dell, will come with the latest software and hardware to make your Internet experience a good one. Better yet, you can usually get everything you need for little more than $1,000.

Q When is upgrading a good idea?

A If you have an older computer and there are aspects of it that need to be improved for your Internet needs, stop before jumping into the upgrading mode. Upgrading is a great idea when it's one or two things that need improving—like a faster modem, some more RAM, or an improved video card.

But lots of people get caught upgrading their computers and end up spending about as much as they would have for a new one. So before you upgrade, make a list of *all* the things you'll want to improve in the next year and compare it to the cost of a new machine. And make sure to add installation costs on anything you might buy that you can't install yourself.

HOUR 3

Getting Connected to the Internet

If you have a mailing address, you probably know about Internet providers, because they're the people who keep cramming free signup CD-ROMs and disks in your mailbox (creasing your *National Geographic*!) and begging you to join. Heck, you don't even need an address—you get free signup disks today in magazines, cereal boxes, and bundled along with any new computer.

The provider you pull out of your cereal box may be a perfectly good choice, but it's not the *only* choice—not by a long shot. In this hour, you'll discover the full range of different ways to get signed up for the Internet, so you can choose the provider that best matches your needs and bank account. You'll also learn the basics of making that connection, so we can get you on your way.

At the end of the hour, you'll be able to answer the following questions:

- What's an Internet provider, and why do I need one?
- What's an Internet account, and what types of accounts are there?
- What are "broadband" Internet accounts, and how do I get one?
- How are commercial online services, like America Online, sometimes different from other Internet service providers?

- How can I find local and national providers from which to choose?
- What types of pricing plans are there, and how do I know if I'm getting a good deal?
- Is there a way I can get Internet access for free?
- How does the process of getting connected work?

Types of Internet Accounts

When you sign up with—*subscribe to*—an Internet service, you get what's called an *Internet account*.

With an Internet account, you get the right to use the provider's Internet service, your very own email address (so you can send and receive email), and all of the other information you need to set up your computer for accessing the Internet through the service. From most providers, you may also get any communications or client software you need, as we discussed last hour.

Dial-Up Accounts

Most Internet accounts are called "dial-up" accounts because you use them by "dialing up" the Internet provider through your modem and telephone line. These are sometimes also described as "IP" accounts because they require your computer to communicate through TCP/IP (see Hour 1, "What Is the Internet and What Can You Do There?"). Dial-up IP accounts are the principal, general-purpose accounts offered by most Internet providers.

Dial-up accounts generally come as what's called a PPP account. With a PPP account, you have access to the full range of Internet activities, and can use any client programs you want to.

An account with an online service like America Online is also a "dial-up" account, but it's not the same thing as a regular Internet PPP or SLIP account. An online service account requires a different kind of communications software (supplied by the service) for accessing the service and its non-Internet content.

When you access the Internet through an online service, the service may temporarily switch you over to a PPP account, or it may funnel you to the Internet using a different communications scenario.

This is why online services often limit you to one or two different Web browsers and other clients, instead of letting you choose the one you want. Any client software used through the service must be specially configured for the service's unique communications system.

Cable Internet and DSL (Broadband)?

In the last few years, a new category of personal Internet account has emerged, sometimes described as *broadband* because it sends and receives information so much faster than a regular dial-up account—as if the information were moving through a nice, fat, "broad" pipe instead of a slow, skinny pipe.

Depending on what's available to you, you have your choice between two different kinds of broadband Internet access, described in the next sections: Cable Internet and DSL. (There are other broadband options, used mostly in business environments. But these two are the popular options for personal users.)

The two options are different from each other, but have seven characteristics in common:

- They are much, much faster than a 56K dial-up account.
- Their speed enables them to carry Internet activities that are simply impractical over a dial-up connection, such as watching a movie online, high-quality videoconferencing, or using a computer somewhere out on the Net as a storage facility for your own files or backups.
- They allow you to use your phone line for telephone calls, faxing, or anything else while you are online.
- They can be set up so that you are always online. You don't have to do anything to get online each time you use the Net (as you must with a dial-up account); you just sit down and get to business.
- They are more expensive, on a monthly basis.
- They require more expensive communications hardware for your computer, rather than relying on the inexpensive modems included in nearly all computers today.
- Once you're online, actually using a broadband account—opening Web pages, exchanging email, and so on—takes the same steps you use on a regular dial-up account, the steps described throughout this book.

> Broadband services are not yet available everywhere. There are many neighborhoods today that cannot get any type of broadband service, even though they may have regular phone and cable service. The hardware in local phone and cable systems must be upgraded in order to support broadband Internet. Phone and cable companies are furiously making these upgrades in order to begin selling broadband service, but it will still take a few years to get broadband availability to everyone.
>
> However, as more and more neighborhoods gain access to both broadband technologies, the monthly cost should drop as the phone and cable companies compete for those customers.

Cable Internet

Supplied by your local cable TV company, cable Internet enters your house through the same cable that TV signals travel through. Cable Internet can support speeds up to 4,096K—more than 70 times as fast as a 56K dial-up connection. Figure 3.1 shows a Web site describing Road Runner, a cable Internet service offered by Time Warner Cable in some (but not all) of the neighborhoods it serves.

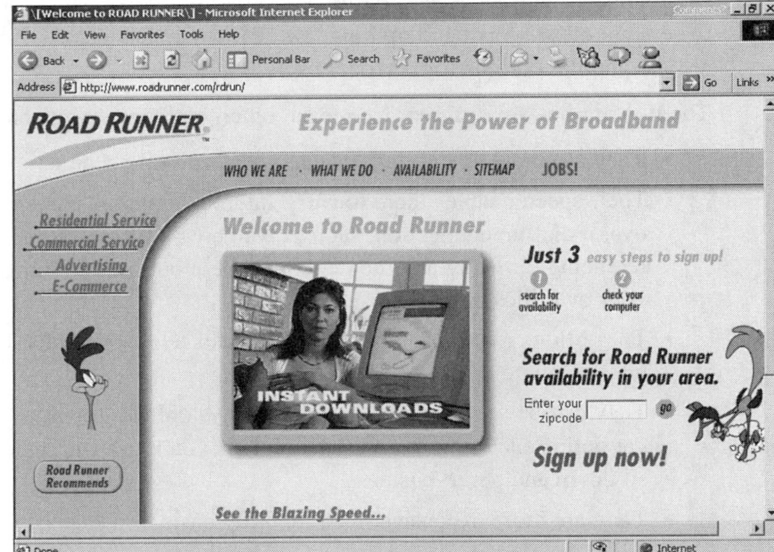

FIGURE 3.1
The Web site of Road Runner, a cable Internet service offered by Time Warner Cable to some of its subscribers.

To use cable Internet, you must have

- A cable Internet account, offered only by the cable TV company that serves your neighborhood.
- A cable modem installed in, or connected to, your PC. A cable modem is not really a modem, but a specialized network adapter. You can usually rent your cable modem from the cable company, which also makes it easy for the cable company to set up your computer for you. You can also purchase cable modems, which run more than $100—but, before buying, be sure to talk first to your cable company to determine the specific hardware required.
- An Ethernet card installed in your computer (or other network adapter). This allows the modem to talk to your computer. Many computer manufacturers are now preinstalling Ethernet cards in their computers.

At this writing, a cable Internet account costs from about $40 to $50 per month—twice the cost of a regular dial-up account. To learn whether cable Internet is available at your home, call your cable TV company.

There are two potential minuses to cable Internet that are worth considering before you take the plunge.

First, the "always-on" nature of a cable Internet connection has been found to make computers using cable connections somewhat more vulnerable to computer hackers than those on regular dial-up lines. You can protect yourself from hackers with a "personal firewall" program such as Black Ice or ZoneAlarm. And, as with any Internet connection, users of a cable Internet connection need to use a good anti-virus program.

Second, cable Internet connections have been shown to become dramatically slower when many people within a neighborhood are using cable Internet simultaneously. At such times, cable would still remain much faster than a dial-up connection. But you might be disappointed by the times when you felt you were not getting all the speed you paid for.

3

DSL

Used through your regular phone line, a Digital Subscriber Line (DSL; also known by various other abbreviations such as ADSL or xDSL) account is supplied by, or in cooperation with, your local telephone company. The fastest broadband option, DSL can support speeds up to 7,270K.

Oddly, DSL can be faster than cable Internet when you are receiving information—such as opening a Web site or video clip. But it is usually slower than cable when you are sending information, such as sending email.

For most folks, these speed distinctions are academic; either broadband option is fast enough to deliver the full broadband benefit.

Note that although DSL uses your regular phone line, it transforms that line into a carrier of multiple services; with DSL, you can use the Internet and talk on the phone at the same time.

Like cable Internet, DSL requires a special modem, typically called a DSL modem, which can cost substantially more than a cable modem. The monthly cost of a DSL account, however, is roughly the same as for a cable Internet account, around $40–$50.

To find out whether you can get DSL where you live, contact your local phone company, or contact an Internet service provider that serves your neighborhood and offers DSL service. (See "Internet Service Providers (ISPs)," later in this chapter.)

If you already have access to the Internet through a library computer or other option, you can look up DSL suppliers online at `http://www.dslmarketplace.com/`.

Email-only Accounts

With an email-only account, you get full access to Internet email, and nothing else—no Web, no newsgroups, no chat, no shoes, no shirt, no service. You will have access to mailing lists, however, which enable you to get through email much of the same discussion content you'd see in newsgroups. (Email, newsgroups, and mailing lists are covered in Part II, "Talking to the World.")

Email accounts can be run from the lowliest of computers, and cost next to nothing. In fact, a few companies now offer you an email account free of charge, in exchange for the right to send you targeted advertisements.

Who Can I Get Dial-up Access From?

You can get your Internet account from any of three main sources:

- A national Internet service provider (ISP)
- A local ISP, one that's headquartered in your city or town
- A commercial online service, such as AOL or CompuServe

Each of these options is explained next.

Whatever service you choose as your provider, make sure the company offers a dial-up telephone number for connecting to the Internet that is a local call from your PC's location. Otherwise, you'll end up paying long-distance fees to the phone company in addition to whatever your provider charges for Internet access.

In most cities, finding local access numbers is no problem—any local ISP, national ISP, or online service will have a local number you can use. In some suburbs and many rural areas, finding a local number gets more difficult. Often your best bet in such circumstances is to find a local ISP (discussed later in this hour), or to see whether your local telephone company offers Internet access. (Many do.)

Some services offer a toll-free number (an 800 or 888 number) that you can use to access the service when the ISP provides no local number. But that number is rarely truly "toll-free." The ISP almost always charges a higher rate for using the service through the 800 or 888 number, kicking the toll back to you.

Commercial Online Services

You've no doubt heard of at least one of the major online services, such as America Online (AOL; see Figure 3.2) or CompuServe (CSi). These services promote themselves as Internet providers, and they are—but with a difference.

In addition to Internet access, these services also offer unique activities and content not accessible to the rest of the Internet community. These services have their own chat rooms, newsgroup-like message boards (usually called "forums"), online stores, and reference sources that only subscribers to the service can use. Setup for an online service is usually very easy: You install the free software the company provides, follow the onscreen instructions, and you're connected.

The principal drawback to online services is flexibility. You often cannot choose and use any client software you want; you must use a single client environment supplied by the service, or one program from among a limited set of options. When new, enhanced releases of client programs come out, ISP users can install and use them right away, whereas most online service users must wait until the online service publishes its customized version.

On the plus side, for Web browsing, most online services do supply a version of either Navigator, Internet Explorer, or both (specially customized for compatibility with the service), making the look and feel of the Web through an online service essentially identical to that of an ISP.

Another beef about online services is capacity. When America Online introduced more attractive pricing a few years ago, it picked up far more subscribers than it was prepared to serve. The result was that subscribers often got busy signals when they tried to connect, and could not get through to the overburdened system for hours. A few times, the system crashed altogether.

This is a legitimate complaint, as are the reports that the online services sometimes tend to supply slow, unreliable Internet access. But to be completely fair, many ISPs also get overloaded, and may be burdened by busy signals and poor performance, too.

Whomever you choose, you must be prepared for the possibility you'll get fed up and switch. You can't expect any provider to be perfect. But the possibility of losing subscribers is the only incentive for providers to continually improve.

Also, try to avoid signing long-term contracts with providers; these deals can cause you great pain if the provider fails to give the level of service you expect.

FIGURE 3.2
Online services such as America Online (AOL) offer Internet access as well as other services available only to their own subscribers.

Online services used to be dramatically more expensive than ISPs. Lately, they've adopted pricing policies that are generally competitive with the local and national ISPs, although you can still usually get a slightly better deal from a regular ISP than from any online service. For example, America Online offers a respectable flat rate of around $20 per month; if you shop around, you can get a flat rate from an ISP for as little as $15.

One final thought: In their advertising, the online services often tout their ease-of-use. That claim refers exclusively to how easy it is to use the service's non-Internet content from its own client software, *not* to ease-of-use on the Internet. For all practical purposes, using the Internet is the same—no harder nor easier—no matter which online service or ISP you choose.

America Online (AOL)

Voice Number: 800-827-6364

America Online is the biggest of the online services (and also, therefore, the single largest Internet provider in the world), largely because of aggressive marketing and the initial convenience of setting up an account from a CD-ROM that came in junk mail. The non-Internet content is indeed the easiest to use of all services. AOL's Internet access, however, is notoriously slow, and busy signals continue to be a problem. AOL offers a wide range of pricing plans, including a flat rate, an annual rate, and several different pay-as-you-go plans. (America Online is covered in detail in Hour 11, "Using AOL 6.0.")

CompuServe (CSi)

Voice Number: 800-848-8199

CompuServe (see Figure 3.3) wasn't the first online service, but it's the oldest still in operation, and it was once the undisputed king. That legacy leaves CompuServe with an unbeatable range of local access numbers. CompuServe is owned by America Online, but still operates as an independent service.

Functionally, CompuServe is similar to America Online in most respects, and it still offers some non-Internet content, exclusively to its own subscribers. Its reputation for providing fast and reliable Internet service is somewhat better than America Online's; its reputation for non-Internet ease-of-use, slightly worse. However, CompuServe can support almost any computer in the world, whereas AOL is essentially limited to popular personals: PCs and Macs.

Microsoft Network (MSN)

Voice Number: 800-FREE-MSN

Microsoft Network started out in 1995 as a service very much like AOL, as the first foray in Bill Gates' ongoing effort to own the Internet. (I guess for some people, having billions of dollars just doesn't seem like enough power.) MSN has since evolved away from the online service model, to the point where it is now more or less a regular national (actually international) ISP, although it still supplies some content accessible only to its subscribers. MSN offers true PPP access, so you can use any browser you want to. (Although, not surprisingly, MSN works best through Microsoft's own browser, Internet Explorer.) The service offers a variety of reasonable flat-rate and pay-as-you-go plans.

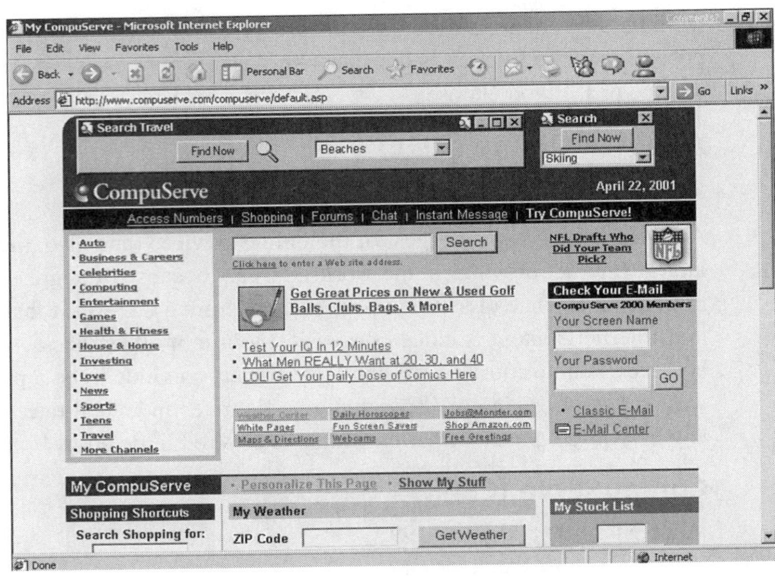

FIGURE 3.3
The Web home page of CompuServe, an online service.

All of the online services, and most ISPs (described next), provide setup software for their service on a disk or CD. This software is required for the online services, but often is optional for an ISP.

Even when it's optional, I strongly recommend getting any signup software your provider offers. The software leads you step-by-step through setting up your PC for the particular provider, and makes setting up your computer properly a no-brainer. As soon as you've selected a provider, call the provider to request the software and instructions for your computer type.

Internet Service Providers (ISPs)

Unlike an online service, an Internet service provider, or ISP, does not offer its subscribers special content that's not accessible to the rest of the Net. You get Internet access, period.

ISPs offer greater flexibility than online services, providing dial-up IP, shell, and email accounts (and often DSL, as well). Through IP accounts, they can enable you to use virtually any client software you want and to add or change that software whenever you feel like it. ISPs also might offer more attractive rates and better service than the online services, although that's not always the case.

There are many large, national ISPs that provide local access numbers all over the United States (and often across North America). Table 3.1 lists a few of the major national ISPs and their voice telephone numbers, so you can call to learn more about the service and also find out whether the service offers a local access number in your area. Just in case you have access to the Net through a computer at school, work, or the local library, the table also shows the address of a Web page where you can learn more about each service.

TABLE 3.1 A More-or-Less Random Selection of National ISPs

Company	*Voice Number*	*Web Page Address*
Earthlink	800-395-8425	`www.earthlink.net`
AT&T WorldNet	800-967-5363	`www.att.com/worldnet`
Prodigy	800-213-0992	`www.prodigy.com`
US Internet	888-873-4959	`www.usinternet.com`

Free Internet!

You may have heard that you can get a completely free Internet account, and that's a fact. In exchange for the right to show you a steady stream of advertising whenever you are online, some companies supply you with free access to the most popular Internet activities: the Web and email.

Free Internet services abounded a year or so ago, but like so many dotcom businesses, these companies fell on hard times and began to charge for access. One of those that still offers free access, NetZero (see Figure 3.4), only allows 40 hours per month for free. It also now offers a low-cost unlimited-access service with no banner ads to clog up your screen.

There are a few others still out there, and it's a great idea, and worth a try. The benefit is obvious: You'll have an extra $20 a month for sandwiches. Here's the potential downside:

- At this writing, the free accounts are somewhat notorious for poor performance and a complete lack of customer service.
- It's difficult to sign up for these accounts unless you are already online and already know how to use the Web, because signing up requires access to the company's Web site. So they make a nice money-saver for those who already know their way around, but may befuddle newcomers to the Internet.
- The ads may grow tiresome.
- You may prefer the features and flexibility of using a real email program instead of the Web-based email the free accounts require.

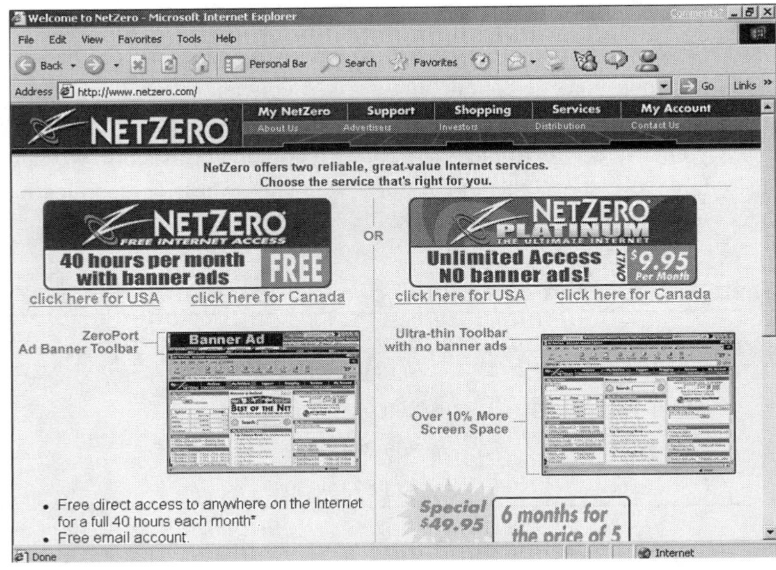

FIGURE 3.4
While it still offers free access at this writing, even NetZero is offering a for-pay service.

Finding a Local ISP

Besides the national ISPs, there are thousands of local ISPs in cities and towns all over the United States and Canada. Typically, a local ISP cannot offer access numbers beyond a small, local service area of a few cities, towns, or counties. But it can provide reliable Internet access, personal service, and often the best rates you can get. If you're having a problem, it can be a terrific help to be able to stop by your Internet provider's office and chat face-to-face. Local providers also play a vital role in keeping the big national providers honest; the continual reduction of rates by the big providers was spurred in large part by competition from even lower-priced local ISPs.

Unlike online services and national ISPs, local ISPs don't have the marketing muscle to advertise heavily or send out free disks. That's what makes them harder to find, but it's also why they're often cheaper. Finding a local ISP is getting easier all the time. Friends, coworkers, and local computer newsletters are all good sources for finding a local ISP. You can also check the Yellow Pages for ISPs: Look first under *Internet*, and then try *Computers—Internet Services*. The folks at your nearest computer store may also know of a good local ISP or two.

If you have access to the Internet (through a friend's computer, your job, a local library, or cyber café), you can search online for an ISP. A Web site called the List (see Figure 3.5) at `thelist.internet.com` is one of several that lists hundreds of ISPs in the United States and in many other countries.

FIGURE 3.5
Using somebody else's Internet account or an Internet terminal at your local library, you can visit the List to find a local ISP.

How Do I Choose a Dial-Up Internet Plan?

Of all the options that are available to you, a dial-up account is still the most popular type of home Internet connection, by a long shot. So, how do you go about picking a dial-up provider and plan?

Beats me. If there were one reliable way to choose the best Internet provider, we would all be using the same one. But different people have different priorities: For some, it's price. For others, it's a range of access numbers; for others, it's speed. Some people have a particular need to use content that's available only through a particular online service; most people don't. You have to check out how each of your available ISP options addresses your own priorities.

Obviously, if you have friends who use the Internet, find out which services they use, and ask whether they're happy. It's always a good idea to use a friend's Internet account to test the service the friend uses, and to explore your other options. Magazine reviews can help, but they rarely cover more than the online services and the largest national ISPs. To judge a local ISP, you need to listen to the word of mouth.

For what it's worth, here's a quick look at a few things to consider:

Stressed out over making a choice? Relax, and remember that—unless you agree to a long-term deal—you can always quit and try another service if your first choice disappoints you.

The only caveat to switching services is that your email address changes any time you switch. But many services will forward your email to your new service for a few months after you quit, and you can always get in touch with all your email partners and let them know your new address.

Of course, switching services also provides an excellent opportunity to *not* tell some folks your new email address, if those folks have been getting on your e-nerves.

- **Plans and Rates**—Most providers offer a range of different pricing plans. The kinds of plans you'll see most often, however, are unlimited access (or *flat rate*) and pay-as-you-go. Flat-rate plans are the most common, because they allow unlimited access for a flat monthly fee. Pay-as-you-go plans charge a low base rate for a small number of hours (such as $10 for the first 20 hours), then an hourly rate after that. I generally recommend that new users first choose a flat rate plan with no long-term commitment, and to keep track of their monthly hours for six months or so. If you do that, you'll know whether you're getting your money's worth at the flat rate or should switch to a per-hour plan.
- **Billing Options**—Most providers will bill your monthly charges automatically to any major credit card. Some local ISPs can bill you by mail, and some others can actually add your monthly Internet charges to your regular monthly telephone bill (itemized separately from your calls to Grandma, of course). All other things being equal, you may lean toward the provider that will bill you in the way that's most convenient for you.
- **Access Numbers**—Obviously, you want a provider that offers a local access number in the area where your computer resides. But what if you need to use your account from both home and work, using two different computers or bringing a portable back and forth? Does the provider offer local access numbers that work from both locations? What if you want to be able to use the Internet when you travel? Does the provider offer local access everywhere you and your computer might go?
- **Software**—The online services require that you use a software package they supply for setting up your connection, using their non-Internet content, and often for using the Internet, too. Most ISPs can also supply you with any communications or client software you require, although using the ISP's software package is optional.

If you need software to get started, you may want to consider what each ISP offers as a software bundle.

- **Web Server Space**—If you think you might want to publish your own Web pages (see Hour 19, "Creating Web Pages and Multimedia Messages"), you'll need space on a Web server to do so. Many ISPs and most online services offer an amount of Web server space free to all customers; others charge an additional monthly fee.
- **Newsgroup Access**—You'll learn all about newsgroups in Hour 7, "Participating in Newsgroups and Mailing Lists." For now, just be aware that there are tens of thousands of newsgroups, and that not all providers give you access to all of them. Some exclude "racy" ones, while others only offer those specifically requested by users.

Getting Connected

So you've chosen an ISP for dial-up access to the Internet. Whether that's an online service like AOL or a local or national ISP, your next step is to actually *connect* to them.

In most cases, the company you've chosen is going to make this as easy as possible for you. They'll either supply you with the software you need—which is often pre-installed on your computer, if you choose a national service—or they'll give you some type of brochure that walks you through the process, step-by-step.

Since the provider usually takes care of that type of thing and there are so many different ways of getting started, we're not going to spend much time on that type of stuff here. Instead, we'll just concentrate on the basics—things that you'll need to understand regardless of which provider you use.

Number, Username, and Password

No matter how you set up your account and computer, you'll wind up with three pieces of information that are essential to getting online:

- **Local access number**. The telephone number your modem dials to connect to your Internet provider.

In this section, we're talking about a typical dial-up connection. If you've chosen AOL, or cable or DSL, your setup will be different. Some dialup providers handle things differently, too. You'd be smart to get setup instructions straight from you provider, to make sure you do it right.

- **Username**. To prevent just anybody from using its service, your Internet provider requires each subscriber to use a unique name, called a username (or sometimes user name, user ID, or userID), to connect.
- **Password**. To prevent an unauthorized user from using another's username to sneak into the system, each subscriber must also have his or her own secret password.

Entering your username and password to go online is called "logging on" (or sometimes "logging in" or "signing in") and the name used to describe that activity is "logon" (or "login," or "sign-in"). If you use a signup program to set up your Internet account and computer as described next, you'll choose your username and password while running the program. If you set up your computer without a signup disk (as described later in this hour), you'll choose a username and password while on the phone with your provider to open your account.

Every user of a particular Internet provider must have a different username. If you choose a large provider, there's a good chance that your first choice of username is already taken by another subscriber. In such cases, your provider will instruct you to choose another username, or to append a number to the name to make it unique. For example, if the provider already has a user named CameronDiaz, you can be CameronDiaz2.

There are rules regarding what you can and cannot use for your username and password.

The rules vary by provider, but, in general, your username and password must each be a single word (no spaces or punctuation) of five or more letters and/or numerals. Nonsense words, like FunnyDad or MonkeyMary, are fine as usernames. For a password, avoid using easy-to-guess items such as your birthday or kids' names. *Total* nonsense—like xkah667a—makes the most effective password, as long as you can remember it.

Your username often doubles as the first part of your email address; if your username is Stinky, your email address might be something like Stinky@serveco.com. Before choosing a username, consider whether you also like it as an email address, which your friends and associates will see and use.

Some systems are *case-sensitive*; that is, they pay attention to the pattern of upper- and lowercase letters. On a case-sensitive system, if your username is SallyBu, you must type SallyBu to log on—sallybu, SALLYBU, or sallyBU won't work.

Using Supplied Software

As I pointed out earlier, a special signup program is required for each online service provider, and many ISPs can also supply you with a signup program for your computer. I *highly* recommend using signup programs whenever they're available, even when they're optional. You can get free signup disks by mail from the providers, just by calling them on the telephone. Also, signup programs often come preinstalled on new computers, and in computer magazines and junk mail. If you choose to go with a local ISP, you can usually pick up a signup CD or disks just by stopping by the provider's office.

Why Use a Signup Program?

Why? Well, first, the signup programs kill two birds at once: They sign you up with a provider *and* configure your computer to access that provider. The program automatically takes care of all the communications configuration required in your computer, some of which can be tricky for inexperienced computer users.

Depending on the provider you select, the signup program might or might not set up all your client software.

After completing any signup program, you'll be able to connect to the Internet and use your Web browser to explore the Web. However, in some cases, your email, news, and other programs may require a little further setup before you can use them. You'll learn about configuring each type of client software in the hour that covers it.

Running a Typical Signup Program

Before running a signup program, make sure your modem is connected to a telephone line, because the signup software usually dials the provider at least once during the signup process. Also, make sure you have a major credit card handy; you'll need to enter its number and expiration date to set up payment.

Signup programs are almost always designed to set up credit card payments for your Internet service. If you do not want to pay by credit card, you may not be able to use the signup program. (Actually, you may not even be able to use a particular provider; some accept payment solely by credit card.)

Call your selected provider to ask about payment terms. If the provider accepts other payment methods, but its signup program handles only credit cards, you can establish your account over the telephone, and then set up your computer without a signup disk, as described later in this hour.

You'll find instructions for starting the program on a page or card that accompanies it, or printed right on the CD or disk.

After you start the program, just follow its lead. The program will prompt you to type in your name, address, phone number, and credit card information, and to choose a logon username and password, email address, and email password. The program may also present you with a list of payment plans from which to choose (see Figure 3.6).

When you choose each of the following during signup, be sure to jot it down for later reference:

- Your logon username and password.
- Your email address.
- Your email password. Sometimes different from your logon password, this is used to retrieve email others have sent to you.
- The telephone number of your provider's customer service and/or technical support departments.

Once or twice during the signup process, the program uses your modem to contact the provider. It does this to verify your payment information, find the best local access number for you, check that your selected username is not already taken, and ultimately to send all of the information it collected to the provider to open your account.

When the program closes, your computer and account are ready to go online and explore.

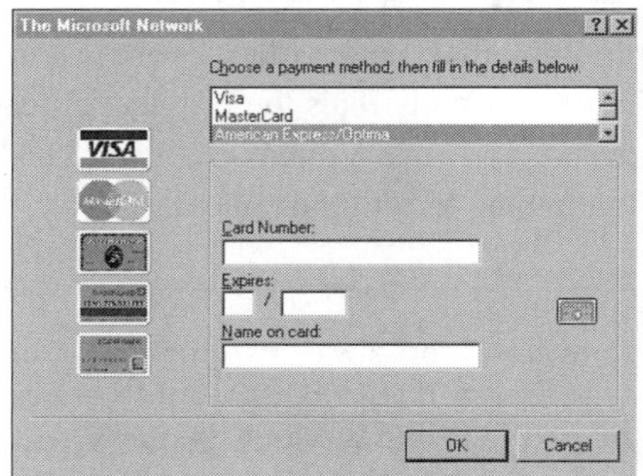

FIGURE 3.6
A typical signup program prompts you for all the info required for setting up your account, such as choosing a payment method.

Using the Connection Wizard on Your Own

Setting up your computer without a signup program is a little more difficult, but well within anybody's capabilities. Often your ISP will provide you with all the instructions you need on a brochure or instruction sheet.

The instructions in this section are for setting up dial-up IP accounts, the most popular type.

When you don't use a signup disk, you must set up your account with your selected Internet provider over the telephone first, then configure your computer. While setting up your account, your provider will tell you all of the communications settings required for the service, and will work with you to select your local access number, username, and password.

3

It's important that you make careful notes of everything your provider tells you. You'll use all of that information when setting up. In addition to your access number and logon username and password, you'll probably come out of the conversation with the following information:

- One or more *IP addresses*—a string of numbers separated by periods—required for communicating with the provider.

More and more Internet providers are set up so that they automatically assign you an IP address whenever you connect to the Internet. This makes it unnecessary to know the IP addresses.

- The addresses of the provider's email and news servers. You'll need these addresses to configure your email program and newsreader. Email server addresses may be described as SMTP and POP3 servers, and news servers may be described as NNTP servers. You don't need to know what the abbreviations mean; just know that if your provider mentions an NNTP server, he's talking about a news server.
- Your own email address, the one others can use to send email to you.
- Your email username and password, required for retrieving email people have sent to you. These may be different from your logon username and password.

- The telephone number and hours of the provider's customer service or technical support departments.
- Any other special communications steps or settings the particular provider requires.

No matter how you go about it, setting up your computer for the Internet is a simple matter of entering this information in your communications software. Once that's done, you can go online.

Running the Connection Wizard

Short of using a signup program, the next easiest way to set up an ISP account on a PC running Windows 95 or 98 is to set up Internet Explorer and run its Connection Wizard. Internet Explorer is included in every copy of Windows 98, Me, and XP, and is often included with Windows 95.

> If your computer is new, you might have the latest version of Internet Explorer already installed: version 6.0. Even if you're using IE5 or IE5.5, however, the Connection Wizard is essentially the same.

The Connection Wizard leads you through each step of the process, prompting you for all of the required information, such as IP addresses. That's almost as easy as using a signup disk, except that the Connection Wizard doesn't sign you up with your ISP—you must take care of that first—and it prompts you for your IP address and other setup information, which a signup program can supply for itself.

To launch the Connection Wizard, simply right-click the Internet Explorer icon on your desktop, choose the Connections tab, and click the Setup button. You'll see a screen like in Figure 3.7. From there, you follow the prompts, filling in the appropriate information. The Wizard walks you through the process quite succinctly.

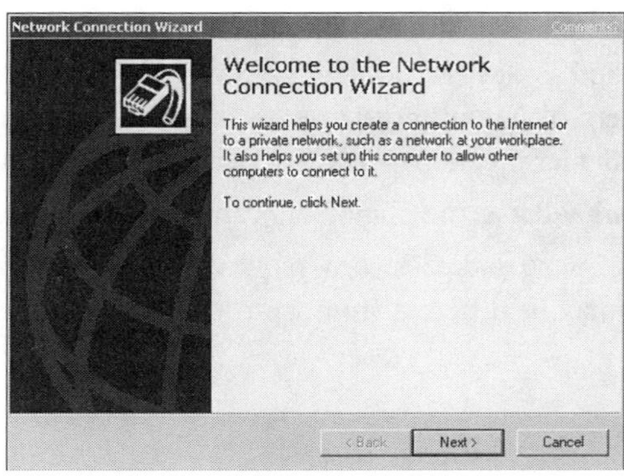

FIGURE 3.7
The Connection Wizard offers easy-to-follow instructions for getting connected to your ISP.

Connecting at Last

When it's done, you'll end up with an icon on your desktop for your connection to your provider. When you want to connect to use the Internet, just double-click that icon. You'll get a dialog box (see Figure 3.8) with your username already included. Just type your password, click Connect, and off you go. Now, you're ready to browse the Web, a topic that (conveniently enough) is covered in the next Hour!

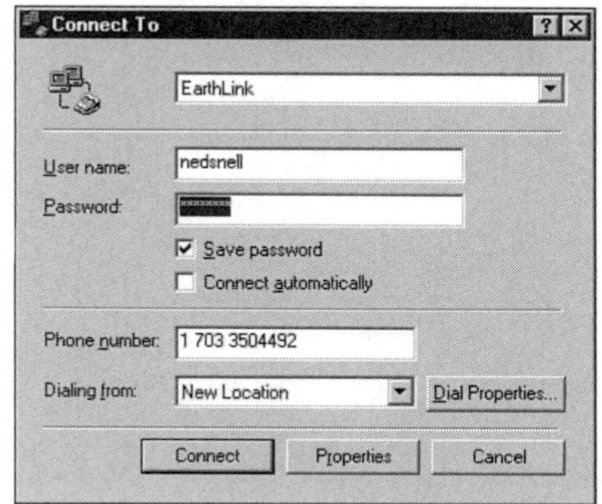

FIGURE 3.8
After opening your connection program, you supply your password to log on to the Internet.

Summary

Well, I'd say you've had just about enough prelude and general fooling around by now. In these first three hours, you've learned what the Internet is, what hardware and software you need to get on the Internet, how to find and choose your Internet provider, and how to get connected.

That's all the preparation you need—it's time to start browsing. You'll do that in Hour 4, "Basic Browsing."

Q&A

Q I saw an ad for an Internet account you can get through one of those pizza-size satellite dishes. What the heck is that all about?

A The same kind of digital satellite dish used by DSS and DBS TV receivers—like those from RCA and Sony—to receive such services as DirecTV and USSB can also be used to receive high-speed Internet transmissions. Many of these services operate only one-way—that is, they can receive data, but you can't send anything, such as email. Some now offer two-way service, allowing you to send and receive, just as you would over a phone or DSL line. These systems cost more than a typical Internet setup. (You must buy a few hundred dollars of extra equipment, and usually pay a higher monthly rate for your Internet account.) But it may be a good option where poor phone lines make it impossible to get acceptable download speed.

Hour 4

Basic Browsing

Whew. You've made it through the first three hours, which are full of all the necessary—yet occasionally mundane—details that provide the background of Internet usage. Alas, you can now rest assured that the remainder of this book will be nothing but fun, fun, fun!

Well, that may be stretching it a bit. But the fact of the matter is that with this chapter, you begin to get into the meat of why you wanted to get on the Internet in the first place—browsing the World Wide Web. The Web is one of the two biggest reasons that the average Joe hops online; the other is email (which is covered in Hour 5, "Sending and Receiving Email").

Over the last six years, the Web has blossomed—okay, make that *exploded*. In this one hour, you'll pick up the basics of getting all around the Web. We'll cover the things that work roughly the same regardless of what browser or ISP you're using. We'll cover specific information on each browser, plus, America Online, in Part III, "Software for Your Journey."

At the end of the hour, you'll be able to answer the following questions:

- What's that Web page that always appears as soon as I open my browser?

- What do all those Web addresses mean, and how do I visit a Web page address?
- How can I use *links* to jump from place to place on the Web?
- How do toolbar buttons like Back and Home make navigating the Web easier?
- What are *frames*, and how do they make getting around a Web page different?

About Your "Home Page"

Most Web browsers are configured to go automatically to a particular Web page as soon as you open them and connect to the Internet. This page is generally referred to as the browser's "home page."

NEW TERM **Home page**. A Web page a browser is configured to go to automatically when you open it, to provide a starting point for your Web travels. It's also sometimes called the "startup page." But remembering that the page is "home" is important, as you'll learn later in this hour.

Note that "home page" has two meanings in Web parlance: It also describes a Web page that serves as the main information resource for a particular person or organization. For example, `www.toyota.com` may be described as Toyota's "home page."

For example, if you get Internet Explorer directly from Microsoft, it opens at the Microsoft Network's home page at `www.msn.com` (see Figure 4.1). If you get Netscape Navigator directly from Netscape, it opens automatically to a similar startup page at Netscape.

However, if you get your software from your Internet provider, your browser may have been reconfigured with a new home page, one that's set up by your provider as a starting point for its subscribers. This home page also serves as a source of news and information about the provider and its services.

A few specific Web sites are used as home pages by a very high proportion of Web users because these pages offer a convenient set of links to the things many folks like to do as soon as they go online: Search for something, check out the latest news, weather, or sports scores, or other common activities.

Some folks call these sites *Web portals* because they function as an everyday point of entry to the Web. Popular portals include such search pages as Yahoo!, Excite, and Lycos, and other sites such as Netscape's Netcenter.

In Part III, you'll find an entire hour devoted to each of the two main browsers, plus an hour on America Online's software. In these hours, you'll learn how to change your home page and set other browser preferences.

FIGURE 4.1
Your browser goes automatically to its "home page." The home page may have been selected by the browser maker or by your Internet provider.

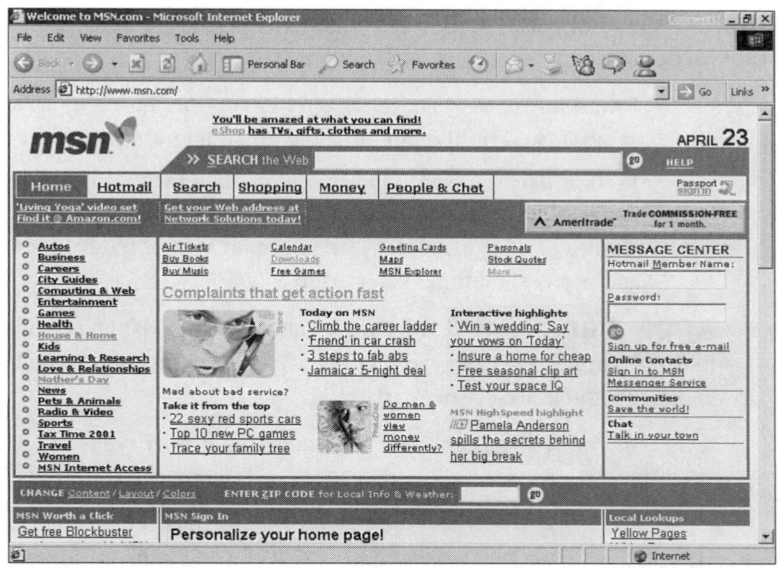

You don't have to do anything with your home page. You can just ignore it, and jump from it to anywhere on the Web you want. But some home pages provide valuable resources, especially for newcomers.

Often, you'll find a great selection of *links* on your home page to other fun or useful pages. If your home page happens to be one set up by your local ISP, the page may even contain local news, weather, and links to other pages with information about your community. Now and then, before striking out onto the Web, be sure to give your home page a glance to check out what it has to offer.

NEW TERM **Link.** A link is an object in a Web page that you can activate to jump to another page, or another part of the page you're on. Links can appear onscreen as a block of text or as a picture or graphic. In most browsers, you go where the link leads simply by pointing to it with your mouse and clicking it. See "Basic Jumping Around," later in this hour.

Understanding Web Page Addresses

Using the Web is easy—that's why it's so popular. But if there's one thing about Web surfing that trips up newcomers, it's using Web page addresses effectively. So here and now, I'll set you straight on Web page addresses so that you can leap online with confidence.

For the most part, you'll deal with only two kinds of addresses for most Internet activities:

- **Email addresses**. These are easy to spot because they always contain an "at" symbol (`@`). You'll learn all about email addresses in Hour 5.
- **Web addresses**. These never contain an `@` symbol. Web page addresses are expressed as a series of letters separated by periods (`.`) and sometimes forward slashes (`/`), for example, `www.microsoft.com/index/contents.htm`. A Web address is sometimes referred to as a *URL*.

NEW TERM **URL.** A URL (Uniform Resource Locator) is the official name for the address format you use when telling a Web browser where to take you. (You can pronounce it "you-are-el" or "earl.")

Although most URLs are Web page addresses, other types of URLs may be used in a Web browser for accessing other types of Internet resources. You'll learn about Web page URLs in this hour, and about other types later in this book.

If you keep your eyes open, you'll see Web page and site addresses everywhere these days. By typing an address in your Web browser (as you learn to do shortly), you can go straight to that page, the page the address "points to." Just to give you a taste of the possibilities, and to get you accustomed to the look and feel of a Web site address, Table 4.1 shows the addresses of some fun and/or interesting Web sites.

As Table 4.1 shows, many addresses begin with the letters "www". But not all do, so don't assume.

TABLE 4.1 A Few Out of the Millions of Fun and Interesting Web Sites

Address	*Description*
`www.cnn.com`	Cable News Network (CNN)
`www.ebay.com`	eBay, an online auction house
`www.epicurious.com`	A trove of recipes
`www.scifi.com`	The SciFi Channel
`www.carprices.com`	A site where you can learn all about buying a new or used auto
`www.uncf.org`	The United Negro College Fund
`www.rockhall.com`	Cleveland's Rock & Roll Hall of Fame Museum
`www.un.org`	The United Nations

TABLE 4.1 continued

Address	*Description*
`www.nyse.com`	The New York Stock Exchange
`college-solutions.com`	A guide to choosing a college
`www.sleepnet.com`	Help for insomniacs
`www.nasa.gov`	The space agency's site
`www.adn.com`	The Anchorage, Alaska, *Daily News*
`www.twinsmagazine.com`	Advice for parents of multiples
`imdb.com`	The Internet Movie Database, everything about every film ever made
`www.amazon.com`	Amazon.com, a popular online bookshop
`www.nhl.com`	The National Hockey League

Appendix A, "Fun Web Sites to Visit," contains a directory of many more fun Web sites you might want to visit.

Anatomy of a Web Address

The address of a Web site is made up of several different parts. Each part is separated from those that follow it by a single, forward slash (/).

The first part of the address—everything up to the first single slash—is the Internet address of a Web server. Everything following that first slash is a directory path and/or filename of a particular page on the server. For example, consider the following fictitious URL:

```
Server address          Directory  Directory   Web page filename
     |                          |          |            |
www.dairyqueen.com/icecream/sundaes/fudge.htm
```

The filename of the actual Web page is `fudge.htm`. (Web page files often use a filename extension of `.htm` or `.html`.) That file is stored in a directory or folder called `sundaes`, which is itself stored in the `icecream` directory. These directories are stored on a Web server whose Internet address is `www.dairyqueen.com`.

Sometimes, an address will show just a server address, and no Web page filename. That's okay—many Web servers are set up to show a particular file to anyone who accesses the server (or a particular server directory) without specifying a Web page filename.

For example, if you go to the address of Microsoft's Web server, `www.microsoft.com`, the server automatically shows you an all-purpose Web page you can use for finding and jumping to other Microsoft pages. Such pages are often referred to as "top" or "index" pages, and often even use `index.htm` as their filename. The extension at the end of a filename (such as .htm) will vary based on the program that created it. You'll see lots of .cfm, .jsp, and .asp extensions along with the .htm and .html ones.

Technically, every Web page address begins with "`http://`" or "`https://`", particularly when described as a *URL,* the technical designation for the address format you use when working in a Web browser.

But the latest releases of Netscape Navigator and Internet Explorer no longer require you to type that first part. For example, using either of those browsers, you can surf to the URL `http://www.mcp.com` just by typing

`www.mcp.com`

(In fact, you don't even need to type the "www" part—if it's required, these browsers will fill it in for you.) Because of this change, Web page addresses often appear in advertising, books, and magazines with the `http://`" part left off.

If you use a browser other than the Big Two, or older versions of the Big Two, however, you probably have to include the `http://` part when typing URLs in your browser. For example, to go to `www.pepsi.com`, you would type

`http://www.pepsi.com`

To Do: Find the Address of Your Home Page

1. Connect to the Internet and open your Web browser. After a few moments, your home page (whatever it may be) appears (see Figure 4.2).
2. Examine your browser's toolbar area. The address you see there is the address of your home page (see Figure 4.3).
3. Make a mental note of the spot where you saw the home page address. That's where you'll always see the address of whatever page you're currently viewing. That's usually also the place where you'll type addresses to navigate the Web, as described next.

FIGURE 4.2
Step 1: *Open your browser to your home page.*

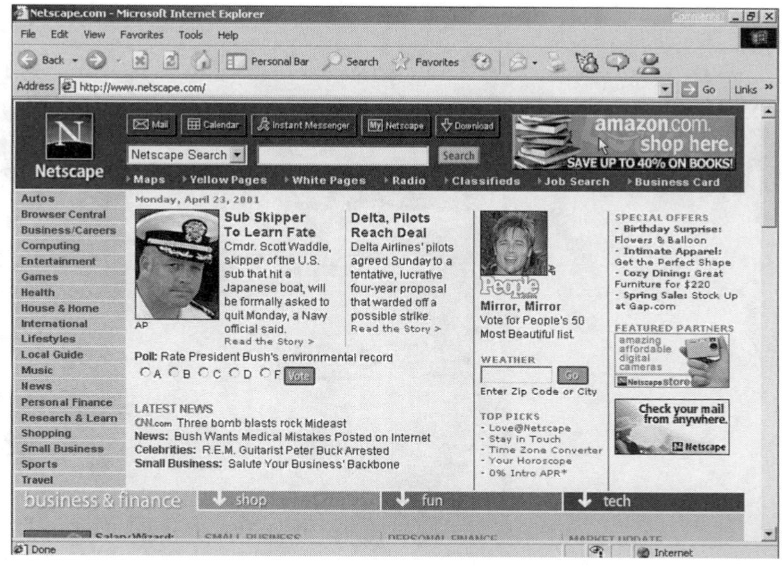

FIGURE 4.3
Step 2: *Find the address of your home page.*

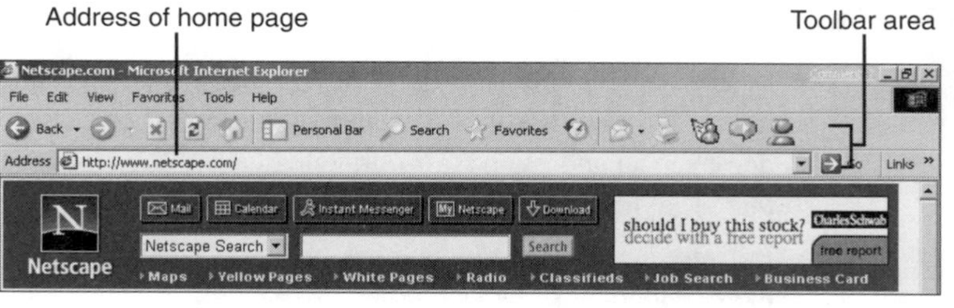

Going Straight to Any Web Address

Before you can jump to a page by entering its address, you must find the place in your browser provided for typing addresses. The term used to describe this area varies from browser to browser, but to keep things simple, I'll just call it the "address box." Figure 4.4 shows the toolbar area of Internet Explorer, with the address box containing an address.

In both Internet Explorer and Netscape Navigator, you'll see the address box as a long text box somewhere in the toolbar area, showing the address of the page you're currently viewing. If you don't see it, the toolbar that contains the address box might be switched off.

Address box showing URL of current page

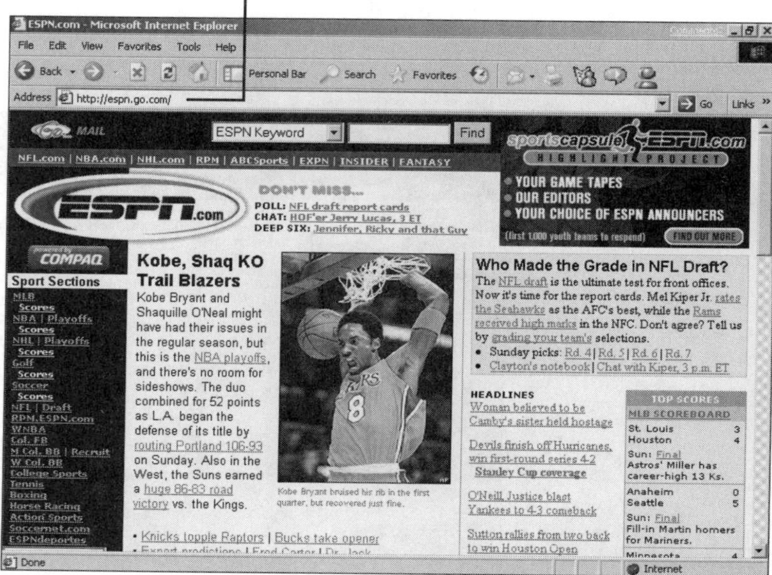

FIGURE 4.4

In most graphical browsers, you'll see an address box in the toolbar area where you type an address to go to a particular Web page or site.

To switch on the toolbar that contains the address box:

- In Internet Explorer, choose View, Toolbars, and make sure a check mark appears next to Address Bar in the menu that appears. If not, click Address Bar. If you still don't see an address box, try dragging each toolbar to the bottom of the stack, so that all toolbars are visible, and none overlap.
- In Netscape, choose View, Show, Location Toolbar. If you still don't see it, it's there, but collapsed so it's not visible. Click at the far-left end of each line in the toolbar area, and it should appear.

> If you use a browser other than the Big Two (Internet Explorer or Netscape Navigator), you may see an address box in the toolbar area, or at the bottom of the browser window. In some browsers, you may have to choose a menu item to display a dialog that contains the address box. Look for a menu item with a name like "Enter URL" or "Jump to New Location."

Entering and Editing URLs

After you've found the address box, you can go to a particular address by typing the address you want to visit in the box and pressing Enter. When the address box is in a toolbar, you usually must click in it first, then type the address, and press Enter.

Before you type an address in the address box, the address of the current page already appears there. In most Windows and Mac browsers, if you click once in the address box, the whole address there is highlighted, meaning that whatever you type next will replace that address.

If you click twice in the address box, the edit cursor appears there so that you can edit the address. That's a handy feature when you discover that you made a typo when first entering the address.

Note that when you type an address to go somewhere, your starting point doesn't matter—you can be at your home page or on any other page.

When typing the address, be careful of the following:

- Spell and punctuate the address exactly as shown, and do not use any spaces.
- Match the exact pattern of upper- and lowercase letters you see. Some Web servers are case-sensitive, and will not show you the page if you don't get the capitalization in the address just right.
- Some addresses end in a final slash (`/`), and some don't. But servers can be quirky about slashes, and many print sources where you see addresses listed mistakenly omit a required final slash, or add one that doesn't belong. Always type the address exactly as shown. But if that doesn't work, and the address appears not to end in a filename, try adding or removing the final slash.
- If you do not use a recent version of Internet Explorer or Netscape Navigator, you may be required to include the "`http://`" prefix at the beginning of the URL. For example, when you see an address listed as `www.discover.com`, you must enter it in your address box as

  ```
  http://www.discover.com
  ```

What happens if you type an address wrong? Nothing bad—you just don't go where you want to go. Usually, your browser displays an error message, reporting that the browser could not find the address you requested. Check that you spelled, punctuated, and capitalized the address correctly. If you discover a mistake, edit (or retype) the address and press Enter to try again.

Note that Web servers and their pages are not permanent. From time to time, an address will fail not because you made a mistake, but just because the page or server to which it points is no longer online, either temporarily (because of a system glitch) or permanently.

To Do: Go to Sams Publishing's Web Site

Honest, I'm not shilling for Sams Publishing here, even though Sams publishes this book. It's just that Web pages come and go. Most Web site URLs for large organizations work fine for years. But addresses can change, and Web pages and sites do disappear from time to time.

I want to give you a reliable set of steps, and I know that the Sams Web site will still be around when you read this.

1. Connect to the Internet and open your Web browser (see Figure 4.5).

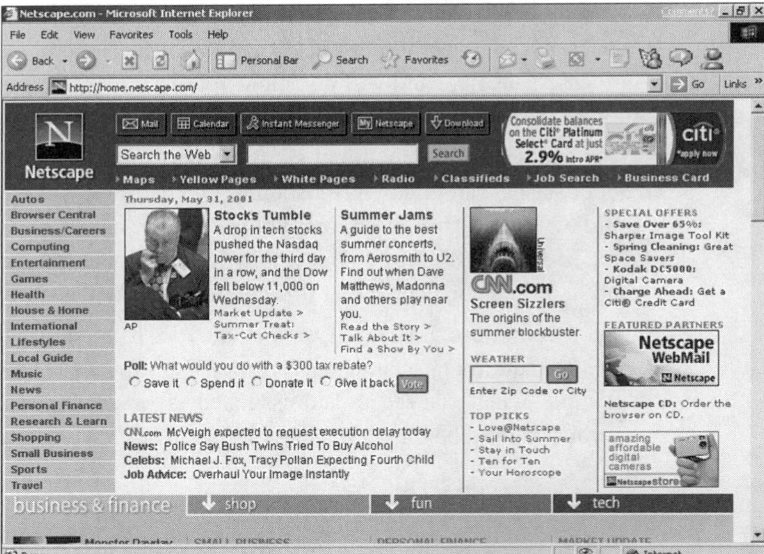

FIGURE 4.5
Step 1: Open your Web browser.

2. Find the address box, and click in it once.
3. Type the URL (see Figure 4.6)

   `www.samspublishing.com`

   (If you are using an older browser, you may have to add the `http://` prefix.)

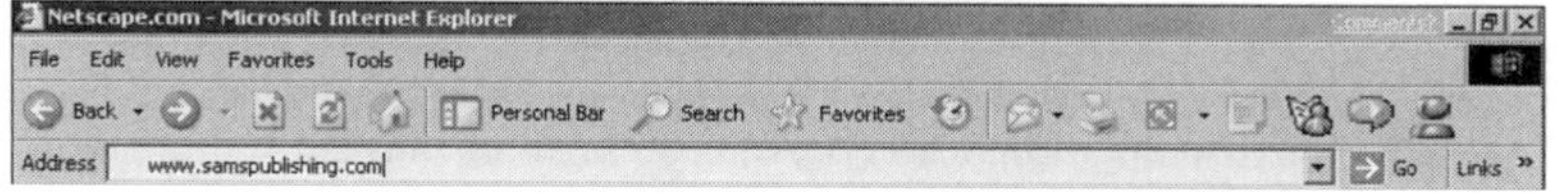

FIGURE 4.6
***Step 3:** Type in the URL* `http://www.samspublishing.com`.

4. Press Enter. Sams's Web site appears (see Figure 4.7).

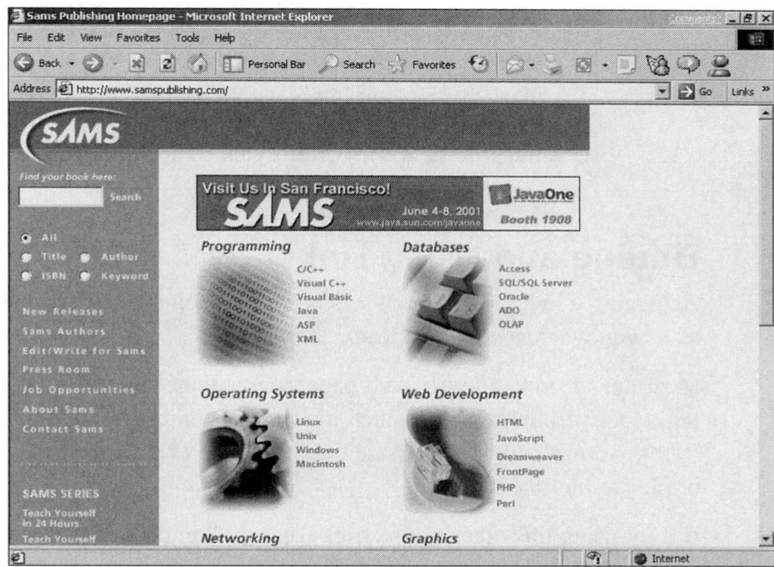

FIGURE 4.7
***Step 4:** Press Enter to see the Sams Publishing Web site.*

Basic Jumping Around

I've shown you first how to move about the Web by entering an address, in part so you could discover along the way a number of important concepts that will help you navigate successfully.

Now I must show you that many—even most—of the times you jump from page to page, you won't type an address. All you'll do is click a link or button.

Sorry to show the hard way before the easy ones, but you must understand that you're not always going to find a link that takes you exactly where you want to go. URLs are like cars—they take you directly to a particular place. Links are like the bus: They often take you just to the right neighborhood.

Here is as good a place as any to point out that some Web pages take a long time to appear, even if you have a fast modem and Internet connection. If some pages do seem terribly slow, don't worry that there's something wrong with your computer, modem, or connection. The problem is probably that the page you're accessing is very complex.

You see, each time you display a particular Web page, the whole page must travel through the Internet to your computer to appear on your screen. A page that's mostly text appears quickly, because text pages contain little data, and thus travel quickly through the Net. Pictures, multimedia, and Java programs balloon the number and size of the files that make up the Web page, and thus take much longer to appear.

Reclicking the link to a page over and over again is only going to slow down the process, and may cause your computer to freeze.

Finding and Using Links

Activating a link in most browsers is simple: Point to the link and click it; your browser takes you wherever the link leads.

Most links lead to another Web page, or to another part of a long Web page you're viewing. However, links can do much more. For example, some links, when activated, may start the download of a software file (see Hour 15, "Downloading Programs and Files") or play a multimedia file.

It's not using links that can be tricky, but finding them in Web pages that aren't designed well enough to make the links obvious. Links appear in a Web page in any of three ways:

As text. You'll notice text in Web pages that appears to be formatted differently from the rest. The formatting differs depending upon your browser, but text that serves as a link is usually underlined (see Figure 4.8) and displayed in a different color than any other text in the page.

As pictures. Any picture you see in a Web page may be a link. For example, a company logo may be a link leading to a page containing information about that company.

As imagemaps. An imagemap is a single picture that contains not just one link, but several. Clicking on different parts of the picture activates different links (see Figure 4.9).

Text links are usually easy to spot because of their color and underlining (see Figure 4.8). Picture and imagemap links can be harder to spot at a glance.

But most browsers provide a simple way to determine what is and is not a link. Whenever the mouse pointer is on a link, it changes from the regular pointer to a special pointer that always indicates links.

FIGURE 4.8
Often, links are indicated by underlined text.

Using Navigation Buttons: Back, Forward, Home, and Stop

In most browsers for Windows and the Mac, you'll see a whole raft of toolbar buttons, many of which you'll examine as this book progresses. But by far, the most important are the Big Four: Back, Forward, Home, and Stop (see Figure 4.10). These buttons help you move easily back and forth among any pages you've already visited in the current online session, and to conveniently deal with the unexpected.

For example, when exploring a particular Web site, you often begin at a sort of "top" page that branches out to others. After branching out a few steps from the top to explore particular pages, you'll often want to work your way back to the top again, to start off in a new direction. The Big Four buttons make that kind of Web navigation simple and typing-free.

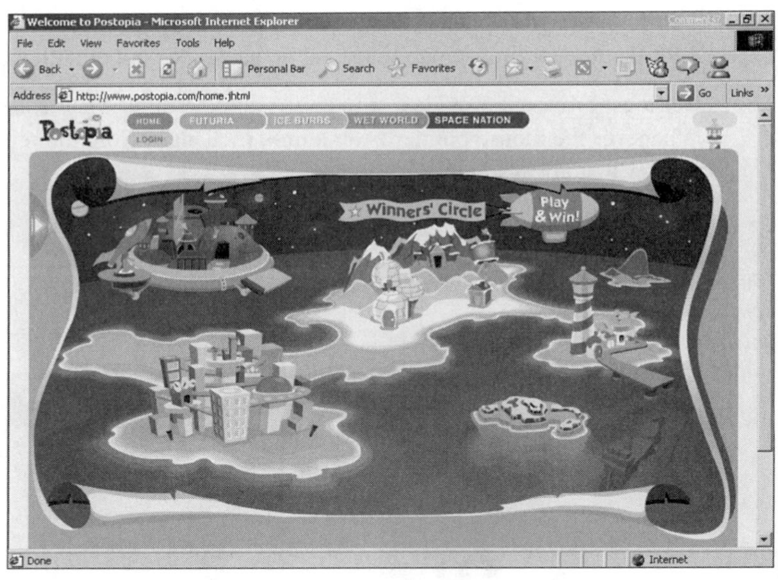

FIGURE 4.9
Each part of this imagemap is a different link. In this case, clicking on any of the signs these people are holding will take you to a different page.

FIGURE 4.10
The main toolbars in Internet Explorer (shown here) and Netscape Navigator prominently feature the invaluable Back, Forward, Stop, and Home buttons.

Here's how you can use each of these buttons:

Back retraces your steps, taking you one step backward in your browsing each time you click it. For example, if you move from Page A to Page B, clicking the Back button takes you back to A. If you go from A to B to C, pressing Back twice returns you to A. When you reach the first page you visited in the current online session, the Back button is disabled; there's nowhere left to go back to.

Forward reverses the action of Back. If you've used Back to go backward from Page B to A, Forward takes you forward to B. If you click Back three times—going from D to C to B to A—clicking Forward three times takes you to D again. When you reach the page on which Back was first clicked, the Forward button is disabled because you can only move Forward to pages you've come "Back" from.

Home takes you from anywhere on the Web directly to the page configured in your browser as "home," described at the start of this hour. Going Home is a great way to reorient yourself if you lose your way and need to get back to a reliable starting point.

Stop immediately stops whatever the browser is doing. If you click Stop while a page is materializing on your screen, the browser stops getting the page from the server, leaves the half-finished page on your screen, and awaits your next instruction.

> Back, Forward, and Home do not care how you got where you are. In other words, no matter what techniques you've used to browse through a series of pages—entering URLs, clicking links, using buttons, or any combination of these—Back takes you back through them, Forward undoes Back, and Home takes you home.

Back and Stop are particularly useful for undoing mistakes. For example, if you click on a link that downloads a file, and while the file is downloading you decide you don't want it, you can click Stop to halt the download but stay on the current page. Click Back to halt the download and return to the preceding page.

To Do: Practice Using Links and Buttons

1. Go to the ESPN Web site at `espn.go.com`, find any interesting-looking link, and click it (see Figure 4.11).
2. A new page opens, the one the link you clicked points to (see Figure 4.12). Click Back to return to the top ESPN page.
3. Click another link on the top ESPN page (see Figure 4.13). On the page that appears, find and click yet another link (see Figure 4.14). (If you see no links, click Back to return to the top ESPN page, and try another route.)
4. Click Back twice (see Figure 4.15) to return to the top ESPN page.
5. Click Forward twice. You go ahead to where you just came back from (see Figure 4.16).

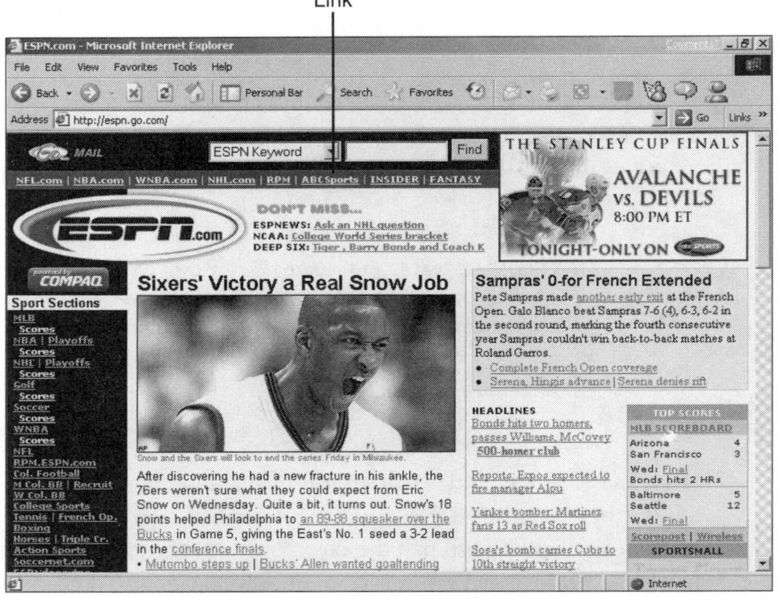

FIGURE 4.11
Step 1: *Go to* `espn.go.com` *and click on a link.*

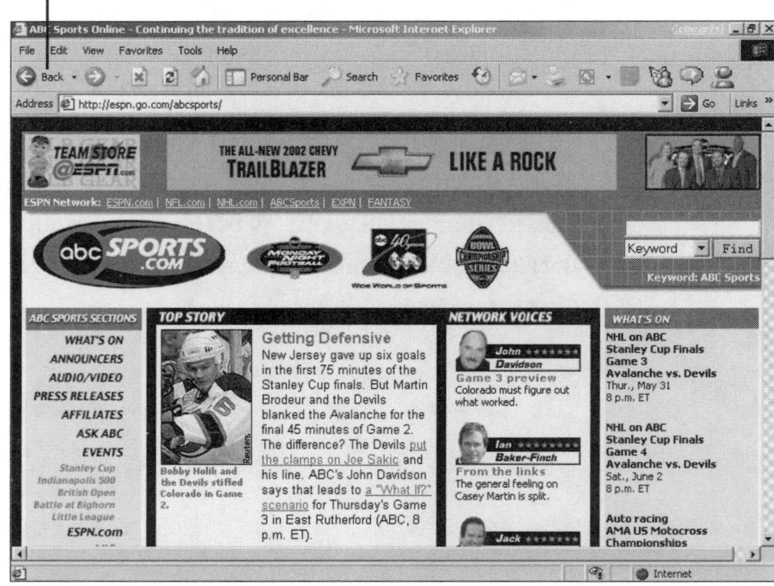

FIGURE 4.12
Step 2: *Click the Back button.*

FIGURE 4.13
Step 3: Click on another link.

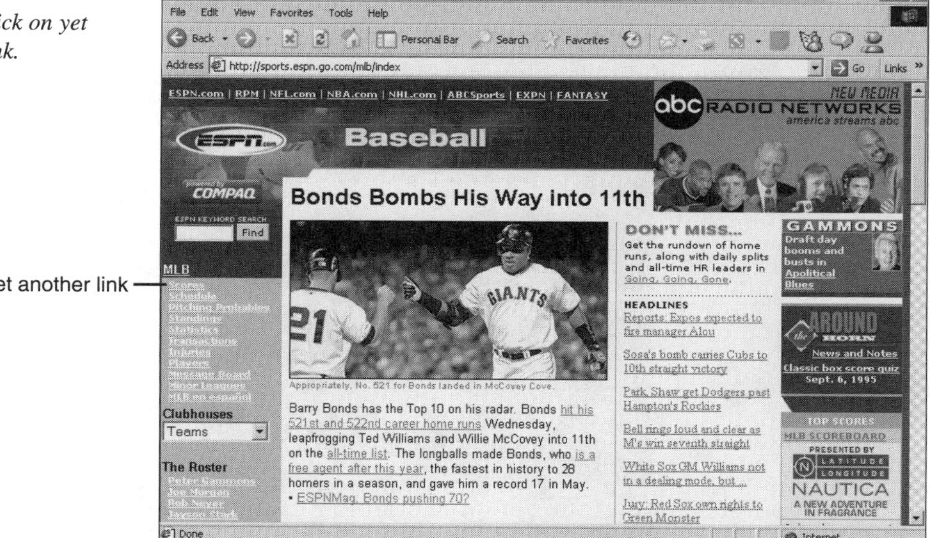

FIGURE 4.14
Step 3: Click on yet another link.

Back button

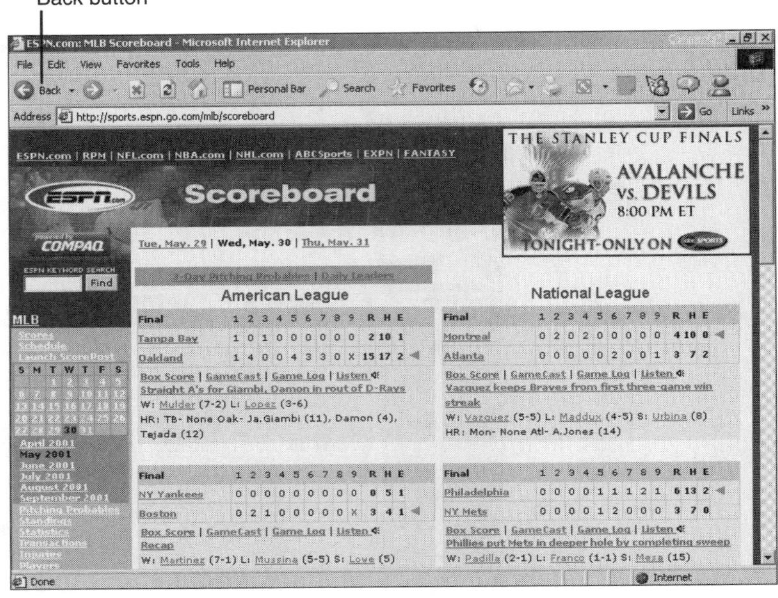

FIGURE 4.15
Step 4: Click Back twice.

Forward button

FIGURE 4.16
Step 5: Click Forward twice.

6. Try a new URL: Enter `www.akc.org` for the American Kennel Club (see Figure 4.17).

FIGURE 4.17
Step 6: *Enter a new URL.*

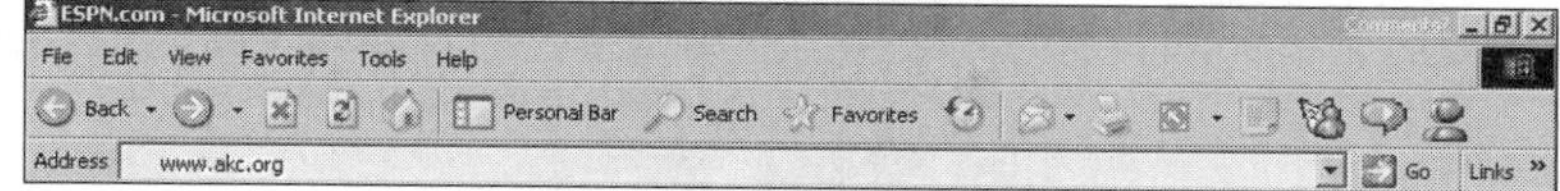

7. From the AKC page (see Figure 4.18), click Back once. You return to a page at ESPN.

FIGURE 4.18
Step 7: *Click Back once.*

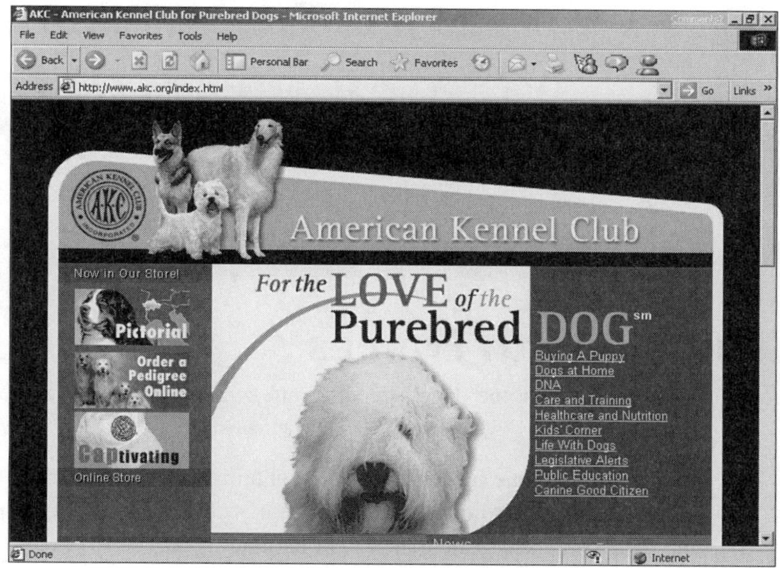

8. Click home, and you'll return to your home page, as you see in Figure 4.19.

Figure 4.19
Step 8: Click home.

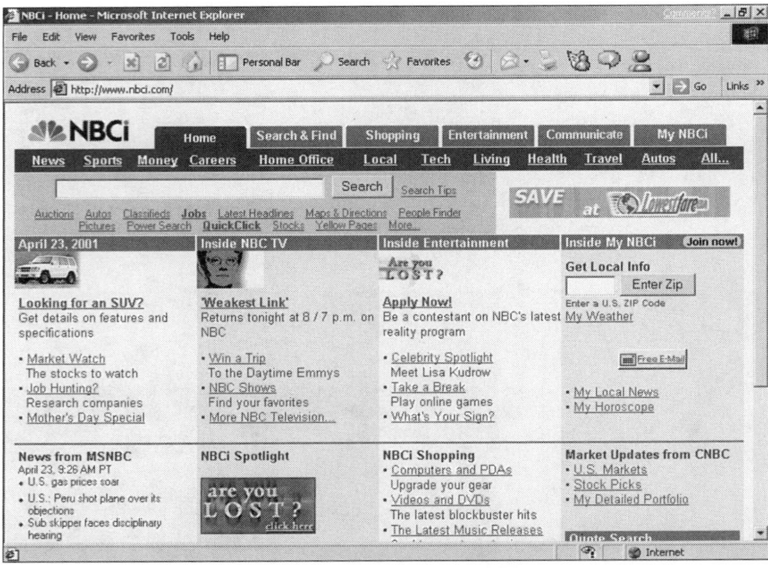

Fussing with Frames

You'll find that some pages are split into *frames*, two or more separate panes (see Figure 4.20).

In effect, each pane in a frames page contains its own, separate little Web page. That enables each pane to operate independently of the others; for example, clicking a link in one pane can change the contents of another.

Some folks get all boxed up by frames, but using a frames-based page doesn't have to be tricky. Just remember the following tips:

- All links within panes are active all the time.
- Some panes have their own scrollbars. When you see scrollbars on a pane, use them to scroll more of the pane's contents into view. If you want to use your keyboard's Up and Down arrows to scroll within a pane, you need to click within the appropriate pane first.
- While you're on a frames page, the Back and Forward buttons take you back and forth among the panes you've used in the current frames page, *not* among pages. Sometimes, it can be tough to use Back to "back out" of a frames page to the page you saw before it; at such times, it's often easier to enter a new URL or click Home to break free of the frames, then go from there.

FIGURE 4.20
A frames page can show two or more separate documents at once, each in its own pane.

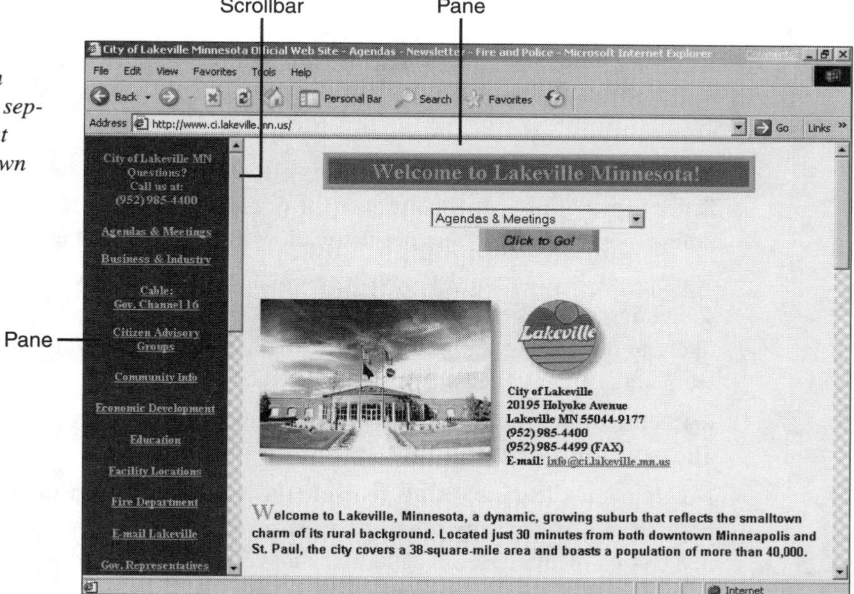

- Some pages use "borderless" frames, and so do not appear at first glance to be frames pages. But after a little experience, you'll quickly learn to identify any frames page when it appears, even when the frames are implemented subtly.

> Internet Explorer, Netscape Navigator, and a few other major browsers support frames, but some others do not.
>
> For this reason, many frames pages are preceded by a non-frames page that provides two links: One for displaying a frames page, and another for displaying the same content in a no-frames version.
>
> If your browser can't handle frames—or if your browser can handle them but you can't—just choose the no-frames version. Life's too short.

Summary

That's all there is to basic browsing. Just by entering URLs, clicking links, and using buttons like Back and Home, you can explore near and far. Little bumps like frames add a little complexity to the mix, but nothing you can't handle.

Q&A

Q I've already started doing a little Web browsing on my own, and from time to time I hit a page that says I need a "plug-in" to continue. What's that all about?

A People are always inventing new kinds of content to put on the Web, such as faster, better forms of online video or interactive gaming. When something new goes online, not all the browsers out there know how to play that new content yet.

A plug-in is a program that adds a new capability to your browser so it can do something new, like play a new kind of multimedia. Most of the plug-ins you're likely to need will be plug-ins for playing new forms of online multimedia. You'll learn about finding and using plug-ins in Hour 12.

Q I was on a page, and suddenly a box popped up reporting some gobbledygook about "Java." What did I do wrong?

A Nothing at all. (Stop blaming yourself!) Another way Web programmers teach a browser new tricks is by running any of several different kinds of program code in it. The two main kinds are called Java and JavaScript. You don't have to know how to do anything to take advantage of Java and JavaScript programs; they run automatically.

However, sometimes the program code contains mistakes, or you are using a browser that has little glitches in its compatibility with the program code. That's when you see these error messages.

The best way to prevent the messages is to try to always use the most recent version of Internet Explorer or Netscape Navigator (see Hour 2). If you do, you'll see such messages rarely. When you do see the messages, just ignore 'em.

Q You said that the `http://` prefix indicates that a URL is a Web page. If URLs are used only in Web browsers, why would a URL need to point to anything *other* than a Web page?

A Web browsers are the Swiss Army knives of the Internet. Many Web browsers are designed to serve as a client for several different types of servers.

Of course, their main gig is showing Web pages on Web servers. But many Web browsers can also show newsgroup messages on news servers, and interact with other server types you can learn about in Appendix B, "Tools for the Serious User: FTP and Telnet." Finally, a Web browser can be used to view various types of files that are stored, not on the Internet, but right on your local computer or network.

For each of the different types of resources a Web browser can access, a different URL prefix is needed. For example, the URL for a resource on an FTP server begins not with `http://`, but with `ftp://`.

In upcoming hours, you'll learn more about accessing non-Web stuff through a Web browser. You'll also learn that it's often better to use a specific client for these activities, rather than your Web browser. A real corkscrew or screwdriver usually works better than the one in your Swiss Army knife.

PART II

Talking to the World

Hour

Hour 5

Sending and Receiving Email

Web browsing is the hottest Internet activity, but email might be the most widely used and most productive one.

Using Internet email—which has become such an everyday fixture that many people now call it plain "mail"—you can easily exchange messages with anyone else on the Internet. An email message typically reaches its addressee within minutes (or at most, within an hour or so), even on the opposite side of the globe. It's faster than paper mail, easier than faxing, and sometimes just plain fun.

It's so easy, in fact, that I know people who haven't written a dozen paper letters in a decade but who write email daily. It's a great way to keep up with friends and communicate with business contacts. In fact, there are some business people so tied to their email that if you contact them in any way *other* than email, you might not get an answer.

At the end of the hour, you'll be able to answer the following questions:

- How do I recognize an email address?
- How do I set up my email program?
- How do I display a message so I can read it?
- How do I compose and send an email message?
- How do I receive messages others have sent to me?
- How can I reply to a message I've received, or forward that message to someone else?
- How can I keep track of all the email addresses I use?

Types of Email Programs

Email can be as complicated or as basic as you want it to be. There are a wide variety of different email programs—some that you have to buy as part of a huge suite of applications, some you get automatically with a browser, and some you can use right over the Web, without installing anything.

Making matters more confusing is the fact that both Microsoft and Netscape, the two companies who hold all the cards when it comes to using the Web, offer a wide variety of choices. Both offer a free program as part of their browser suite, but both also offer free Web-based email (Microsoft has Hotmail, Netscape has Netscape Webmail). Web-based email allows you to read messages right off a Web page, just like you are browsing. It is covered later in this chapter.

This chapter can't possible cover all the options for email. It's designed to cover the most commonly used features. After you're comfortable with those, we figure, you'll be ready to pick up your program's little nuances on your own.

Understanding Email Addresses

The only piece of information you need to send email to someone is that person's Internet email address. An email address is easy to spot: It always has that "at" symbol (`@`) in the middle of it. For example, you know at a glance that

```
sammy@fishbait.com
```

is an email address. In most email addresses, everything following the `@` symbol is the domain address of a company, Internet service provider, educational institution, or other organization. The part before the `@` is the name (or user ID) of a particular employee or user. For example, the addresses

```
SallyP@genco.com
mikey@genco.com
Manager_of_Sales@genco.com
```

obviously belong to three different people, all of whom work for the same company or use the same Internet service provider (whatever Genco is).

Each online service has its own domain, too: For example, America Online's is `aol.com`, and Microsoft Network's is `msn.com`. So you can tell that the email address

```
neddyboy@aol.com
```

is that of the America Online user named `neddyboy`.

> Online service users usually can omit the `@` symbol and anything that follows it when sending to other users on the same service. For example, suppose you want to send email to
>
> `allieoop@aol.com`
>
> If you use a regular Internet ISP or any online service other than America Online (`aol.com`), you would use the address as shown. However, if you use America Online, you can address the message simply to
>
> `allieoop`

Setting Up Your Email Program

5

There are many different email programs out there. Internet suites such as Internet Explorer and Netscape Communicator include an email program—but you must take care when installing these programs not to optionally omit the email component of the suite. Choosing the "full" installation option when setting up a suite ensures that you include all the suite's client programs.

In the suites, the email programs are called

- **Messenger,** in Netscape Communicator. You can open Messenger from within the Navigator browser by choosing Communicator, Messenger (see Figure 5.1).
- **Outlook Express,** in Internet Explorer. You can open Outlook Express from within the Internet Explorer browser by clicking the Mail button on the toolbar and choosing Read Mail from the menu that appears (see Figure 5.2).

Don't confuse the free Microsoft email program Outlook Express with another Microsoft program, Outlook (no "Express").

Like Outlook Express, Outlook is an email program. But Outlook also does many other things Outlook Express does not do, such as personal scheduling and contact management. And, of course, Outlook is not free. Most people who use Outlook buy it as a part of Microsoft's Office suite.

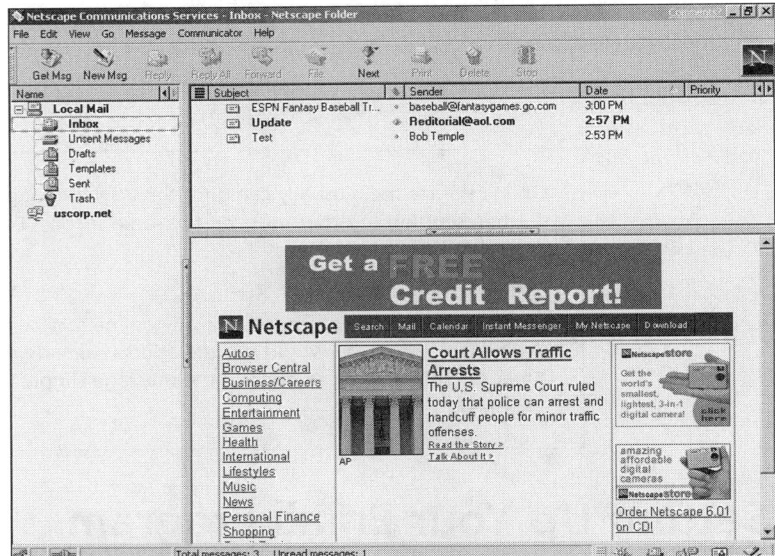

FIGURE 5.1
Netscape Messenger, the email program that's included in the Netscape Communicator suite.

If you don't already have an email program, you can jump ahead and apply the file-finding techniques from Hour 14, "Downloading Programs and Files," to search for one, or check out the Tucows directory of Internet software at `www.tucows.com`.

Among the links you'll likely find in any search for email programs are links to various versions of a program called Eudora, one of the most popular email programs outside of the suites. If you simply want to go straight to learning about and downloading Eudora, visit the site of Eudora's maker at `www.eudora.com`.

If you use an online service, such as America Online or CompuServe, you might not be able to easily choose just any email program you want to use; you might be required to use the online service interface—the tool you use for accessing the service's non-Internet content—to send and receive email.

However, using an online service interface for email is similar to using an Internet email program, as described in this hour. And from the online service interface, you can send email both to others on your service and to anyone on the Internet.

You need not configure email, as described next, for an online service. Email configuration is handled automatically when you sign up for the service and install its software.

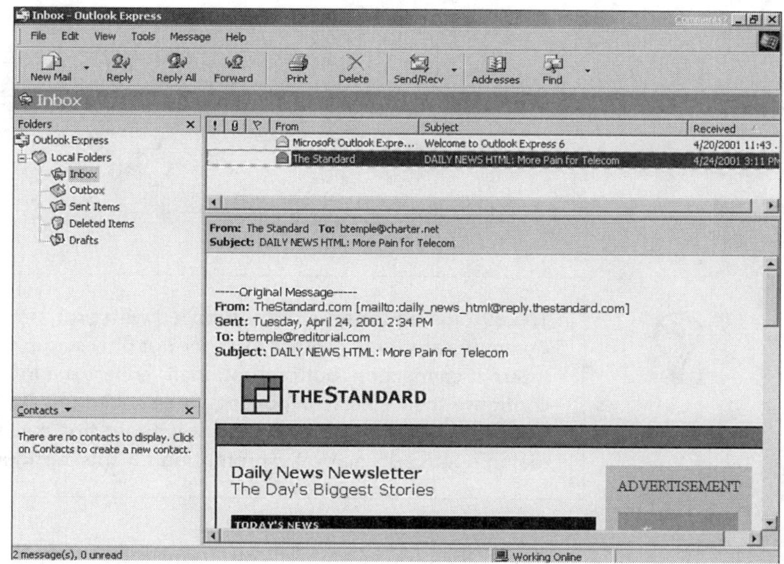

FIGURE 5.2
Outlook Express, the email program that's included with Microsoft Internet Explorer.

Configuring Email

After installing an email program, you need to configure it before you can use it. All email programs have a configuration dialog of some kind (or a series of dialog boxes) in which you can enter the information required for exchanging email. You'll find the configuration dialogs

- **In Netscape Messenger,** by choosing Edit, Preferences to open the Preferences dialog box. In the list of Categories, choose Mail & Newsgroups. Complete the configuration settings in the Mail & Newsgroups category's Identity and Mail Servers subcategories (see Figure 5.3).
- **For Outlook Express,** by completing the Mail dialogs of the Windows Internet Connection Wizard (see Hour 3). If you open Outlook Express without having

configured it first, the Connection Wizard opens automatically to collect configuration information from you.

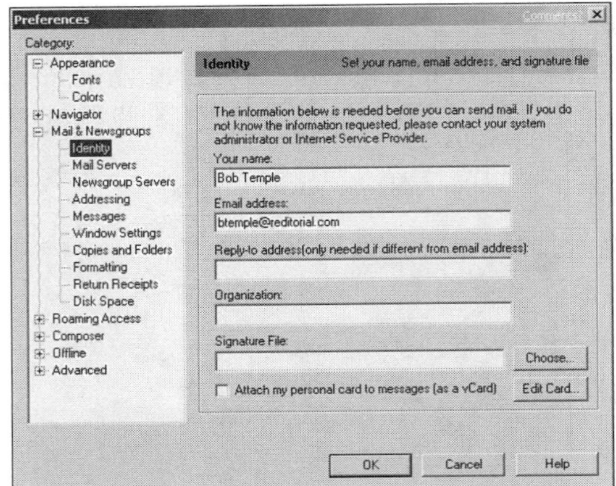

FIGURE 5.3
In Netscape Messenger, configure email settings in the Mail & Newsgroups category of the Preferences dialog box.

The automated setup routines supplied with programs such as Netscape Communicator and Internet Explorer not only set up your browser and Internet connection, but can optionally collect the information required to configure their email components (Messenger and Outlook Express). If you open Messenger or Outlook Express without first having configured them, a dialog opens automatically, prompting for the configuration information.

The configuration dialogs for most email programs require most or all of the following information, all of which your Internet service provider will tell you:

- Your full name. (Okay, so you don't need your ISP to tell you this one.)
- Your full email address. (Some configuration dialogs make you indicate the two parts of your address separately: the *username*—the part of the email address preceding the `@` symbol—and your *domain*—the part of the email address following the `@` symbol.)
- The address of your service provider's *outgoing mail server*, sometimes called the SMTP server.
- The address of your service provider's *incoming mail server*, sometimes called the POP3 server (some ISPs use another type of server called IMAP4). The POP3 address is sometimes (but not always) identical to the SMTP address.

Also, to ensure that no one but you gets your email, most ISPs require you to choose and use an email password. Some email programs let you enter that password in the configuration dialog so you needn't type a password each time you check your email.

Getting Around in Your Email Program

Before jumping right into sending and receiving messages, it's a good idea to learn how to get around in your email program, move among its *folders* (lists of messages), and display messages you select from a folder.

When working with email, the only time you need to be connected to the Internet is when you actually send messages—transmit them to the Internet—or receive messages—copy them from the Internet to your computer. You can be online or offline while composing messages, reading messages you've received, or managing your messages.

You'll learn more about using email offline in Hour 16, "Working Smarter by Working Offline."

Choosing a Folder

Netscape Messenger and Outlook Express divide their messaging activities into a family of folders. In each folder, you see a list of messages you can display or work with in other ways. The folders are

- **Inbox.** The Inbox folder lists messages you have received.
- **Outbox** (called Unsent Messages in Messenger). The Outbox folder lists messages you have composed but saved to be sent later.
- **Sent.** The Sent folder lists copies of all messages you've sent, for your reference.
- **Deleted** (called Trash in Messenger). The Deleted folder lists messages you've deleted from any other folder.

Outlook Express and Messenger both handle two different jobs: email and newsgroups. Each therefore has folders not only for email, but also for newsgroups. Before performing an email activity in one of these programs, always be sure first that you're in an email-related folder, such as Inbox, and not a newsgroup folder.

You'll learn about using newsgroups in Hour 7, "Participating in Newsgroups and Mailing Lists."

To switch among folders in either Outlook Express or Messenger, click a folder name in the panel along the left side of the window (see Figure 5.4).

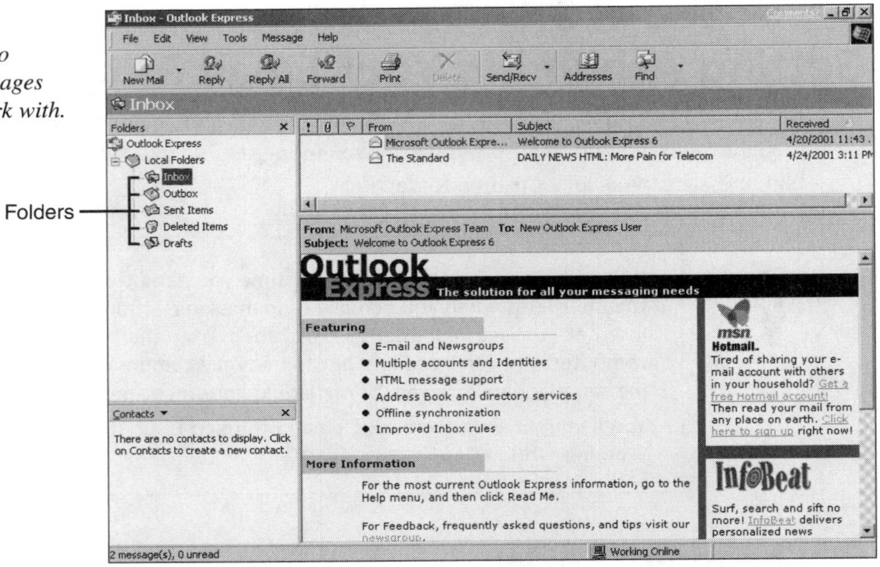

FIGURE 5.4
Select a folder to choose the messages you want to work with.

Displaying a Message

From the list displayed by each folder, you can display any message. You do this in either of two ways (the steps are the same in both Outlook Express and Messenger):

- Single-click the message in the list to display it in the preview pane (see Figure 5.5) in the bottom of the window.
- Double-click the message in the list to display it in its own message window (see Figure 5.6).

In general, the preview pane is best when you're simply scanning messages, and need to move quickly from one to the next. Use a full message window to read a long message, or to read a message you will reply to or forward (as described later in this hour).

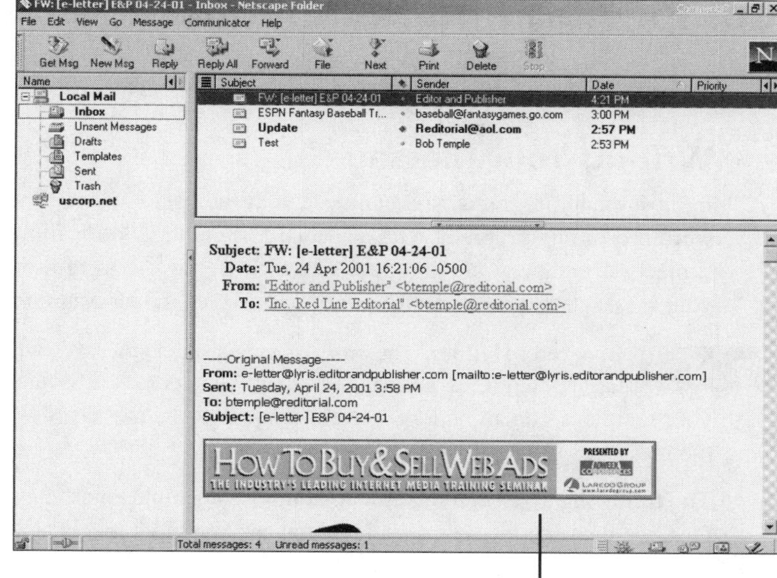

FIGURE 5.5
Single-click a message in a folder to display the message in the preview pane.

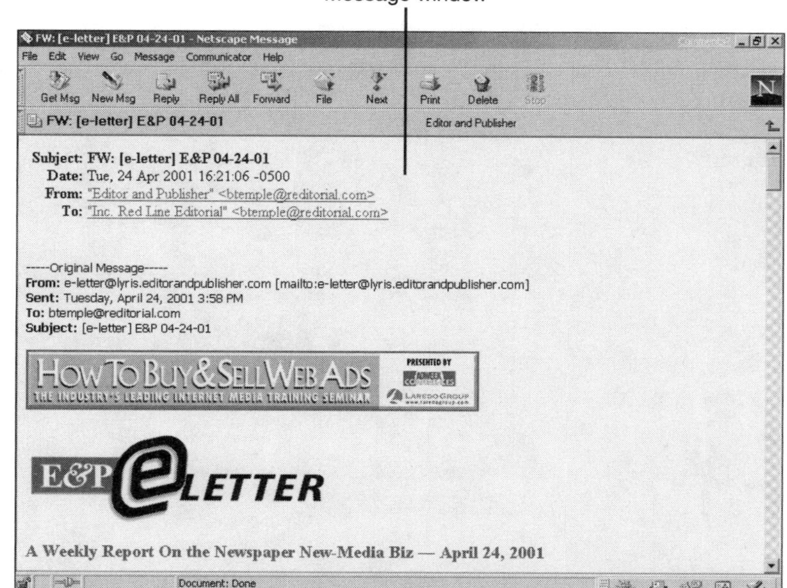

FIGURE 5.6
Double-click a message in a folder to display the message in a message window.

5

Composing and Sending a Message

When you have something to say, and the email address of someone to whom you want to say it, you're ready to go.

Writing Your Message

In most email programs, you compose your message in a window that's very much like a word processing program, with a special form at the top for filling in the address and subject information—the message's *header*. Below the form for the header, you type your message text in the large space provided for the message *body*.

NEW TERM **Body** and **Header.** The *body* of a message is the text, which you compose in the large pane of the message window. The address information you type—including your recipient's email address and the subject of the message—is called the *header* of the message.

The following To Dos show how to compose a simple email message. Following the To Dos, the next section describes how you can send that message.

To Do

To Do: Compose a New Message in Outlook Express

1. Click the New Mail button (see Figure 5.7).

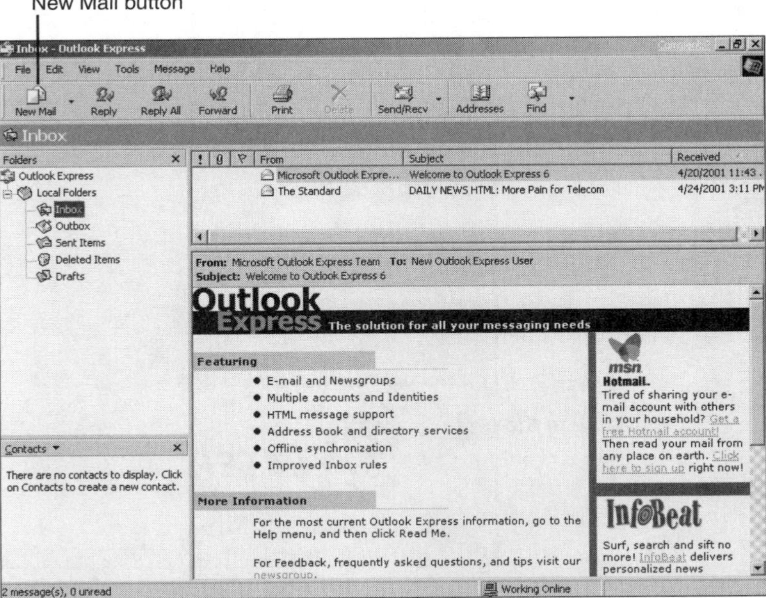

FIGURE 5.7
Step 1: *Click the New Mail button in Outlook Express.*

2. In the To line (near the top of the window), type the email address of the person to whom you want to send a message (see Figure 5.8).

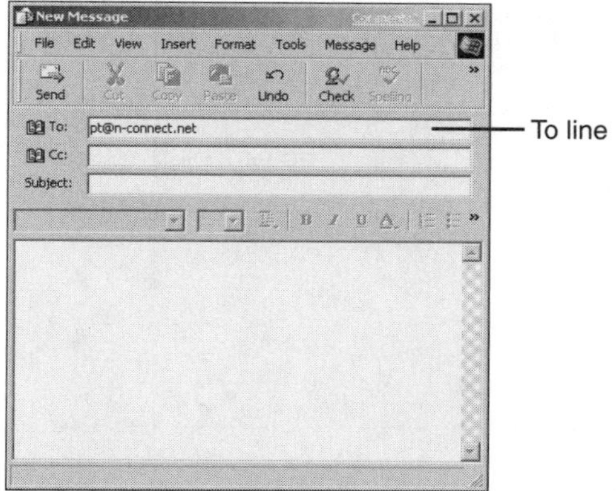

FIGURE 5.8
Step 2: *Type in the recipient's email address.*

3. Click in the Subject line, and type a concise, meaningful subject for your message (see Figure 5.9). (The subject appears in the message list of the recipient, to explain the purpose of your message.)

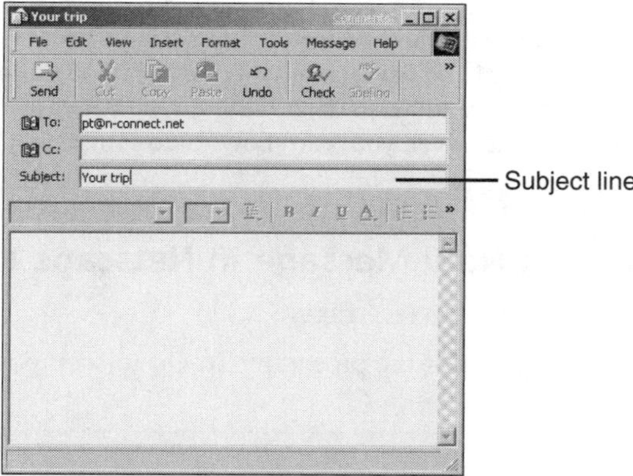

FIGURE 5.9
Step 3: *Type in a subject for the message.*

5

4. Click in the large panel of the new message window and type your message, just as you would in a word processor (see Figure 5.10).

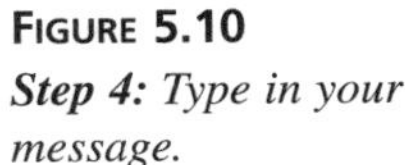

FIGURE 5.10
***Step 4:** Type in your message.*

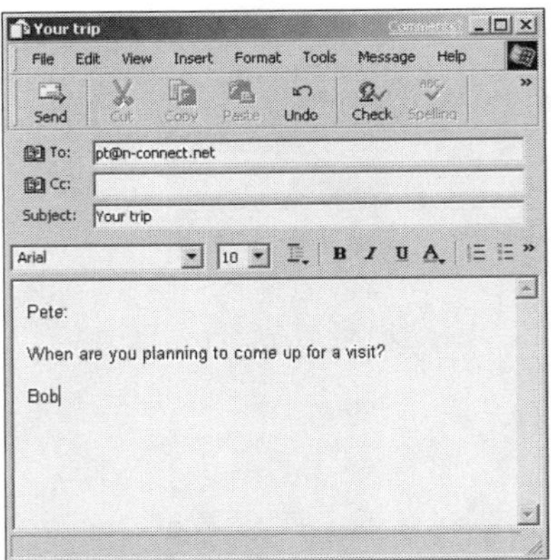

It used to be that email programs automatically created text-only messages, because many email readers weren't configured to display HTML messages. The latest versions of both Outlook Express and Netscape Messenger allow you to create messages in HTML format.

What does this mean to you? Simply put, it allows you to format the text, using bold, italics, different fonts, and so on, so the message can have a personal touch. Be aware, however, that some of those who receive your messages might still be using email clients that don't allow them to display HTML messages. In Hour 19, "Creating Web Pages and Multimedia Messages," however, you learn how to do some fancy message formatting.

To Do

To Do: Compose a New Message in Netscape Messenger

1. Click the New Msg button (see Figure 5.11).
2. Follow steps 2, 3, and 4 of the preceding To Do for composing a message.

You can send one message to multiple recipients in several different ways. For example, you can "cc" (carbon copy) your email to recipients other than your primary addressee(s). To do this, just enter their email addresses into the CC: field of the New Message window.

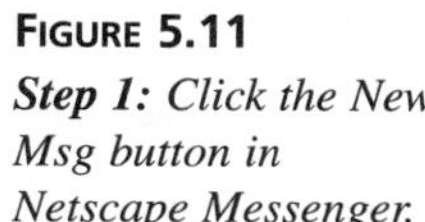

FIGURE 5.11
***Step 1:** Click the New Msg button in Netscape Messenger.*

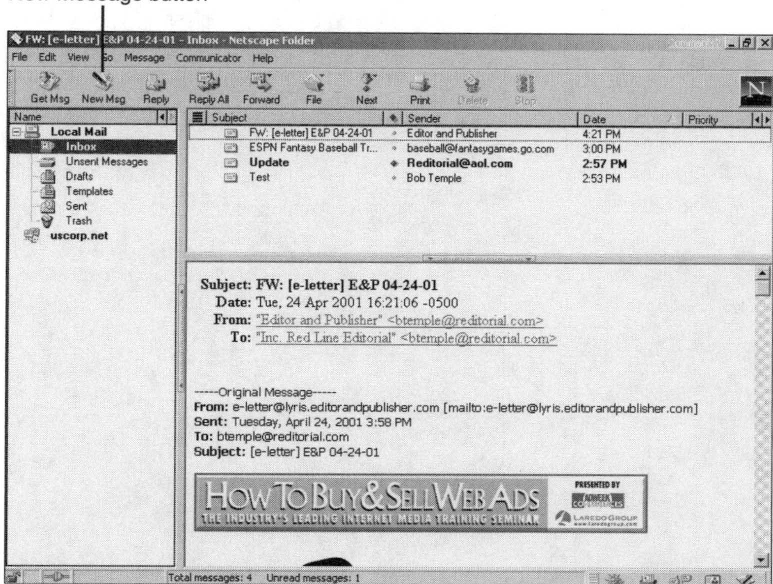

Sending a Message

After the header (To and Subject) and body (what you have to say) of the message are complete, you send your message on its way. In most programs, you do so simply by clicking a button labeled Send in the toolbar of the window in which you composed the message.

What happens immediately *after* you click Send depends upon a number of different factors:

- The email program you use
- Whether you're online or off
- How your program is configured

The message can be sent immediately out through the Internet to its intended recipient. If you're offline when you click Send, your email program can automatically connect you to the Internet to send the message. Otherwise, you must connect before sending.

However, instead of sending your message the instant you click Send, your email program can instead send the message to your Outbox (or Unsent Messages) folder, to wait. After clicking Send, you can open your Outbox or Unsent Messages folder to see whether the message is there (see Figure 5.12).

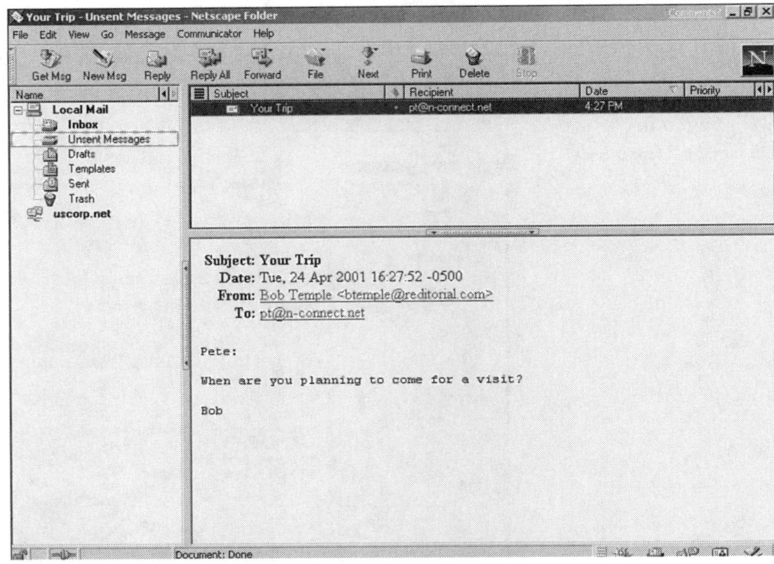

FIGURE 5.12
In some programs, messages are sent to wait in the Outbox or Unsent Messages folder, then finally go out to their recipients at a later time.

Why does this happen? Well, actually it's pretty smart. This Outbox scenario enables you to do all your email composing offline, saving as many messages as you want in your Outbox folder. Then, when you're all done, you can send all the messages in one step.

> In Hour 16, you'll learn how to make the most of this "delayed send" scenario, along with other offline techniques.
>
> You'll also learn how to configure both Outlook Express and Messenger to do what you want: Either send messages right away, or send them to the Outbox or Unsent Messages folder for sending later.

Here's how to send waiting messages:

- In Outlook Express, click the Send/Recv button (it might be labeled "Send/Receive" in your copy) to send all messages in the Outbox folder.
- In Netscape Messenger, click the Get Msg button (short for Get Messages) to send all messages in the Unsent Messages folder.

If you are offline when you click the Send/Recv (Send/Receive) or Get Msg button, Outlook Express and Messenger connect you to the Internet automatically (or prompt you to do so) to send your messages.

The Send/Recv and Get Msg buttons not only send all waiting messages, but also receive any new messages sent to you.

Receiving Messages

When others send messages to you, those messages go to your service provider's mail server, and wait there until you choose to receive messages. To receive messages

- **In Messenger,** click the Get Msg button on the toolbar.
- **In Outlook Express,** click the Send/Recv (or Send/Receive) button on the toolbar.

If you are offline when you click the Send/Recv or Get Msg button, Outlook Express and Messenger connect you to the Internet automatically (or prompt you to do so) to retrieve your new messages.

As I mentioned earlier, your ISP provides you with a special password you use only when receiving email (you don't need it to send email). When you click the button to receive mail, a dialog might appear to prompt for your password. Just type your password and press Enter to continue receiving email.

In the configuration dialogs of some email programs, you can type your email password; this enables the email program to automatically enter your password for you when you receive messages, saving you a step. This feature is handy, but should only be used if your computer is located where no one else might try to retrieve and read your email if you leave your desk while connected to the Internet.

Your email program contacts your ISP, and checks for any new messages addressed to you. If there are none, the words "No new messages on server" appear in the status bar at the bottom of the window. If there are new messages, the messages are copied to your PC and stored in your Inbox folder, where you can read them any time, online or off.

In the message lists displayed by most email programs, the messages you have not yet read appear in **bold** (see Figure 5.13).

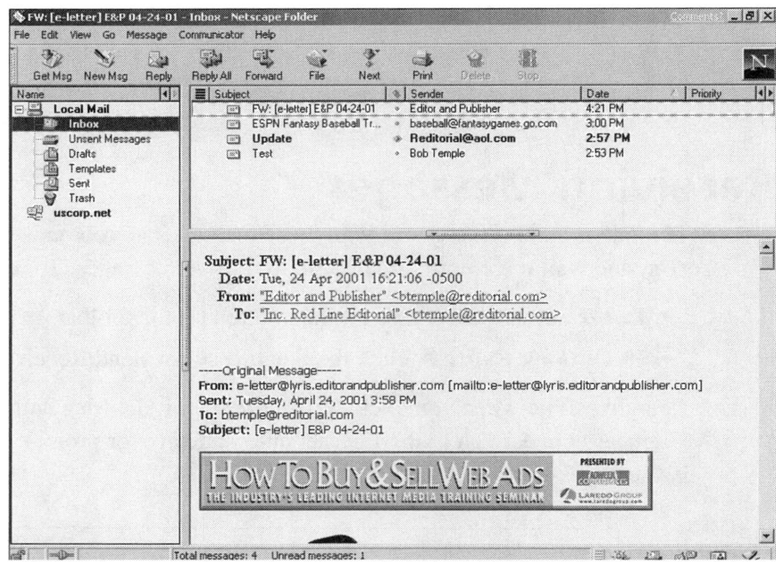

FIGURE 5.13
Messages listed in the Inbox in bold type are those you have not read yet.

Messages you receive can contain computer viruses, particularly (but not exclusively) when those messages have files attached to them or they come to you from strangers. The best way to protect yourself from these files is to have a good anti-virus protection program installed on your computer; keep it updated to protect against newer viruses; never open an email or attachment from someone you don't know. Two of the top anti-virus programs are Norton AntiVirus (`www.norton.com`) and McAfee VirusScan (`www.mcafee.com`).

Replying and Forwarding

Most email programs provide you with two easy ways to create new messages by using other messages you have received: *reply* and *forward.*

NEW TERM **Replying** and **forwarding.** *Replying* means sending a message back to someone from whom you have received a message, to respond to that message. *Forwarding* is passing a copy of a message you've received to a third party, either because you want to share the message's content with the third party or because you believe that, although the message was originally sent to you, the third party is a more appropriate recipient for it.

To reply or forward, you always begin by opening the original message. From the message window's toolbar, you then click a button or menu item with a label like one of the following (see Figure 5.14):

- **Reply.** Reply creates a reply to the person who sent you the message.
- **Reply All.** Reply All creates a reply to the person who sent you the message and to everyone else in the email's recipient list.
- **Forward.** Forward creates a new message containing the entire text of the original message, ready for you to forward.

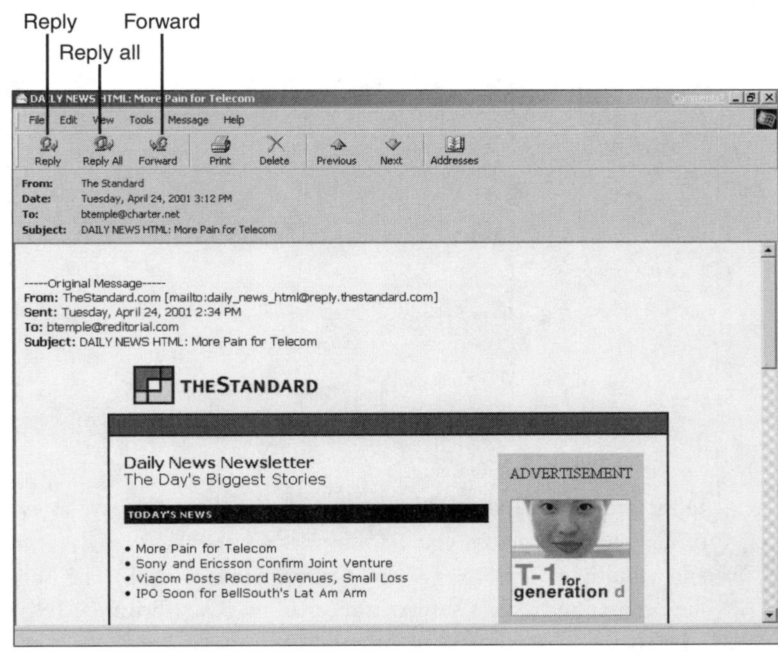

FIGURE 5.14
The Reply, Reply All, and Forward buttons offer different ways of responding to messages you've received.

Whichever button you click, a new message window opens. In the body of the message, a complete quote of the original message appears (see Figure 5.15).

NEW TERM **Quote.** A quote is all or a portion of a message you've received, included in a reply to indicate what you're replying to, or included in a forward to carry the message you're forwarding.

You can edit the quote, cutting out any parts that aren't relevant and inserting your own comments above, below, or within the quote.

In the message window of a reply, the To line is automatically filled in for you, with the address of the person from whom you received the message (or multiple addresses, if you chose Reply All). The Subject line is filled in with the original message's subject, preceded by Re:, to indicate that your message is a reply to a message using that subject.

5

To complete the reply, all you have to do is type your comments above, below, or within the quote, and then click Send.

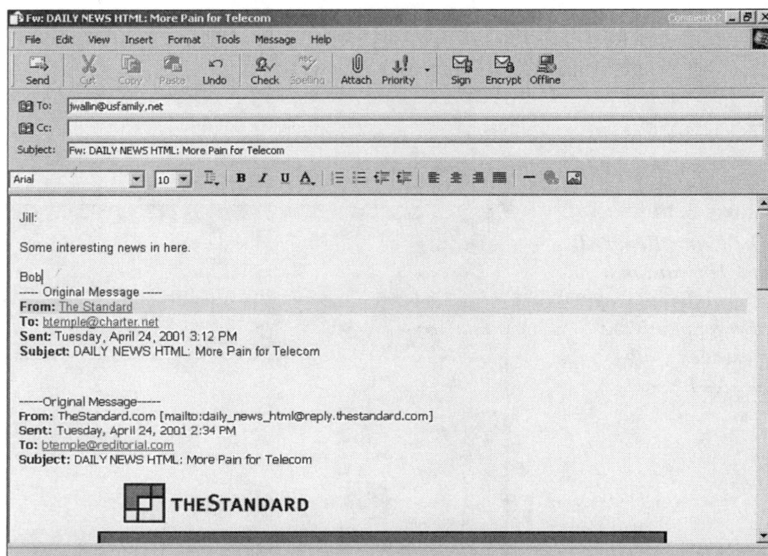

FIGURE 5.15
A reply or a forward includes a quote from the original message.

In the message window of a forward, the To line is empty, so you can enter the address of the person to whom you want to forward the message. (As with any message, you can enter multiple To recipients, and Cc recipients as well.) The Subject line is filled in with the original message's subject, preceded by FW: (*forw*ard). To complete the forward, address the message, type your comments above, below, or within the quote, and then click Send.

Using an Address Book

Most folks find that there's a steady list of others to whom they email often. Keeping track of those all-important names and addresses, and using them, is easier when you use your email program's *address book*.

NEW TERM **Address book**. A directory you create, containing the names, email addresses, and often other information (mailing address, phone, notes) about your contacts.

When an addressee's information is in your address book, you needn't type—or even remember—his or her email address. Instead, you can simply choose the person's name from the address book, and your email program fills in the address for you. Some address books also support *nicknames*—short, easy-to-remember names you type in the To line of a message instead of the full email address.

Adding to Your Address Book

In both Outlook Express and Messenger, the easiest way to add to your address book is to copy information from messages you've received. For example, if you've received a message from Sue, you can use that message to quickly create an address card you can use to send messages to Sue.

To create a new address book entry from a message, begin by displaying the message in its own window. Next…

- **In Netscape Messenger,** from the message window's menu bar, choose Message, Add Sender to Address Book. A New Card dialog opens (see Figure 5.16). Make sure the name and email address boxes on the Name tab have been filled in, and complete any of the other, optional boxes you want. Click OK to save the new entry.
- **In Outlook Express,** from the message window's menu bar, choose Tools, Add Sender to Address Book. Make sure the name and email address boxes on the Name tab have been filled in, and complete any of the other, optional boxes and tabs you want. Click OK to save the new entry.

FIGURE 5.16
When you use a message you have received to add someone to your address book, that person's name and email address are entered for you, automatically.

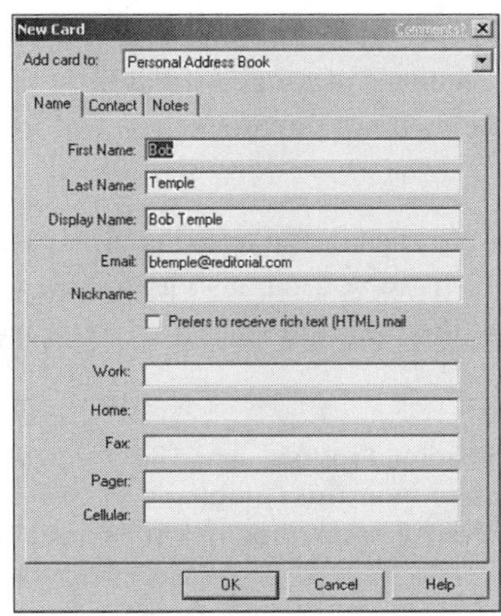

5

To create an address book entry from scratch (without beginning from a message you've received)

- **In Outlook Express,** choose Tools, Address Book, click the New button, then choose New Contact from the menu that appears.

- **In Netscape Messenger,** choose Communicator, Address Book, then click the New Card button.

Addressing a Message from the Address Book

To use an address book entry to address a message (in Netscape Messenger or Outlook Express), begin by opening the new message window as usual. Then open the address book list:

- **In Netscape Messenger**, by choosing Communicator, Address Book.
- **In Outlook Express,** by clicking the little icon in the To line that looks like an open address book.

In the list, click the name of an addressee, and click the To button to add the addressee to the To line.

When done choosing recipients, click OK to close the address book, and complete the Subject line and body of your message.

Attaching Files to Email Messages

Once new Internet users get the hang of using their Web browsers and email programs, nothing causes more frustration than file attachments.

Attachment. A file (any type—a picture file, word processing document, anything) that's attached to an email message so that it travels along with the message. The person who receives the message can detach the file from the message and use it.

The following To Do shows how to attach a file to an email message in Outlook Express. You'll send that message to yourself, so you can also learn how to detach and use a file attachment you receive. Note that the steps are similar in Netscape Messenger.

In Hour 14, "Downloading Programs and Files," you will learn about the risk of catching a computer virus from programs and other files you download from the Internet. Well, you can pick up a virus just as easily from an email attachment.

If you're like most people, most email attachments you receive come from people you know, so you may think that those files are safe. But what if your friend is just passing on a file they received from someone else, maybe a stranger? That's one way email viruses spread; innocent, well-meaning people catch them and spread them around.

> You can use most major virus protection programs, such as Norton AntiVirus and McAfee VirusScan, to check email attachments for viruses. Just save the attachment as a file separate from the message (as described in step 5 of the following To Do), then scan the file for viruses.
>
> *DO NOT* open the file (by double-clicking its file icon or right-clicking it and choosing Open or Run) until *after* you have scanned it for viruses and determined that it's safe.

To Do

To Do: Attach a File to an Email Message

1. Compose and address your message (to yourself) as you normally would. Then click the Attach button (see Figure 5.17).

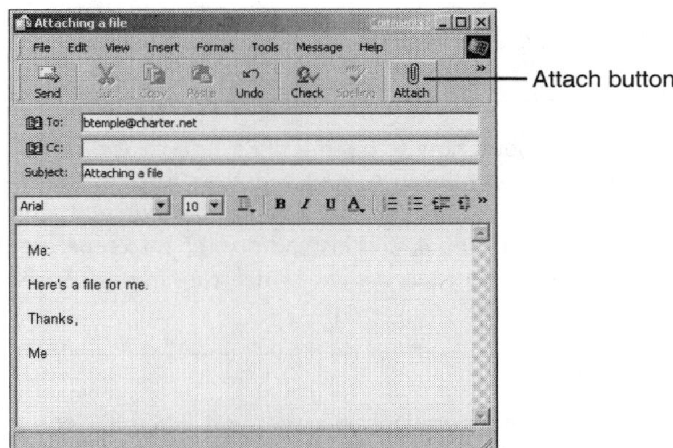

FIGURE 5.17
Step 1: *Click the Attach button in a new message.*

2. Use the dialog to navigate to and select the file to attach, and then click the dialog's Attach button (see Figure 5.18).

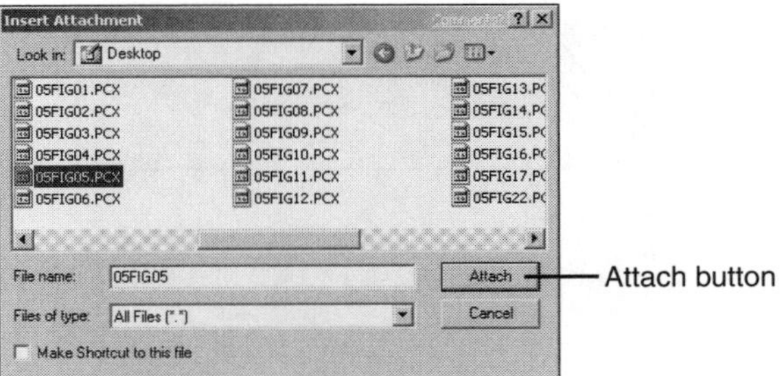

FIGURE 5.18
Step 2: *Find the file, and then click the Attach button.*

5

3. Send the message (see Figure 5.19). If you do not immediately receive it, click Send/Recv again to receive the message.

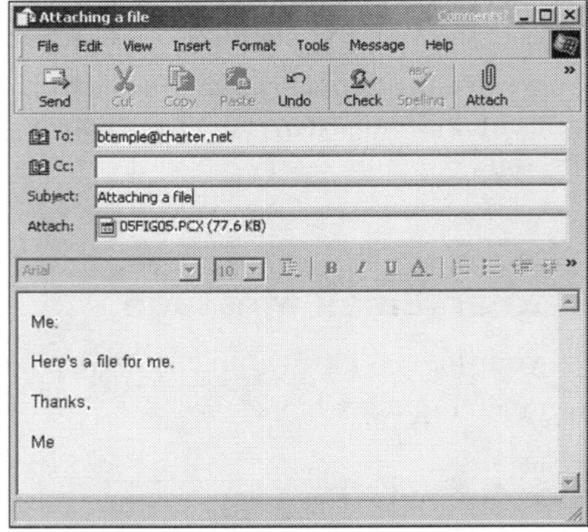

FIGURE 5.19
Step 3: *Send the message.*

Step 4 shows how to open a file attachment directly from the message, which is okay because you know the source of the file (you). But as a rule, unless you're very confident about the source of a file attachment, you should skip step 4, and instead do step 5 to separate the file from the message. Then you can use your virus-scanning software to check the file for viruses before you open it.

4. In the header of the received message, you'll see an icon and a filename representing the attached file. To view the file, double-click the icon (see Figure 5.20).

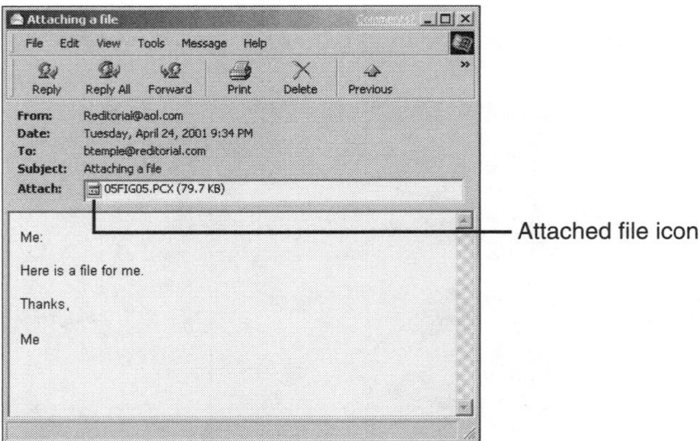

FIGURE 5.20
Step 4: *To read the attachment in the received message, double-click the file's icon.*

5. If you want to save the file separately from the message (for use later), right-click the icon, and choose Save As (see Figure 5.21).

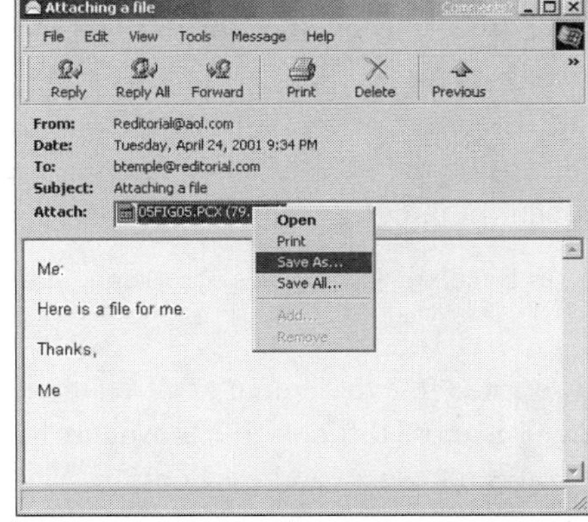

FIGURE 5.21
Step 5: *To save the file, right-click and choose Save As.*

If you have your email program configured for formatting fancy, HTML-based messages (see Hour 19, "Creating Web Pages and Multimedia Messages"), when you attach a picture file (such as a photo you've scanned) to a message, you might see the actual picture displayed in the message instead of an icon.

Not to worry: Anyone you send to who has a similarly configured email program will see the picture the same way, and anyone who does not have such an email program will receive the picture as an attachment.

Keep in mind that unless you have a broadband connection, big file attachments can dramatically increase the length of time it takes you to send a message, and the length of time it takes the recipient to receive messages. Avoid sending really large files (more than 300K), and before sending an attachment to someone you haven't sent to before, send a message describing the file and its size, asking if it's OK to send it.

Using the Web for Email

Increasingly, people are using Web-based email to communicate. Web-based email allows a user to send and receive messages directly from a Web page, rather than opening a separate email program.

The advantages of this type of email are twofold: You can access your email and send and receive messages from any computer connected to the Internet, so it's great for travelers; and typically, the email account is free.

They are available all over the Web; Yahoo! and Hotmail, the Microsoft Network's Webmail offering, are the two biggest. But lots of sites offer free email as a way to increase visitors to their site. The more people sign up for it, the more people visit the site, the more people see the ads on the site, the more the site owner can charge for the ads. Free enterprise is a wonderful thing!

Heck, even the Major League Baseball site (`www.majorleaguebaseball.com`) offers free email to its users.

The primary drawback, however, is that these aren't full-featured email programs. Handling attachments to email is more difficult, if it's available at all. Saving emails is harder, too. And typically, you can't use an address book.

After you've been on the Web a while, you will encounter some sites that want you to "register" with them in order to be able to use certain features. Although registering is often free, you usually have to supply an email address, so they can send you "special offers" and the like. Many people sign up for one of these free email accounts simply so they have an alternate email address to give to these sites. That way, your regular email account will receive less junk mail.

There is a combination of regular email and Web-based email that's a wonderful thing, however. Some ISPs offer a Web-based mail client to their regular members, so you can access your email if you're away from your regular computer.

America Online is one of these. AOL members can read their email from anywhere in the world, simply by logging on to the AOL site at `www.aol.com`. You simply sign in with your screen name and password, click the Check Your Mail! button, and you'll be able to read your messages. You can also reply, forward, or create new mail messages, right from the site (see Figure 5.22).

Each message appears as a highlighted and underlined link. Clicking on the link opens the message. It's pretty simple.

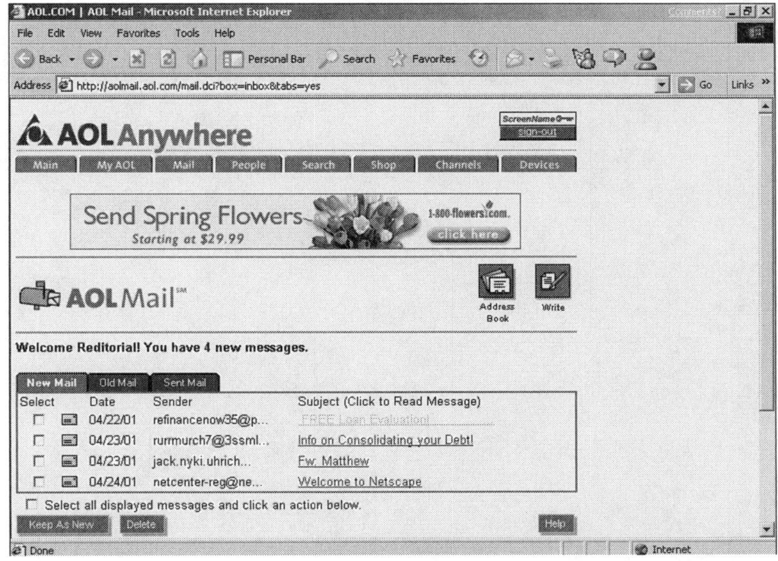

FIGURE 5.22
America Online offers a Web-based email option so its members can access their email from anywhere in the world.

Summary

Wow! You learned a lot this hour. As you saw, the hardest part about email is getting yourself set up for it. Composing, sending, and receiving messages is a breeze, and techniques that can make you even more productive—such as using an Outbox or Address Book—are also pretty easy, and always optional.

Q&A

Q Can I look over messages I've already sent, to recall what I wrote to someone?

A Sure. Most email programs include a Sent (or Sent Messages) folder, in which a copy of every message you send is saved. If you need to refer later to a message you've sent, find its copy in your Sent folder.

Q If you use a Web-based email option, can other people see your emails?

A Not unless they have your username and password. While those pages with your messages on them are part of the Web, they are secure pages. So a person can't just enter the Web address and get your messages. They'd have to enter your username and password, just like you do.

HOUR 6

Chatting and Instant Messenger

Feel the need to reach out and touch someone, live and (almost) in person? Chat puts you online in a live conversation with other Internet users anywhere in the world.

And whereas chatting used to require a high degree of technical understanding, that's no longer the case. It used to require downloading a software program—a chat client—and installing it on your computer. Now, however, more and more people simply chat using their browser, through one of hundreds of sites that offer it.

Instant messaging is another way of reaching out and touching someone. What began as an America Online–only exercise is now available to anyone on the Web.

At the end of the hour, you'll be able to answer the following questions:

- What is Internet chatting?
- Where can I find a good chat to join?

- How do I join in an online chat session?
- How is Microsoft Chat different from a typical chat program?
- How do I enhance my contributions to the chat with expressions, gestures, and other touches?
- How do I exit one chat and enter another?
- How do I chat through my Web browser?
- What is Instant Messenger?
- How do I use IM?

You might as well know that a substantial amount of chat traffic on the Internet is dedicated to sex chats of various persuasions and fetishes. There are many sex chat rooms, and sex-chat–oriented chatters often wander into non–sex-oriented rooms looking for new friends.

If that's okay with you, have fun. Live and let live, I always say, especially between consenting adults. But if you have an aversion to such stuff, tread carefully in chat. If you have a *severe* aversion to it, it's best to stay out of chat altogether.

And regardless of your own interests, I strongly advise against permitting children to use chat, especially unsupervised. My warning isn't about sex, but about safety. You'll find more about kids and chat in Hour 17, "Enjoying Safe Family Fun and Games."

Understanding Internet Chatting

You may have heard people refer to chatting on the Internet as being in a "chat room." Well, you don't have to go into a special room in your house that you designate only for these chats. Chats are divided by subject matter, and the term *chat room* really refers to the subject area you have entered on the Internet.

Room is an appropriate word to use, however, because it's very much like being in a room full of people, all talking about the same subject. Everything you "say" by typing it into your computer can be "heard" by everybody else in the room—they will see your words appear on their computer screen. That can be a very small group of people, or dozens.

Thousands of different chats are under way at once, each in its own chat room. When you join a chat, you enter a room, and from then on you see only the conversation that's taking place in that room.

NEW TERM **Chat room.** This is a space where a single conversation is taking place. In Internet chat parlance, a chat room is sometimes known as a *channel.* This can be a confusing term, however, because it has several other meanings on the Internet. Stick with *chat room.*

In most chat rooms (or channels), the conversation is focused on a given subject area. In a singles chat room, participants chat about stuff singles like to talk about. In a geology chat, people generally talk about rocks and earthquakes.

When you're in a chat room, everything that everyone else in the same room types appears on your screen. Each participant's statements are labeled with a nickname to identify who's talking. Those participating in a chat (known as *members*) choose their own nicknames and rarely share their real names. In a chat, you can be whoever you want to be, and so can everyone else.

NEW TERM **Nickname.** Your nickname, which you choose yourself, is how you're known to others in a chat. Your nickname appears on every statement you make so everyone knows who's talking.

Chatting Through Your Browser

Chatting through your browser is the simplest way to get involved in chatting online. For that reason, it's also the most commonly used type of chat online.

All kinds of sites offer chats for their users. Big portals like Yahoo! offer chats on a wide variety of topics. Specialized sites also offer chats for their users. Heck, even the Weather Channel (`www.weather.com`) offers chats. Hot enough for ya?

There are really two different kinds of chats. There are open chats that can involve anyone and everyone from around the globe, all talking about a particular subject of interest. These are sometimes moderated by someone whose job it is to keep the discussion clean and on-topic. The other kind of chat is a celebrity chat, in which a particular person appears in a chat room at a specified time to answer questions. For example, a local TV news crew might have its anchorperson online in a chat room for an hour one night a week to talk with viewers.

Finding Sites with Chat Rooms

It's not very difficult to find sites that offer chats for their users. Simply go to any site that interests you, and look around for a chat button. Some sites will call it "interact" or "forums" or the like, but it's often there if you want to find it. The chances are pretty good that the site you've been visiting all along has a chat area, and you didn't even know it.

Chatting at Yahoo!

If you're really interested in chatting, however, a great place to start is at the Yahoo! site or that of another major portal. These sites will typically offer chat rooms on a wide variety of subject, giving you the opportunity to get chatting and change "rooms" easily.

We'll use Yahoo! as our example of a portal with good chat capabilities. They make it pretty easy to get started, too. All you have to do is sign up, choosing an ID and a password, provide some other basic information, and you're ready to go. To get started, go to the chat area at Yahoo! (`chat.yahoo.com`), and click on the Sign Up for Yahoo! Chat! Link (see Figure 6.1).

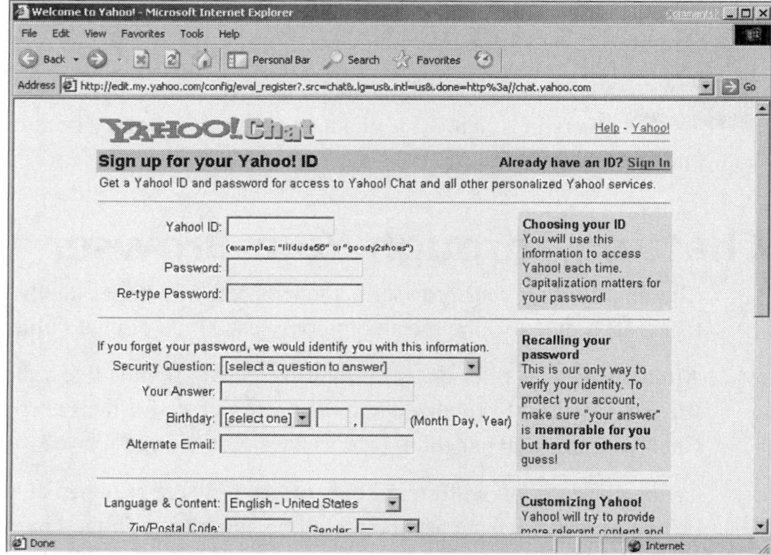

FIGURE 6.1
Signing up for chatting on Yahoo! is quick and easy.

> The hardest part of signing up for Yahoo! or any other popular service is picking a username (or ID) that hasn't already been chosen. Because signing up for Yahoo! chat also registers you for a free Yahoo! email address, you're in the mix with the millions who have already joined. So you may end up with an ID that's a little nonsensical.

Signing up only takes a minute (after you've found an ID that's not already in use). Once your information has been accepted, click on the Complete Room List button to get an idea of what's out there in terms of chat.

Yahoo! chats are broken into categories, and each category contains several different rooms. For example, under the Music category, you'll find chats on subjects ranging from Britney Spears to jazz (see Figure 6.2).

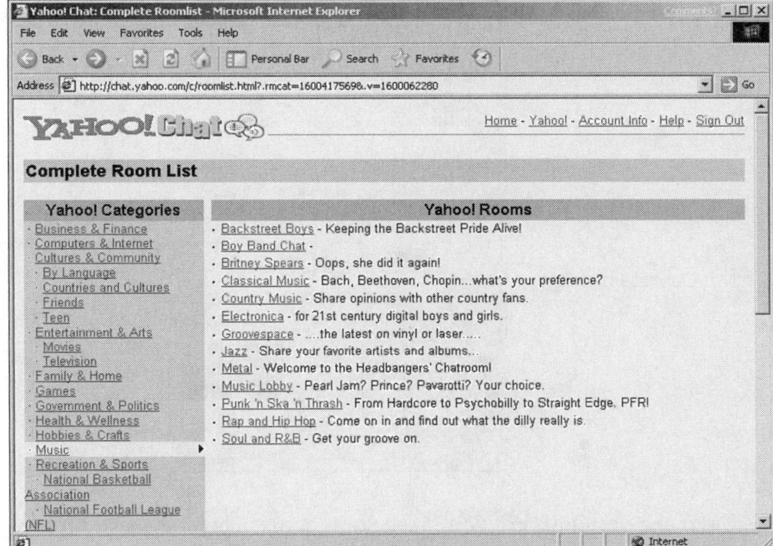

FIGURE 6.2
Yahoo! chat offers a wide variety of rooms from which to choose.

After you've found a subject that interests you, just click its link to enter the room. Now, it's time to chat!

The Chat Window

Before you can be a successful chatter, you need to know the ins and outs of the chat room itself. Yahoo! is a good example, because its chat rooms appear much like those at many other sites.

After you've entered a chat, you'll see the chat window (see Figure 6.3). It's divided neatly into different frames, and each has its purpose.

The biggest pane in the window, in the upper left, is the viewing pane. This is where all the messages appear, including those that you write. Below that, you will see some formatting buttons that allow you to change the way your text appears, and the Chat: pane. This is where you will type any messages you write in the chat. Type it out, click the Send button, and they'll appear in the viewing pane, for you and all the others in the room to see.

Speaking of the others, they are listed in the member list pane, at the upper right. The list is by ID.

FIGURE 6.3
The Yahoo! chat window is similar to those of many other chats.

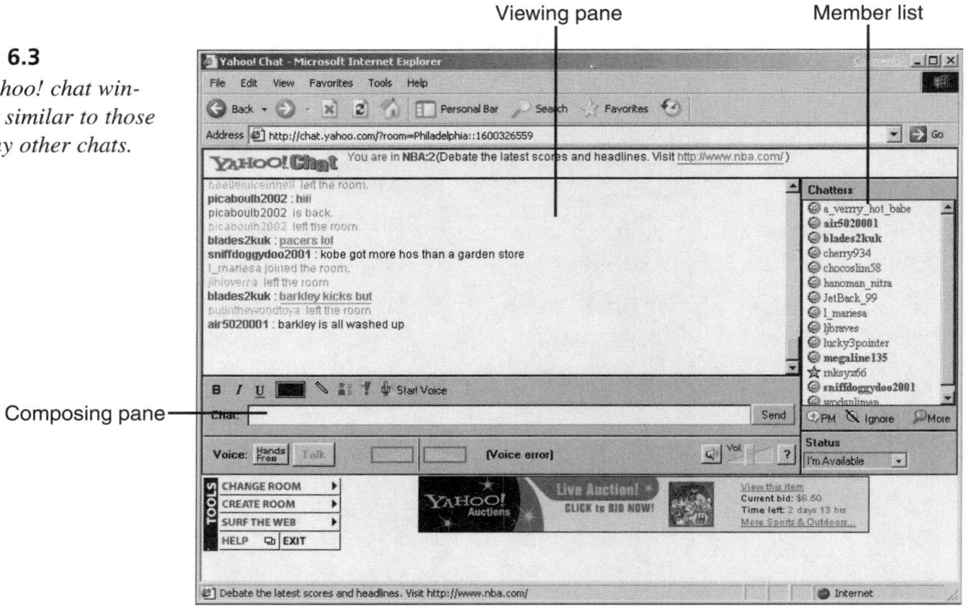

At the very bottom, you'll see some tools. There are also other special tricks you can do, as well:

- Create Room—You can create your own chat room if you wish. This is great if you want to have a private chat with a group of people, say for business purposes. Or, if you want to have the entire extended family all in one place to announce a baby on the way! You can set up your own chat room, make it password-protected so the ordinary Joes can't enter, then set a time for the chat and give the appropriate people the room name and password.
- PM—Under the member list, you see the PM button. Use this to send a private message to someone in the chat room. Just highlight their name, click PM, and type your message to them.
- Ignore—If there's one person in the room who really bugs you, highlight their ID and click Ignore. You will no longer see any messages posted by that person.
- Voice—If your computer is properly equipped, you can participate in a voice chat by clicking the Start Voice button. You need a good sound card, speakers, and a microphone to participate.

Chatting in AOL

America Online's chats are one of the service's most popular features. Chat rooms are all over AOL. You'll find chat rooms in forums to discuss just about any topic the service offers.

Just choose a channel from the list on the left side of your AOL screen and you'll be able to find chats within that area of interest. For example, take the Parenting channel. If you click on the Parenting button, you'll find a special "Moms" area inside. Go there, and you'll find a Chat Now button. Click it, and you'll have a wide range of chatting options (see Figure 6.4—everything from a special chat for disabled moms to chats about dealing with teenagers (good luck), and so on.

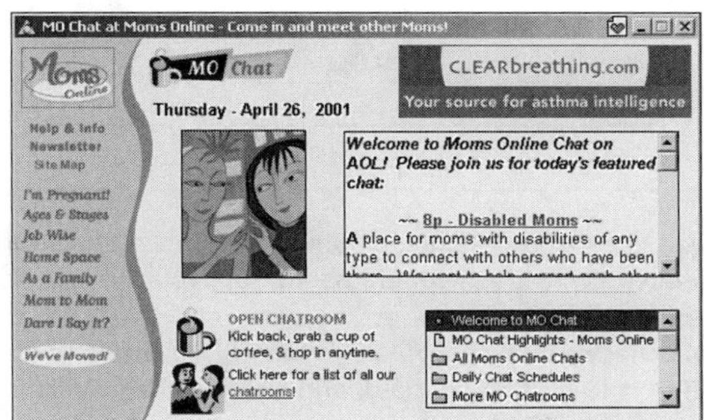

FIGURE 6.4
AOL's chats are specialized by topic, so you can meet with people of similar interests.

Using the People Connection

As many chat rooms as there are in the Channel forums, you'll find many more in the People Connection. The People Connection is abuzz with chat 24 hours a day, seven days a week. These are different than the chats in the various channels.

Chat rooms are so popular that there's a Chat button on the Welcome window that greets you when you sign on. You can click that or select People Connection from the People menu on the toolbar—either way, you'll go to the People Connection.

When you click the Chat button, you move into the People Connection screen. There are many options here; choose Chat Now, and you're dropped into a lobby chat room in Town Square (see Figure 6.5). Town Square is the generic chat category online—there are others (you'll see them in a moment). A lobby is just that: a waiting room where you can chat or move on to a room with a more defined topic of conversation.

At any given moment, there can be *hundreds* of lobbies in the People Connection. They are all given a number—the one shown in Figure 6.5 is Lobby 75.

On the right side of the chat window is a list of the people who are in the lobby with you (your screen name is there, too). You can find out a little something about the folks in your room by seeing if they have a Member Profile. To read a Member Profile, double-click a screen name from the room list and then click Get Profile on the dialog box that appears.

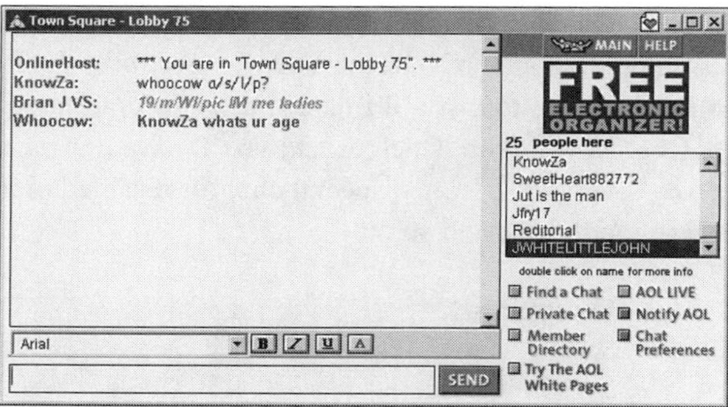

FIGURE 6.5
Your basic chat room—this one's a lobby.

Just like in Yahoo! chat, if someone is getting on your nerves in a chat room and you wish they would just shut up, you can shut them up—as far as you're concerned at least. The same Info dialog box that lets you read another member's profile also has a little check box labeled Ignore Member. Click it so that it's checked, and nothing that person says will appear on your screen. You're ignoring him; perhaps he'll lose interest and go away.

When you first start out in a chat room, it's a good idea to sit and read the chat scrolling up your screen. It gives you a notion of what's being talked about, who's doing the talking, and whether you want to join in. If you want to participate in a lobby chat, simply type what you want to say in the text box at the bottom of the window and then press Enter (or click Send). Your chat appears in the chat window, and you can carry on a conversation.

If there isn't much going on in the lobby, you might want to move to a room with a more specific chat theme.

Moving to Another Room

To see a list of the currently active chat rooms in the People Connection, click the Find a Chat button at the bottom-right side of the chat window. A list of categories and chat rooms appears in the Find a Chat dialog box, as shown in Figure 6.6.

In the Find a Chat dialog box, you'll see a list of room categories in the box on the left side of the screen. When you highlight a category name and click the View Chats button in the middle of the window, the list box on the right of the screen shows all the rooms that are available for that specific category. At peak chatting hours, you might need to click the List More button a couple of times to see all the chat rooms in a given category.

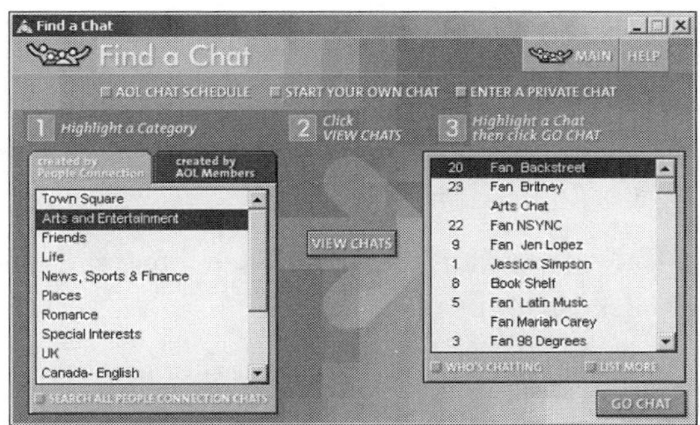

FIGURE 6.6
Find a Chat helps you find rooms of interest.

To enter a room, double-click its name in the list. You can also peek in and see who's chatting in a room. Click on the room's name in the list and then click the Who's Chatting button. A list of the members in the room appears, much like the room list in an actual chat room. You can use it to see who's around before you drop in for a chat.

You might notice that the categories list on the left side of the Find a Chat window has two tabs. The second tab reveals the same category list as the first tab, but the chat rooms listed in the right side are instead those that have been created by AOL members, not AOL staff. The list looks, and works, exactly the same as the one shown previously in Figure 6.6, but the rooms have all been created by AOL members.

You can create your *own* chat room from the list of Member Chats by clicking the Start Your Own Chat button (top middle of the Find a Chat window).

These member-created rooms can be much wilder and woollier than the AOL sanctioned rooms—consider that a warning, or a piece of advice, depending on your mood.

Using Microsoft Chat

Another type of chat involves downloading and using a chat client software program. These programs used Internet Relay Chat, or IRC, to conduct their chats. There are many such programs, but one of the best is Microsoft Chat—it's free, and it's a little bit unusual in that it makes the chat look like a comic strip.

If you don't have Microsoft Chat, you can download it free from the Tucows software directory at `www.tucows.com` or directly from Microsoft at `www.microsoft.com`.

Like any chat program, Microsoft Chat—henceforth to be known simply as *Chat* with a capital *C*—lets you communicate with chat servers. You can view the list of chat rooms, join a chat room, read what everyone says in the chat room, and make your own contributions to the discussion. What's different about Chat is the way it displays the conversation.

Most chat clients show the text of the conversation a line at a time and label each line with the speaker's nickname.

Chat, however, can display the conversation as text or as a comic strip, using little cartoon characters to represent members and showing their words in cartoon word balloons (see Figure 6.7). The folks at Microsoft think this approach makes chatting feel more human, more fun. In its first versions, Chat was actually named Microsoft Comic Chat.

Balloon. This is the little bubble you see in comics in which the words or thoughts of a character appears.

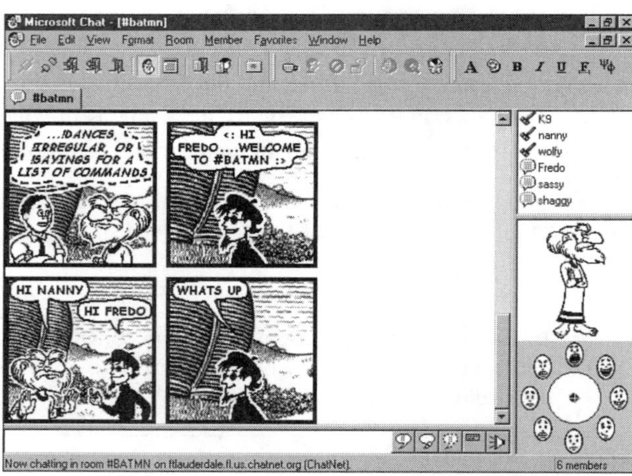

FIGURE 6.7
Microsoft Chat can make a chat session look like a comic strip, with a different cartoon character for each participant.

It's important to understand that most folks you'll end up chatting with probably won't use Microsoft Chat. Many will use ordinary text chat clients; they'll see your statements labeled with your nickname but won't see your comic character.

On your display, Chat converts all statements in a chat—even those made by users of text-only clients—into comics. Other Chat users in the same room appear as their chosen cartoon characters. For users of other chat clients, Chat automatically assigns and shows unused characters.

Joining a Chat Room

It's time to hit a server and see it for real. On the way, though, you'll perform some automatic configuration that Chat needs to operate properly.

> Before you open Chat, you can be online or off. If you're offline when you begin, Chat connects to the Internet automatically. Also, your browser need not be open for you to use Chat, although it won't hurt anything if it is open.

To Do: Start Chat and Display the Chat Rooms List

1. Open Microsoft Chat. In Windows 95/98/NT, you do so by choosing Programs, Microsoft Chat.
2. Select the Show All Available Chat Rooms option, and then click OK to connect to the chat server listed in the dialog (see Figure 6.8).

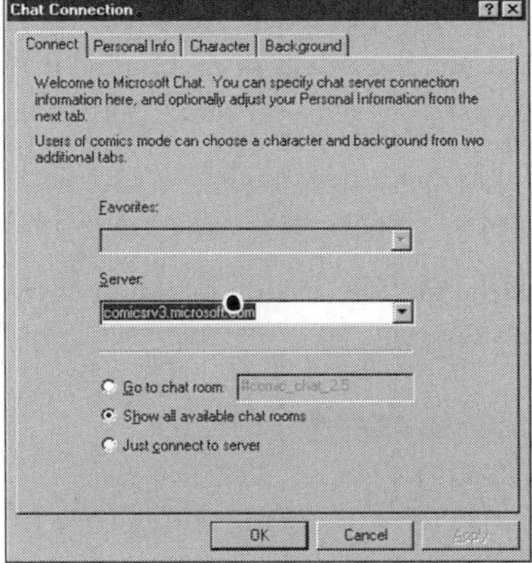

FIGURE 6.8
***Step 2:** Select Show All Available Chat Rooms and then click OK.*

3. A message appears. This message differs by server, but typically it contains any special rules or instructions for the server, plus any disclaimers in which the server operator reminds you that he's not responsible for what people say there.
4. A list of all chat rooms available on the server appears (see Figure 6.9). You are now connected to a chat server and are ready to chat—except that, as a new user, you have not yet selected a nickname and a comic character, as described next.

6

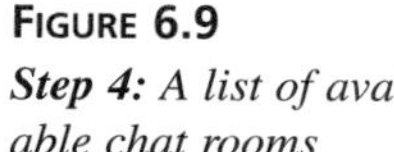

FIGURE 6.9
Step 4: A list of available chat rooms appears.

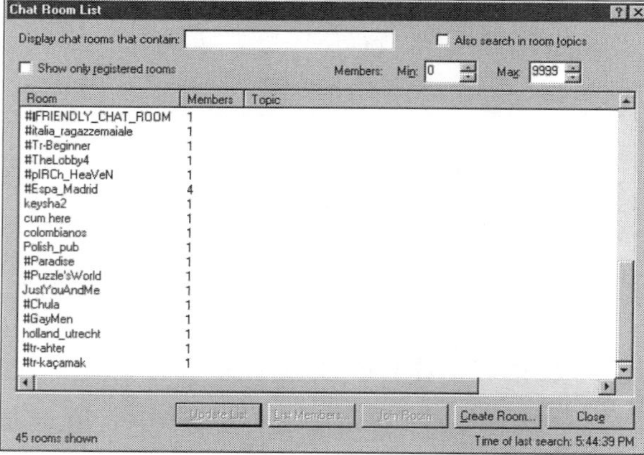

Choosing an Identity

Before you can join in a chat, you must create a nickname. And because of Chat's unique presentation style, you must choose a comic character, too. In addition, you can select a background that appears behind the characters in each panel of the comic, as you see it on your screen.

After you choose a nickname, character, and background, Chat remembers them for future sessions. You do not need to choose them again unless you want to change them.

Choose View, Options to open the Options dialog box, and choose the Personal Info tab if it is not already selected (see Figure 6.10).

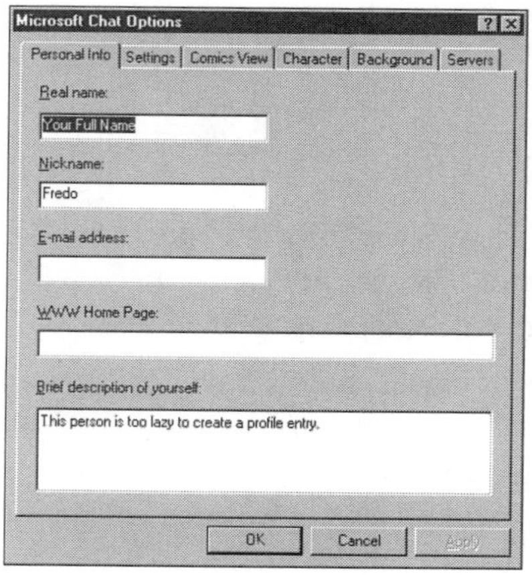

FIGURE 6.10
The Personal Info tab allows you to set your preferences.

Click in the Nickname box and type a nickname for yourself. Your nickname should be one word with no spaces or punctuation, and it should also be unusual enough that another member hasn't chosen the same nickname. (If you attempt to enter a room where someone is already using the same nickname as you, Chat prompts you to change your nickname before entering.)

On the Personal Info tab, you can enter other information besides your nickname, such as your real name and email address. Think carefully before doing so, however. Any information you supply here can be seen by other members whose clients (like Chat) can display member profiles. If you want to keep your anonymity, enter your nickname and *nothing else*.

To choose the character you would like to use for your likeness, click the Character tab and click a name in the Character column (see Figure 6.11). The Preview column shows what the selected character looks like—what *you* will look like to other Chat users if you stick with that character.

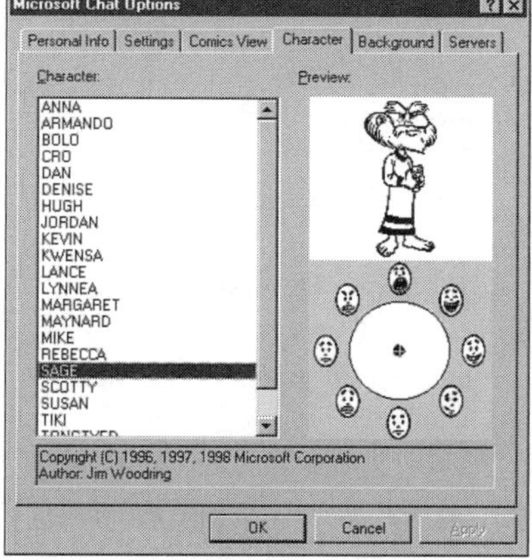

FIGURE 6.11
Select a character for your likeness.

When you're choosing a character in the Character tab, you can click the faces in the emotion wheel (beneath the character preview) to see what the character will look like when you apply a given emotion to it when making a statement. You'll learn about choosing emotions later in this hour.

You can also specify a background to use by clicking the Background tab and selecting one.

Entering a Room

To enter a chat room, you select a room from the chat room list. Figure 6.12 shows the list of chats available on the server. Each server has its own list, and the lists change often.

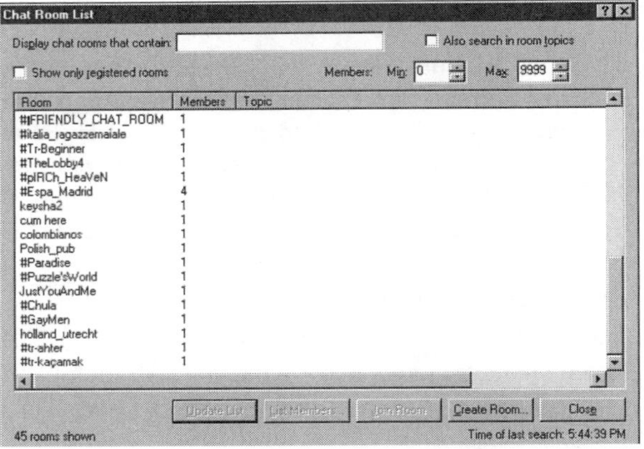

FIGURE 6.12
To enter any room in the list, double-click its name.

The chat room list reappears after you finish selecting your identity, but you can open the chat room list anytime you're connected to the server by clicking the Chat Room List button on Chat's toolbar.

In the list, the name of each room begins with a pound sign (#). The name of the room is followed by the number of members currently in the room, and sometimes also by a description of the conversation that usually takes place there.

When you first arrive in a room, you might not see any comic panels right away. The server shows you only what's been said since you entered the room. After you enter, statements begin appearing one by one as members make them.

Now that you're in a room, you can just *lurk* or listen in on the conversation, or you can contribute to it by sending your statements for all the others to see. Note that you are not obligated to add anything to the conversation. In fact, just lurking in a chat room is a great way to learn more about chats before diving in.

When you're ready to contribute your comments to the chat, just type them in as you did in the browser-based chats we discussed earlier.

While you're typing and editing your statements in the Compose pane, no one sees them but you. A statement is sent to the chat only when you press Enter. This gives you a chance to choose your words carefully and correct typos before committing your statement to the chat.

After you press Enter, those in the room who are using regular chat clients see your statement labeled with your nickname, so they know you said it. Those in the room who are using Microsoft Chat see your chosen comic character speaking the words in a *say balloon,* the type that surrounds words that comic characters say aloud.

You can format your words by picking a special balloon from the right side of the Compose pane. The balloons allow you to indicate you are thinking (bubbles) or whispering (dotted outline). You can also have your character express emotions by picking the appropriate face from the Emotion Wheel in the lower-right corner.

There are lots of other chat clients out there. If you want to look for others, you can always check the Tucows directory at `www.tucows.com`.

Because some members in the room might not be using Chat and therefore can't see expressions, be sure your words alone carry your meaning.

What Is Instant Messenger?

Instant messaging is a lot like chat, with a few key differences. One, most instant messages are sent to or received from people you know. Two, the conversations are just between you and one other person.

6

America Online members automatically get AOL's Instant Messenger and can use it within the service. If you know another person's screen name, you can use Instant Messenger to check to see if they are online. If they are, you can type them a quick message, and it automatically pops up on their screen.

Those who don't have AOL can still use Instant Messenger. You can download it from the Netscape Web site (`www.netscape.com`). It's a quick download, and it walks you through the steps of setting it up.

Sending "Instant" Messages

Instant Messenger lets you see, from among a list you set up yourself (a "Buddy List"), which of your friends are online at the same time you are (see Figure 6.13). You can exchange typed messages with those friends—but unlike email, those messages show up instantly. The moment you send a message to a friend who's online, he or she sees it, and vice versa. So you can carry on a live, interactive conversation, much like chat.

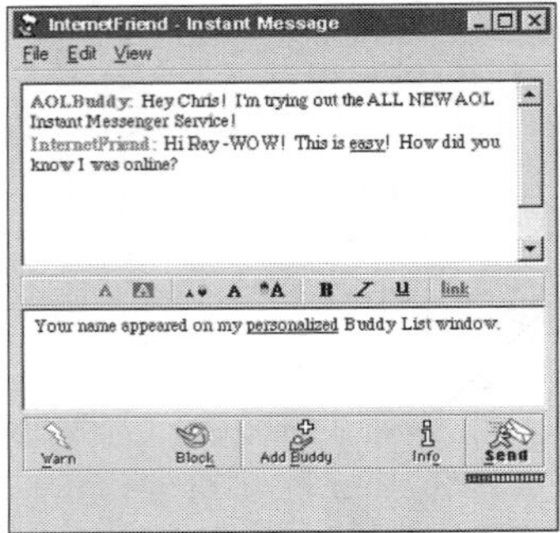

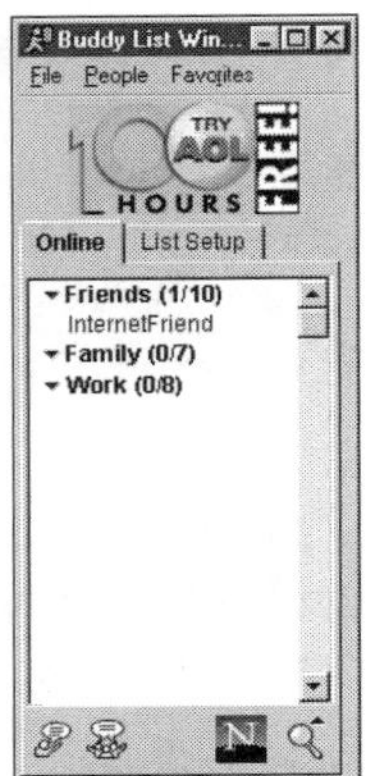

FIGURE 6.13
AOL Instant Messenger lets you exchange live messages with friends who are online at the same time you are—even if neither of you uses AOL.

The easiest way to sign up for Instant Messenger is to install Netscape Communicator. From Navigator's menu bar, choose Communicator, AOL Instant Messenger Service, and then follow the prompts to sign up.

Note that AOL Instant Messenger is not the only such service available. Another is Yahoo! Messenger, which you can learn about at `messenger.yahoo.com`. Internet Explorer offers a similar instant messaging system, called MSN Messenger. There are other instant message systems, but these are the main ones, and they are all free and fun.

You might think it's cool that you can know whether or not a friend is online by using your Buddy List. However, that means others can know if you're online as well. If you want to limit who knows you're online and who can contact you, open the My IM menu and select Edit Options, Edit Preferences. Then click the Privacy tab, and you can create a more-private setup for yourself.

Summary

Chat and instant messages are fun, as long as you stay among people whose reasons for chatting are the same as yours. Like a carnival or circus, chat is an entertaining place with a seedy underbelly and should be enjoyed with caution. But if you're careful, you can have safe, interactive fun with chat and instant messages.

Q&A

Q Sometimes the sequence of statements in a chat looks all jumbly to me. Like, somebody asks a question, and then three unrelated statements appear, and then someone answers the question a few panels later. What's the deal?

A In a chat with three or more members, the conversation often appears out of order. This jumbling happens because each member's words take a different amount of time to reach the server, and some members take more time composing their statements than others.

After you've used chat for a while, you'll get used to the jumbling, and your brain will develop the ability to sort out the conversation intuitively.

Q My teenage daughter comes home from school, goes online and trades instant messages with her friends. They are all in the same city. Are they nuts?

A They're teenagers; of course they're nuts. Seriously, though, when we were kids we used to come home from school and call our friends on the telephone. That's not nearly as "cool" today—unless you're using a cell phone—as sending instant messages across town. Plus, they can be sending messages to numerous friends at once!

HOUR 7

Participating in Newsgroups and Mailing Lists

Now that you've gotten started with email and chat, it's time to look at a couple of other ways of communicating: newsgroups and mailing lists. They both share aspects of emailing and chatting, but they work in different ways. And they both offer great ways to get involved with a subject that interests you, or to just have fun.

At the end of the hour, you'll be able to answer the following questions:

- What are newsgroups?
- How do I find and open a newsgroup?
- How do I navigate among and read the messages in a newsgroup?
- How do I contribute to a newsgroup?
- What are the two kinds of mailing lists, and the two different email addresses I need to use most mailing lists?

- How can I find the addresses for mailing lists covering topics that interest me?
- How do I join a mailing list and contribute to it?

Getting Started with Newsgroups

When you know how to use an email program, you know 90 percent of what you need to know to use newsgroups. Reading a message, composing a new message, and replying are all very similar in an email program and a newsreader.

Where a newsreader differs is that it retrieves messages from and posts messages to Internet newsgroups, sometimes known as discussion groups or, collectively, as Usenet. The newsgroups and their messages are stored on a family of servers called *news servers* or *NNTP servers*.

NEW TERM **Post**. Sending a message to a newsgroup is known as *posting*, because you're publishing the message in a public forum, just as if you had "posted" a paper note on a bulletin board.

Your ISP or online service has a news server that you are authorized to use for reading and contributing to newsgroups. Access to one news server is all you need; the messages sent to any news server on the Internet are automatically copied—at regular intervals—to all news servers.

On any news server, you can open any newsgroup and read any current message posted to that newsgroup, no matter which news server the message was originally posted to. That's why a newsgroup on an ISP's server in New York has messages from folks in Canada, California, and the U.K.

Before you can open newsgroups and display their messages, you must configure your newsreader to contact your ISP's news server, and you must download the complete list of newsgroups from the server.

In general, all news servers carry the same newsgroups and current messages—but not exactly.

First, a few ISPs or online services do not carry all newsgroups, omitting those they deem potentially offensive to their customers, such as sex-oriented groups. A few ISPs carry only newsgroups specifically requested by their subscribers, instead of all of the thousands of groups out there. And some ISP's servers carry special newsgroups of local interest that are not copied to other news servers.

Beyond those differences, note that it takes a day or so for a message posted to one server to be copied to all the others. At any given time, a new message might be on some servers, but not yet on others.

Finally, no news server keeps messages forever. After a set number of days, a newsgroup message is automatically deleted from the server. Each server has its own schedule for removing these old—*expired*—messages, so a message that's been deleted from one server might remain on others.

Configuring Your Newsreader

As with other types of Internet programs, there are many different newsreaders out there. In the Big Two Internet suites, the programs are the same ones you use for email: Netscape Messenger and Outlook Express. You just have to switch these programs from email mode to newsgroup mode.

There are a number of good newsreader programs available on the market. If you have the Microsoft Office suite, you could use Microsoft Outlook as a newsreader. Forte, Inc., offers two good newsreader products, a freeware program called Free Agent, and a commercial program called Agent. You can check them out at `www.forteinc.com`.

To switch either program to newsgroup mode, you simply click your news server's name near the bottom of the folder list (see Figure 7.1). Observe that choosing the server changes the toolbar buttons and menu choices from those used for email to those you need for newsgroups.

You can open Outlook Express directly in newsgroup mode from Internet Explorer by clicking the Mail button on IE's toolbar, then choosing Read News from the menu that appears. You can open Netscape Messenger directly in newsgroup mode by choosing Communicator, Newsgroups from within any Communicator component (such as Navigator).

If you use an online service, such as America Online or CompuServe, you might not be able to choose your own newsreader; you might be required to use the online service interface—the tool you use for accessing the service's non-Internet content. However, this will still allow you to access the newsgroups on the Internet just like another newsreader would.

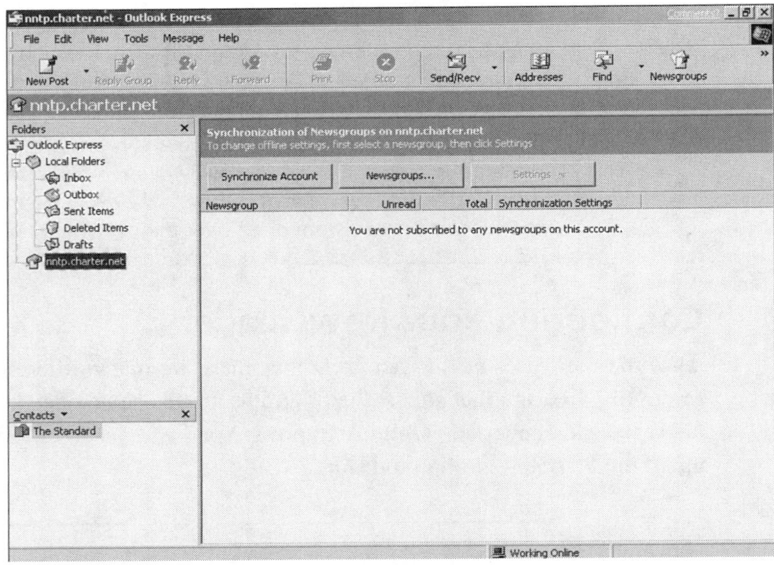

FIGURE 7.1
To use Outlook Express (shown here) or Netscape Messenger for newsgroup activities, click your news server's name in the folder list.

All newsreaders have a configuration dialog in which you enter the information required for communicating with your ISP's news server. That dialog always requires the address of your ISP's news server. If your newsreader is not part of a suite (and thus cannot copy configuration information from the email component), the configuration dialog also requires your email address and full name.

You'll find the configuration dialog

- **For Netscape Messenger** by choosing Edit, Preferences to open the Preferences dialog. In the list of Categories, choose Mail & Newsgroups. Complete the configuration settings in the Mail & Newsgroups category's Newsgroup Servers subcategory.
- **For Outlook Express** by completing the News dialogs of the Connection Wizard (see Hour 3, "Getting Connected to the Internet"). If you choose your news server folder in Outlook Express without having configured first, the Internet Connection Wizard opens automatically.

Instead of using the Internet Connection Wizard, you can configure newsgroup access in Outlook Express by choosing Tools, Accounts, then clicking the Add button on the Internet Accounts dialog.

Downloading the Newsgroups List

After your newsreader knows how to contact the server, you must download the complete list of newsgroups, which usually takes just a few minutes. If you open some newsreaders (including Netscape Messenger and Outlook Express) without first having downloaded the list, a prompt appears, asking whether you want to download the list.

If your newsreader does not prompt you, find a button or menu item for downloading the list by doing one of the following:

- **In Netscape Messenger,** make sure you are in newsgroup mode by clicking the name of your news server or choosing Communicator, Newsgroups. Choose File, Subscribe and, on the dialog that appears, click the Refresh List button.
- **In Outlook Express,** click the name of your news server, and then click the Newsgroups button. On the dialog that appears, click Reset List.

The list of newsgroups changes periodically, adding new groups and removing others. Netscape Messenger, Outlook Express, and some other newsreaders detect automatically when the list changes, and display a prompt asking whether you want to update your list.

If your newsreader does not detect changes in the list, it's smart to redownload the full list once a month or so, to keep current.

Finding and Subscribing to Newsgroups

Once the list has been downloaded to your computer, you can find and subscribe to any newsgroups you want. While exploring Web pages devoted to topics that interest you, you'll probably come across the names of related newsgroups. But newsgroups are easy to find, with or without a Web page's help.

Unlike mailing lists, you are not required to subscribe to a newsgroup in order to use it. All subscribing really does is add the group to an easy-access list in your newsreader, to make visiting it convenient.

Most people have a small list of groups they visit often, so subscribing makes sense. But in most newsreaders, you can pick a newsgroup out of the full list, or enter the group's name in a dialog, to open the list without subscribing.

Newsgroups are perhaps the one Internet activity where names are a reliable indicator of content. Newsgroups are organized under a system of names and categories. The leftmost portion of the name shows the top-level category in which the group sits; each portion further to the right more narrowly determines the subject of the group.

For example, the top-level category `rec` contains recreational newsgroups, those dedicated to a recreational—rather than professional—discussion of their topics. So the hypothetical newsgroup name

```
rec.sports.basketball.womens
```

indicates that the discussion focuses on a recreational interest in women's basketball. There are thousands of `rec` groups, many `rec.sports` groups, several `rec.sports.basketball` groups, and just one `rec.sports.basketball.womens` newsgroup. See how it works?

Some of the other major top-level categories include the following:

- `alt`—Alternative newsgroups, those in which the most freewheeling conversations are accepted
- `biz`—Business newsgroups and ads
- `comp`—Computer-related newsgroups
- `k12`—Education-related groups
- `misc`—Miscellaneous
- `sci`—Science-related groups

To Do: Choose, Subscribe To, and Open Groups in Outlook Express

1. Connect to the Internet, open Outlook Express, and click the news server's name in the left-hand column (see Figure 7.2).

> If you are using Netscape as your newsreader, the steps are very similar. To get started, open the Communicator menu and select Newsgroups.

2. Click the Newsgroups button to open the list of newsgroups available to you. (See Figure 7.3).

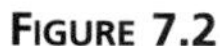

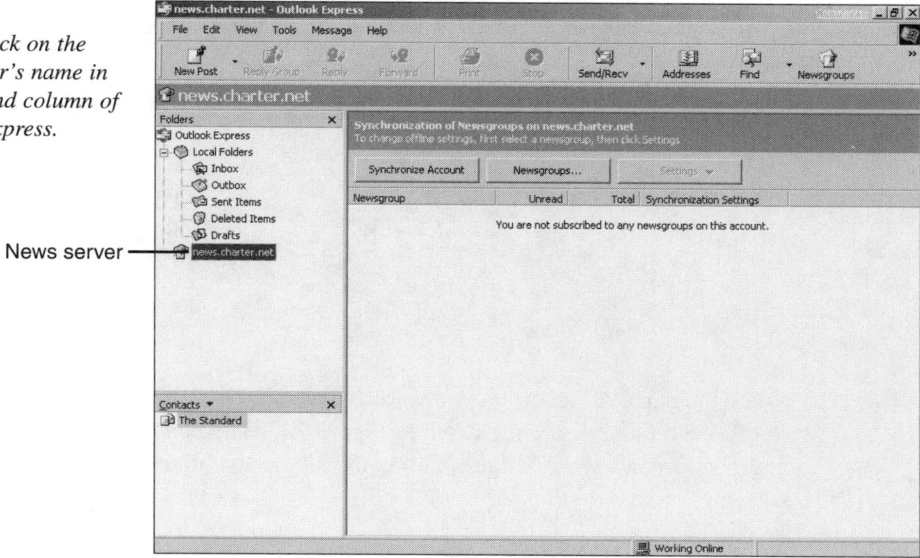

FIGURE 7.2
Step 1: *Click on the news server's name in the left-hand column of Outlook Express.*

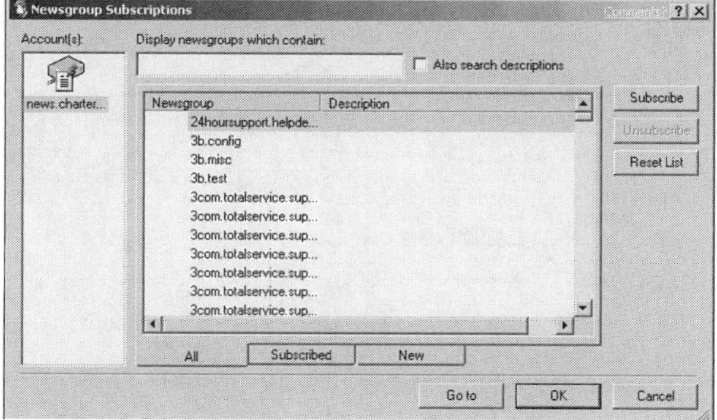

FIGURE 7.3
Step 2: *Click the Newsgroups button to open the list.*

3. In the All tab, display the group's name in the Newsgroup box (see Figure 7.4). There are several ways to do this:
   - If you know the exact name of the group you want to subscribe to, type the name in the box.
   - Use the list to scroll to the group name, then click it. In the list, the groups are presented alphabetically.
   - Enter a search word or phrase in the box and click OK to search for newsgroups of a particular topic.

7

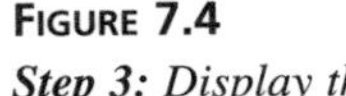

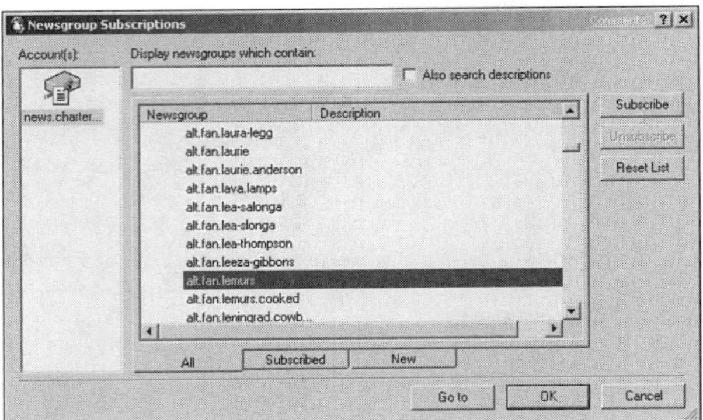

FIGURE 7.4
Step 3: *Display the group's name in the Newsgroup box.*

4. When the name of the group you want to subscribe to is highlighted, click the Subscribe button, then click OK (see Figure 7.5). The newsgroup's name appears under your news server's name, and in the bigger list of newsgroups on your screen.

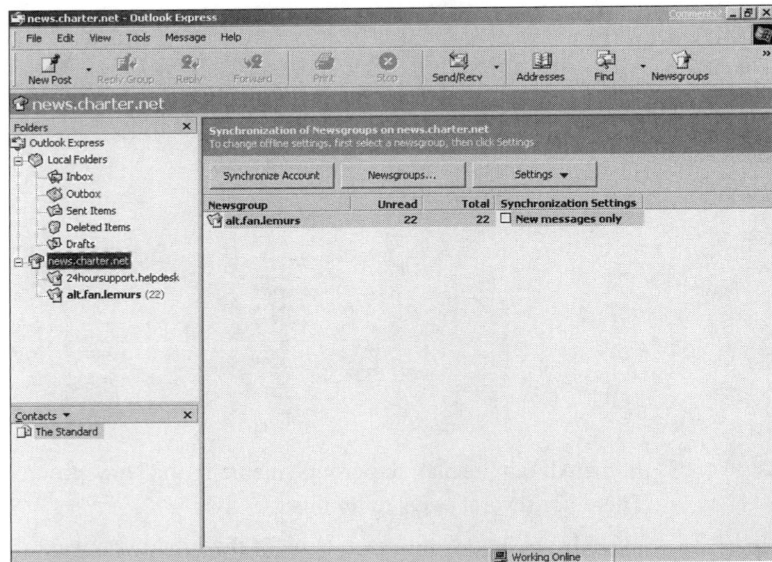

FIGURE 7.5
Step 4: *The subscribed newsgroup appears in your list.*

5. To open a newsgroup, click its name in the list (see Figure 7.6).

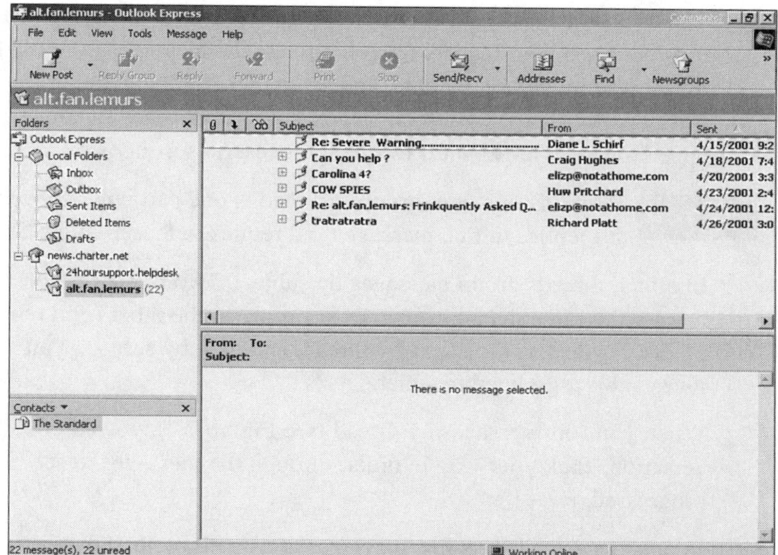

FIGURE 7.6
***Step 5:** Click the newsgroup name to open a list of messages.*

Reading Newsgroup Messages

Once you open and display a newsgroup's message list, reading messages is just like reading email messages in an email program. Single-click an item in the list to display it in the preview pane (as shown in Figure 7.7), or double-click it to display the message in its own window.

The message lists you see in an email program generally show messages that have been copied to your computer. But in most newsreaders, the messages in the list you see when you open a newsgroup are not on your computer; they're on the news server.

All that's been copied to your computer are the message headers, to make up the list. When you display any particular message, that message is then copied to your computer. Because the messages aren't copied until you request them, you must stay online while working with newsgroups.

Some newsreaders—including Netscape Messenger and Outlook Express—support *offline news reading*. You can configure them to automatically download messages from newsgroups so you can read them later, offline. You learn how to do this in Hour 16, "Working Smarter by Working Offline."

The tricky part about reading news messages is organizing the list in a way that works for you. Most newsreaders let you arrange the messages in myriad ways: Alphabetically by subject, by author, by date, and so on. (The options for sorting the message list in Netscape Messenger, Outlook Express, and most other Windows and Mac newsreaders appear on the View menu.) But the most useful sorting is by *thread*.

NEW TERM **Thread.** In a newsgroup, a thread is one particular conversation—a message and all replies to that message (and replies to those replies, and so on).

In effect, threads group messages by subject. Two messages can have the same subject but not the same thread, if neither is a reply to the other (or a reply to a reply to the other). If you sort messages by thread, and then by subject, you'll get all threads on a given subject grouped together.

When you sort messages by thread (see Figure 7.7), you can follow the flow of the conversation, click your way in order, through the messages to see how the discussion has progressed.

In most newsreaders, when messages are sorted by threads, the replies to a message do not appear automatically in the list; instead, a plus sign (+) appears next to the message's listing, to indicate that there are sub-messages—replies—to that message. To display the replies, click the plus sign.

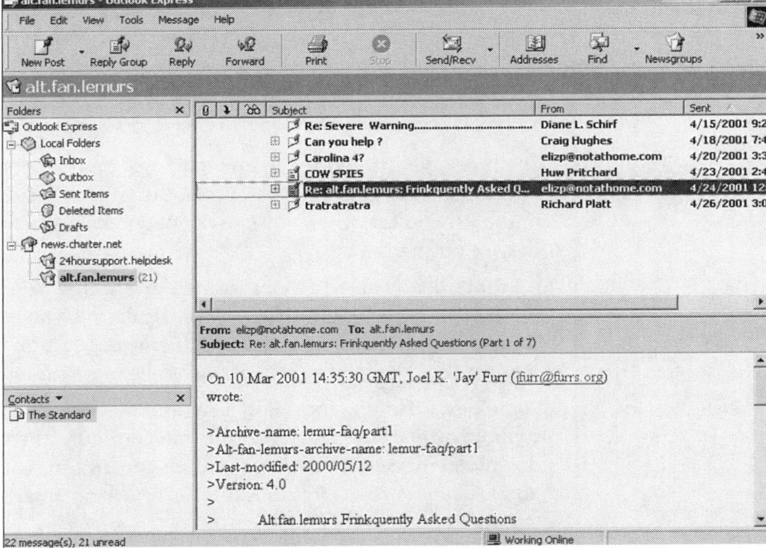

FIGURE 7.7
You can organize your newsgroup message list by thread, to better follow the flow of individual conversations.

Composing and Replying to Messages

You compose and reply to messages in a newsreader exactly as you do in an email program. The only differences are in the message header, because instead of addressing a message to a person, you're addressing it to a newsgroup.

The only other important difference between sending email and newsgroup messages is the terminology you see applied on buttons and menu items:

- In email, you click Send to send a message; in a newsreader, it's either Send or Post.
- In email, you click Reply to reply to a message; in a newsreader, it's either Reply or Respond.

The easiest way to deal with that difference is to start in the right place. For example, when you want to compose a new message (not a reply) and post it to a newsgroup, begin by opening that newsgroup, then clicking your newsreader's button for comp
a new message. (It's New Msg in Netscape Messenger, New Post in Outlook Expr
When the message window opens, you'll see that it's preaddressed to the current
newsgroup.

When you first join a newsgroup, it's a good idea to "lurk" for a
before posting. Lurking is the act of reading other people's pos
"getting the lay of the land" before jumping in head-first. A c
the dos and don'ts of online communication is included in Hc
Communication Tricks and Tips."

When replying, open the message to which you want to reply, and
(or Respond) button on the message window in which that messa
sage window that opens, the message is preaddressed to the app
subject line is correctly phrased to add the reply to the same th
sage, and the original message is quoted in the message area
your comments, and edit the quote as necessary.

After completing a new message or reply, send the messa
menu item labeled Send or Post.

When you choose to reply, most newsreaders provide the option of replying to the newsgroup or sending an email reply directly to the author of the message you're replying to. The email option is handy when your reply is really intended only for the author, not the whole group.

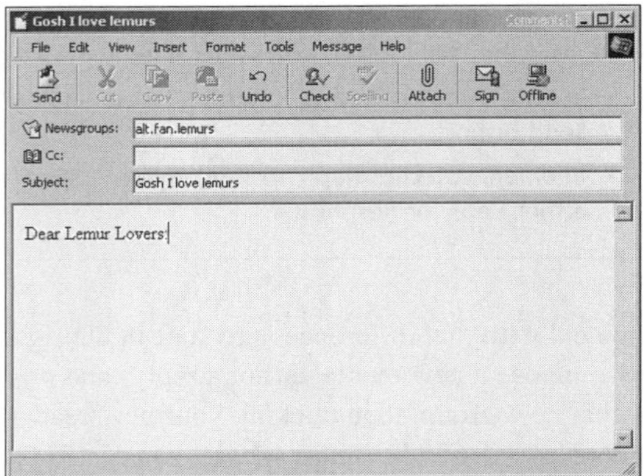

FIGURE 7.8
Start a new message or reply while viewing the message list of a newsgroup, and that message is preaddressed to the open newsgroup.

The Basics of Mailing Lists

A mailing list is much like a newsgroup in that you subscribe to a list based on its topic. The primary difference is that instead of visiting the newsgroup and reading messages of your choice, a mailing list will automatically send every post to the group to your email address.

For a mailing list to work, someone has to handle its management and administration: mostly signing up new members and removing members who have asked to be removed.

In a few mailing lists, that administrative task is handled by a real person. However, most mailing lists are managed not by a person, but by a *list server*. Sometimes, the mailing lists managed by people are called *manual* mailing lists, to distinguish them from the lists automated by list servers.

NEW TERM **List server.** A program that automatically manages a mailing list. Actually, there are several different programs that manage mailing lists, including Listserv, Listproc, and Majordomo. They are often grouped generically under the term "listserv."

Working with Mailing Lists

The first step in using mailing lists is finding one that interests you. When visiting Web pages devoted to your favorite topics, you'll often see mention of related mailing lists, along with the email address required for signing up: the *subscription address*.

You can also visit any of several Web pages that help folks find mailing lists related to a particular subject. A good first stop is Liszt (`www.Liszt.com`), a search tool dedicated to helping you find and use mailing lists (see Figure 7.9).

You can browse through Liszt's categories to find a list, or use its search engine to find lists related to a search term you enter.

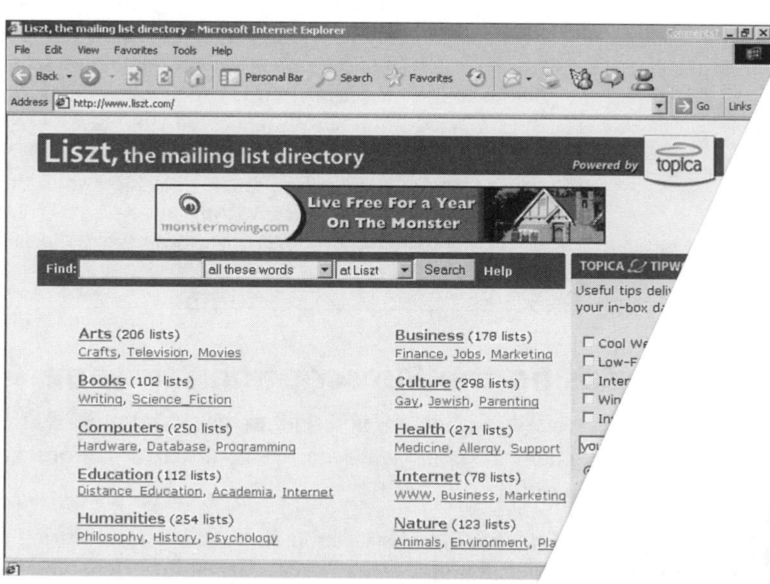

FIGURE 7.9
Use Liszt to browse for a mailing list, or search for one.

Besides Liszt, other good places to find mailing lists (and instruct
include the following:

- The list of Publicly Accessible Mailing Lists at `http://`
- The List of Lists, at `catalog.com/vivian/interest-`
- Yahoo!'s directory at `www.yahoo.com/Computers_an` `Mailing_Lists/`

Subscribing to a Mailing List

To use any mailing list, you need to know two different email addresses:

- The address of the person, or program, that manages the list. This address might be called the "management" or "subscription" address.
- The list address, an email address to which you send all your contributions to the list, the comments or questions you want all others in the list to see.

Sorry, sorry... Hate to break into an easy topic like mailing lists with a big fat Caution. But I really want to alert you to the one major mailing list mistake: Mixing up the *list* address with the *management* address, and vice versa.

If you accidentally send your list contributions to the management address, the others on the list won't see them. And if you send management commands to the list address, those commands will not be carried out. Worse, the message containing those commands might show up in the mailing list of everyone in the list, which won't win you any friends.

Never forget: Contributions to the discussion go to the list address, commands for managing your subscription go to that other address (subscription, management, whatever), which is usually the same one you used to subscribe.

Composing the Subscription Message

When you're ready to sign up, you send to the subscription address a simple email message that contains the command required to subscribe. Unfortunately, the command differs from list to list.

Most references to mailing lists—including those you'll turn up in the directories described earlier—include subscription instructions. Those instructions typically tell you the command you must send, and also *where* in the email message—the Subject line or the message body—you must type that command.

Command instructions use a *syntax diagram* to tell you what to type. Even manually managed lists generally require a particular command syntax, although they're more forgiving of command mistakes than automated lists are.

EW TERM **Syntax diagram.** A syntax diagram shows what you must type in order to properly phrase a command to control a computer program, such as a listserv. In a syntax diagram, the exact words you must type are shown in normal type, while any parts of the command you must add are surrounded by brackets or shown in italics.

For example, to phrase the command indicated by the syntax diagram

```
subscribe lastname firstname
```

or

```
subscribe [lastname] [firstname]
```

I would type

```
subscribe Snell Ned
```

Notice that I replace any portions in italics or brackets with the information indicated, and that I do not type the brackets.

To subscribe to a list, read the instructions to find the following:

- The syntax diagram for subscribing
- The part of the message where the command should be typed (either the Subject line or body)
- The subscription address

Compose an email message containing only the command indicated by the instructions, and send it to the subscription address. Figure 7.10 shows a typical subscription message in which the command appears in the message body.

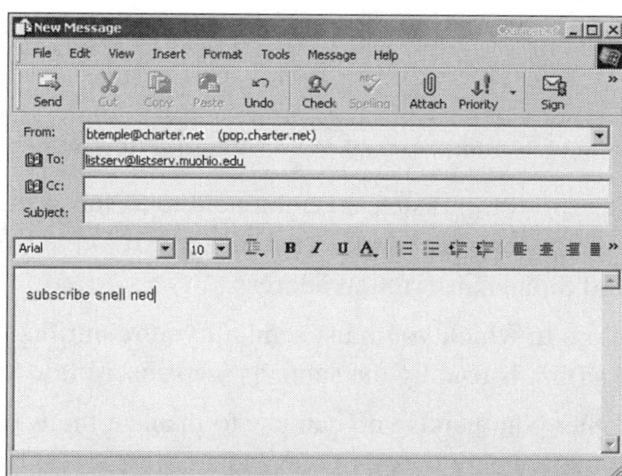

FIGURE 7.10
You subscribe to a mailing list by typing a subscription command in an email message and sending it to the list's subscription address.

When composing your message, don't type anything the instructions don't ask for. If the instructions tell you to put the command in the message's Subject line, leave the message body blank. If the command belongs in the message body, leave the Subject line blank, and put nothing but the command in the body. (Many lists don't care whether you follow this rule, but because you can't predict which lists *do* care, it's best to follow the rule always.)

Because many automated list management programs manage more than one list, the subscription command syntax often includes the name of the list, so the program knows which list you're subscribing to, for example:

`subscribe` *`listname firstname lastname`*

Reading the Welcome Message

Shortly after you send your subscription message, you'll receive a reply message from the list. An automated list might reply within a minute or two. After sending a subscription message to an automated list, stay online, wait a few minutes, and then check your email—the reply will probably be there. (Some automated and manual lists might take a day or more to reply, so be patient, and don't resend the subscription message if you don't receive an immediate reply.)

If you did not phrase your subscription message properly, the reply reiterates the subscription command syntax and usually includes instructions. You must compose and send another subscription message, carefully following any instructions in the reply.

Always, always, always read *and save* the Welcome message, if for no other reason than that it contains the instructions for *unsubscribing*—quitting—the mailing list if you choose to do so later.

The Welcome message contains lots of very valuable information, particularly:

- A syntax diagram for phrasing the command to *un*subscribe. If and when you decide you no longer want to receive messages from the list, you'll need to send this command to the subscription address.
- The list address to which you must send all your contributions, and the management address (that is usually the same as the subscription address, but not always).
- Syntax for other commands you can use to manage the way messages come to you. For example, many lists let you send a command to temporarily pause—stop sending you messages—if you go on vacation or want messages paused for any other reason.
- Any other rules or policies all members of the list are required to observe. These typically include the basic rules of netiquette (covered in Hour 8).

> Sometimes, the Welcome message includes instructions to send a reply to the Welcome, to confirm your subscription. In such cases, you're not officially subscribed until you send a reply as instructed.

Always read and save the Welcome message, so you can refer to it when you need to know a command or policy or want to unsubscribe. If your email program lets you organize your messages in folders, create a special folder for Welcome messages (or a folder for each list you subscribe to), so they're easy to find and you don't accidentally delete them when cleaning up your Inbox. You might also want to print the Welcome message and file it.

Shortly after you receive the Welcome message (and reply to it, if so instructed), you'll begin receiving email messages from the list. How many and how often depends on the list, but it's not unusual to receive a dozen or more messages per day. Read anything that looks interesting; ignore (or delete) the rest.

> Some mailing lists are purely informational. They're designed not as a discussion forum, but to keep you abreast of news and developments in a particular company or other organization.
>
> Usually, such lists don't have list addresses to which you can contribute. It's a one-way conversation; you just subscribe, and then read whatever shows up.

> Mailing lists can send dozens of messages a day, which can clutter up your Inbox and make it hard to find other messages. If your email program supports a facility called *filtering*, you can set up a separate folder where all messages from the list are stored automatically as soon as they're received, leaving your Inbox for other mail.

Contributing to a Mailing List

You are not required to contribute to a mailing list. Many people simply read and enjoy the messages they receive, and never add their own comments or questions.

If you do feel inspired to contribute, just send a message to the list address. If the contribution is related to a previous message, use your email program's Reply feature to reply to the group. In the reply, include a quote of any portion of the original message that's relevant to your comment or question.

When using Reply to send a message to a mailing list, always double-check the To: line in your message to be sure that it shows the correct list address. Many lists are configured so that when you click Reply, the message is addressed not to the list, but to the individual sender of the message. In such cases, you'll want to type the actual list address in the To: line (or choose that address from your Inbox).

Summary

Newsgroups and mailing lists are both great ways to keep up with a subject that's of interest to you. You can jump in and participate and, better yet, unsubscribe any time you want. Take some time to subscribe to one or two mailing lists and a few newsgroups, just for fun.

Q&A

Q Lots of sites say I can subscribe to their newsletter and get it delivered to my email box. Is this a mailing list?

A Sort of. These are really e-newsletters. The site owner creates them for people who sign up, and you receive them in your email. This is one-way communication; you cannot reply to an e-newsletter. They are great for trade publications; I'm subscribed to about 12 different newsletters related to the publishing industry.

Q I heard that some newsgroups and mailing lists are "moderated," and some aren't. What does that mean?

A Those lists have a "moderator," a person who reads every message and tries to ensure that messages follow some general rules set forth for the group (usually the rules of netiquette; see Hour 8). If you break the rules in a group, the moderator might send you a warning or two. In a mailing list, if you break rules repeatedly, the moderator might kick you off the list.

Of course, some folks object to moderators, saying that a moderator inevitably imposes his or her values on the whole group, preventing a truly free-flowing dialog from taking place. There are many "unmoderated" newsgroups; for example, many of the "alternative" newsgroups (those whose names begin with alt) are unmoderated. There are fewer unmoderated mailing lists, but of course, some moderators are so lenient that the list seems unmoderated anyway.

Personally, I don't pay much attention to whether a list or group is moderated or not. But if you're particularly bothered by petty squabbles and off-color remarks, you might find that the moderated lists and groups are more to your liking.

HOUR 8

Online Communication Tricks and Tips

We've come to the last hour in this section of the book. The previous three chapters have all dealt with communications modes on the Internet: email, chat, instant messages, newsgroups, and mailing lists.

Internet communication is very simple to understand and to use. But a few key mistakes can cause you lots of trouble. That is, if you're not careful.

There is a different form of etiquette that is followed on the Internet. It's called *netiquette*, and if you don't understand the basic principles of it, you run the risk of offending people, or worse.

And, after you've opened yourself up to Internet communication, the chances that you'll receive unwanted mail are pretty good. Just like all those credit card solicitations you get in your mailbox at home, the Internet can fill up your email box pretty quickly with unwanted offers for this or that.

This hour is a clearinghouse for the little nuances of Internet communication. Now that you know *how* to communicate over the Net, this hour will help clean up the loose ends, so your communications can remain as enjoyable as possible.

By the end of this hour, you will:

- Understand netiquette and know how to observe it
- Know how to add "emotion" to your communications using symbols and shorthand
- Find out how junk emailers find you
- Learn how to weed out the junk mail before it gets to you
- Know your options for dealing with difficult people in all forms of Net communication

Observing Proper *Netiquette*

How you communicate with private friends in email is between you and your friends. But after you begin contributing to discussion groups—mailing lists and newsgroups—you're participating in a public forum, and have an obligation to follow a code of conduct that keeps the conversation pleasant and productive for all.

Netiquette—the unofficial online code of conduct—boils down to the Golden Rule: Do unto others. As you gain experience, you'll begin to notice things others do that bug you, such as quoting too much or writing sloppily. Obviously, those are the things you must remember not to do yourself.

Here are the basics of being a good cyber-citizen, particularly in discussion groups. Note that none of this stuff is law; if you skip a rule, the cyber-police will not show up at your door. (Although there are a few strictly managed lists that will kick you out if you break certain rules—another reason to read and follow the Welcome message!) Like all forms of courtesy, netiquette is often not strictly required, but always highly recommended.

- **Don't shout.** SOME FOLKS LIKE TO TYPE ALL MESSAGES ONLY IN CAPITAL LETTERS, and some others overuse capital letters FOR EMPHASIS! On the Internet, capitalizing letters means you are SHOUTING. Capitalize like you would in a typed letter, and use your word choices and phrasing for emphasis, saving the all-caps trick for rare, EXTREME EMPHASIS.
- **Stay on topic.** Nothing is more aggravating than subscribing to a list and then receiving all sorts of messages that veer off on tangents. If your message does not pertain directly to the discussion group's stated topic, don't send it.
- **Keep current.** Newcomers to a list or group, or folks who only drop in occasionally, tend to ask questions that have already been asked and answered a dozen

times, which annoys the regulars. Keep up with the conversation so you know what's going on. Read the FAQ, if one is available.

NEW TERM **FAQ.** *Frequently Asked Questions*, a file that contains a general list of common questions and answers pertaining to a particular list, newsgroup, Web page, or other topic.

By reading FAQs (pronounced "faks" so that computer book authors can make stupid puns with "fax"), you can quickly bring yourself up to speed on the background information shared by others in the group.

When a FAQ is available for a mailing list, you'll find instructions for obtaining the FAQ in the Welcome message.

- **Don't use sarcastic language.** It's very difficult to communicate sarcasm effectively in a written message. Often, exaggerated messages intended as sarcasm are taken literally by those who read them, and confusion or arguments ensue.
- **Keep personal discussions personal.** Before sending any message, ask yourself, "Would this message interest the whole list, or is it really a personal message to just one member?" If the message is really for one person, you can find that person's email address in the header information quoted in all list and newsgroup messages, and send your comment or question directly to that person, in private.

Avoid small, conversational contributions that add little information. For example, if someone posts a message with a great idea in it, don't send a reply to the group just to say "Great idea!" No one wants to go to the trouble of receiving and opening a message with so little to say.

- **Don't over-quote.** When replying, cut quotes down to just what's necessary to show what you're replying to. When a series of replies builds up and nobody cuts the quotes, each message can be pages long even if it contains only one new sentence. Try to leave enough information so that a newcomer to the conversation can tell what's being discussed, but cut everything else.
- **Write and spell well.** In the name of speed and efficiency, some folks boil their msg.s down to a grp. of abbrev.'s &/or shorthnd, or write toooo quikly and sloppilly. Do your readers the courtesy of writing whole words and complete sentences, and fix mistakes before you send.
- **Neither flame nor counter-flame.** A *flame* is an angry tirade or attack in a message, the kind that flares when a debate grows into a spat. No matter how hot the

argument gets, try to keep your cool. When flamed personally, don't rise to the bait: Flame wars only escalate, and no one ever wins.

Some folks flame others for breaches of netiquette, but that's hypocritical. Take responsibility for your own online behavior, and let others worry about theirs.

- **Fit in.** Usually, I'm no fan of conformity. But every mailing list and newsgroup has its own, insular culture. After reading messages for a while, you'll pick up a sense of the general technical level of the group, whether they're experts or novices (or both) on the topic at hand, the overall tone, catch phrases, vocabulary, and so on.

  By all means, be yourself—any group needs fresh ideas, new personalities. But try to be yourself within the style and culture of the group, to ensure that you can be understood by all.

Adding Personality with Smileys and Shorthand

Over the years, a system of symbols and shorthand has developed to enable folks to be more expressive in their messages: *Smileys* and *shorthand*. You'll see both used online often, in discussion groups and in email.

Although I show you smileys and shorthand next, I'm doing so mainly to help you understand them in messages you receive. Except for the occasional, simple smiley face, I don't recommend using these in your contributions to discussion groups.

There are many newcomers online today who don't know smileys or shorthand, so if you use these, many of your readers won't understand you. Try to put all your meaning in your words, so everybody gets the message.

Smileys

Smileys are used to communicate the tone of a message, to add an emotional inflection. (In fact, smileys are sometimes called *emoticons*—emotional icons.) They're little pictures, usually of faces, that are built out of text characters.

To see the picture, you tilt your head to the left. For example, tilt your head to the left (or tilt this book to the right) while looking at the smiley below, which is made up of three characters: a colon, a dash, and a close parenthesis:

```
:-)
```

Looks like a little smiling face, doesn't it? Folks follow a statement with this smiley to indicate that the statement is a joke, or is made facetiously (see Figure 8.1).

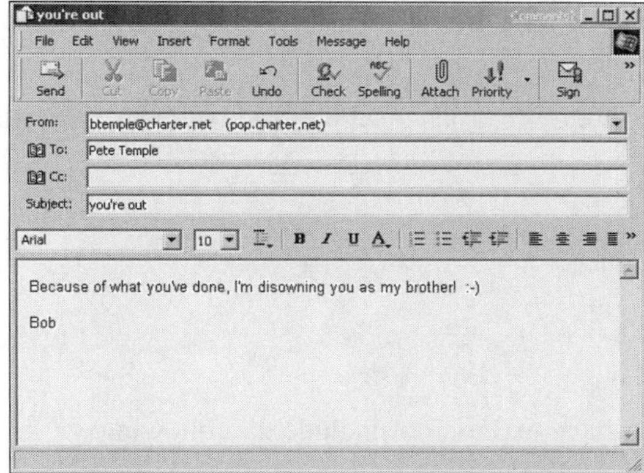

FIGURE 8.1
Using emoticons allows you to add a little personality to your messages.

There are many different smileys, some so obscure that only the real Net jocks use or understand them. But you're likely only to see the basics, including the basic smile shown earlier and also:

`:-(` —Frown

`;-)` —Wink

`:-0` —Surprise

`8-)` —Smile with glasses or bug-eyed

`:'-(` —Crying

`:-D` —Laughing

> Some folks omit the nose from their smileys; for example:
>
> `:)` `;)` `:0`

Shorthand

Shorthand abbreviations are used to carry a common phrase efficiently, to save space and typing. Some of these are commonly used offline, every day, such as ASAP (as soon as possible). Another shorthand expression used commonly online is IMO (in my opinion) and its cousin, IMHO (in my humble opinion). Figure 8.2 shows an example.

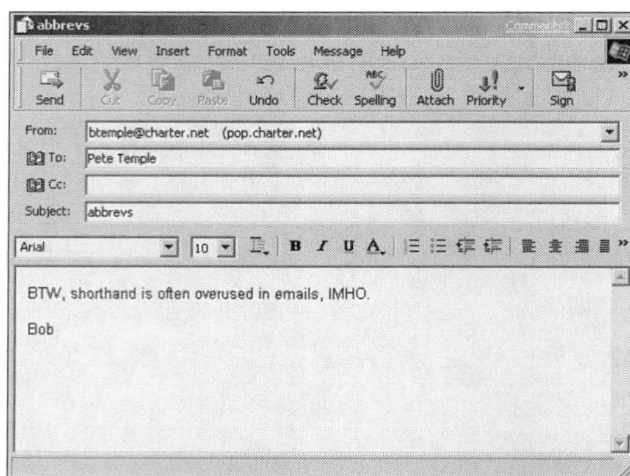

FIGURE 8.2
Shorthand allows you to communicate more succinctly.

Other popular shorthand expressions include the following:

BTW—By the way

B4—Before

FWIW—For what it's worth

IBTD—I beg to differ

IOW—In other words

LOL—Laughing out loud (generally used to declare that a statement is laughable)

OTOH—On the other hand

ROTFL—Rolling on the floor laughing (generally used to declare that a statement is extremely laughable)

Stopping Junk Email (Spam)

Within a few weeks after you begin using the Internet, you'll make an unpleasant discovery: The same sort of take-no-prisoners direct marketing types who telemarket you at suppertime and stuff offers in your mailbox have found you online. Over time, you'll see an ever-increasing number of ads, offers, chain letters, pyramid schemes, and other such scams in your Inbox. This mountain of unwanted crapola is collectively known as *spam*.

NEW TERM **Spam.** Unsolicited email sent out to a large group of strangers for purposes of advertising products and services, promoting political causes, or making mischief. (Senders of spam are called *spammers*.) The name might derive from the fact that the messages multiply the way the word "spam" does in an old *Monty Python* skit, but the term's origin is unconfirmed.

It's easy and cheap for an advertiser to automatically crank out an email ad to thousands—millions, even—of Internet users all at once. These messages often have subject lines designed to entice you into reading the message (FREE $$$) or to trick you into doing so (MESSAGE FROM AN OLD FRIEND). As the Internet population has grown, so has the spam problem.

The next few pages offer advice for dealing with the spam problem.

I should say right up front that nothing today can prevent or eliminate spam altogether—the problem is too pervasive. But by following the advice in this chapter, you can reduce spam to a tolerable amount. Until and unless it's outlawed, spam will remain as sure a fact of life as death, taxes, and telemarketing.

How They Get You

The more widely known your email address is, the more spam you'll get—it's that simple. So a logical first step in stopping spam is being very careful about how and when you reveal your email address.

Unfortunately, you cannot fully enjoy the Internet while keeping your email address a secret. Many online activities, such as shopping or posting to newsgroups, create an online record of your email address. In fact, anytime you send email, an unscrupulous spammer might harvest your address by intercepting messages on their way across the Net.

Still, you can effectively reduce the extent to which your address is known by making some smart surfing choices. In particular, be careful about

- **Forms.** Be very careful how and when you fill out online forms or surveys. A growing number of Web sites request that you complete a form to "register" in order to use the site; the form data is almost always used for marketing, and often for spam. On any site where you might complete a form, look for a link to a privacy policy; some Web sites promise in that policy not to spam you or to sell your information to spammers.

Some folks use a secondary email address—such as a Web-based email address—on all forms and other activities that are not part of their personal communications. That way, any spam resulting from filling in forms goes to the secondary address, where it's easier to ignore.

You still need to check messages on the secondary address from time to time, in case you do get a legitimate message there, and to clean out old messages. But at least you can minimize the day-to-day spam intrusion.

- **Newsgroup postings.** When you post to a newsgroup, a spammer can easily learn two things about you: your email address, and that you're interested in the newsgroup's topic.

  That's valuable direct marketing information; if you post a message to a newsgroup about a particular kind of product, you can expect to receive spam trying to sell you such a product. If you post to a sex-related newsgroup, you will soon receive spam selling phone sex or other sex-related stuff. You can read newsgroup messages anonymously—but when you post, you reveal your address. So watch where you post.

Again, all of the suggestions offered here are ways to reduce spam—nothing yet can truly eliminate it. So even if you never visit a sex-related newsgroup and never, ever post to one, you probably will receive spam from sex-related advertisers from time to time.

It's not your fault; receiving such messages does not necessarily mean that you did something to bring it on yourself. It's just that the merchants of sex and the merchants of get-rich-quick schemes are the two most aggressive kinds of spammers, and they spam anyone—and everyone—they can find.

- **Cookies.** Cookies are files on your computer stored there by a Web site, such as an online store, to record information about you that the page can access next time you visit. Unfortunately, the cookies on your computer—which might contain your email address and other personal data—might be read not only by the servers that put them there, but by other servers you visit, who might use that information for spam.
- **Mailing lists.** When you subscribe to mailing lists, your name, email address (and your interest in the list's topic) are recorded in a database that might be accessed and copied very easily by a spammer, particularly if the list is managed by an automated program. (Some mailing lists let you keep your address private; read the list's Welcome message for information about a CONCEAL command.) See Hour 7, "Participating in Newsgroups and Mailing Lists."

A newsgroup covering the same topic is a safer choice, as long as you don't post to it. If you contribute to the discussion, the mailing list is still less spam-risky than the newsgroup.

> Stopping spam is a little trickier for users of online services than for users of ISPs. The online services derive some of their revenue from advertisers, for providing access to you. So they're not too keen on letting you block those ads.
>
> Experts on AOL and spam advise users to avoid posting messages on AOL's forums, and to use Internet newsgroups instead. Despite the spam exposure risk in newsgroups, AOL's forums are notoriously harvested by spammers.

Report 'Em!

The people who run Internet servers are generally described as system administrators (*sysadmins*) or as system operators (*sysops*). These folks usually hate spam as much as you do, because it dramatically increases the traffic on their servers, taking up room needed for legitimate communications. There are two times you should contact sysops about spam:

- If you do not want to receive spam, always let the sysop of your Internet provider know how you feel. He or she might be able to take steps to minimize (but not eliminate) spam to your account. You can email your sysop by sending a message to the technical support address for your account.
- You can report spammers to the sysops of their Internet providers, who might then cancel their accounts or issue a warning. To address the message, take the part of the spammer's email address following the `@` symbol, and put `system@` or `sysop@` or `support@` in front of it. For example, if you get spam from `jerko@serv.com`, address messages to

  ```
  support@serv.com
  system@serv.com
  sysop@serv.com
  ```

  reporting that the user named Jerko is sending spam. This technique won't work all the time, because spammers are savvy about hiding their real server names. But it's a start.

In Newsgroups, Spoof 'Em!

Ultimately, having to restrain yourself from posting to newsgroups can severely hamper your ability to enjoy the Net. Here's a technique that some folks use to post to newsgroups while foiling spammer's efforts to cull their addresses: *spoofing*.

NEW TERM **Spoofing.** Also known as *munging*, the practice of scrambling your return email address in newsgroup postings just enough so that if it's harvested by one of the programs spammers use, the resulting spam will never reach you (it'll be sent to the spoofed address, not your real one).

A properly spoofed email address fools the automated harvesting programs that spammers use, but enables real folks on the group to still send you messages. For example, suppose your address is

```
shirley@aol.com
```

You can use your newsreader's configuration dialog boxes to change the Reply to address to

```
shirleytake_out_this_part@aol.com
```

If you use a signature at the bottom of your messages to identify yourself, change the address there, too. You can even add a note to your signature telling readers of your postings how to decode your address to send you email. The programs spammers use aren't smart enough to decode the address or read the note.

To spoof your newsgroup return address in Outlook Express, choose Tools, Accounts from the menu bar. On the dialog box that appears, click the News tab, then click Properties. In the box labeled Email Address, type the spoofed address (see Figure 8.3).

Spoofing your newsgroup return address in Netscape Mail is not recommended, because doing so also spoofs your return address on your email messages. That makes it difficult for people to make legitimate replies to your email messages.

At the time of this writing, spoofing works pretty well. But inevitably, spammers will smarten up their harvesting programs so that they recognize and decode spoofed addresses. Spoofing is only one step in reducing spam; you still need to do the other stuff described here, too.

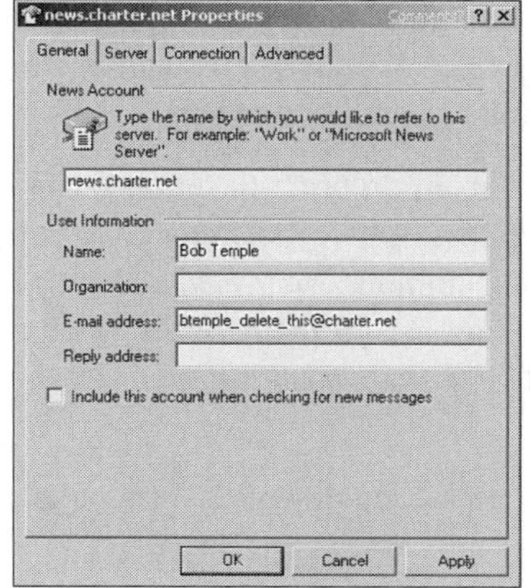

FIGURE 8.3
Use this dialog box in Outlook Express to spoof your return address on newsgroup postings.

Never Reply! Never! *Never!*

Many spam messages include "removal" instructions, telling you that if you reply to the message and include the words "REMOVE ME" or a similar phrase in the subject line, you'll receive no further messages.

In some cases, doing so might work. But in many cases, the "REMOVE ME" bit is actually a trick intended to make you verify your email address, so that the spammer knows he has a live one. In such cases, following the removal instructions won't remove you from the spammer's list, and might even increase the amount of spam you get.

Some folks also try to stop spam by sending angry replies to spammers. This approach never works. Often, the "From" line in the spam is left empty, or filled with a dummy or spoofed email address, so a reply won't even reach the real spammer. When angry replies do reach spammers, spammers ignore them. (They know full well that they are bothering some folks. They don't care. If they must annoy a million people in order to make a sale or two or three, they're happy with that.)

The moral? Never do anything an unsolicited email tells you to do, even if the instruction claims to be for your benefit. Never.

Filter 'Em Out!

If you can't stop the spam from coming, your next best bet is to avoid having to look at it. A variety of programs and techniques *filter* your incoming email to remove unwanted messages.

NEW TERM **Filter.** Settings in your email program (or a special utility) that automatically delete or move messages under specified circumstances. For example, if there's a person whose messages you never want to read, you can configure a filter so that all messages from that person's email address are deleted automatically upon receipt; you'll get them, but they'll be gone before you ever see them.

Filters cannot completely remove spam. In order to set up filters to delete all spam messages, you'd have to know the address of every spammer. No complete master list of spammers exists (new folks start spamming every day, and slippery spammers change addresses often), but you can pick up lists of many of the worst offenders, and then import or manually copy the lists into your email program so you can create filters to block messages from them.

Use the following URLs to learn about and download lists of spammers for filtering:

- The BadMail from Spam List: `www.webeasy.com/w2/spam/`
- The Network Abuse Clearinghouse: `www.abuse.net/`
- The Blacklist of Internet Advertisers: `www-math.uni-paderborn.de/%7Eaxel/BL/#list`

> You can pick up utilities that combine a filtering system with a spammers database, for fast and easy configuration of anti-spam filters. Check out
>
> Spambuster at `www.contactplus.com`
>
> Spameater Pro at `www.hms.com/spameater.htm`

Finding Filters in Your Email Program

Most full-featured email programs have their own built-in filtering systems you can apply to manage incoming mail and, to a limited extent, control spam.

If you don't have a list of spammers, or if creating filters for a long list is too difficult, you can deal with spam by creating filters for your legitimate contacts.

It works like this: If you have a steady group of people you communicate with regularly, create a filter that automatically stores all messages from those people in a separate folder. When you receive email, all of the important messages are automatically stored in the folder, while all of the spam stays in your Inbox, where you can ignore it. (You'll still want to scan your Inbox from time to time to check for legitimate messages from folks you haven't added to your filters.)

You can find the filters dialog boxes

- **In Messenger** by choosing Edit, Message Filters.
- **In Outlook Express** by choosing Tools, Message Rules.

In Outlook Express, you can choose Tools, Message Rules, Mail to open a dialog box in which you can set up all sorts of rules for how incoming messages are handled (see Figure 8.4).

But when all you want to do is prevent certain senders from sending you email, just choose Tools, Message Rules, Blocked Senders List, click Add, and type the address of the person from whom you will no longer accept email.

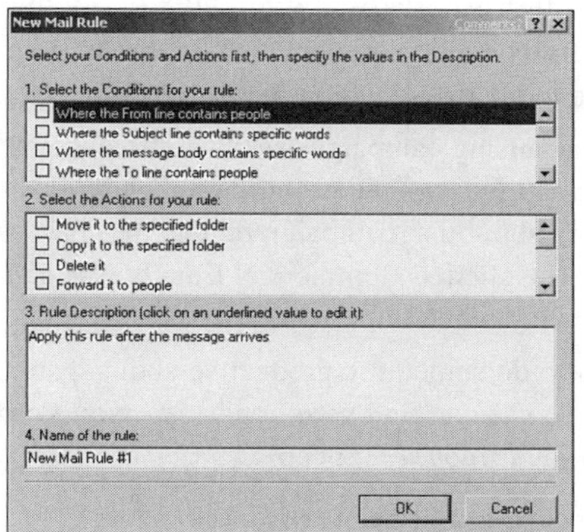

FIGURE 8.4
Email programs use filters (which Outlook Express, shown here, calls Rules) to automatically deal with certain incoming messages in whatever way you choose.

The Last Resort: Move

When all else fails, if you're still getting too much junk mail, there's one reliable (albeit temporary) solution: Change ISPs, or ask your current ISP to change your email address.

When you change your email address, spam directed to your old address can't reach you. (Be sure to inform all of your legitimate email partners of your new address, and instruct your old ISP not to forward email to your new address.) If your address has found its way into lots of spam databases, you can get a clean start this way.

Changing your email address is an extreme measure, especially if you have been using your address for important purposes, be it business or otherwise. No matter how diligent you are in informing your contacts about the move, some won't notice and you'll miss others. This action should be reserved for only the most severe circumstances.

Eventually, spammers will find you. But if you start clean with a new address, and then diligently apply the steps you learned in this hour, you might be able to keep the spammers at bay for a time.

Summary

Before this hour, you knew everything you had to know about messaging on the Internet. Now that you know how to stop spam, use emoticons, observe netiquette, and so on, you know even more than you really have to. Doesn't that make you feel special?

Q&A

Q You mentioned outlawing spam. Is that going to happen?

A There are many efforts underway to control or eliminate spam through legislation, but it's impossible today to say which, if any, of these efforts will succeed.

One of the most promising campaigns seeks not to enact new laws against spam, but to extend an existing law—the prohibition of junk faxes—to also cover email. You can learn more about that campaign on the Web page for CAUCE, the Coalition Against Unsolicited Commercial Email (`www.cauce.org`), which also provides links to many other anti-spam resources.

If you really want to do something productive about spam, let your congressperson know how you feel. You can find your congressperson's email address from the Web page at `www.house.gov/writerep/`.

Q Why should I be careful not to overuse emoticons?

A Well, you should be careful not to overuse anything, really. But emoticons, while they may be cute to you, are often annoying to some people. They shouldn't really be used in business communications at all. Most people save them for when they are communicating with a friend or relative.

PART III

Software for Your Journey

Hour

Hour 9

Using Internet Explorer 6.0

We've already spent a fair amount of time talking about browsing and Web communications, and you've seen a lot of figures that include screens from Microsoft Internet Explorer.

There might be a part of you wondering why those screens don't look *exactly* like the screens you see on your computer. That's an easy one—you're probably using a different version of Explorer than I am.

In this hour, we'll take a look at the Explorer program. We'll cover its features and offer some tricks and tips for using the program. After all, if you're going to be using the Internet, you might as well get accustomed to the software through which you'll view it. (Netscape Navigator is covered in Hour 10.)

In this hour, we will cover:

- Reasons for choosing Internet Explorer as your primary browser
- Where and how to get Internet Explorer

- Some of the features of the program
- What Favorite Places are, and how to organize them
- How to work with Explorer's toolbars and views
- How to set your preferences
- How to protect your privacy online using Explorer

Why Choose Internet Explorer?

A better question than the above might be, "Why not?" Internet Explorer is, along with Netscape Navigator, one of the two most-often used Web browsers. That alone isn't reason to pick it as your browser of choice, of course. What that brings along with it is, however.

Depending on where you stand on Microsoft in general, the company is either a behemoth trying to devour the computing world in general (and online communications in particular), or a forward-thinking, revolutionary, and creative genius, forever pushing the envelope of new technology to improve our lives.

Maybe both.

At any rate, say what you want about Microsoft. The fact is the company is big enough and smart enough to continually offer updates to its software, constantly improve it, and back it up. So there are some good reasons to choose Explorer.

Beyond that is the program itself. Explorer is a full-featured browser with some great new additions in its latest version, 6.0. It's also free, which doesn't hurt matters.

Where and How to Get Internet Explorer

How's this for some good news: You probably already have Internet Explorer. How do I know? Two reasons. First, if you're running a Windows-based computer, virtually all versions of Windows in recent history came with a version of Explorer included. You may not know you have it, but chances are you do. Second, we did some Web browsing back in Hour 4, and unless you cheated and were reading without using your computer, you must've been using a browser. Chances were good it was Explorer.

Regardless, the chances are also good that you don't have the latest and greatest version of Explorer. How do I know that? Well, Microsoft—like most software manufacturers—is constantly updating its software. These updates often add a new feature, but even more often they fix a little glitch or two that's been found in the works somewhere. Gotta get rid of those gremlins!

So, even if you bought your computer yesterday, and it came with a pre-installed version of Explorer 6.0, Microsoft might have come out with version 6.0.1 or 6.0.2 by now. Heck, depending on when you bought this book, Microsoft might even be on 6.2!

All those little numbers in the version of a software program may not mean that much to you, but they can be important. Let's say you're using version 6.0.1, for example. Any time the first number (in this case, the 6) changes, that means the software has undergone a remake that is fairly significant. Usually, this will mean a new look to the software, its buttons, icons, and so on. The second number reflects changes to the software that might offer improvements or new features, but not changing the basic way it functions. When the third number changes, it usually means that the updated version has fixed some bugs.

So, for example, if you are using Explorer version 5.5 (the last revision before 6.0 came out), you'll notice a new look to the software when you download version 6.0.

9

Downloading the Latest Version

There's one great way to make sure you have the latest version of Explorer: Go to the Microsoft Web site and download the latest version available. It doesn't take long, is easy to accomplish, and guarantees you're up to date.

Hour 14, "Downloading Programs and Files," gives a more detailed look at downloading. Consider the following tutorial a little preview to that hour.

So, let's give it a try!

To Do: Download and Install the Latest Version of Internet Explorer

1. Open your browser and go to the Microsoft Web site at `www.microsoft.com`. From the menu across the top of the page, click Downloads, then click Download Center (see Figure 9.1).
2. Using the pull-down menus on the Download Center page, select the most recent version of Internet Explorer (the one with the highest number) and your operating system. Leave the Show Results For box set at "Most Recent." Click Find It, and the page will display a list of the most recent versions of this software (see Figure 9.2).

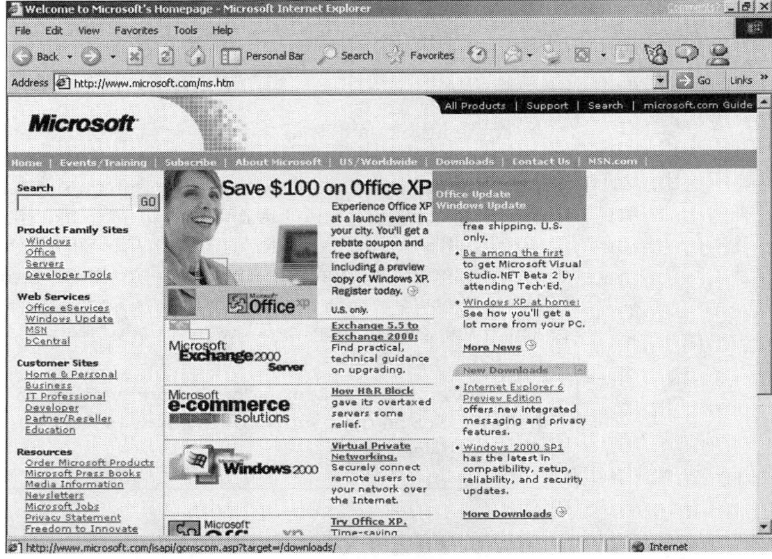

FIGURE 9.1
Step 1: *Click on the Download Center link from Microsoft's home page.*

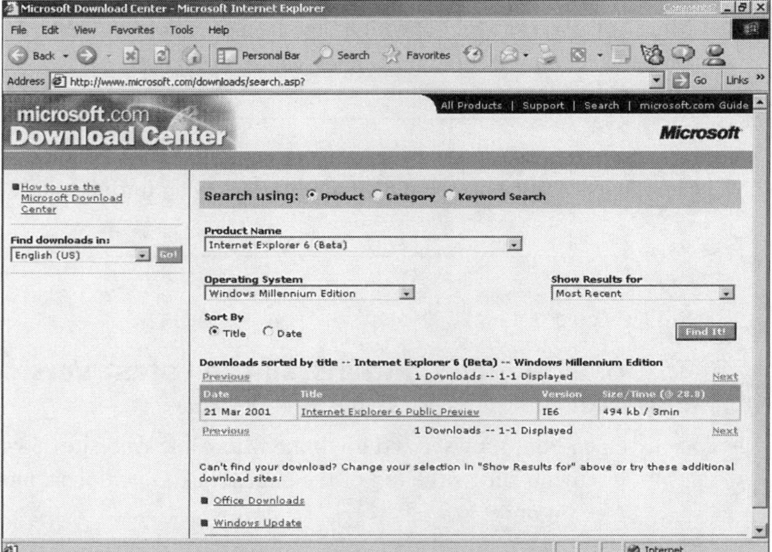

FIGURE 9.2
Step 2: *Display the most recent versions of Internet Explorer.*

Because Explorer 6.0 wasn't yet released to the public at the time of this writing, you see the word "Beta" in parentheses in the Product Name field in Figure 9.2. This was a public preview version of the software that was available prior to the official launch. You should be aware that "beta" software can be unstable and can cause problems with your computer. By the time you read this, version 6.0 will have been released, so you shouldn't see that word when you download.

3. Click the link to the latest version of the software that is not a "beta" version. On the screen that appears, select your language (I'm guessing it's English) from the drop-down menu, and click the Download Now button (see Figure 9.3).

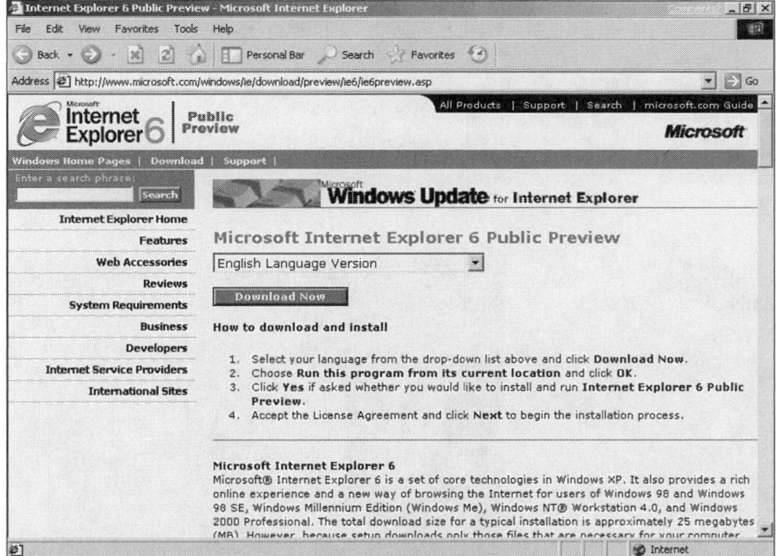

FIGURE 9.3
Step 3: *Choose your language and click Download Now.*

4. Click the button to "Run this program from its current location," then click OK (see Figure 9.4).
5. After a brief download of setup files, a Security Warning appears. Click the Yes button (see Figure 9.5).
6. Read the license agreement, click the "I accept the agreement" button, and click Next (see Figure 9.6).

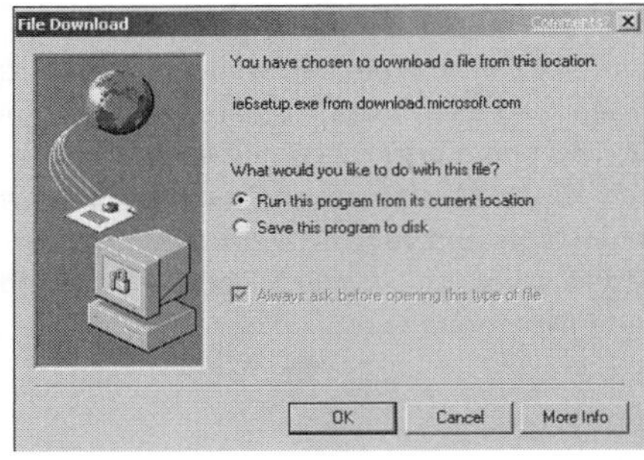

FIGURE 9.4
Step 4: *Select "Run this program from its current location."*

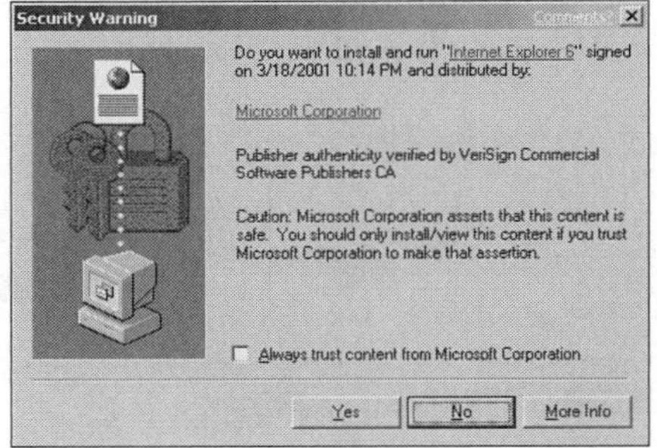

FIGURE 9.5
Step 5: *Click the Yes button.*

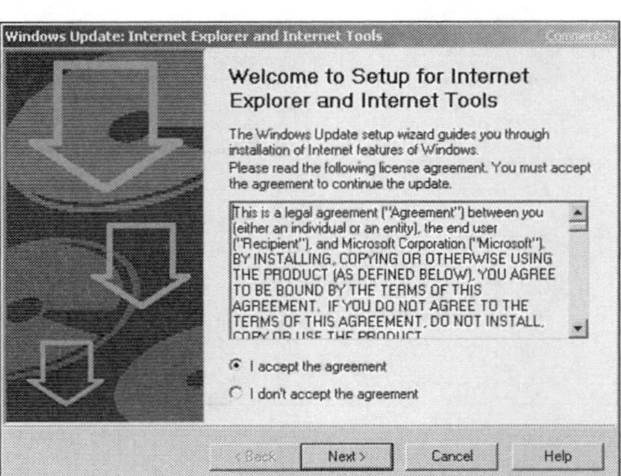

FIGURE 9.6
Step 6: *Accept the license agreement, and click Next.*

7. The program name appears, and you click Next again. The program begins to download and install automatically (see Figure 9.7).

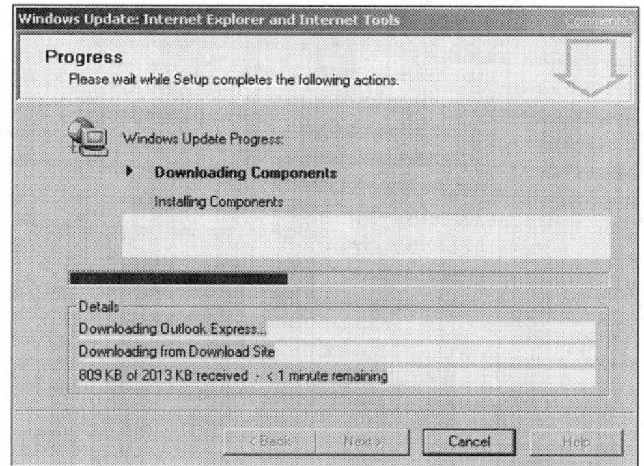

FIGURE 9.7
Step 7: The program downloads and installs automatically.

8. When the install is complete, you will be asked to restart your computer. Do so, and you're ready to go!

> Depending on the speed of your connection, this download/install can take anywhere from about 15 minutes (on a DSL or cable connection) to more than an hour (on a 56K). Be patient; it's worth the wait.

Starting Up Internet Explorer

Now that you've downloaded the latest version of Explorer and restarted your computer, all that's left is to connect to the Internet, start up Explorer, and off you go.

During the install process, Explorer probably created an icon on your desktop that you can simply double-click to launch the program. If not, just click on the Start button, and choose Internet Explorer from your list of programs.

As discussed in Hour 4, Explorer opens automatically to its predetermined home page, `www.msn.com` (see Figure 9.8). You can change that home page to any page you like (covered later in this hour).

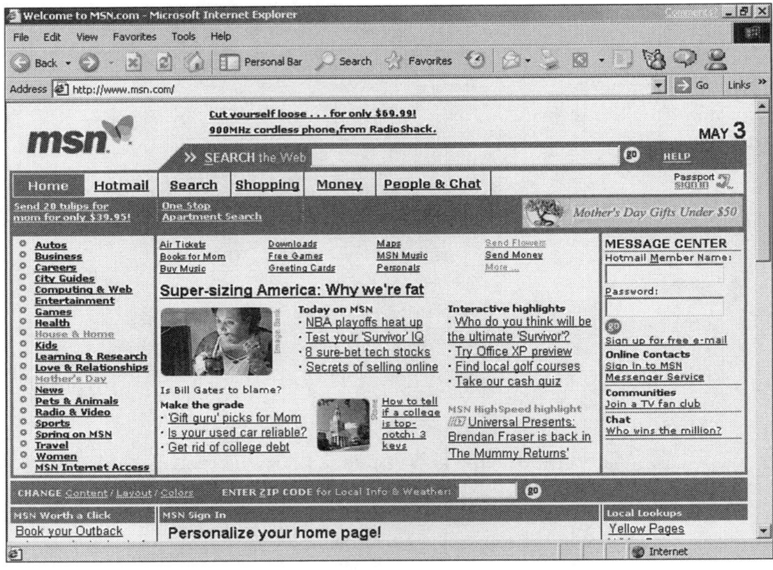

FIGURE 9.8
Explorer opens automatically to the Microsoft Network's home page.

Features of Internet Explorer

Whether you're familiar with past versions of Internet Explorer or not, you'll find a lot to like about version 6.0. But before we delve too deeply into the advancements that have been made for 6.0, let's look at some of the basic features of the software that have been available in older versions (and continue in 6.0).

Basic Features of Explorer 6.0

Because of Microsoft's position on the cutting edge of Internet technology, Internet Explorer has always been able to display pages that contain advanced programming. Microsoft continues to keep pace with new advancements in software design (if not making those advancements themselves).

There's not enough space here to go over all of the many features of the software, but I'll do my best to highlight some of the ones that are most likely to come into play for you. Some of these are discussed in greater detail later in this hour.

- **IntelliSense**—Explorer senses the direction you're heading in many different ways and helps you get there faster. For example, if you're typing in the address of a site you've visited before, Explorer fills in the rest of the address and opens a History window for you to choose other possible options (see Figure 9.9).

IntelliSense options

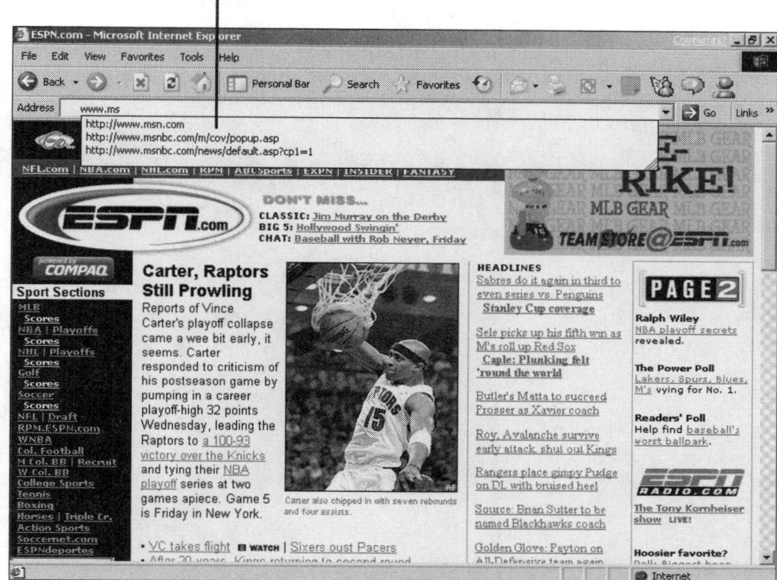

FIGURE 9.9
As soon as you start typing an address, Explorer offers options based on your browsing history.

- **AutoSearch**—There are lots of ways to conduct a Search in Explorer. You can click the Search button, open the Search bar from the View menu, or simply type in a search word or phrase directly into the Address box. (Searching is covered in detail in Hour 13, "Searching for Information.")
- **Related Links**—No matter what site you visit, Explorer is ready to offer you some options for other sites just like it. On the Tools menu, just select Show Related Links, and the links appear in the Explorer bar to the left of the main browser window (see Figure 9.10). This window, called Search Companion, also gives you valuable info about the site you're seeing, such as an address and phone number.
- **One-click Email, Printing**—Buttons to print the page or to quickly open Outlook Express for email are available on the main toolbar. Many Web pages don't print out like they appear onscreen, however, so Explorer offers a Print Preview option from the File menu that allows you to see how the page will print before you waste the paper.

There are many more features available in Explorer, and some of them are discussed throughout the rest of this chapter.

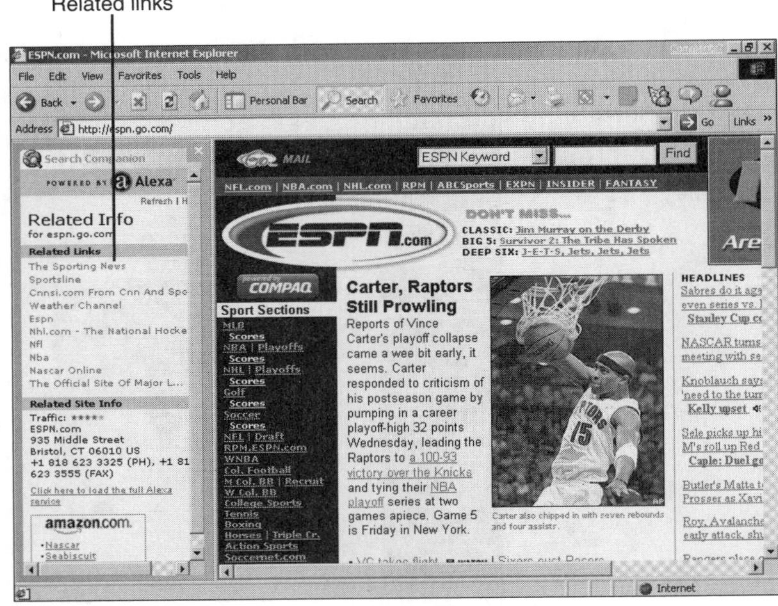

FIGURE 9.10
Related Links offers users options for other content similar to what they are viewing.

Using the Explorer Bar

One of the many things you'll notice is the Explorer bar. Although it's not visible when you first start up the program, you might soon find that it's a valuable part of your surfing experience. It displays on the left side of the browser window, taking up as much as half the screen if you expand it.

Best of all, the information it presents is up to you. To get to the Explorer bar, open the View menu, select Explorer bar, and here are your options:

- **Personal Bar**—This feature, new for version 6.0 allows you to use the left portion of the browser window to display personal information (see Figure 9.11). You can use the Search feature at the top, display news and weather from your area in the middle, and use the bottom portion to play and/or manage media files. The first time you use the Personal bar, you can enter your ZIP code and the symbols of your favorite stocks and your personal information will be displayed.

The three choices on the Personal Bar—news, search, and media— can also be used to fill up the entire Personal bar if you select them individually as options from the Explorer bar menu.

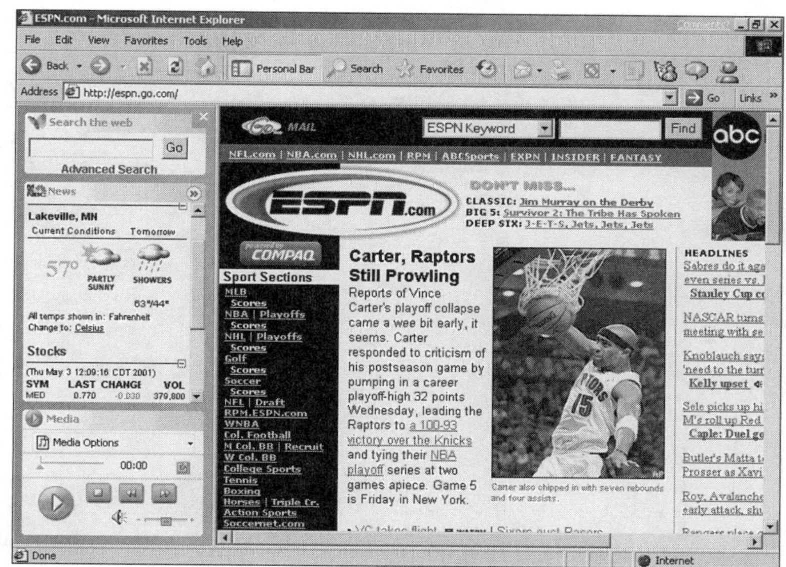

FIGURE 9.11
The Personal Bar offers gives you the ability to display information you choose in Explorer.

- **Search**—The Search Companion displays in a couple of different circumstances. If you choose Search from the Explorer bar menu, you can type a question into the Search box and use it to search the Internet or your own hard drive.
- **Contacts**—This is a handy feature to have on your screen while surfing the Web. You can create a list of Contacts that you regularly interact with (see Figure 9.12), and by double-clicking on a name, a New Message window opens with the contact's email address included, so you can send them a quick email.
- **Favorites**—Your Favorite Places are the Web sites you have stored for quick access later (there's more information on Favorite Places in the next section of this hour). You can display them in the Explorer bar, too, so you can jump to them quickly.
- **History**—As you travel around the Web, Explorer keeps a little record of your travels for you called History. This is a useful feature in that it allows you to return to these sites more quickly, even if it's been a few days since you last used your computer. Sites you've visited are stored in History for 20 days by default.
- **Folders**—You can use the Explorer bar to display folders on your computer, so you can access them quickly.

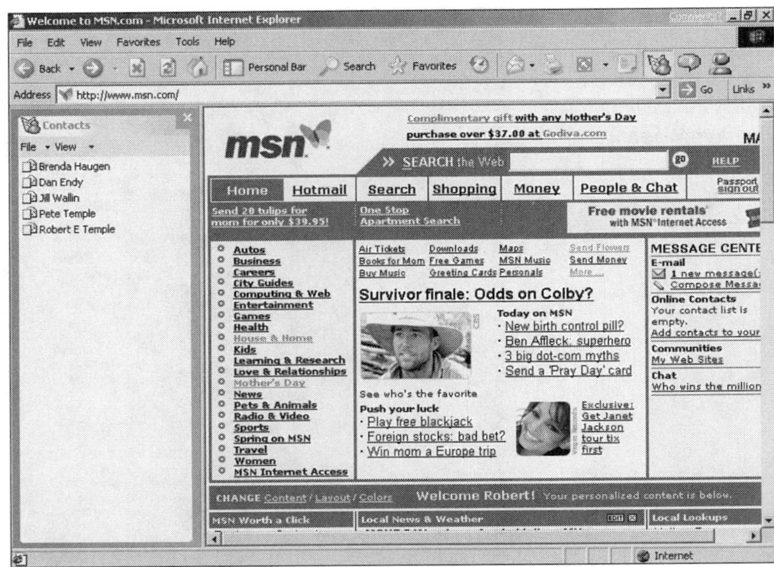

FIGURE 9.12
Viewing your Contacts in the Explorer Bar allows you to send off a quick email.

Customizing the Personal Bar

The center panel of the three in the Personal Bar displays the News view by default. However, you can change that so your Personal Bar is, shall we say, more personal. The two right-pointing arrows in that center panel lead to a list of Explorer bar options that you can display in that panel (see Figure 9.13). Simply select the one you would like to display from the list.

Adding/Removing Explorer Bars

Another option on the list of Explorer bars you can display in the center panel is Add/Remove Explorer Bars. There are a number of different bars that can be added for services offered over the Internet, and more are expected.

You can get travel information from Expedia, or you can use the MSN Calendar to display your appointments for the day. Simply click the Add/Remove Explorer Bars option, then click “Add new Explorer Bar” to get a list of options.

They load quickly, and you can change your display to show them almost immediately (see Figure 9.14).

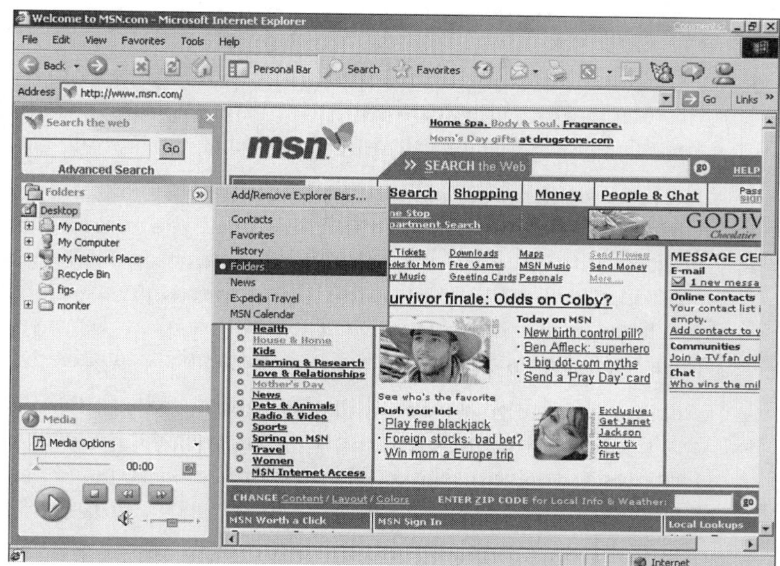

FIGURE 9.13 *The Personal Bar can be customized to show other views.*

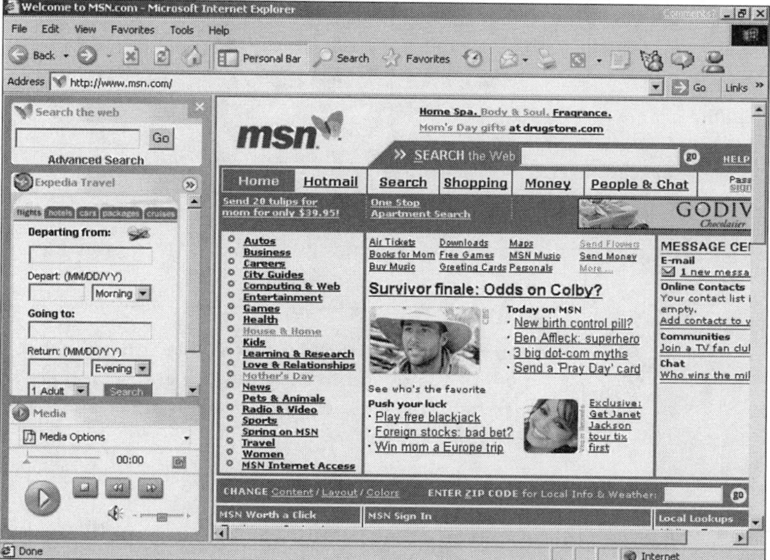

FIGURE 9.14 *Displaying Expedia in the Personal Bar allows quick access to flight and other travel information.*

Working with Favorite Places

As you travel around the Web, you're going to find a lot of sites that you like. In some cases, you'll know right away that you're going to want to return. In others, you might find yourself going back to the site a few times before you realize it's one of your favorites.

Explorer makes it easy for you to return to those places over and over again, by allowing you to add them to a list called—cleverly enough—Favorite Places.

It's very simple to use, and it's a great resource. It eliminates the need to remember the URL of the sites you like to go to. Even better, you're not just limited to home pages for your Favorite Places list. If you've found some obscure page deep within a Web site, you can add it to your list. Then, you'll be able to return to it with one click, instead of going to a home page and navigating your way back to your favorite spot. It's a little like leaving a bookmark in the book—in fact, in Netscape Navigator, they're called Bookmarks.

Adding a page to your Favorites list is extremely easy. All you have to do is go to the exact page you want to jump back to. Then, open the Favorites menu and select Add to Favorites (if you've displayed your Favorites in the Explorer bar, you can just click the Add button there). The Add Favorite window opens, as you see in Figure 9.15.

A name is provided for the Favorite, but you can change it to whatever you want by clicking in the box and typing. Then click OK, and the next time you open your Favorites list, it will be there.

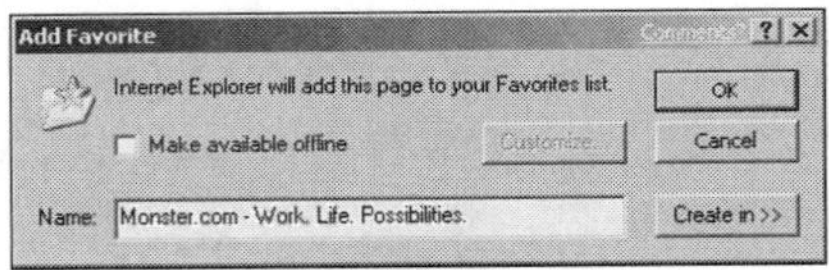

FIGURE 9.15
Adding a page to your Favorites list makes it easy to get back there.

To go back to that page next time, just select it from your Favorites list.

You may notice the "Make Available Offline" check box in Figure 9.15. This feature allows you to view this site even if you are not connected to the Internet. This feature is explained in detail in Hour 16, "Working Smarter by Working Offline."

That list will grow pretty long, pretty quickly, and you'll need to pare it down some. You can create folders for Favorites by category, delete those that have fallen out of favor (excuse the pun), move your Favorites into different folders, and rename them by using the Organize Favorites option from the Favorites menu (see Figure 9.16).

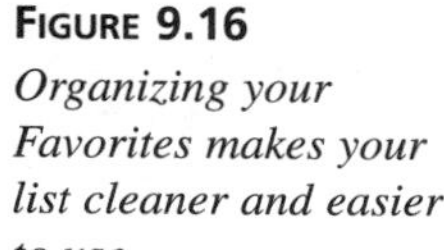

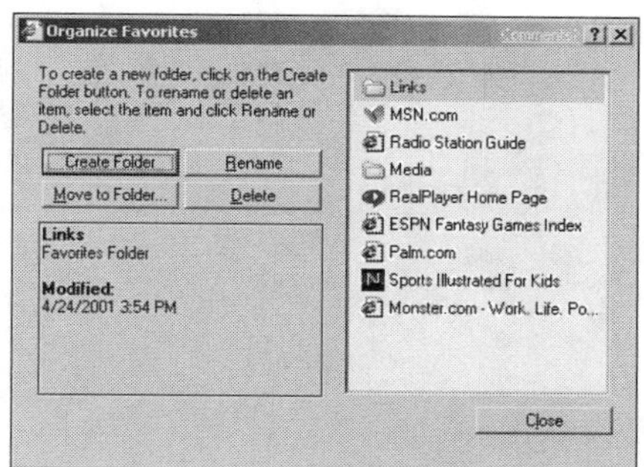

FIGURE 9.16
Organizing your Favorites makes your list cleaner and easier to use.

Creating folders is easy—click the Create Folders button—and you can move Favorites by dragging and dropping them on folders or by highlighting them and clicking the Move to Folder button. Take a few minutes every couple of weeks to clean up this list; if it's not organized well, you won't save much time by using it!

Setting Your Internet Options

Every piece of software known to man these days comes with a complete set of options. These options, depending on your perspective, either make using the program easier or make it a complex web that is beyond human comprehension. Your call.

Explorer's options are viewable by opening the Tools menu and selecting Internet Options. You'll find a myriad of possibilities here; for our purposes, we'll concentrate on the General and Content tabs.

General Options

On the General tab (see Figure 9.17), you'll find basic options settings, as you might expect. The top panel allows you to select a new home page (the page that appears when you first start Explorer). The Use Blank button opens a blank page, and the Use Current button allows you to select whatever page is currently displayed on your browser. The Use Default button sets it back to Explorer's default page, `www.msn.com`.

As you surf, a variety of files get saved on your computer. These Temporary Internet Files can, over time, take up a lot of room on your hard drive. From time to time, you may want to delete the files and cookies that are consuming your hard drive. It'll make some pages load slower when you visit them the next time, but it will also remove pages from your hard drive that you never intend to visit again. The Settings button allows you to determine exactly how much room on your drive can be consumed by these files.

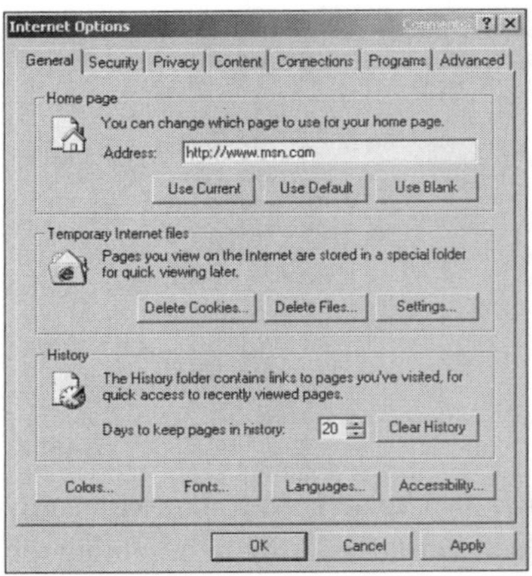

FIGURE 9.17
The General tab allows you to change basic settings.

Your History is also kept as you surf, and you can specify in the bottom panel how many days worth of sites you want kept on your computer. The Clear History button will completely clear out your surfing trail.

You can use the buttons along the bottom to specify colors, fonts, languages, and accessibility options as well.

Content Options

The Content tab offers one major feature for parents: the ability to limit what can be seen over the Internet using Explorer.

The Content Advisor (see Figure 9.18), as it's called, comes disabled by default. But any parent whose child might spend time on this computer without supervision should probably enable at least some of these controls.

FIGURE 9.18
The Content Advisor allows you to set boundaries for objectionable content.

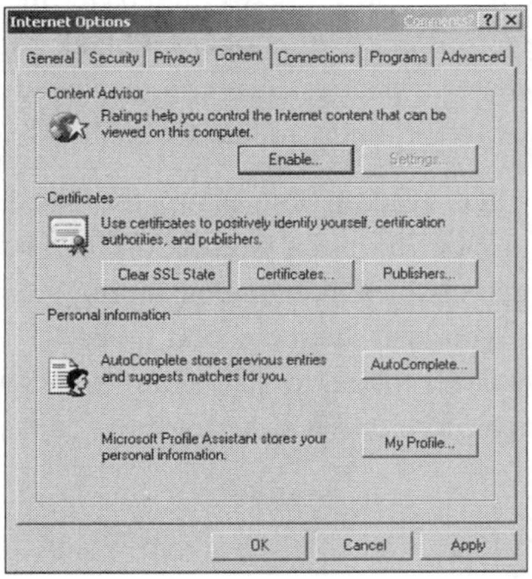

Using a sliding scale, you can select from a four-point scale the level of language, nudity, sex, and violence you will permit on this computer. Setting the levels low allows little or no potentially dangerous content; setting them higher allows more content; not setting them at all allows a free-for-all.

Not to put on the Ward Cleaver hat here, but I strongly urge parents to set these controls if their children are going to spend *any* time online unsupervised. I'm not saying you have naughty kids; it's just very easy to stumble onto objectionable content on the Internet. One link leads to another, and another, and before you know it, little Jimmy's at a porn site. Or, it can be more direct—a youngster looking for information on the White House for a research paper might type in `www.whitehouse.com`, which is a porn site. The one for the president's residence is `www.whitehouse.gov`.

Summary

Internet Explorer is one of the two best options for you to use when browsing the Web. Netscape Navigator, covered in the next hour, is the other. I recommend you go through both chapters and have the latest version of both browsers on your computer. Then you can use them both, and decide for yourself!

Q&A

Q Can I add more than one page from a given site to my Favorite Places?

A Sure you can, you darn goof. You can add as many pages as you want. For example, say you really like the Los Angeles Lakers. You could add the individual pages for all the Lakers players on `espn.com` to your Favorites list, then organize them all into a folder called Lakers! Now doesn't that sound like fun?

Q What's the one key difference between Internet Explorer and Netscape Navigator?

A That's a trick question. The vast majority of stuff you can do in one, you can do in the other; it's just called by a different name (Favorite Places are "bookmarks" in Navigator). The biggest difference is in look and feel of the products, and in the names of the companies who make them. It's really just a matter of personal preference as to which one you choose.

HOUR 10

Using Netscape Navigator 6

So you've learned all about Internet Explorer in the last hour, and now you're ready to really jump into the Internet and take off, right? Hold on a minute there, pardner.

There's another choice. Netscape, which is now under the umbrella of America Online, offers its Navigator browser as Explorer's chief rival. Navigator has undergone a recent facelift, adding new features and taking on a new look. It's just as functional as ever, if not more, and it's every bit as good a browser choice as Microsoft Internet Explorer.

So, take the time to walk through the Netscape browser with me, and you'll have both of them to try out for a while. Then, you can make your own choice.

By the end of this hour, you will have learned

- Some reasons for choosing Netscape Navigator as your primary browser
- Where and how to get a copy of the latest version of Navigator

- Some of the basic features of the program
- How to bookmark your favorite sites and pages
- How to work with Navigator's toolbars and views
- How to set your preferences
- The uses for Navigator's Sidebar
- How to change the look of Navigator using Themes

Why Choose Netscape Navigator?

In the last hour, this section indicated that one of the reasons to pick Internet Explorer was that it was from Microsoft. That means it's backed by the largest software company in the world, and that carries with it a certain degree of clout.

So, why choose Navigator? Well, that's a funny one. Navigator has just as many features as Explorer. The two programs mirror each other in a number of ways, with similar features that are called by different names.

To be frank, one reason that some people choose to go with Navigator is that Explorer is produced by Microsoft. There is a sizable faction out there that believes that Bill Gates and his boys have gotten a little too big for their britches (the U.S. government included), and that using Navigator, in some way, helps prevent Microsoft's stronghold on the consumer software industry.

But there are much better reasons to pick Navigator than that. Like Explorer, Navigator has added features that make it more customizable for the user. In fact, Netscape has gone a step farther than Microsoft in allowing users to set up user profiles, so that different people using Navigator on the same computer can automatically view the browser the way they want to, without having to reset a bunch of preferences.

In the rest of this hour, you will learn about many of Navigator's options and features.

Where and How to Get Netscape Navigator

Like Explorer, you might already have a copy of Navigator on your computer. Navigator isn't as widely preinstalled as Explorer, but the chances are still pretty good, especially if you've purchased your computer within the last year or so.

But like we discussed last hour, it's also very likely that you don't have the latest version of the browser on your computer. Netscape can take care of that for you by allowing you a free download of the software from its Web site.

Download the Latest Version

Even if you're pretty sure that you have the most recent version of Netscape Navigator on your computer, it can't hurt to check. Besides, if you do have the latest and greatest Navigator, the Netscape Web site will sense that and tell you not to download another one. Pretty cool, huh?

So, using your old, antiquated version of Navigator (or Explorer if you don't have Navigator on your computer at all), log on to the Netscape site at `home.netscape.com`, and we'll get started.

To Do: Download and Install the Latest Version of Netscape Navigator

1. At the Netscape home page, click on the Download button on the top of the page. This opens the main download page (see Figure 10.1). As you can see, you can also use this area to order a free CD, but let's download instead. Click on the Netscape Browsers link.

Whenever you plan to download or install anything you'll need to make sure you have sufficient disk space available for the files. Most installation programs perform a check for you before installing files. It will let you know how much room the files will take up, and how much space you have available.

To suite or not to suite? At the time of this writing, there were two different browser versions available for Netscape. If you download the entire Netscape Communicator suite, it comes with Netscape Messenger for email, Composer for creating Web pages, and Navigator. But at this writing, the Communicator suite was in version 4.77, as was the version of Navigator that came with it. You could also download Navigator 6.01, which offers Netscape Mail (instead of Messenger). Netscape Mail now supports multiple email addresses, but Messenger is a more full-featured email program. For purposes of this hour, we'll be using the latest version of Navigator, 6.02, because it offers more features and functionality as a browser.

2. This page shows you the version of the browser you are now using (see Figure 10.2). Click the Download button under the name of the latest version of the Navigator browser (not the Communicator suite).

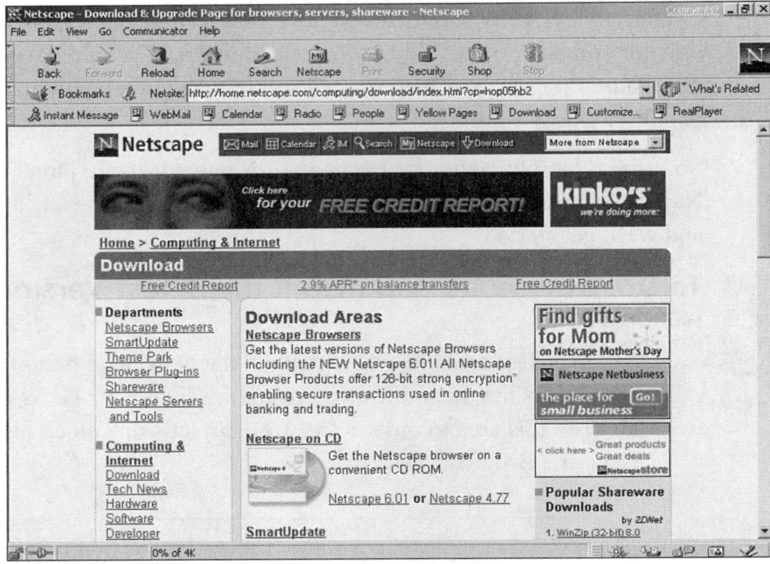

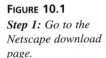

FIGURE 10.1
Step 1: Go to the Netscape download page.

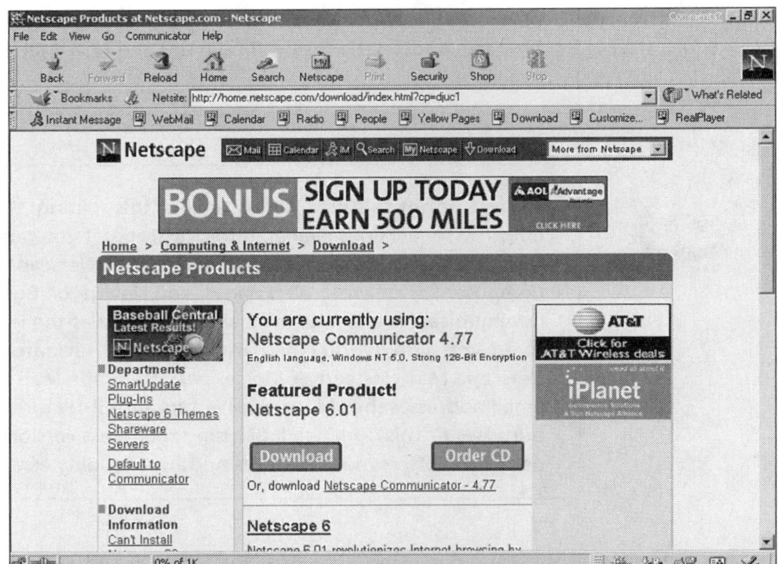

FIGURE 10.2
Step 2: Click on the Download button.

3. Choose a location for the file you are going to download (see Figure 10.3). The Desktop is a convenient location, because the file will be easy to find later.

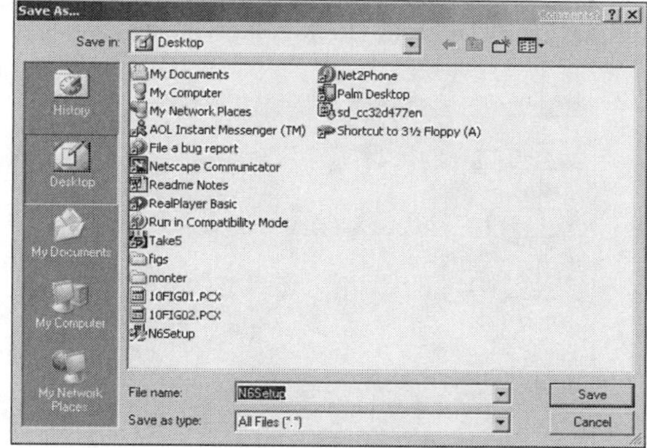

Figure 10.3
Step 3: *Choose a location for the file.*

4. When the file is done downloading (it is a relatively small file), double-click its icon on your desktop. This launches the Netscape Setup program (see Figure 10.4).

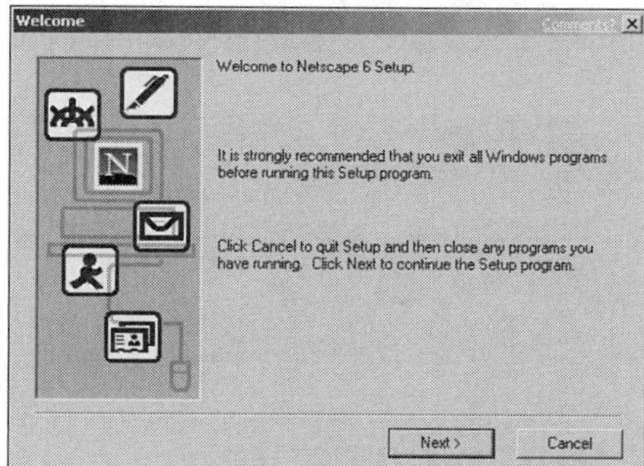

Figure 10.4
Step 4: *Launch the Setup program.*

5. Click the Next button, read the license agreement, and click the Accept button (see Figure 10.5).

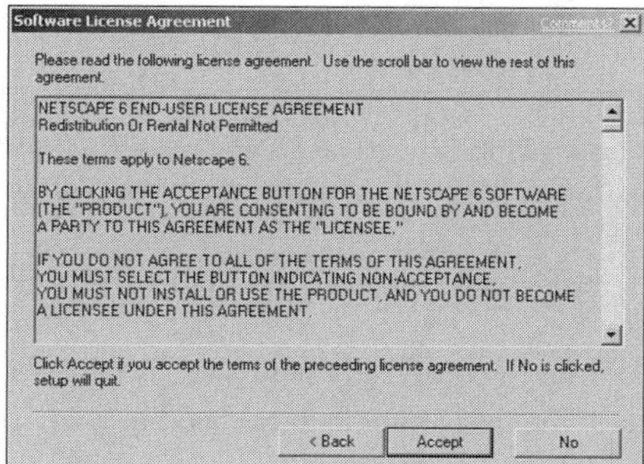

Figure 10.5
Step 5: *Read the license agreement and click Accept.*

6. Choose the Recommended installation, and click the Next button (see Figure 10.6). Netscape asks you where you want to download the program from; I recommend leaving this setting at Default. Click Next. On the Start Install screen, click Install.

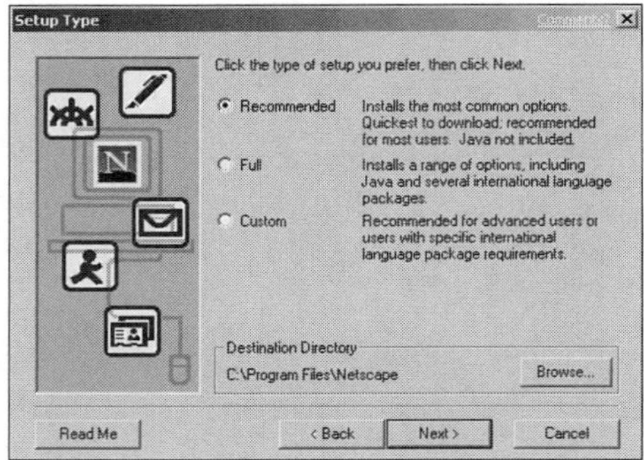

FIGURE 10.6
Step 6: *Select the Recommended installation.*

7. The program begins to install on your computer (see Figure 10.7). This may take a few minutes (or longer, depending on the speed of your connection). When it's completed, you'll have a Netscape 6 icon on your desktop.

FIGURE 10.7
Step 7: *The program begins to install on your computer.*

Starting Up Netscape Navigator

A simple double-click on the icon you now have on your desktop will launch the Navigator program. By default, Navigator opens to the Netscape home page at `home.netscape.com` (see Figure 10.8). You'll learn later in this hour how to change that home page to one of your choosing, if you want.

> You may be asked to activate a screen name the first time you launch Netscape. If so, follow the on-screen prompts to do so; it won't cost you anything.

Version 6.01 of Navigator has a completely new look over previous versions of the program. As a result, some of the basic buttons have been moved.

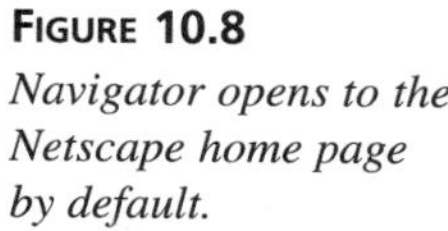

FIGURE 10.8
Navigator opens to the Netscape home page by default.

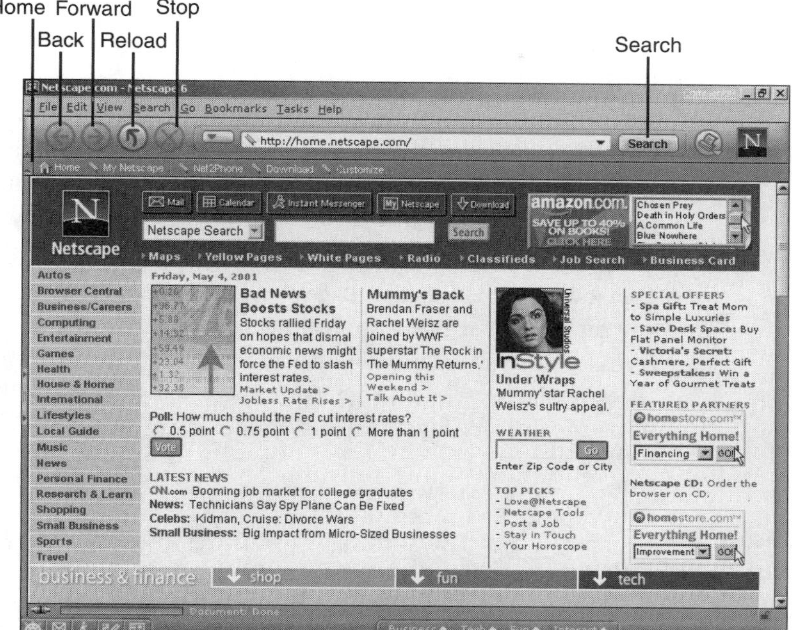

As you can see from Figure 10.8, the Back, Forward, Reload, and Stop buttons are all in their usual locations. The Home button, however, has been moved to the Personal Bar, a toolbar that you can customize (discussed later in this hour). Meanwhile, the Search button has been moved to the right of the address box.

Features of Netscape Navigator

Netscape (like Microsoft) is working to make everything on the Internet more personal. Customizable this, customizable that. The goal is to make you feel more at home, and to allow you to set up things so that when you return next time, it's just the way you left it.

One of the biggest complaints of newcomers to the Internet is that it is such a vast wonderland, the difficulty in finding the information they are looking for makes it seem more like a vast wasteland. Netscape has attempted to boil everything down for you, so you can get where you want to go in fewer clicks.

Basic Features of Netscape

The basic functionality of Netscape is very similar to Microsoft Internet Explorer. Let's take a few minutes to look at some of the basic features that make up Navigator.

- **Task Toolbar**—Along the bottom of the screen, there's a Task toolbar in the lower-left corner, giving you access to Mail, Instant Messenger, Composer, and Address Book.
- **Advanced Search**—There's a reason that Search button is to the right of the address box. You can use the address box as a search tool, by entering any search word or phrase directly into the box and clicking Search. Click on the Search button when the Address box is empty, and it brings you to the search page on Netscape's site.
- **Quick Access to Netscape Pages**—At the bottom of the screen, near the center, you see menus for Business, Tech, Fun and Interact. These menus offer one-click access to specific areas within the Netscape site. So, for example, if you wanted to check on the latest news from Hollywood, you would open the Fun menu and select Movies (see Figure 10.9).

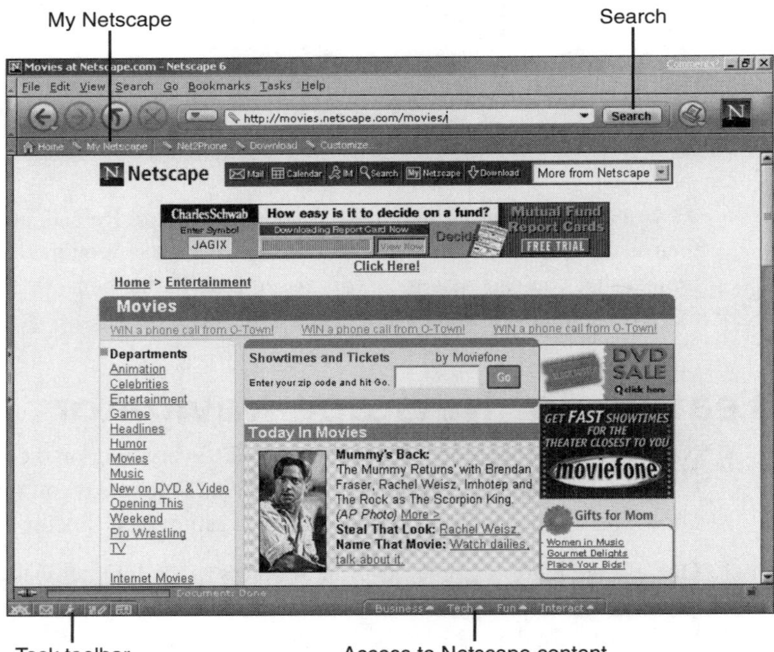

FIGURE 10.9
You get quick access to Netscape content from the toolbar at the bottom of the screen.

- **My Netscape**—The button leads you to a personalized home page. The first time you visit, you are asked for your ZIP code and birth date. Enter it, and you're on your way. On the My Netscape page (see Figure 10.10), you can choose the types of content you would like to appear, how you want the layout to look, and other settings. The ZIP code is used to provide local news and info.

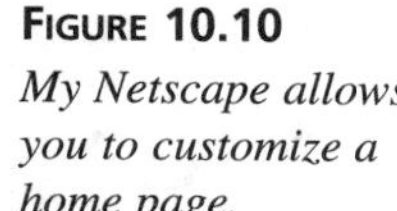

FIGURE 10.10
My Netscape allows you to customize a home page.

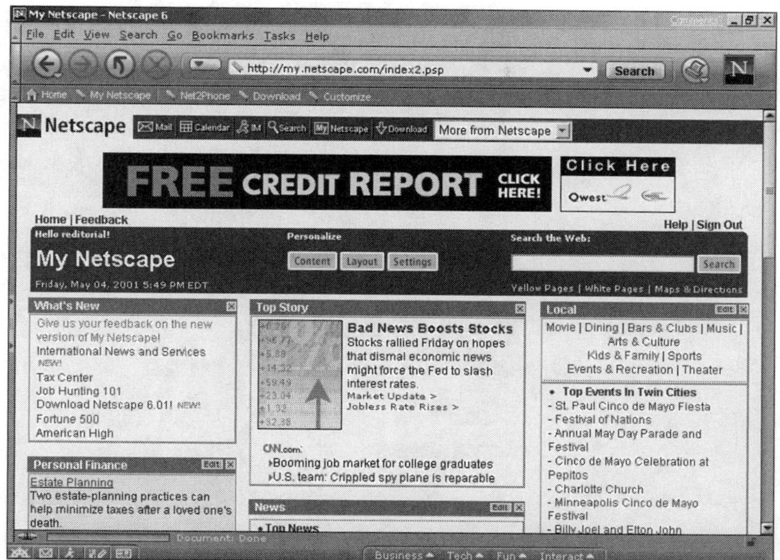

Working with My Sidebar

Explorer had the Explorer bar on the left side of its browser window, Netscape Navigator offers My Sidebar. If you haven't seen it yet, it's because it's hidden. And cleverly, too.

Along the left side of the default browser window, you'll notice a little button with a couple of arrows. That's where your Sidebar is hiding. Just a single click on that button, and the Sidebar appears (see Figure 10.11). It's very similar to the Explorer bar, but it offers some additional functionality.

> Lots of people don't like these frames that run down the left side of their pages, because the frames force the image of the Web page they are viewing off the right side of the screen. That can be annoying, but Sidebar has such great features and it's so easy to quickly tuck it away, it's a great option to use in Navigator. And if you don't like it, you can always close it, by clicking the same button you used to open it.

By default, the tabs that appear are Search, What's Related, Buddy List, Stocks, News, and Today's Tips. A quick click on any of the tabs will reveal its content. For example, What's Related will show you links to other Web sites that have content similar to the site you are currently viewing.

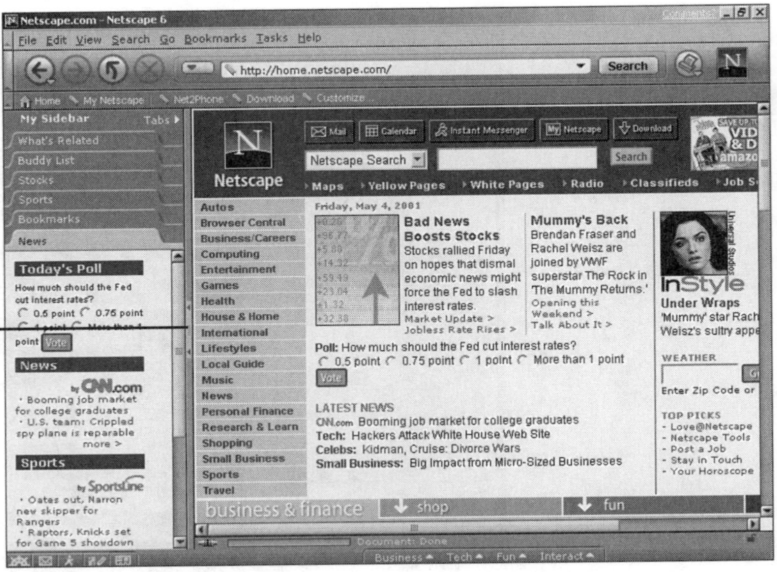

FIGURE 10.11
Navigator's Sidebar offers a variety of information at a glance.

Click to show/hide My Sidebar

The Buddy List tabs needs to be customized with your Instant Messenger screen name and password the first time you use it. After that, it brings instant messaging to within a single click, any time you're using Navigator.

You can make Sidebar fill up to half of your screen if you want by dragging the right-hand border over to the center of the screen. But this pushes your browser window further to the right.

Changing the Sidebar Tabs

What if you don't like the choices that Netscape gives you for tabs? Now you don't think they would leave you high and dry for choices, do you?

Of course not.

Right at the top of the My Sidebar tabs is a button called Tabs. Click it, and you'll display a list of tabs the Netscape has provided for you (see Figure 10.12). The ones that are checked are the ones currently displayed. Clicking on a checked name will deselect it; clicking on an unchecked name will select it.

Customizing Your Sidebar

Still haven't had enough of the Sidebar, eh? Well, Netscape offers more options for you. If you look back at Figure 10.12, you'll notice that at the top of the Tabs menu, there's an option called Customize Sidebar. Click it, and you'll see the window that appears in Figure 10.13.

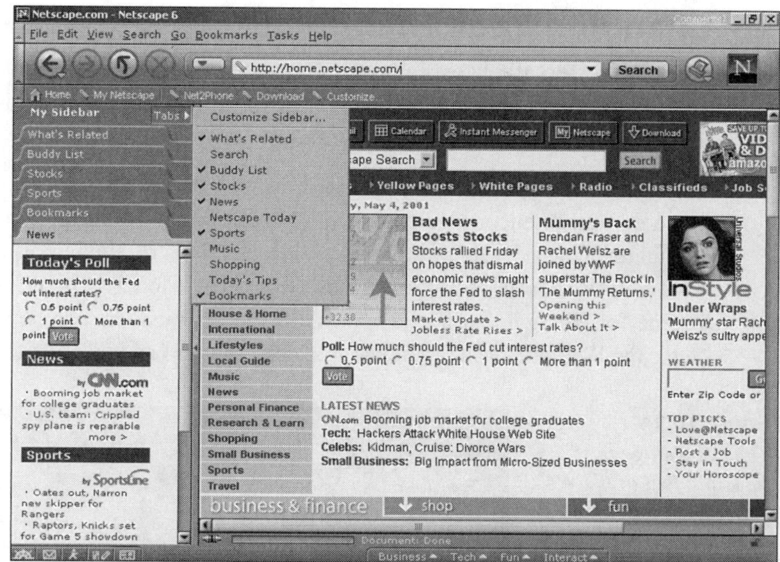

FIGURE 10.12
Netscape offers different tabs for you to choose from.

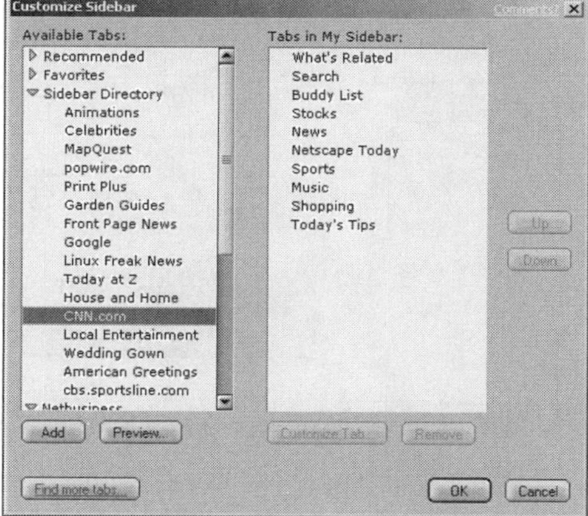

FIGURE 10.13
You can customize your Sidebar with tabs developed by non-Netscape providers.

In the right pane, you'll see a list of the tabs that are currently available to you from Netscape. In the right pane, you'll have a list of other possible tabs you can add to your browser. Just highlight the name of the tab, and you can get a preview of it by clicking the Preview button. When you're ready to implement it, click Add.

Also, in the lower-left corner, there's a Find more tabs button. Click there, and you'll be taken to a Web site that will include tabs from all kinds of different sources. There are literally hundreds available, with more being offered all the time.

Changing Your Theme

Navigator offers the latest in browser customization, an option called Themes. It allows you to change the entire look and feel of the Navigator program, including such basic things as the Back and Forward buttons.

These different options can be created by Web developers anywhere—in fact, Netscape had a contest to encourage designers to create more Themes. Two Themes are offered in Navigator: Classic, which looks like older versions of Navigator; and Modern, which is what you've seen in the figures in this hour. The Modern Theme is also the default Theme for Navigator 6. The Themes created by outsiders can be downloaded from the Netscape Web site at `home.netscape.com/themes/index.html` (see Figure 10.14).

FIGURE 10.14
Themes change the look and feel of the entire Navigator program.

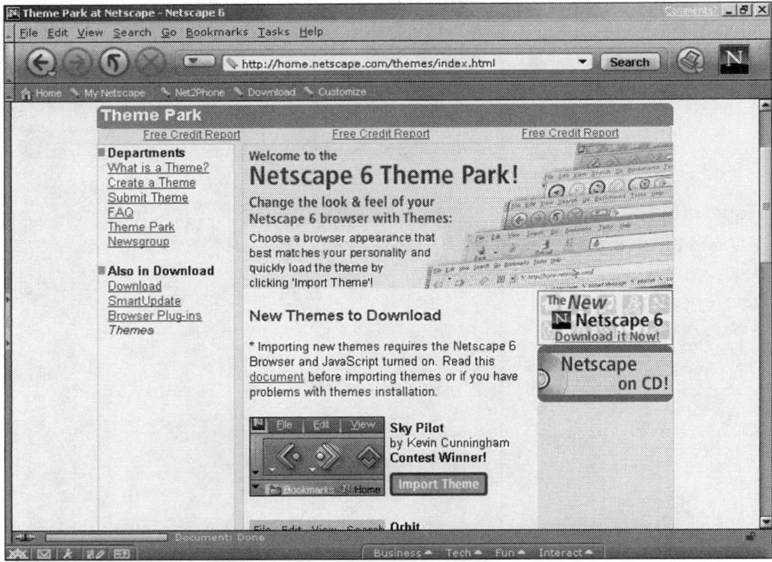

Just click the Import Theme button next to the Theme(s) of your choice, and it will download. Navigator automatically changes to the new Theme immediately. You can change it back by selecting Preferences from the Edit menu. In the window that appears, highlight Themes, then highlight the name of the Theme you would like to use (more on Preferences in the next section).

Working with the Preferences

Preferences in Navigator are like Internet Options in Explorer. You can use them to set and change all manner of settings within the program. You can alter how the program displays information, captures information, the length of the history of Web sites you've visited, and more.

To open the Preferences window, open the Edit menu and select Preferences (see Figure 10.15).

FIGURE 10.15

The Preferences screen allows you to change basic settings in Navigator.

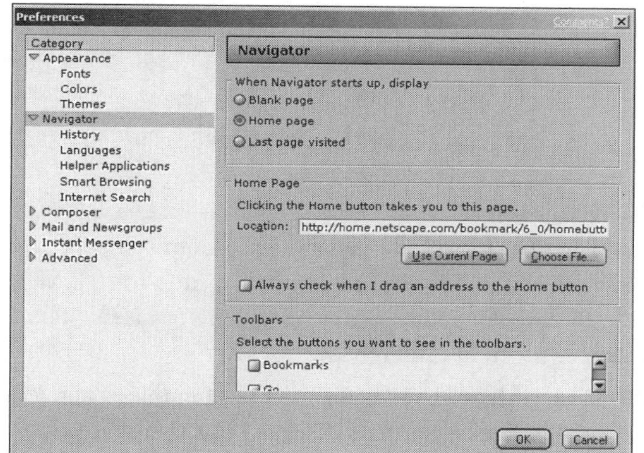

On the right side of the Preferences screen, you can select the page you want for your home page (middle pane) and a different page (if you want) to appear each time you start Navigator. For example, a lot of people want to pick up their surfing where they last left off, and you can do that by selecting "Last page visited" in the top pane of the Preferences window. In the bottom pane, you can select the items you want to appear in your toolbars.

Here's a look at some of the other features you can alter using Preferences:

- **Internet Search**—You'll learn more about searching in Hour 13, "Searching for Information." Suffice it to say, there are a lot of options for search sites on the Internet. You've no doubt heard of or used Yahoo!, Lycos, and many others. Netscape offers its own search tools, but it also realizes you might want to use a different site. By clicking Internet Search (under the Navigator menu in Preferences), you can tell Navigator which site you want to use for your searches (see Figure 10.16).

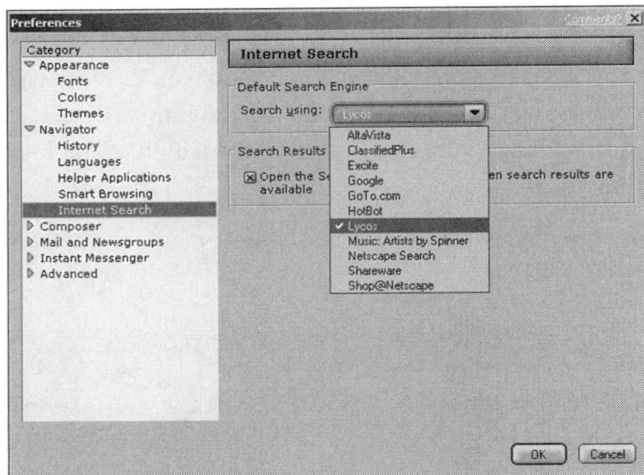

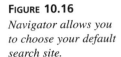

FIGURE 10.16
Navigator allows you to choose your default search site.

- **Instant Messenger**—Instant Messenger is integrated into Netscape Mail. So much so, in fact, that when you open an email from someone who is an Instant Messenger user and is currently online, a little Instant Messenger icon shows up next to their email address. You can enable or disable this function in the Instant Messenger menu in Preferences.
- **Collecting Addresses**—One of the least fun things about emailing is entering all those email addresses into an address book. Netscape allows you to automatically save email addresses from incoming and outgoing emails in a special address book called Collected Addresses. Then, if you want, you can easily drag them into your regular address book. This option is enabled by default; you can disable it in the Address Books window in the Mail and Newsgroups menu in Preferences.

Working with Bookmarks

Bookmarks are a great way to keep your favorite sites handy all the time. Netscape makes bookmarking sites easy, and offers a couple of ways for you to have one-click access to those bookmarked sites.

There are a couple of different ways to bookmark a site in Navigator. One is the old-fashioned way: Go to a site you like, open the Bookmarks menu and select Add Current Page. Without hesitation, the page jumps into your Bookmarks list.

Earlier in this chapter, you learned how to add a tab to your Sidebar. One of the tabs that you can add is Bookmarks. After you've added it, if you have that tab displayed on your Sidebar, you can drag the address of the site you're visiting (by grabbing the icon to the left of the address) onto the Sidebar, and it will drop into your Bookmarks list automatically.

Putting Bookmarks in Your Personal Toolbar

Okay now, try not to get confused. We know there's a Personal Bar in Explorer, but this is different. In Navigator, the Personal Toolbar is that thin bar that runs right above the top of the browser's main window; it includes the Home and My Netscape buttons (see Figure 10.17).

FIGURE 10.17
The Personal Toolbar can be personalized in Netscape.

You can add your most important Bookmarks to this toolbar. To do so, open the Bookmarks menu and select Manage Bookmarks (see Figure 10.18). Now, simply drag any bookmark you have into the Personal Toolbar folder area, place it in the order you want it to appear, and release it.

When you close the Manage Bookmarks window, your Personal Toolbar will contain any of the bookmarks you put there. Now, the next time you want to go to that page, it's literally one click away!

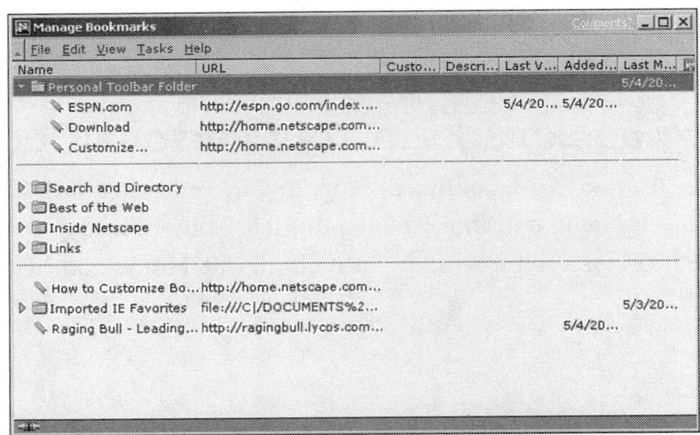

FIGURE 10.18
You can add bookmarks to your Personal Toolbar.

Removing Bookmarks from the Personal Toolbar

Okay, so that site you used to visit all the time just doesn't do it for you anymore. And it's just taking up space on the Personal Toolbar. You can remove it just as easily as you put it there in the first place.

Just go back to the Manage Bookmarks window. There, you can either drag the offending bookmark to the bottom pane, thus relegating it to a spot among the "regular" bookmarks, or you can highlight and press your delete key, thus getting rid of it altogether.

Summary

Netscape Navigator is an outstanding browser that offers all the basic functionality of Microsoft Internet Explorer, plus some extra bells and whistles. Now that you've seen both programs, you can take the time to try them both out and see which one best fits your style.

Q&A

Q I have my Personal Toolbar mixed up with my Explorer bar and my Sidebar. Maybe I spend too much time in bars. What do you think?

A Well, I won't comment on your free time. However, your problem is based on the similarities between Explorer and Navigator, and the different names they use for similar features. What each item is called really isn't that important. What matters is whether you like the feature or not, and how it fits into your Web browsing.

Q On my Personal Toolbar, there's a Net2Phone link. What's that?

A Net2Phone is a program that allows you to make phone calls over the Internet, using your computer. We'll talk about it more in Hour 12, "Plug-in and Add-on Programs."

Hour 11

Using AOL 6.0

You can hardly turn on the television anymore without hearing something about America Online. If it's not a commercial for the service itself, then you'll hear it mentioned at the end of a commercial for something else, such as, "Visit us at www.microsoft.com; AOL keyword 'Microsoft.'"

AOL was once a part of a three-way national online service war with CompuServe and Prodigy. Today, however, AOL is the undisputed king. It seems like a hundred years ago when AOL struck the key blow in that war when it offered unlimited access to its customers for $19.99/month. Before that, all the services were offering "packages" such as 40 hours for this price, with additional charges for additional hours.

When AOL made its bold move, it walked out on a dangerous ledge. At first, customers signed up in droves, only to encounter busy signals when they dialed in because AOL wasn't ready to handle the demand created by the success of their new pricing structure. For a while, it appear AOL's own success would doom it to failure.

But largely, its members stuck with the service. Those who left were likely to return after the connection problems were solved. Today, Virginia-based AOL is the largest Internet service provider in the world. But it's more than an ISP, too.

AOL offers content—lots of it—that only its members can see. And, members get full access to the Internet as well, making AOL the largest ISP in the world.

In this chapter, we'll give you an introductory look at AOL 6.0, the latest version of the software, and the services that AOL offers, so you can decide whether AOL is right for you.

By the end of this hour, you'll be able to answer the following questions:

- Why should I choose AOL?
- What does AOL offer that the browsers don't?
- What's the difference between AOL content and the Internet?
- What are the features of AOL?
- How can I set my AOL preferences?
- Where can I find the software and how do I sign up?

In the preceding two hours, you learned about the two primary browsers, Internet Explorer and Netscape Navigator. In both cases, I walked you through downloading the latest version of the software and then its features.

AOL is different, because it's not just a browser. AOL offers its own content, and it requires a subscription (typically in the low $20s per month). As a result, this chapter will be presented backward from the previous two. First, we'll look at the features and advantages of AOL. Then, if you're interested in signing up, you can read about where to get the software and how to sign up.

Understanding AOL

It's a question I get asked all the time: What's the difference between AOL and the Internet? It's a good question, too. The truth is that by using AOL, you get everything that the Internet has to offer, plus content that is only available to AOL members. After all, you can get to the Internet using AOL and browse any site in the world. Plus, you have access to AOL content: channels, chat rooms, email, instant messages, a calendar feature, forums, shopping, and so on.

AOL is a little pricier than many local ISPs would charge. But you do get more for the money, too.

Why Should I Choose AOL?

So the question then becomes, "Why should I choose AOL?" Here's a quick look at some of the top reasons:

- **People**—AOL's slogan, "20 million people can't be wrong," says it all. Many people you know (or many kids your children know) are using AOL. Joining gives you quick access to them through Instant Messenger, email, chat, and so on.
- **Ease**—AOL makes it simple. Getting the software is easy, as is logging on and setting up your account. After you've done that, your Internet access, email, and everything else is all ready to go for you. That's why tons of first-time Internet users gravitate toward AOL to get themselves online.
- **Content**—AOL's content is divided into 20 different areas of interest, which AOL calls Channels. Channel topics range from Women to Sports to Shopping to Personal Finance to Kids Only to Health to Games. Some are serious, some are just for fun, some offer a little of both. But they all are packed with content.
- **Worldwide access**—This one's often overlooked. AOL makes it easy to log on to someone else's computer somewhere else in the world and still get on to your account. This allows you to access your own email (you can also access from AOL's Web site) and do everything just as you would at home.
- **Multiple Users, One Account**—AOL allows up to seven screen names on one account. This means that you and your spouse, plus little Billy, Johnny, Pookie, Muffin, and The Beav can all have your own email accounts.
- **Parental Controls**—This is perhaps the biggest reason (along with "multiple users") that AOL is so popular with families. Although there are other ways to limit what your kids see on the Internet, AOL's Parental Controls allow you many options for setting what each child, based on age, can see. So, have 8-year-old Muffin's settings at a more restrictive level than 16-year-old Billy's and make sure Muffin doesn't know anyone else's password, and Muffin won't see any naughty stuff.

Why Shouldn't I Choose AOL?

This one's a little tougher, because AOL does have a lot to offer. Here's why some people stay away:

- **It's For Beginners**—Some "serious" Internet users, especially business people, don't want an `@aol.com` email address because they wrongly believe it is an indication they are novices. The truth is, a lot of these "serious" types have their business account and keep an AOL account as well for personal reasons, and for its worldwide access. However, do know that the perception that "AOL is for beginners" is very much alive, but AOL offers plenty for new and experienced users.

- **Email Compression**—AOL compresses automatically any emails that have multiple attachments. This can make them difficult to open and use for non-AOL members. Not a big problem, really, but something to consider if you send or receive lots of attachments.
- **Advertising**—Having a captive audience of 20 million does come with its drawbacks, including lots of advertising. Every time you sign on to AOL, you'll get a pop-up ad before you ever hear the friendly, "Welcome!" or the ubiquitous "You've Got Mail!" The ads, though, can be limited through your preferences.
- **Junk Mail**—If you're an AOL member, you're going to get a fair amount of junk mail.

Taking a Quick Tour of AOL

AOL has a lot more to offer than can be covered in one hour of this book. If you decide to become an AOL subscriber, I strongly recommend that you pick up a Sams book on using AOL.

Let's take some time, however, to take a quick look around the service to see what it offers.

Remember now, AOL also allows you full access to the Internet, so you can get everything that's on the Web, too. This section just covers the stuff that's only available to AOL members.

The Welcome Screen

When you first log on to AOL, you're greeted by a warm, "Welcome!" (assuming you have a sound card and speakers in your system). The Welcome screen (see Figure 11.1) appears.

Here you'll find quick access to lots of great AOL content, including:

- **You've Got Mail**—If the little mailbox icon shows a letter sticking out and the words, "You've Got Mail," well, you've got mail. If you don't, it shows a closed mailbox and the words, "Mail Center." A double-click gets you to your mailbox either way.

- **You've Got Pictures**—A relatively new service that allows you to drop off your film at a participating processing center, check a box on the envelope and, for a small fee, be able to access your pictures online through AOL.
- **My Calendar**—AOL's calendar service allows you to input your personal (or professional) schedule and be able to track it from any computer with AOL installed on it.
- **My Places**—A customizable list similar to Favorite Places or Bookmarks. You can choose what appears in the list and have one-click access to those features.

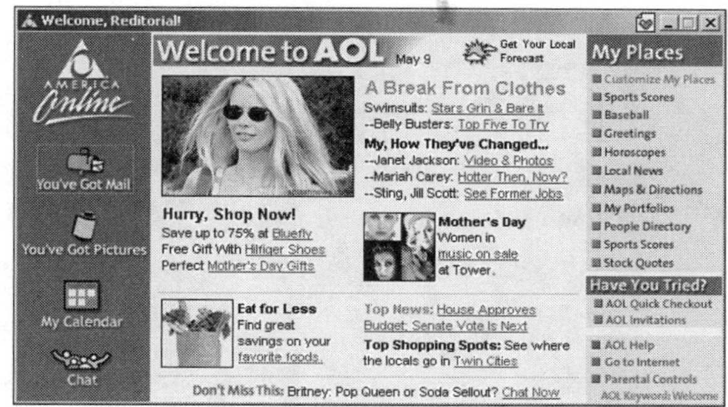

FIGURE 11.1
AOL's Welcome screen offers quick access to AOL features.

The Channels

AOL's Channels are the foundation upon which the service is built. You can get access to any area of AOL through the Channels.

The Channels list appears down the left side of the screen when you log on to AOL (see Figure 11.2). The list gives you easy access to AOL's 20 different content areas. To visit a Channel, just click on its name and a new window pops into the middle of the screen, opening that Channel (see Figure 11.3).

One of the nicer features of AOL 6 is that when you switch between channels, the rest of the channel options remain on the left side of the window. Only the content area changes, leaving you with access to all the other channels. To get back to the Welcome screen, simply click the Welcome bar at the top of the Channels list.

Let's take a brief look at some of the Channels and what they offer.

Entertainment

The Entertainment channel, as shown in Figure 11.3, provides information on all things entertaining—from music and musicians to movies, television, and books. Every day, you'll find a couple of entertainment items in the spotlight (see the Today's Top Features area), as well as buttons for the channel's main departments.

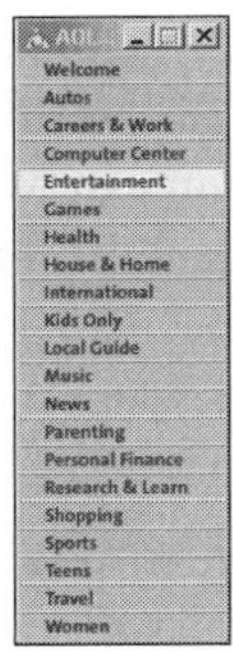

FIGURE 11.2
Click on Entertainment in the Channels list …

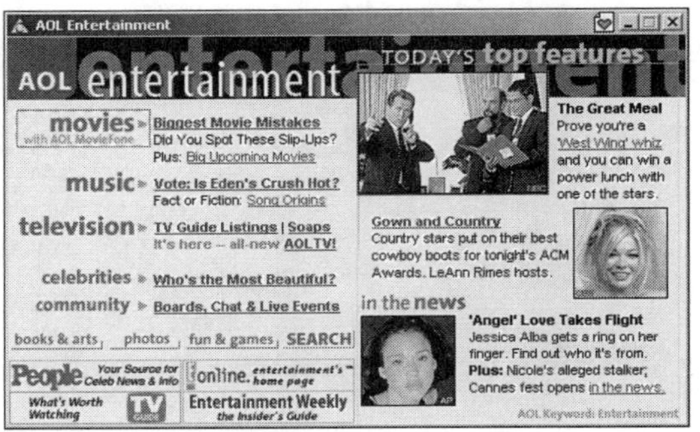

FIGURE 11.3
… and the Entertainment Channel opens in a new window.

The Entertainment channel departments are Movies, Music, Television, Celebrities, Books & Arts, Photos, and Fun and Games. Each covers what the name implies.

Speaking of clicking and going, go ahead and explore the Entertainment channel. Don't be shy—click a department button or check out one of the Top Features. Poke around and have some fun. It is the Entertainment channel, after all. Pick a topic that interests you and go nuts.

The Welcome screen *can't be closed.* You can minimize it, but you can't close it. Don't let it throw you.

Kids Only

AOL is a great place for kids—there's lots for them to see and do, and there are other kids online with whom they can share their thoughts and ideas. The Kids Only channel (shown in Figure 11.4) is like a mini-AOL that preteen kids have all to themselves.

The Kids Only channel is a collection of fun, entertainment, and education just for kids. Your children can chat with some online friends, play a game, or even get help with their homework.

FIGURE 11.4
Kids Only—it really is just for kids.

As you saw with the Entertainment channel's main screen, the Kids Only screen gives you a few highlights of what's going on online for kids today, plus buttons with which you can access the Kids Only departments.

11

The departments include the following:

- **News and Sports**—Profiles of athletes, up-to-date stories, and news from a kid's point of view.
- **Art Studio**—Kids get an opportunity to draw, write, and create.
- **Clubs**—There are clubs for everything from cartoons to movies for kids to join.
- **TV, Movies, and Music**—Keep up with Britney Spears, the latest Disney offerings, and more.
- **Games**—This department is fairly self-explanatory.
- **Homework Help**—Help from *real* teachers no less.

At the bottom of the Kids Only channel's main window, you also see a chat button that leads you to the Kids Only chat areas.

Personal Finance

After the kids are done playing and learning on America Online, you might want to hop online yourself to see whether you can send them to college someday…yikes!

The main Personal Finance screen offers all manner of financial resources, including the latest market reports, stock quotes, mutual fund information, stock and insurance brokers, banking, and a vast array of advice and financial services. In the My Portfolios area, you can build a portfolio of investments for yourself and track their progress. You can also get the latest Business News or do some research on companies in the Stocks area.

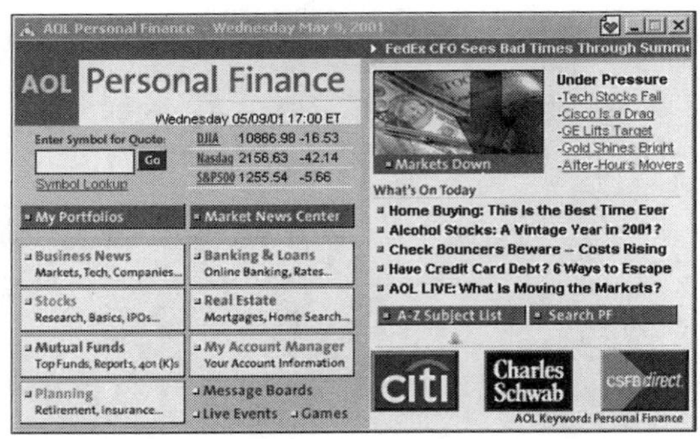

FIGURE 11.5
The Personal Finance channel allows you to keep up with the markets and monitor your portfolio.

Computer Center

The Computer Center channel, shown in Figure 11.6, is a Mecca for computer lovers, but is also a good resource for newbies. It's the source of all sorts of computer news, information, and even software. Whether you're an old hand with computers or just learning your way around one, the Computer Center channel has something for you.

Newbie—A slang word for someone who is new to the Internet, America Online, or any online service.

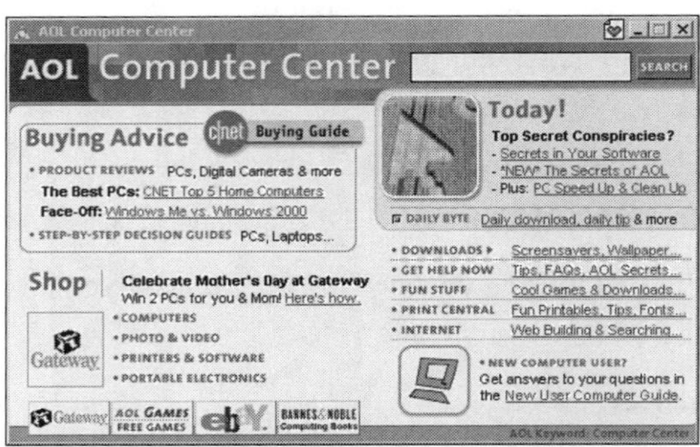

FIGURE 11.6
The Computer Center Channel has software and information for new and experienced computer users.

As with the other channels we've seen so far, the Computer Center main screen features a breakdown of the channel's departments as well as highlights of popular areas. The departments include Downloads (where you can search for and copy to your computer actual software you can use), Get Help Now, Fun Stuff, Print Central, and Internet.

News

A lot is happening in the world, but most people have little time to keep up with it—unless there's some *major* calamity or hot news topic, the electronic media reduce everything to eight-second sound bites. If you want news with a little more depth, you can find it on AOL. Nearly every channel offers a News button or index: entertainment news, software news, kids' news, Internet news, weather news…you get the idea.

An entire News channel is also available, shown in Figure 11.7, which you can flip through rather like a newspaper.

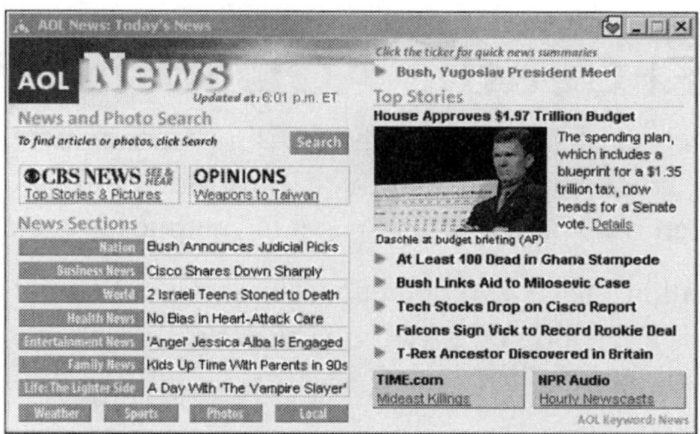

FIGURE 11.7
AOL News acts a little like your local newspaper.

From the News main window, you can access the hour's headlines and news by department: Nation, Business News, World, Health News, Entertainment News, Family News, Life, Weather, Sports, Photos, and Local.

Getting Places, Saving Places

AOL offers a quick way to get from place to place, called Keywords. Almost all of the places you can go within the service are identified by a Keyword. If you know the Keyword, or can hazard a guess, you can type in the word and go directly to that area.

To do this, just click the Keyword button near the upper-right corner of the AOL screen. A Keyword box appears, as you see in Figure 11.8.

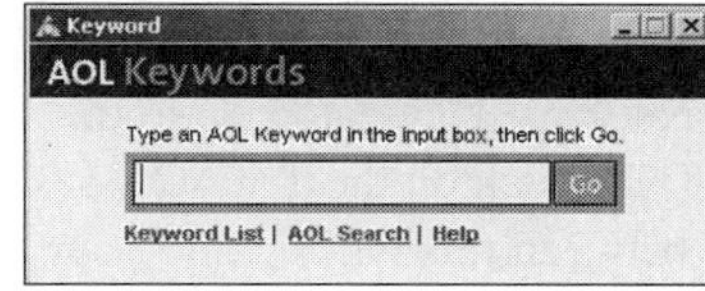

FIGURE 11.8
Enter your Keyword, and jump right to that area within AOL.

There are several keywords that work for each area. For example, if you type in the word "genealogy," you go right to the genealogy section within AOL. You would also get there by typing in the word "genealogy."

After you've found places you like within AOL, there are a couple of ways you can bookmark them. AOL's My Favorites allows you to keep a list of bookmarks—just like Internet Explorer or Netscape Navigator—for Web pages. But you can also mark favorite areas within the AOL services, giving you quick access to them. As stated earlier in this hour, your My Places area on the Welcome screen can also be customized with your most-used places and sites.

Where Can I Get the AOL Software?

If you haven't received a free copy of the AOL software by now, you're the one person they missed. AOL routinely sends out free CDs with its software. Sometimes it's stuck in a magazine, sometimes with your newspaper, sometimes it comes on its own.

However, if you didn't have a computer before or weren't interested in AOL when you got it, the chances are good you tossed it in the trash (or made a drink coaster out of it). So, what do you do now?

Well, almost every computer retailer, especially the electronics superstores, offer the AOL software for free (they sometimes charge a penny) on CD. You can also get it at libraries and other major stores, like Wal-Mart or Target.

You can also get it online, direct from AOL. If you're interested in signing up for the AOL service, take the following To Do and download the latest version of the AOL software.

In the following exercise, you will download the latest version of AOL. All this does is load the software on your computer. You are not required to sign up yet. So completing this exercise won't hurt a bit!

To Do: Download the Latest Version of AOL

▼ To Do

1. Using Internet Explorer or Netscape Navigator, go to the AOL Web site at `www.aol.com` (see Figure 11.9). Click on the Try AOL 6.0 button (the version number may have changed between this writing and your visit to the site).

FIGURE 11.9
Step 1: Go to the AOL Web site and click the Try AOL button.

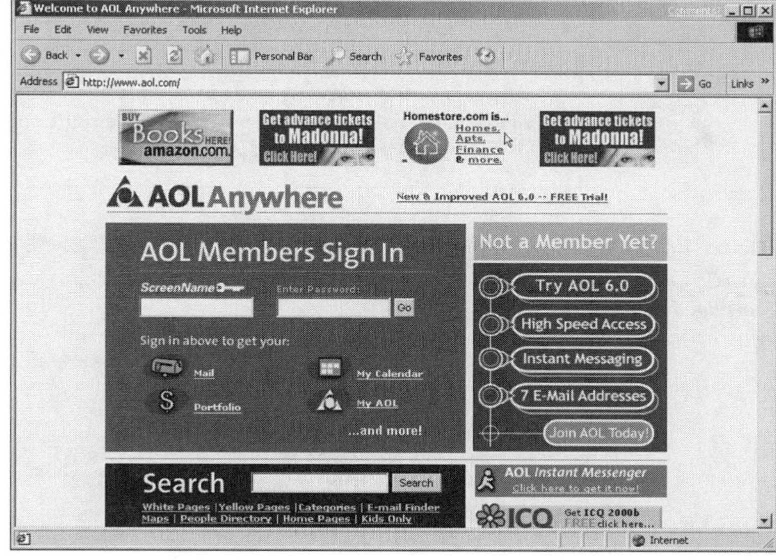

2. On the download page (see Figure 11.10), click the Download Now button.

FIGURE 11.10
Step 2: Click the Download Now button.

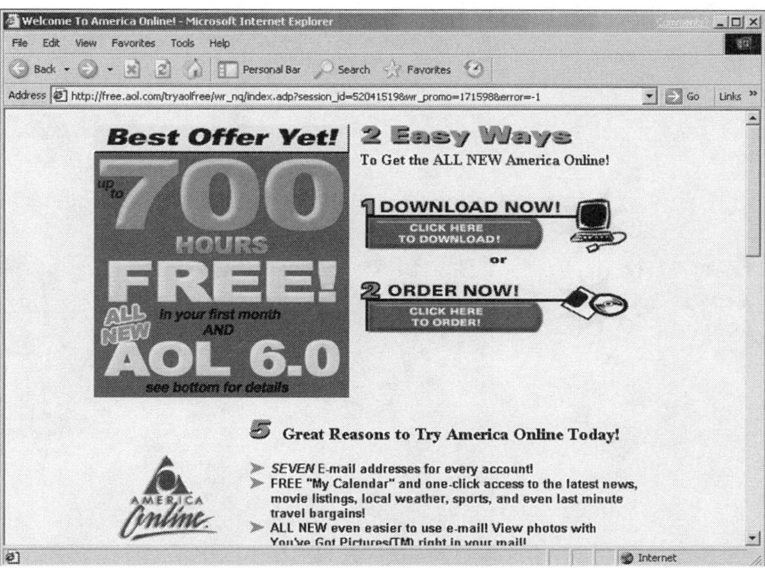

3. Click the download button that is appropriate for your operating system (see Figure 11.11).

Some versions of AOL may not operate properly on some versions of Windows, so make sure you're choosing the right one.

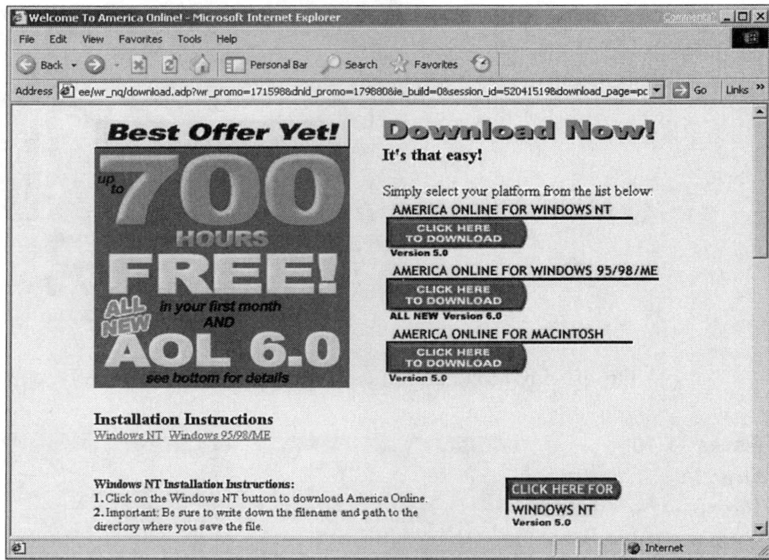

FIGURE 11.11
Step 3: Click the download button for your system.

4. Choose a location to save the download file (see Figure 11.12).

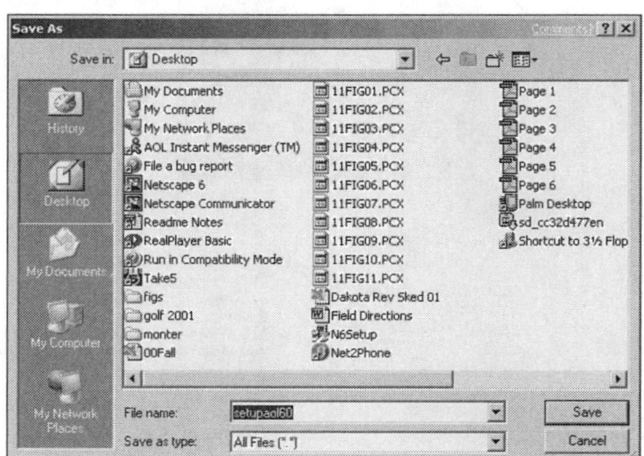

FIGURE 11.12
Step 4: Choose a location for the file.

5. The file begins to download to the location you specified (see Figure 11.13).

FIGURE 11.13
***Step 5:** The file downloads.*

After the file has completed its download, all you need to do is decide whether you are ready to sign up to be an AOL member. If you are ready to give it a try, just double-click the icon for the file (from the location where you saved it), and the AOL setup program will launch (see Figure 11.14).

AOL does a great job of walking you through the process of registering and getting started. The hardest part of the process is deciding on a screen name. Because there are already millions of members, a lot of screen names are taken!

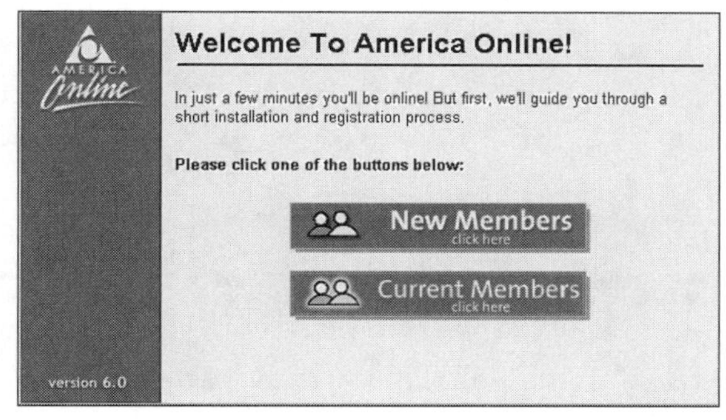

FIGURE 11.14
The AOL setup program walks you through the process of signing up and getting into the service.

11

Summary

America Online is full of great content and features, and it also gives you access to the full Internet. It's a great choice as an ISP for both novices and experienced Internet types. And, it's easy to use!

Q&A

Q So, if I'm reading you right, I can get all of the Internet through AOL, but I can't get all of AOL through the Internet, right?

A That's correct. Because AOL bought Netscape, some content appears to be merged. For example, a look at Netscape's home pages reveals a list of categories down the left side that looks an awful lot like AOL's Channels. But it's different. You can't get all of AOL's content through the Internet, unless you're an AOL subscriber.

Q How is AOL's Instant Messenger different from the one I got with Netscape?

A Actually, they're the same. You can send instant messages to friends who have downloaded the program through Netscape and aren't AOL members, and they can send them to you. So if you're an AOL member, and you have a friend who isn't, have them download Instant Messenger from Netscape, and you can send instant messages to each other.

HOUR 12

Plug-in and Add-on Programs

It may have happened to you already—surfing around the Internet, you come across a link that looks particularly promising. You click it, and a screen pops up telling you that in order to run this or see or hear or use it, you must have a program that is not currently installed on your computer.

"Would you like to download it now?"

You might, and you might not. That's up to you. But the fact of the matter is, as the Web develops and becomes more interactive and more multimedia-oriented, you're going to need more of these programs.

These additional programs function with your browser to allow you to view certain types of files, hear music, view video, have a conference call, and so on.

Your PC is not really your TV yet. But it's getting there. Already, you can watch live or recorded video through the Internet and listen to live radio broadcasts and CD-quality recorded music, too.

Your ability to do that depends on your browser. Good, up-to-date browsers come pre-equipped to play most of the multimedia content on the Web (sometimes with a little help from programs built in to the Windows or Macintosh operating systems). Good browsers are also *extensible*; that is, they can be refitted to deal with new file types and Internet services as they come along. New stuff always does come along, all because petulant teenage geniuses keep inventing new multimedia formats (like CD-quality music files) and putting 'em online.

Taking advantage of today's hottest multimedia—and tomorrow's—requires an understanding of the accessory programs—often called *plug-ins*, *players*, or *helper programs*—that endow your browser with new powers. In this hour, you discover not only how to fit your browser to play the coolest online multimedia, but also how to make your browser play anything even newer and cooler that may come along.

At the end of the hour, you'll be able to answer the following questions:

- How does the Web teach my browser new tricks?
- What are *plug-ins*, *players*, and *helper programs*, and how do I use them to help my browser do new things?
- How do I play audio and video files I've downloaded from the Internet?
- How do I watch *live* video and hear *live* radio broadcasts on the Internet?
- How can I get CD-quality music from the Internet and listen to it online or offline, anytime?

You'll hear a lot about "downloading" files in this hour. If you're not already familiar with downloading files, fear not: You'll learn all about it in Hour 14, "Downloading Programs and Files."

In the meantime, you may find that you can figure it out on your own. Simply put, to download a file, you click a link (you already know how to do that!), and then do whatever your browser tells you to do.

Understanding Plug-Ins, Java, and Other Programs in Pages

Up-to-date versions of Internet Explorer and Netscape Navigator come pre-equipped to play most (but not all) of the stuff you'll encounter online. So the most important step in preparing to play multimedia is making sure you have the latest version of your browser, so it supports native play of those file types.

NEW TERM **Native.** When a browser has the built-in capability to play a particular kind of file, the browser is said to include *native* support for that file type. Anything the browser can do without help from another program is native; any capability in which the browser must call on another program (such as those in this chapter) is *non-native*.

As part of being extensible, Netscape Navigator and Internet Explorer can, in effect, be reprogrammed through the Web to acquire new capabilities. This happens chiefly through four types of program files:

- **Plug-ins.** A plug-in is a program that implants itself in the browser to add a new capability. Usually, after you install a plug-in, that new capability appears to be a native, built-in part of the browser, as if it had always been there.
- **Helper programs.** A helper program is a separate program that the browser opens automatically to deal with a particular type of file. For example, when you play a video file from within Internet Explorer in Windows, the browser typically opens up the Windows Media Player—a separate program—to show you the file.

In practice, there's often not a whole lot of difference between a helper and a plug-in. In fact, the terms are often used interchangeably (and therefore incorrectly).

The main difference is that a plug-in is generally more tightly integrated with the browser and usually can't play if the browser is closed. A true helper is self-contained—it can be opened as needed by the browser, but can also be used when the browser is closed.

- **Applets and scripts (Java, JavaScript).** Both Big Two browsers can run program code delivered to them from servers—in effect, little programs that run once and then go away. This code—sometimes described as a script (when in JavaScript) or an applet (Java)—is used increasingly to enable advanced multimedia and other cool, interactive stuff on Web pages.
- **ActiveX controls.** An ActiveX control is a file of program code that teaches the browser how to do new things.

In general, you don't have to do anything special to take advantage of scripts, applets, or ActiveX; they're delivered to the browser automatically by Web sites. You just have to make sure that you use the most up-to-date version of Internet Explorer or Netscape Navigator, and you'll be all set.

Most other capabilities are delivered today through plug-ins (or plug-in–like helpers). Although plug-ins are occasionally delivered automatically, more often than not you must deliberately download and install a particular plug-in to enjoy whatever it does.

Finding Plug-Ins and Helpers

Usually when you come across a Web site or a file that requires a particular plug-in or other program, it's accompanied by a link for downloading the plug-in.

In fact, when you first enter the site, a message may appear on your screen informing you that a particular program is required and giving you a link for downloading it. On some sites requiring a specific program you do not have, your browser may show you a message telling you about the program. Often, that message includes a button you can click to get the program right away (see Figure 12.1).

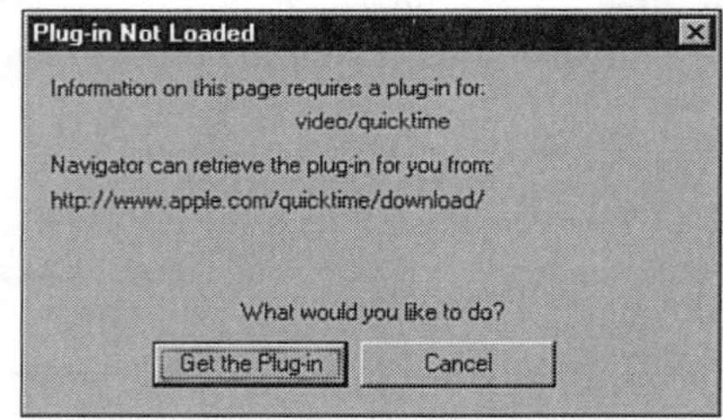

FIGURE 12.1
Sometimes, when you enter a site that requires a particular plug-in or other program, you'll see a message that provides a handy way to go get the program you need.

Occasionally, though, the site doesn't help you get the right program, and you have to go hunting for it.

Fortunately, several excellent indexes are devoted to these programs. The logical first stop is Netscape, where a full directory of plug-ins is maintained, along with links to the latest, coolest ones to come out (see Figure 12.2). You can reach Netscape's Plug-Ins index at `home.netscape.com/plugins/`.

The simplest way to find out what file types your computer is already equipped to play is to simply try files as you find them. If, when attempting to play a particular file type, you see a message telling you that your computer or browser doesn't know what to do with that file, you need to find and install a player program for that file type. Before trying any files, however, make sure you have an up-to-date virus protection program installed and operating on your computer.

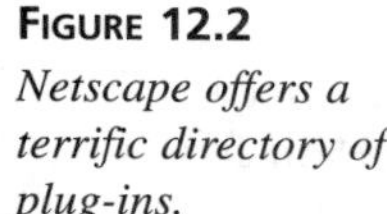

FIGURE 12.2
Netscape offers a terrific directory of plug-ins.

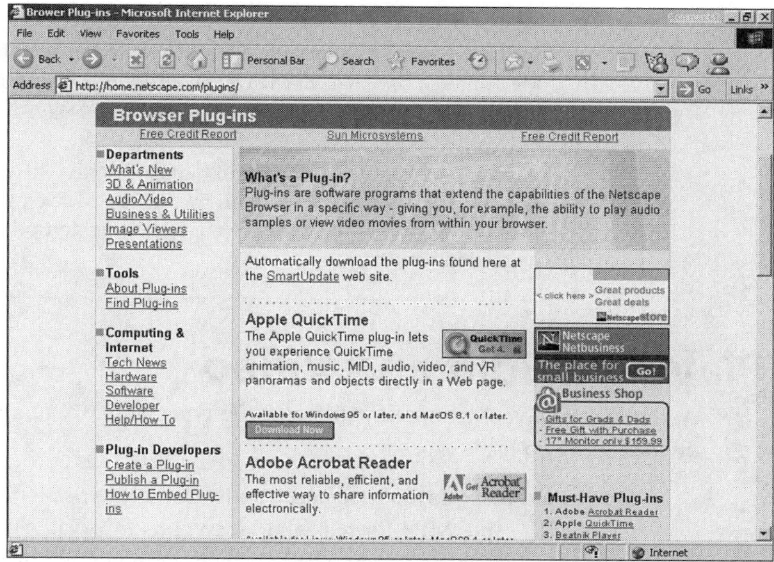

Installing and Using Plug-Ins and Helpers

Because these programs can come from any software publisher, no single method exists for installing them. Typically, though, you have to run some sort of installation program and then specify the directory in which your Web browser is installed.

When you come across a link to a plug-in or helper program a site requires, carefully read any instructions you see, click the link, and follow any prompts that appear.

After you install the program, you really needn't think about it any more. Any time you initiate an action in your browser that requires the plug-in or other program, it springs into action automatically. For example, if you've installed a plug-in that plays a particular kind of audio file, any time you click a link for that type of file, the plug-in kicks in to play it.

If you keep up with the latest release of your browser, you may not come across many occasions when you need to add anything to it, and you can deal with the rare situations one by one, as they arise.

Still, there are a few enhancements you're likely to need fairly soon. One is RealPlayer, described later in this hour. Two more are the programs for playing two types of advanced media online: Flash (which enables you to see certain kinds of animation in Web pages) and Shockwave (which enables you to use certain advanced interactive features in some Web pages). Players for both Flash and Shockwave are available for download free from Macromedia (`www.macromedia.com`), although sites containing Flash and Shockwave content nearly always include an easy-to-find link for downloading the necessary programs.

Internet Explorer (versions 5 and higher) comes with a built-in Flash player, so you might not need a plug-in for Flash. However, the types of content these kinds of plug-ins play are constantly being updated, necessitating upgraded players.

Playing Audio and Video

Audio and video come in many different file types online. But all audio and video can be divided into two basic types:

- **Download and play.** These audio and video file types—including sounds in .WAV, .AU, .MID, and .MP3 formats and video clips in .AVI, .MOV, .QT, and .MPG formats—are generally downloaded to your computer and then played. After they are downloaded, these files play anytime, whether you're online or off.
- **Streaming.** *Streaming* audio and video begin to play a few moments after the audio or video data begins arriving at your computer; in other words, while you're watching or listening to a few seconds of audio or video, the next few seconds are being transmitted to your computer. Streaming is essential for live broadcasts, but is also used to give you faster gratification with some non-live audio and video.

In the next two sections, you'll learn about playing each type.

Besides the aforementioned Windows Media Player and the about-to-be-mentioned RealPlayer, another important program for playing video clips is the QuickTime player. Available both as a Netscape plug-in and as a separate helper program, it equips a computer to play video clips stored in .MOV and .QT formats, of which there are many online.

This free player is not quite as critical as the two I just mentioned, though. All Macintoshes include native support for QuickTime files (they can play them without a separate player program), and some Windows systems already have a QuickTime player installed that browsers will automatically use as a helper. (Recent versions of Windows Media Player play QuickTime, and on older systems, a QuickTime player has usually been installed at some time or other by a multimedia CD-ROM program that featured QuickTime video.) If you have a Macintosh, or if your PC already has a player, Internet Explorer or Netscape Navigator will probably use the existing player to play MOV files.

If you have trouble playing .MOV video, however, get the player at `www.apple.com/quicktime/`.

Playing Downloaded Audio or Video Files

If you have a computer equipped with the latest operating system (Windows 98/Me/2000/XP on a PC or OS8/OS9/OS X on a Macintosh) and an up-to-date version of Internet Explorer or Netscape Navigator, you will find that you already have everything you need to play all of the common video and audio file types (non-streaming) you can download from the Web.

When you click a link that downloads an audio or video file, a dialog box generally appears (see Figure 12.3), asking whether you want to save the file on disk or open it as soon as it finishes downloading.

FIGURE 12.3
When downloading a media file, you can choose to save it (for later play) or open it (play it as soon as it finishes downloading).

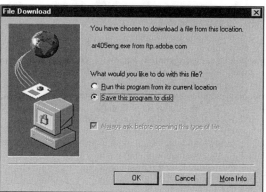

- Choose Save to save the file on disk, so you can play it later (online or offline). A regular Save dialog box opens, just as it does when you download any file. On that dialog box, you choose a location where the file will be stored. After downloading, you can play the file at any time by going to the folder or directory you chose to store the file in and double-clicking the file's icon.
- Choose Open to play the file as soon as it finishes downloading, so you can watch it right away and you don't have to fiddle with choosing where the file will be stored.

When you play a file (whether online or off), your computer automatically uses whatever program it has that's registered (assigned) to play that type of file. For example, in Windows, nearly all audio and video file types play in the Windows Media Player program (see Figure 12.4). (The version of Windows Media Player you have may differ, depending on which version of Windows you run and how long ago you got it.)

Observe that Windows Media Player has buttons that look like the buttons on a VCR or tape recorder. You use these buttons the same way you would on those devices: The Play button plays the file, Stop stops play, Fast-Forward skips ahead, and so on.

FIGURE 12.4
Programs that play audio and video files typically show buttons that mimic the functions of similar buttons on a VCR or tape recorder (Play, Stop, and so on).

Whether or not you have Windows Media Player already depends on your version of Windows. Windows ME, 2000, and Windows XP include it. But early shipments of Windows 98 did not include an up-to-date version of the Windows Media Player. On top of that, the Media Player is updated and improved from time to time.

No matter which Windows version you use, the best way to ensure that you always have the latest player is to use Windows's Update feature. Just click the Start button and then choose Windows Update; Windows contacts Microsoft through your Internet connection to see whether there are any updates available for your version (including Media Player upgrades and other enhancements).

If updates are available, you will be presented with the option to easily download and install them (free), right then and there.

The latest version of Windows Media Player, version 8, acts not only as a player, but also as a sort of media-specific browser. As Figure 12.4 shows, buttons along the left side of the window offer access to a Media Guide (a Web page, displayed within Windows Media Player, that offers links for playing the hottest music video, film clips, and more), a Media Library of stuff you have downloaded and saved, and more.

Playing "Streaming" Files

Streaming audio and video is the fastest-growing type of multimedia content on the Internet. It enables you not only to enjoy various multimedia programs designed for delivery through the Internet, but also to experience broadcast TV and radio programs from all over the world—programs you could not otherwise see or hear without first jumping on a plane to the places where these programs are actually broadcast.

NEW TERM **Streaming** media is audio or video (or both together) that begins to play on your computer before it has been completely downloaded. The main use of streaming audio and video is to present live Web broadcasts of audio or video content or to reduce your wait when playing a very large audio or video file.

Windows Media Player plays most popular streaming audio and video types currently in use, so if you have Windows 98 or newer, you may not need another program for streaming audio/video.

But if you have another type of system, you'll need a player program to play streaming audio and video. And even if you do have Windows Media Player, it never hurts to pick up another streaming audio/video player (as long as it's free). In either case, the best choice is RealPlayer, at `www.real.com`. RealPlayer is available in a free, scaled-down version and also in a version you pay for—RealPlayer Plus. It's also available in a "Real Entertainment Center" suite that includes other tools, such as Real Download, a program for making downloads of any type of file more convenient. But for playing streaming audio and video online, all you really need is the free RealPlayer.

RealPlayer enables you to play streaming video and audio feeds from television and radio broadcasts to news updates to live music. The RealPlayer home page (see Figure 12.5) also provides links to fun places where you can try out RealPlayer.

After you have a streaming audio/video player properly installed, it opens automatically anytime you click a link in a Web page that opens one of the streaming audio or video file types for which the player is built (see Figure 12.6). Like regular audio/video play programs, streaming audio/video players feature the familiar VCR buttons (Play, Fast Forward, and so on) for controlling playback.

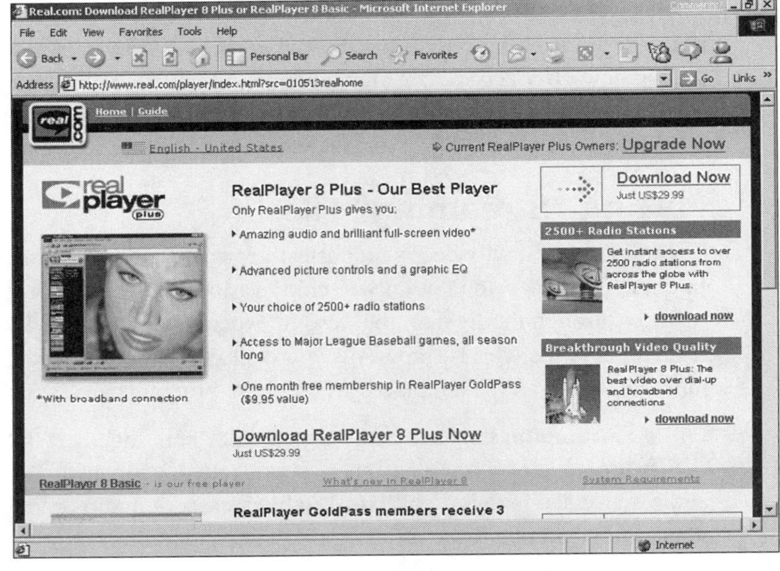

FIGURE 12.5
Download RealPlayer to play streaming audio and video from the Web.

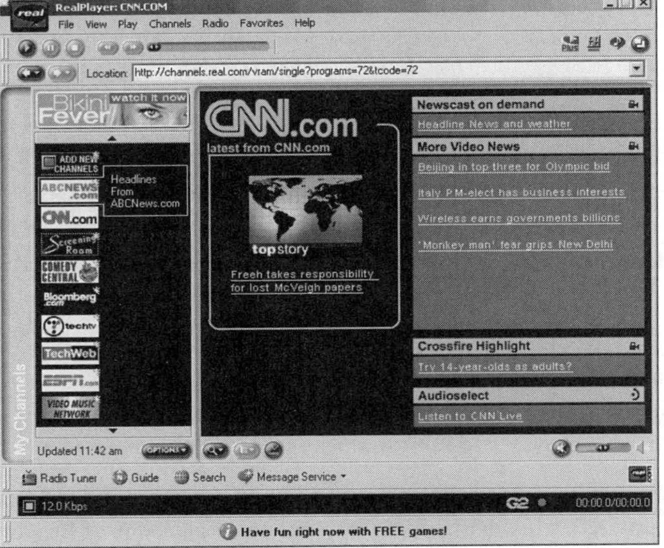

FIGURE 12.6
Like Windows Media Player, RealPlayer plays streaming audio/video.

Windows Media Player and RealPlayer both play most of the common streaming media file types online. But there are special "Real" files that play only through RealPlayer. Many people use both programs to be sure that they can play anything they come across.

Note that when you install either RealPlayer or Windows Media Player, the program may automatically set itself up as the default media player—the program that opens automatically when you click a link to a media file online. For example, if you already have Windows Media Player and you install RealPlayer, the next time you open a media file, you'll see RealPlayer.

If this happens and you would prefer to have your old player remain the default, no problem... The next time you open the displaced player, it will display a note asking whether you would like to make it the default player again. Check the check box provided, and you have your old default player back.

Taking Advantage of Media Options in Internet Explorer

In Internet Explorer 6's Personal Bar, you can display a Media pane, which puts buttons for playing radio broadcasts and controlling the volume within easy reach (see Figure 12.7). Note that broadcasts you open and control through the Personal Bar are ones you could also play from RealPlayer—it doesn't give you access to anything special but rather makes accessing the regular stuff easier.

To open the Personal Bar, just click the Personal Bar icon from the toolbar at the top of Internet Explorer. By opening the Media Options menu, you can explore other possibilities available to you, including a list of radio stations from which you can choose.

Where Can I Get Streaming Audio/Video?

You'll come across it all over the Web in sites devoted to other subjects. But the following are a few good starting points for getting to some of the good stuff:

- RealGuide (`www.realguide.com`)—One-stop access to lots of great sites with streaming content
- Film.com (`www.film.com`; see Figure 12.8)—Film clips and movie trailers
- Cinemapop.com (`www.cinemapop.com`)—Free, streaming full-length movies through the Internet
- CSPAN (`www.cspan.org`)—Live Congressional action
- Emusic (`www.emusic.com`)—Live (and prerecorded) streaming music programming

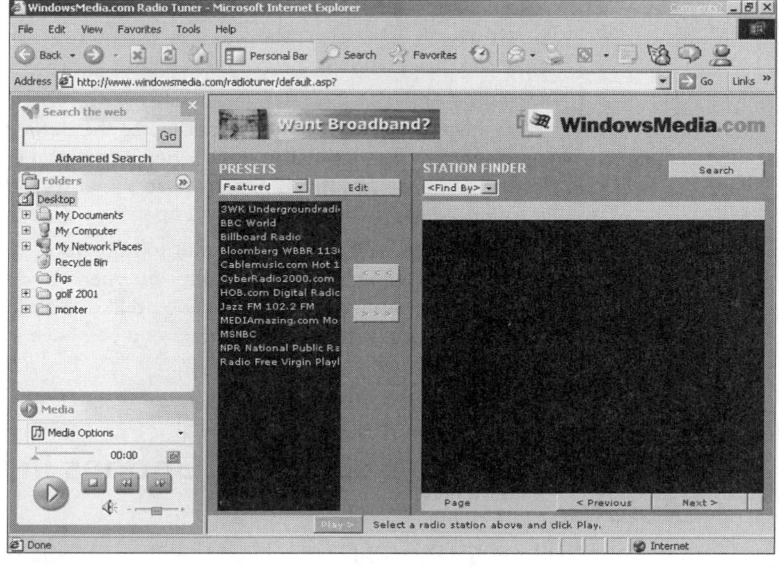

FIGURE 12.7
Internet Explorer's Personal Bar can make accessing and controlling live Web radio broadcasts more convenient.

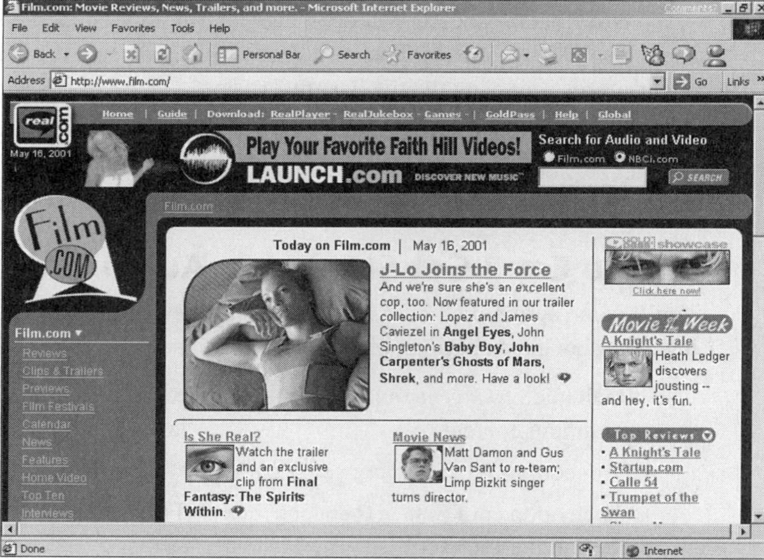

FIGURE 12.8
Film.com offers streaming film clips.

Downloading and Playing CD-Quality Music (MP3 Files)

Although most audio and video you can get online is pretty small and scratchy, one file format online supplies top-quality sound—MP3. MP3 files, which have the filename extension .MP3, are downloadable files containing CD-quality music or other high-quality audio.

Getting MP3 Files

Downloading MP3 files is like downloading any other type of file; you typically click a link in a Web page and then wait for the file to download to your computer. After the file is on your computer, you can play it anytime, even offline. A typical MP3 file containing one pop song is between 3MB and 4MB; over a 56K connection, it typically takes no more than about 15 minutes to get the file.

Of course, the trick with MP3 files isn't downloading them—it's finding the exact song you want to hear from among the thousands available online. To help with that, there are MP3 search pages, which you use just like regular search pages, but which are specifically designed to find MP3 files online when you supply all or part of the song's title or the artist's name. Check out `music.lycos.com` (see Figure 12.9). Using the Search box at the top of the page, you can search for MP3s by clicking the MP3 radio button.

FIGURE 12.9
There are MP3 search engines that help you find exactly the song you want to hear.

There are lots of sites with MP3 files and players. But a good place to start with MP3 is (you guessed it) `www.mp3.com`.

Playing MP3 Files

If you use Windows and have a recent version of Windows Media Player, you'll find that it plays MP3 files you've downloaded from the Web. Otherwise, you'll need to pick up an MP3 player to hear MP3 files. Good shareware and freeware players are available all over the Web; the following are a few sites to check out for good players:

- Sonique (see Figure 12.10) at `sonique.lycos.com`
- Winamp at `www.winamp.com`
- Macamp (for Macintosh) at `www.macamp.net`

Most MP3 players not only play MP3 files, but also serve as all-purpose sound players playing other sound file formats (such as .WMA) and also audio CDs in your CD-ROM drive.

FIGURE 12.10
Sonique is one of many great freeware and shareware MP3 players available online.

Summary

If you have the latest version of Netscape Navigator or Internet Explorer, your browser comes equipped to do so much that you'll rarely come across a situation in which it needs enhancement. Still, no matter how fast developers enhance their browsers, the new file types and programs stay one step ahead. Knowing how to deal with plug-ins and helper programs ensures that you don't get left behind when something new and wonderful hits the Web.

Q&A

Q Should I go out and get as many plug-ins as I can find, so I'm ready for anything?

A Nah. For the most part, outside of streaming audio/video, Flash, and Shockwave, plug-ins are rarely necessary. Smart Web developers want to reach as many people as possible, and they know that forcing people to get a plug-in may scare some folks off. Also, plug-ins are known to drag your browser's performance; there's no sense bogging down your browser (and filling up your hard disk) with plug-ins you may not use. Besides, not all plug-ins are free.

When you come across something you really want to see or do and it requires a plug-in, make your move. Otherwise, don't worry about it.

Q I read in the paper something about MP3 and piracy. Am I breaking the law when I listen to an MP3 file?

A Yes and no…(Why do you ask these difficult questions? What do you *want* from me? I just write computer books. That alone should tell you how little I know about ethics.)

Early in the MP3 boom, a large number of copyrighted songs began circulating the Internet in MP3 files on sites such as Napster (`www.napster.com`). The music publishers—rightly feeling that they were losing a royalty on all these free files—got wise and started to crack down on sites that distribute these files. But many MP3 files are still available online, and new ones are put online every day in spite of the record companies' efforts. When you download one of these "bootleg" MP3 files, you're aiding and abetting a violation of copyright law.

The legal issues are still being worked out, so don't hold me to this, but it appears a model is evolving wherein record companies would permit (even encourage) the distribution of MP3 files of a very few, select songs from a CD as samples in the hope that these would encourage listeners to buy the whole CD. This is especially the case, obviously, with groups that aren't well-known and want people to listen to their songs. A number of well-known artists have also embraced MP3 to distribute their songs, recognizing that although they won't collect as much per song as by selling CDs, they'll benefit in the long run from jumping on the MP3 bandwagon early.

To support this concept (and keep the sharks at bay), a growing number of MP3 sites are featuring links to online CD stores, such as CDNow (`www.CDnow.com`) and CD Universe (`www.cduniverse.com`), so visitors can jump straight from the site where they heard the song to a place where they can buy the CD.

Q Whither Napster?

A Why do you have to use words like "whither"? Napster was easily the most popular online music site, building a huge following of people who used it to upload and download music. Its ongoing court battles have changed the company somewhat, and it's since been purchased by a larger firm. Recently, Napster's been reaching agreements with recording labels for the rights to distribute music, but the end results of these agreements are still difficult to discern.

PART IV

Needles in a VERY Big Haystack

Hour

Hour 13

Searching for Information

There's just too much on the Web. It's like having a TV set with a billion channels; you could click the remote until your thumb fell off and still never find the *Law & Order* reruns.

Fortunately, a number of search sites on the Web help you find exactly what you're looking for, anywhere on the Web, and even *beyond* the Web in other Internet arenas. In this hour, you'll discover what searching the Web is all about, and discover a simple but effective searching method: cruising categories. You'll also learn how to use search terms, and how to phrase them carefully to produce precisely the results you need.

At the end of this hour, you'll be able to answer the following questions:

- What are *search sites*, and where can I find them?
- How do I use features in my browser that can make searching more convenient?

- How can I conduct a simple search by clicking through a series of links?
- What's a *search term*?
- How do I use a simple search term to produce a list of *hits*, Web pages related to the term?
- How do I phrase more complex search terms, for power-searching?
- How can I conveniently use multiple search tools all from one place?
- How can I search for information just among the contents of a particular site?

What's a Search Site?

Put simply, a search site—which you may also see variously described as a *search page*, *search tool*, or *search service*—is a Web page where you can conduct a search of the Web. Such pages have been set up by a variety of companies that offer you free Web searching and support the service, at least in part, through the advertising you'll see prominently displayed there. Figure 13.1 shows a popular search site, Excite.

> The term *search engine* is sometimes used to describe a search site. But this term more accurately describes the program a search site uses, behind the scenes, to perform searches. When you hear someone refer casually to a "search engine," just remember that they probably mean "search site."

FIGURE 13.1
Excite, a popular search site.

No matter which search site you use, and no matter how you use it, what you get from a search site is a page of links, each pointing to a page the search site thinks might match what you're looking for. When using a search site, your job is to provide that tool with enough information about what you're searching for, so that the resulting "hit list" (see Figure 13.2) contains lots of good matches or you to explore.

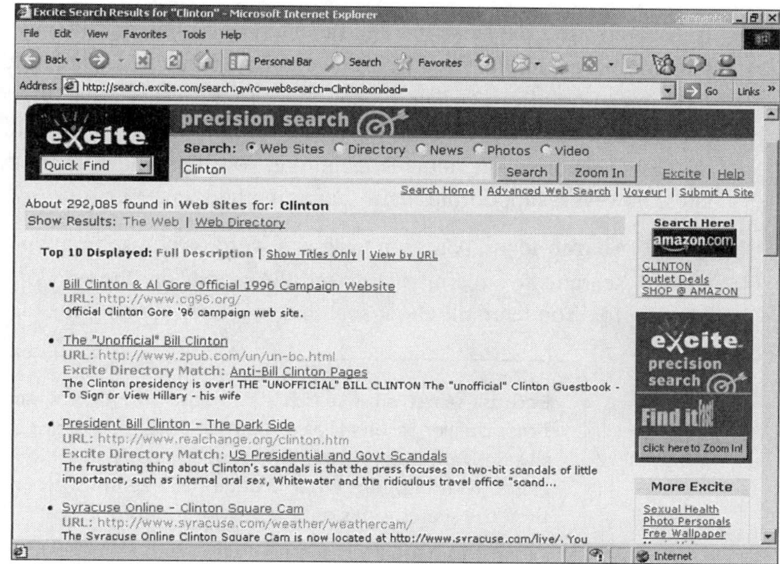

FIGURE 13.2
Search sites show you list of links—a "hit list"—of Web pages and other resources that match what you told the search site you were looking for.

Can I Really Search the Whole Web?

Well, yes and no…. (Don't you *hate* that answer?)

Although using the various search sites works similarly, each has its own unique search methods. But, more important, each has its own unique set of files—a *database*—upon which all searches are based.

You see, no search site actually goes out and searches the entire Web when you ask it to. A search site searches its own index of information about the Web—its database. The more complete and accurate that database is, the more successful your searches are likely to be.

The database for a search site is created in either (or both) of two ways:

- **Manually.** Folks who've created Web pages, or who've discovered pages they want the world to know about, fill in a form on the search site's Web site to add new pages (and their descriptions) to the database. If the search site's editors deem the site to be worthy of inclusion, it gets added.

- **Through a *crawler* (or *spider*, or *worm*).** All of these creepy-crawly names describe programs that systematically contact Web servers (at regular intervals), scan the contents of the server, and add information about the contents of the server to the database. (They "crawl" around the Web, like spiders—get it?) It takes the crawler a month or so to complete each of its information-gathering tours of the Web.

If a search site's database has been created by a crawler, the tool tends to deliver results that are more complete and up-to-date, whereas manually built databases tend to contain more meaningful categorization and more useful descriptive information. Also, most search sites with crawler-built databases do not offer you a way to search by browsing through categories—a valuable technique you'll pick up later in this hour. All search sites, however, support the main search method: entering a *search term*.

NEW TERM **Search term.** A search term is a word or phrase you type in a text box on a search site's main page, to tell the search site the type of information you're looking for. You learn all about search terms later in this hour.

Because search sites search a database and not the actual Web, they sometimes deliver results that are out of date. You might click a link that a search site delivered to you and find that the page to which it points no longer exists. That happens when a page has been moved or deleted since the last time the search site's database was updated.

When this happens, it's no big whoop. Just click Back to go back to the list of results, and try another link.

How sites are ranked within their categories also varies from search site to search site. Some will simply list sites in alphabetical order. Some sell higher placement for a price, then list the rest in alphabetical order. Some display results based on the likelihood that the site matches your search term. One site, Google, uses a unique page-ranking system that examines the Internet's elaborate system of links to determine a site's "value" based on the number of other sites that link to it.

Despite differences and strengths and weaknesses among the available tools, the bottom line is this: Any of the major search sites might locate a page or pages that meet your needs, or it might not. If you can't find what you want through one tool, try another. Because each tool has its own database, and each tool applies a different technical method for searching its database, no two search sites turn up exactly the same results for any given topic.

Where Are the Major Search Sites?

There are about a dozen, general-purpose search sites out there, and many, many more specialized search sites (more about those in upcoming hours).

Table 13.1 lists the major players. You can visit any search site by entering its URL.

TABLE 13.1 The Top Search Sites

Tool	*URL*
Yahoo!	`www.yahoo.com`
Excite	`www.excite.com`
AltaVista	`www.altavista.com`
Lycos	`www.lycos.com`
Google	`www.google.com`
WebCrawler	`www.webcrawler.com`
Ask Jeeves	`www.askjeeves.com`
GoTo	`www.goto.com`

Note that a few of the search sites listed in Table 13.1 are also Web portals, pages that are popular as home pages because they provide easy access to searching, news, and other popular services. Two other popular portals not only offer searches, but actually let you use several different popular search sites, all from the portal page. These are

- Netscape: `home.netscape.com`
- MSN: `msn.com`

For example, right from the Netscape portal, you can submit a search term to Netscape's own search engine, or to Infoseek, AltaVista, and other popular search sites (see Figure 13.3).

13

There's a confusion about search sites, created by some ISPs and browser sellers. In part to simplify their sales pitch for novices, these folks sometimes tout their products as "featuring all the best search sites," or words to that effect. That implies that a search site is a feature in a browser, or a service provided by an ISP.

That claim is, oh, what's the word... hooey. A search site is a Web page, and anyone with a browser can use it. Browsers sometimes include features that can make accessing search sites easier, but no browser has a real built-in search engine, and no ISP can claim ownership of any of the important search sites.

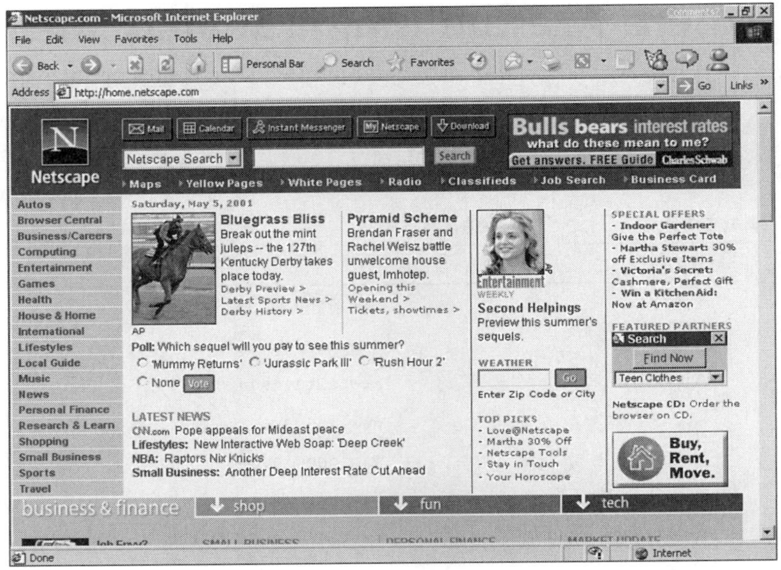

FIGURE 13.3
Some Web portals, such as the Netscape portal shown here, provide one-stop access to multiple searches.

Before beginning to use search sites, take a peek at a few from the list in Table 13.1. While visiting these pages, watch for helpful links that point to

- Instructions for using the search site, often called Help.
- A text box near the top of the page, which is where you would type a search term
- Links to categories you can browse
- Reviews and ratings of recommended pages
- "Cool Sites"—a regularly updated, random list of links to especially fun or useful pages you may want to visit just for kicks
- Other search engines

Simple Searching by Clicking Categories

These days, all the major search sites accept search terms. But a few also supply a directory of categories, an index of sorts, that you can browse to locate links to pages related to a particular topic. Tools that feature such directories include Yahoo!, Excite, and Infoseek.

Directory browsing is something of a sideline for other search sites, but it's the bread and butter of Yahoo!. When you want to search in this way, Yahoo! is almost always your best starting point.

Why Use Categories Instead of a Search Term?

When you're first becoming familiar with the Web, forgoing the search engines and clicking through a directory's categories is not only an effective way to find stuff but also a great way to become more familiar with what's available on the Web. As you browse through categories, you inevitably discover detours to interesting topics and pages that you didn't set out to find. Exploring directories is an important part of learning how the Web works and what's on it.

Also, the broader your topic of interest, the more useful categories are. When you use a search term to find information related to a broad topic (cars, dogs, music, plants), the search site typically delivers to you a bewildering list containing hundreds or thousands of pages. Some of these pages will meet your needs, but many will be pages that merely mention the topic rather than being *about* the topic.

Some links that a search term delivers will match the term, but not your intentions; a search on "plant" will likely turn up not only botany and houseplant pages, but others about power plants, Robert Plant, and maybe the Plantagenet family of European lore. Categories, on the other hand, help you limit the results of your search to the right ballpark.

Using a Directory

Everything in a directory is a link; to find something in a directory, you follow those links in an organized way.

You begin by clicking a broad category heading to display a list of related subcategories (see Figure 13.4). Click a subcategory heading, and you display its list of subsubcategories.

You continue in this fashion, drilling down through the directory structure (usually through only two to five levels), until you eventually arrive at a targeted list of links to pages related to a particular topic. You can explore those page links one by one, and after finishing with each, use your Back button to return to the search site's list and try another link.

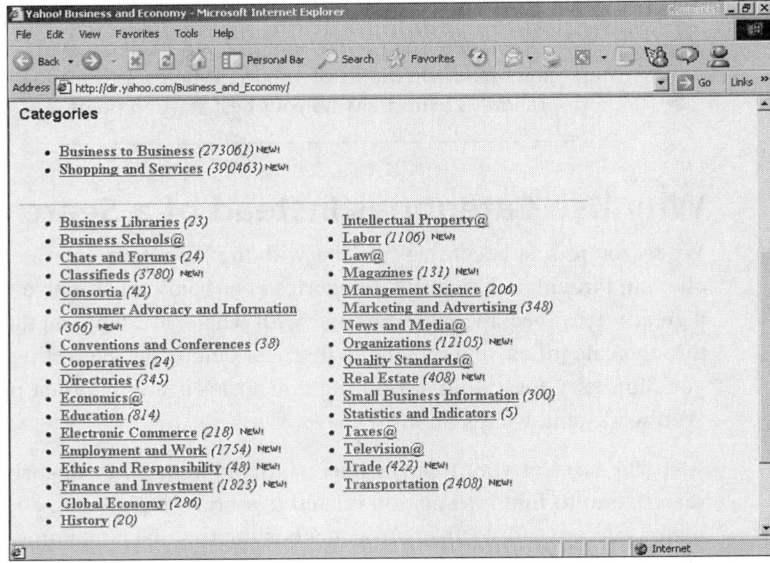

FIGURE 13.4
A subcategory list in Yahoo!.

To Do: Exploring Categories

To Do

1. Go to Yahoo! at `www.yahoo.com` (see Figure 13.5).

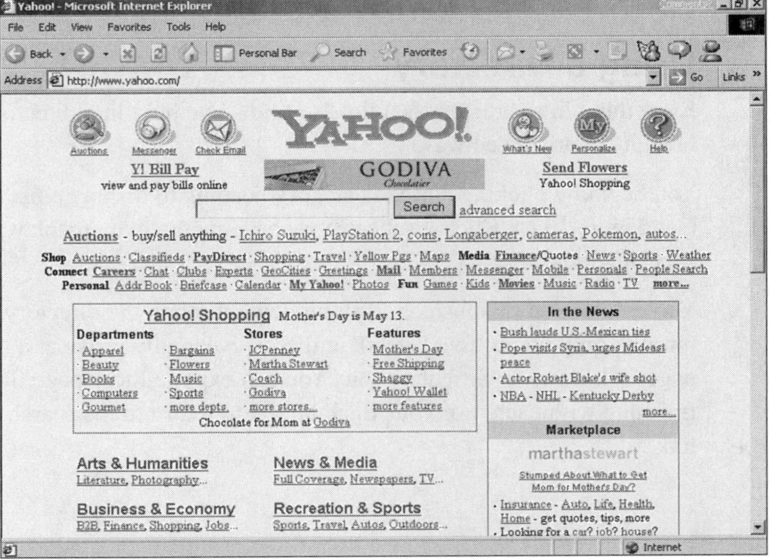

FIGURE 13.5
Step 1: *Go to Yahoo!.*

2. In the list of categories, click Entertainment (see Figure 13.6).

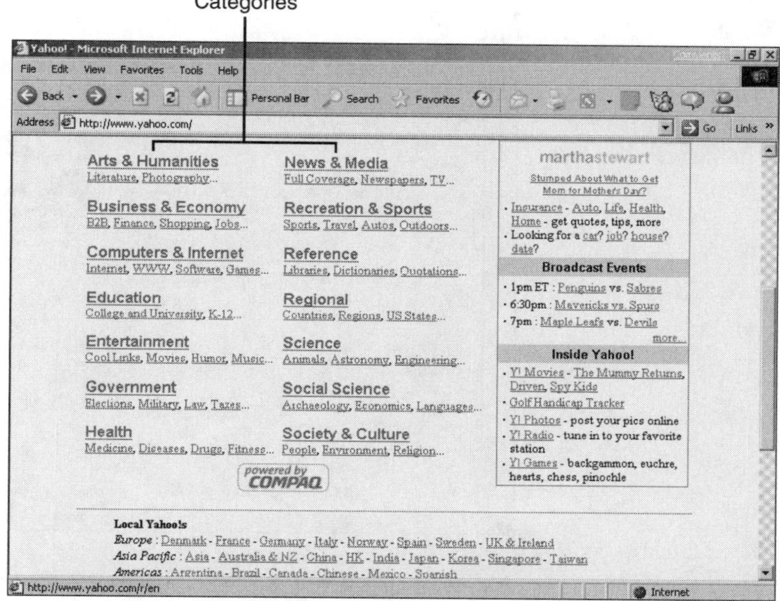

FIGURE 13.6
Step 2: *Click Entertainment.*

3. In the list of subcategories that appears, click Amusement and Theme Parks (see Figure 13.7).
4. Scroll down to reveal links leading to pages about amusement parks. You can click one of the preceding subcategories to see more options, or visit one of the following pages (see Figure 13.8).
5. If you choose a site, such as Adventureland USA, you'll get to that home page (see Figure 13.9).
6. Click Back until you return to the top Yahoo page. Observe that you can try any path or page and then back out by as many levels as you want to so that you can try a different path.
7. Explore on your own, clicking down through the directory and then back up again with Back.

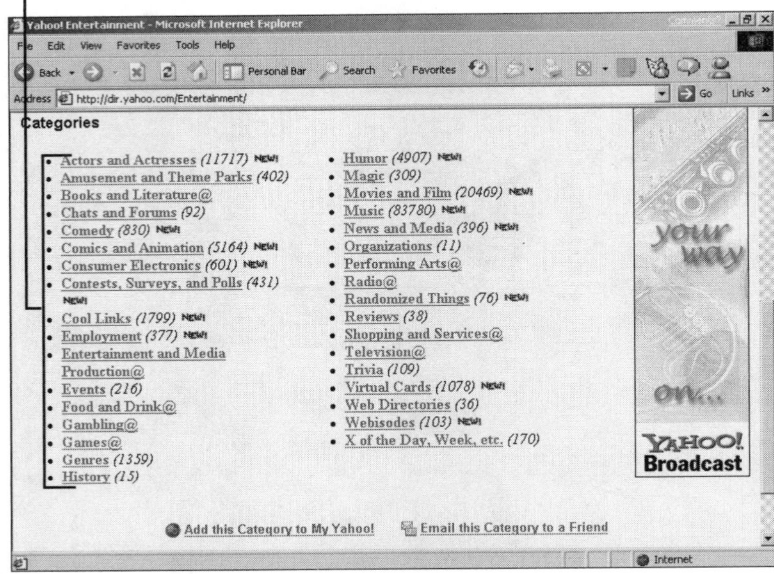

FIGURE 13.7
Step 3: *Click Amusement and Theme Parks.*

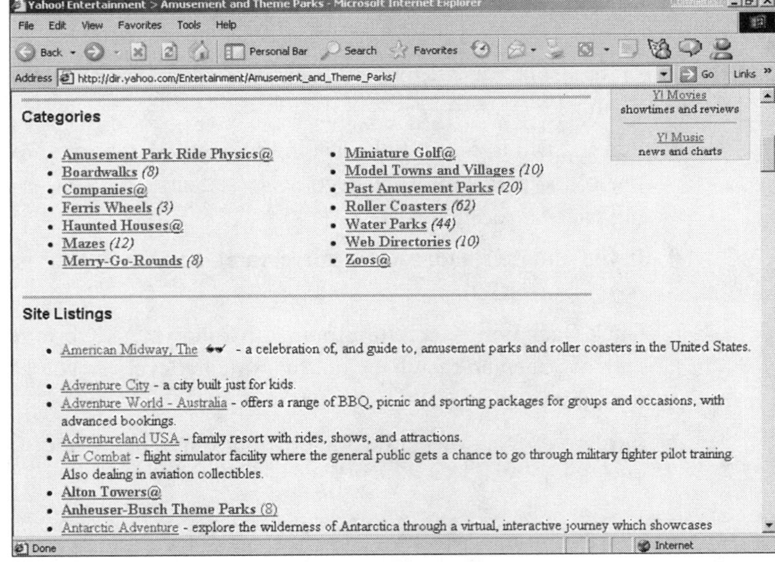

FIGURE 13.8
Step 4: *Choose a subcategory or visit a site.*

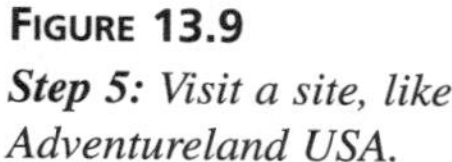

FIGURE 13.9
Step 5: *Visit a site, like Adventureland USA.*

Understanding Searches

Each of the search tools described thus far, and just about any other you might encounter on the Web, has a text box featured prominently near the top of its main page (see Figure 13.10). That text box is where you will type your search terms. Adjacent to the box, there's always a submit button, almost always labeled "Search."

Typing a search term in a text box and then clicking the submit button to send the term to the search tool is known as *submitting a search term.* Such searches are sometimes also described as *keyword* searches, because the search term serves as a key to finding matching pages.

When you submit a search term, the search tool searches through its database of information about pages, locating any entries that contain the same combination of characters in your search term. Although the contents of the various search tool databases differ, the record for each page typically contains the page's URL, title, a brief description, and a group of keywords intended to describe the page's contents. If your search term matches anything in that record, the search tool considers the page a match.

After searching the whole database (which takes only a moment or two), the search tool displays a list of links to all the pages it determined were matches: a *hit list*.

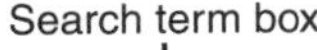

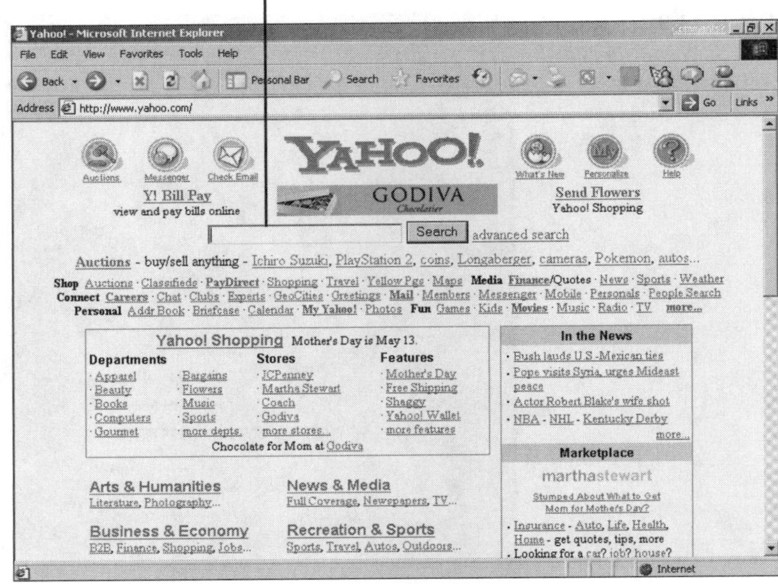

FIGURE 13.10
The text box you see on all search tool pages is where you type a search term.

NEW TERM **Hit list.** A *hit list* is a list of links, produced by a search engine in response to a search term you have entered. Each link is a "hit": a page that contains a match for your search term.

Each hit in the list is a link (see Figure 13.11). You can scroll through the hit list, reading the page titles and descriptions, to determine which page might best serve your needs, and then click the link to that page to go there. If the page turns out to be a near miss, you can use your Back button to return to the hit list and try a different page, or start over with a new search.

> A hit list may show no hits at all, or it may have hundreds. Zero hits are a problem, but hundreds or even thousands of hits really aren't. Remember, most search engines put the best hits at the top of the list, so even if your hit list has thousands of links, the links you want most likely will appear somewhere within the top 20 or so.
>
> Regardless of the number of hits, if you don't see what you want somewhere in the first 30 to 50 links, you probably need to start over with a new search term. And if your first search turned up hundreds of hits, use a more specific term in your second try.

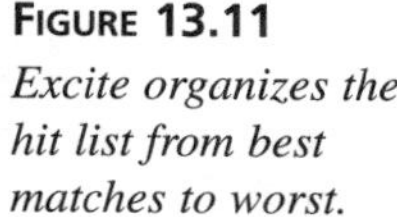

FIGURE 13.11
Excite organizes the hit list from best matches to worst.

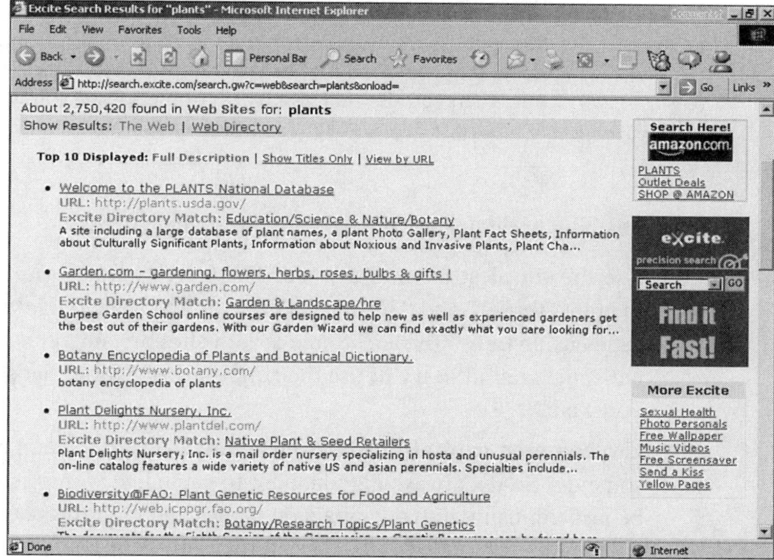

Some tools organize the hit list in smart ways, attempting to put the best matches at the top of the list so you see them first, and weaker matches lower in the list.

For example, suppose you use *Godzilla* as your search term. A particular search tool would tend to put at the top of the hit list all pages that use the word "Godzilla" in their titles or URLs because those are the pages most likely to be all about Godzilla. Matches to keywords or the page's description come lower in the list, because these might be pages that simply mention Godzilla, but aren't really *about* Godzilla. Even lower in the list, a tool might show links to "partial" matches, pages to which only part of the search term, such as those containing the word "God" or the partial word "zilla."

Phrasing a Simple Search

You can get awfully artful and creative with search terms. But 9 times out of 10, you needn't get too fancy about searching. You go to the search site, type a simple word or phrase in the text box, click the submit button, and wait a few moments for the hit list to show up.

If the list shows links that look like they hold what you're after, try 'em. If not, try another search term.

You can use multiple words in a search term; for example, someone's full name (*Michael Moriarty*) or another multi-word term (*two-term presidents*). But when you use multiple words, some special considerations apply. See "Phrasing a *Serious* Search," later in this hour.

Here are a few basic tips for improving your search success:

- **Use the simplest form of a word.** The search term *Terrier* will match references to both "Terrier" and "Terrier*s*." However, the term *Terriers* may fail to match pages using only "Terrier." Some search sites are smart enough to account for this, but some aren't. So try to use the simplest word form that's still specific to what you want.
- **Use common capitalization.** Some search sites don't care about capitalization, but some do. So it's always a good habit to capitalize words as they would most often be printed, using initial capitals on names and other proper nouns, and all lowercase letters for other words. Be careful to observe goofy computer-era capitalizations, such as AppleTalk or FrontPage.
- **Be as specific as possible.** If it's the German shepherd you want to know about, use that as your search term, not *dog*, which will produce too many hits, many unrelated to German shepherds. If the most specific term doesn't get what you want, then try less specific terms; if *German shepherd* fails, go ahead and try *dog*. You may find a generic page about dogs, on which there's a link to information about German shepherds.
- **Try partial words.** Always try full words first. But if they're not working out, you can use a partial word. If you want to match both "puppies" and "puppy," you can try *pup* as a search term, which matches both.

When you use a search term in Yahoo! (`www.yahoo.com`), the hit list typically shows not only pages, but Yahoo! categories related to the search term. You can try one of the pages, or start exploring related category headings from the head start the search provides.

To Do

To Do: Try a Simple Search

1. Go to AltaVista at `www.altavista.com` (see Figure 13.12).
2. Click the search term box, and type *DaVinci* for a search term (see Figure 13.13).

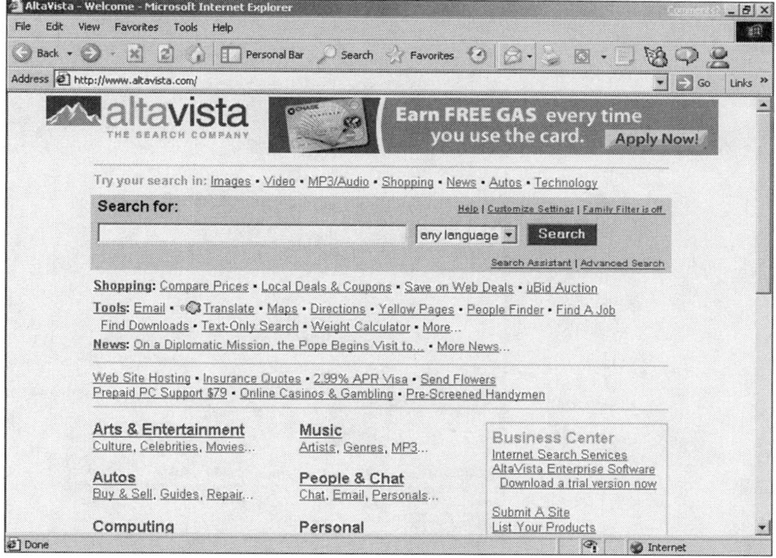

FIGURE 13.12
Step 1: *Go to AltaVista.*

FIGURE 13.13
Step 2: *Type DaVinci into the search term box.*

3. Click the submit button, labeled Search to reveal the hit list (see Figure 13.14).

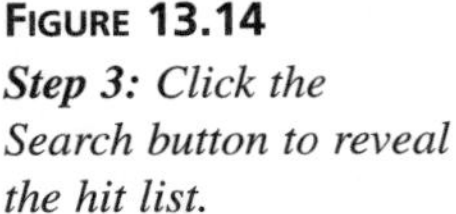

FIGURE 13.14
Step 3: *Click the Search button to reveal the hit list.*

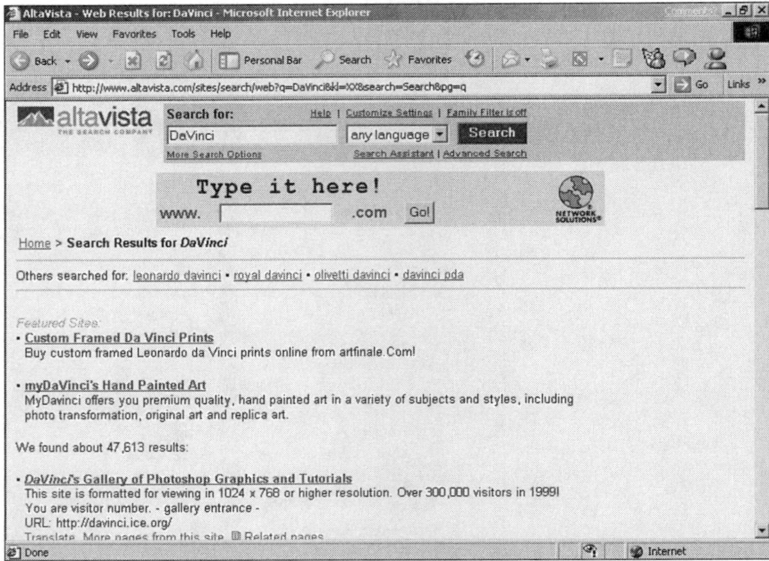

4. Click any link in the hit list, to see where it leads (see Figure 13.15).

FIGURE 13.15
Step 4: *Try a link to see where it leads.*

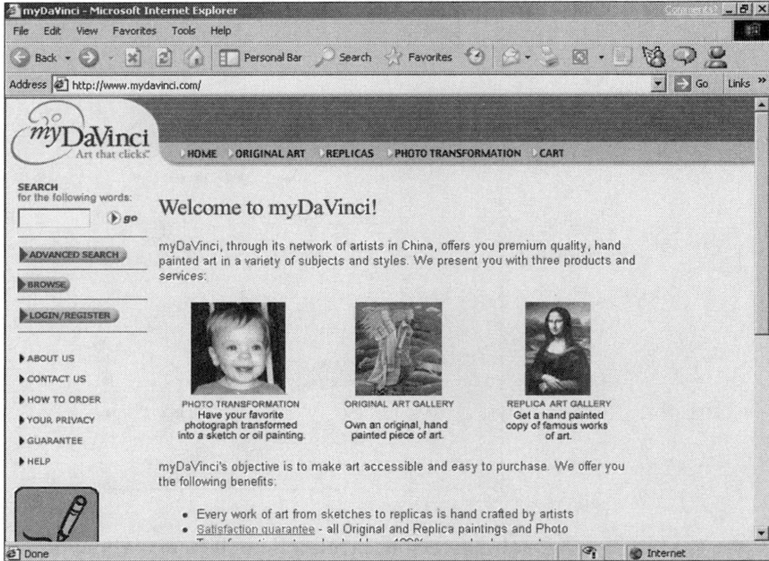

5. Click Back to return to the hit list. Scroll to the bottom of the page, and observe that there are links for moving ahead to more pages of the hit list (see Figure 13.16).

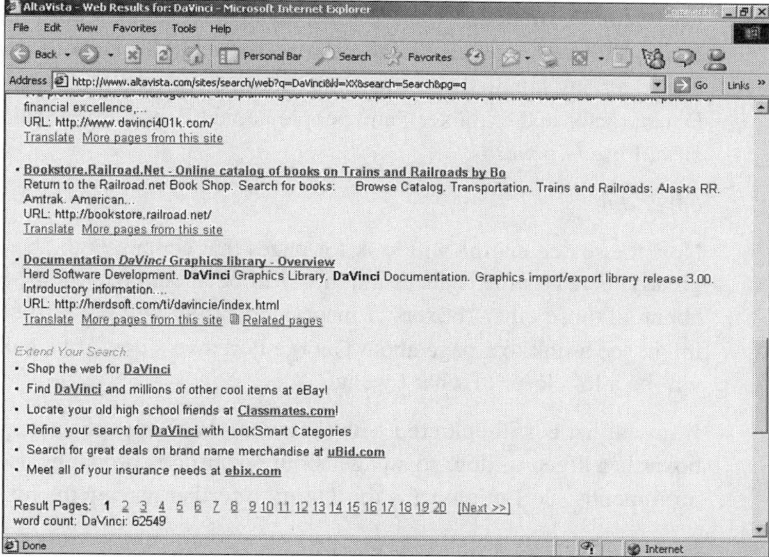

FIGURE 13.16
Step 6: *Scroll down to the bottom of the page.*

> Observe that the search term box appears on every page of the hit list. You can start a new search at any time, from any page of the hit list, by entering a new search term.
>
> Some search sites display the search term box only on the top page; to start a new search in those, just click Back until you return to the top page.

Phrasing a *Serious* Search

Sometimes, in order to phrase a very specific search, you need multiple words. And when you use multiple words, you may need to use *operators* to control the way a search site works with those words.

NEW TERM **Operator.** In mathematics, an operator is a word or symbol used to specify the action in an equation, such as plus or minus. Operators are used in search terms to express a logical equation of sorts that tightly controls how a search engine handles the term.

Using Multiple Words in a Search Term

In a search term, you can use as many words as you need in order to make the term specific.

For example, suppose I want to learn about boxer dogs. I could use the search term *boxer*. Although that term might turn up some hits about boxer dogs, those hits may be buried among hundreds of other links about prizefighters, China's Boxer rebellion, Tony Danza (actor and ex-boxer), and people named Boxer. So to make my search more specific, I use two words:

boxer dog

Now the search engine will look for pages that contain both "boxer" and "dog," which greatly increases the chances that hits will be about boxer dogs, because most pages about all those other "boxers" I mentioned earlier will not also be about "dogs." I still might see a link to a page about George Foreman's dog, if he has one. But the hit list will be a lot closer to what I want.

If my hit list is still cluttered with the wrong kind of pages, I might remember that a boxer is a breed of dog, so a page about boxer dogs probably also uses the term "breed" prominently. So I might try a third term to further narrow the hit list:

boxer dog breed

Get the idea? Now, if you get *too* specific, you may accidentally omit a few pages you want—there may be boxer dog pages that don't use "breed" anywhere that would show up in a search database. So it's best to start off with a happy medium (a term that's specific but not overly restrictive), see what you get, and then try subsequent searches using more or less specific terms, depending on what's in the hit list.

A few search engines support *natural language queries*. In a natural language query, you can phrase your search term as you might naturally phrase a question; for example, you might use the search term *Who was the artist Leonardo da Vinci*, and the search site applies sophisticated technology to determine what you're asking.

Natural language queries are a good idea, and they're worth experimenting with. But in my experience, their results are usually not as good as you would probably get with a really smartly phrased search term.

Using Operators to Control Searches

Whenever you use multiple words, you're using operators, even if you don't know it. Operators are words you use between the words in a multi-word search term to further define exactly how the search site will handle your term. Using operators in this way is sometimes described as *Boolean logic.* There are three basic operators used in searching:

- **And.** When you use *and* between words in a search term, you tell the search engine to find only those pages that contain *both* of the words—pages that contain only one or the other are not included in the hit list.
- **Or.** When you use *or* between words in a search term, you tell the search engine to find all pages that contain *either* of the words—all pages that contain either word alone, or both words, are included in the hit list.
- **Not.** When you use *not* between words in a search term, you tell the search engine to find all pages that contain the word before not, then to remove from the hit list any that also contain the word following not.

Table 13.2 illustrates how *and*, *or,* and *not* affect a search site's use of a term.

TABLE 13.2 How Operators Work in Search Terms

Search Term	*What a Search Tool Matches*
Dodge and pickup	Only pages containing both "Dodge" and "pickup."
Dodge or pickup	All pages containing either "Dodge" or "pickup," or both words.
Dodge not pickup	All pages that contain "Dodge" but do not also contain "pickup". (This gets all the Dodge pages, and then eliminates any about pickups.)
Dodge and pickup and models	Pages that contain all three words.
Dodge or pickup or models	Pages that contain any of the three words.
Dodge not Chrysler	Pages that contain "Dodge" but do not also contain "Chrysler." (This gets all the Dodge pages, and then eliminates any that also mention Chrysler.)

Before using operators in search terms, check out the options or instructions area of the search site you intend to use (see Figure 13.17). Most search sites support *and*, *or,* and *not*, but some have their own little quirks about how you must go about it. For example, Excite and AltaVista prefer that you insert a plus sign (+) at the beginning of a word rather than precede it with *and.*

Another powerful way to use multiple words is to do an *exact phrase match*, which most search sites support. In an exact phrase match, you surround the multi-word term with quotes to instruct the search to match only pages that show the same words as the term, in the same order.

For example, suppose you want to know about the film *Roman Holiday*. A search on *Roman Holiday* will probably match any page that uses both of those words anywhere, in any order, together or separately. That'll still get you some good hits, but a lot of bad ones, too. A search on *"Roman Holiday"* (in quotes) matches only pages that use the exact phrase Roman Holiday, so the hit list will be much better targeted to what you want.

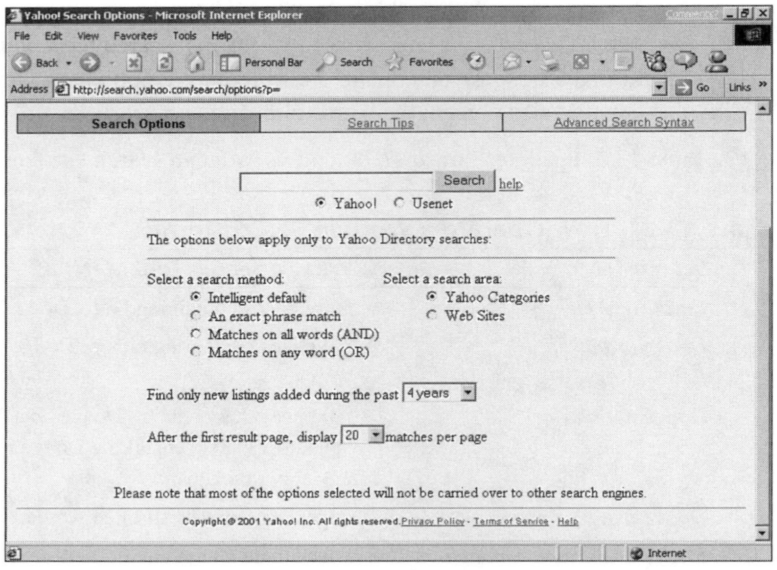

FIGURE 13.17
Click the Advanced Search link near Yahoo!'s search term box to learn how Yahoo! supports operators and other advanced search techniques.

When you use multiple words and don't include operators, most search engines assume you mean to put "and" between words. (See, you are using operators, even if you don't know it.)

For example, if you use the term *candy corn*, most search engines assume you mean "candy *and* corn" and match only pages that contain both words.

Some engines will apply *and* first, and then use *or*. The *"and"* hits go to the top of the hit list, and the *"or"* hits go to the bottom, as lower-rated hits.

Conducting a Super Search

In high school, they warned you that you'd need algebra one day. If you ignored that warning (like I did), then you've forgotten all of that stuff about grouping parts of equations in parentheses.

If you remember algebra, then note that you can apply those techniques for super searches. For example, suppose you wanted to find pages about pro boxers (the kind that hit each other). You would need a hit list that matched all pages with *boxer* or *prizefighter*, but eliminated any that matched *dog* (to weed out the boxer dog pages). You could do that with either of the following algebraic terms:

(boxer or prizefighter) not dog

(boxer not dog) or prizefighter

If you can apply these techniques, drop your old math teacher a note of thanks for a job well done.

About Site Searches

The major search sites mentioned in this hour are for finding information that may reside anywhere on the Web. Because they have that enormous job to do, they can't always find everything that's on a particular server.

However, large Web sites often provide their own search tools, just for finding stuff on that site alone. For example, Microsoft's Web site is huge, encompassing thousands of pages. So Microsoft supplies a search tool (you can open it from a SEARCH link atop most pages) just for finding stuff at Microsoft. Even fairly small sites may have their own search tools; Figure 13.18 shows one for *Discover* magazine.

You use a site's search tool just as you would any search site, by entering a search term. Many such search tools even support multi-word searches and operators—but always check the instructions accompanying the search tool to find out whether it supports fancy searches.

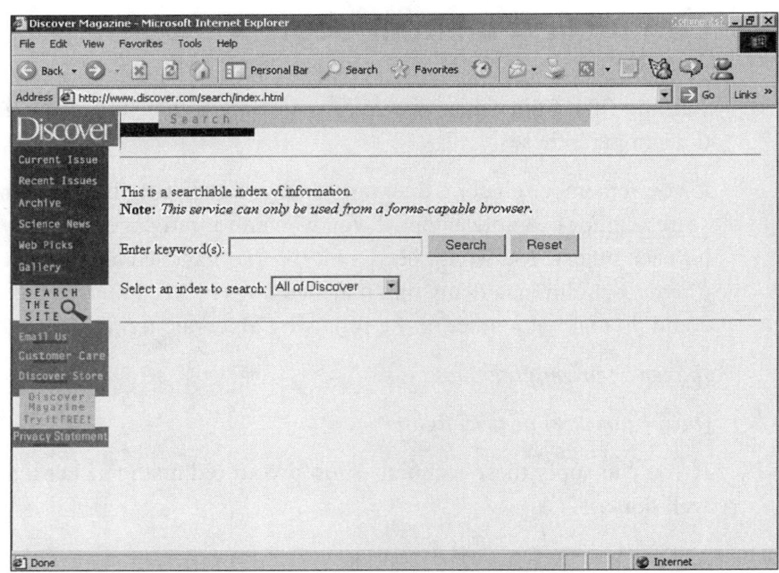

FIGURE 13.18
Discover *magazine supplies its own search tool just for finding stuff on its site.*

Summary

Most of the time, a search is a snap. Just type a likely sounding word in any search tool's text box, click the submit button, and wait for your hits. But the more you know about narrowing your searches by choosing just the right word, using multiple words, and using operators, the better your odds of always finding exactly what you're looking for.

Q&A

Q When searching for a name, like "Bill Clinton," should I use that old last-name-first gag and use *Clinton, Bill* as my search term?

A It doesn't matter. Search tools pretty much ignore commas, so whichever way you do it, the tool sees *Bill and Clinton* and comes up with the same hits. By the way, if you're searching for whom I think you're searching for, note that A) He's not the only Bill Clinton in the world, and B) He sometimes goes by William, not Bill. The term *President Clinton* is a better choice.

Q Why would I ever need more than one search site? Can't I just pick my favorite, and always use it?

A Every search site has a different database, and uses a different technical method for extracting results from that database. Although there will be overlap, you'll never see the same results from two different search sites.

Sure, if you have a search site you're comfortable with, it makes sense to try it first. But to ensure the best hope of finding exactly what you're looking for, it's important that you know how to get to several different search sites, and how to operate each one.

Portals such as MSN and Netcenter can make trying the same term in multiple search sites easier, as can Internet Explorer's search sites in its Explorer bar or Netscape Navigator's Related Sites.

Q I like exploring Yahoo!'s directory, but find it tiresome after exploring one branch to Back my way back upward a few levels to try another route. Is there a shortcut?

A If you look carefully at any listing in Yahoo!, you'll notice that a complete path appears in a large heading at the top, showing the full list, left to right, of the category and subcategories under which the list you're viewing appears. You can click on the name of any subcategory in that path to jump directly back to that subcategory's listing.

Hour 14

Downloading Programs and Files

The huge, diverse group of people who use the Internet have only one thing universally in common: They all use a computer. So it's no surprise that computer programs and files are the most common "things" you can acquire through the Internet. You can find online all kinds of Internet software, other kinds of programs (like games or word processors), documents (such as books or articles), and other useful files such as utilities and plug-ins.

To find a particular file or program you want, you can apply the search techniques you've already picked up in Hour 13, "Searching for Information." But in this hour, you'll learn how to use search techniques that are better focused and faster so that you can find exactly the files you want. You'll also learn all about *downloading* the files you'll find, and about preparing those files for use on your computer.

At the end of the hour, you'll be able to answer the following questions:

- What's downloading?
- What kinds of files can I download and use on my computer?

- Where are the sites that can help me find and download files, and how do I use them?
- What's a compressed archive—or *Zip* file—and what must I do with it before it will work on my computer?
- What's a computer virus, and how can I avoid catching one when downloading files?

What's Downloading, Anyhow?

Downloading is the act of copying a computer file from a server, through the Net, to your computer so you can use it there, just as if you had installed it from a disk or CD-ROM. (Incidentally, you can also *upload*—send a file *to* a server. You can learn about that in Appendix B, "Tools for the Serious User: FTP and Telnet.")

Click a Link, Get a File

Whether you've thought about it or not, when you're on the Web, you're really downloading all the time. For example, every time you open a Web page, the files that make up that page are temporarily copied from the server to your computer.

But here we're talking more deliberate downloading: You locate a link in a Web page that points to a file or program you want (see Figure 14.1). To download the file, click the link, and then follow any prompts that appear. It's really that simple.

> Observe that most of the file links in Figure 14.1 have the filename extension `.zip`. This extension indicates that these files are compressed archive files, also known as *Zip* files. You'll learn more about Zip files later in this hour.

How Long Does Downloading Take?

The larger the file, the longer it will take to download. That's why the size of the file is usually shown somewhere in or near the link for downloading it (refer to Figure 14.1). The size is expressed in kilobytes (K or KB) for smaller files, or in megabytes (M or MB) for larger files. One M equals 1,024K.

How long does it take to download a file of a given size? That depends on many factors, including the speed of your Internet connection, and how busy the server is. But over a connection of 28.8Kbps, a 1MB file typically downloads in around 10 minutes, give or take.

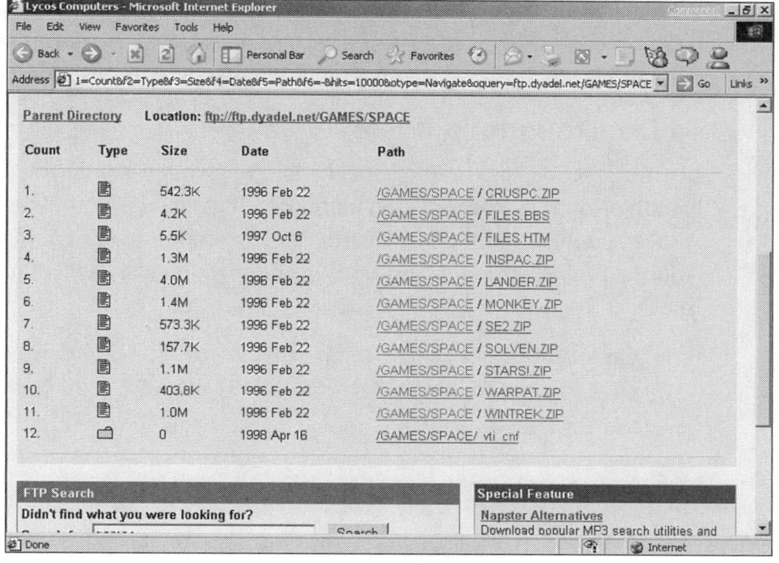

FIGURE 14.1
You can download files from the Web simply by clicking links that lead to files, such as those shown here.

You might expect that downloading a file through a 56Kbps connection would take half as much time as doing so through a 28.8Kbps connection, but that's never the case.

Even in the best case, current regulations limit the download speed over phone lines to 53Kbps, even if the modem handles 56Kbps. More importantly, a noisy phone or other factors can make a 56Kbps modem perform way below its top speed.

Finally, other factors—pauses in the downloading caused by overly busy servers, the speed of your computer's hard disk, and so on—can affect download speed.

In general, though, the faster your connection, the faster the download. A cable or DSL connection allows downloads to occur much more quickly than a dial-up connection.

You'll find lots of great stuff to download that's less than 1MB. However, many programs or multimedia files can be much, much larger. A download of the entire Internet Explorer program from Microsoft's Web site can take several hours, even through a 56Kbps connection.

With experience, you'll develop a sense of how long downloading a file of a given size takes on your system. After you have that sense, always carefully consider the size of the file and whether you want to wait that long for it, before starting the download.

To Do: Download a File

Just for practice, and to understand what to do when you locate a file you want, download the Adobe Acrobat reader, a program that enables you to display documents in the Adobe Acrobat (`.pdf`) file format, which are common online. If you already have an Adobe Acrobat reader, or just don't want one, you can cancel the download before it finishes.

1. Go to Adobe's Web site at `www.adobe.com`, scroll to the bottom of the page, and click the button labeled Get Acrobat Reader (see Figure 14.2).

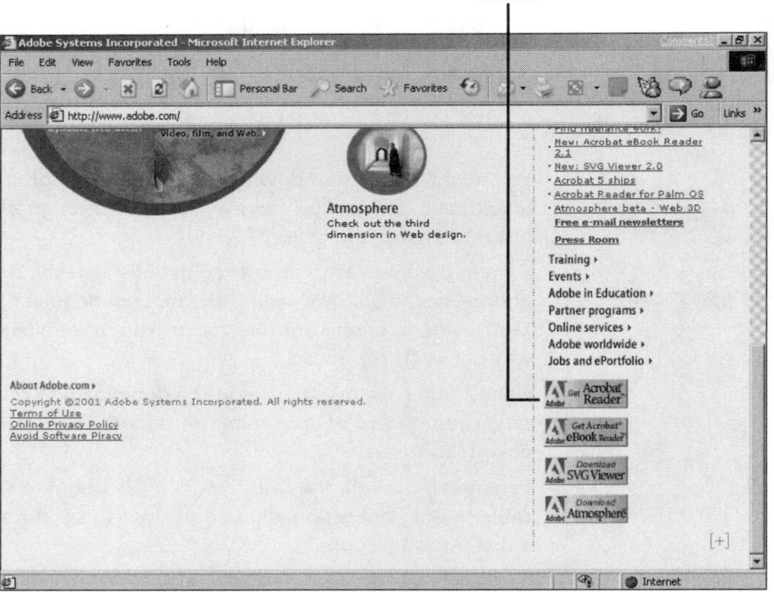

FIGURE 14.2
Step 1: Click the Get Acrobat Reader icon.

2. The first page you see (see Figure 14.3) will compare Acrobat Reader's functions with the full-featured Adobe Acrobat, which costs $249 retail. Because we just want to download a free program for now, click Get Acrobat Reader at the bottom of the page.
3. Complete the choices on the form, and then click the Download button (see Figure 14.4).

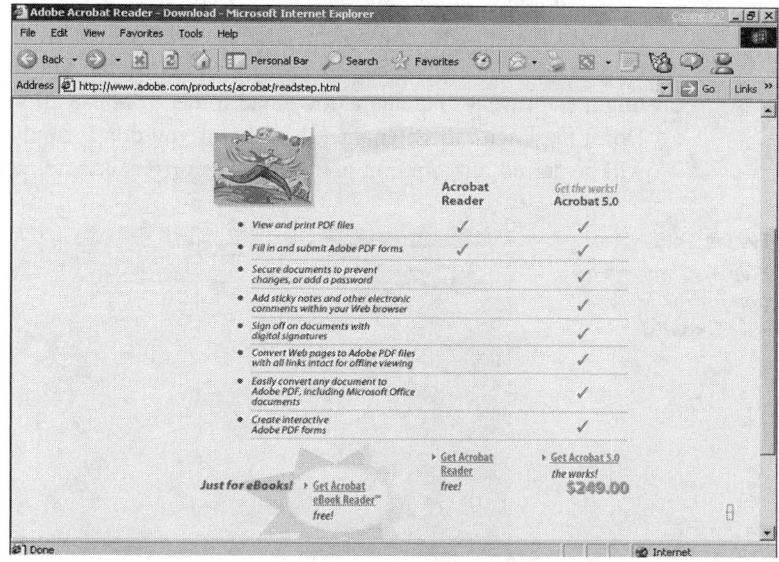

FIGURE 14.3
***Step 2:** Click the Get Acrobat Reader button.*

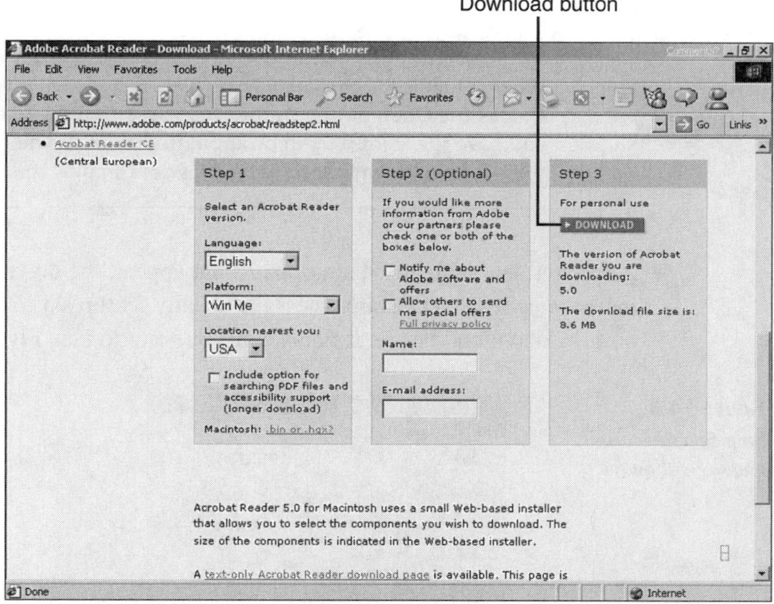

FIGURE 14.4
***Step 3:** Fill in the form, and click Download.*

4. The exact dialog boxes you'll see differ by browser and computer type. Sometimes you may be asked whether you want to save it or run it from its current location.

Usually it's smartest to choose the Save option, and then to open the file later. The next dialog box you might see prompts you to select the location (folder or desktop) and filename for the downloaded file (see Figure 14.5). Choosing a location is a good idea so that you can easily locate and use the file after downloading (you might even want to create a download folder to house all your downloaded files). Don't mess with the filename, though—if you don't supply a new filename, the file will be stored on your computer under its original name, which is usually best.

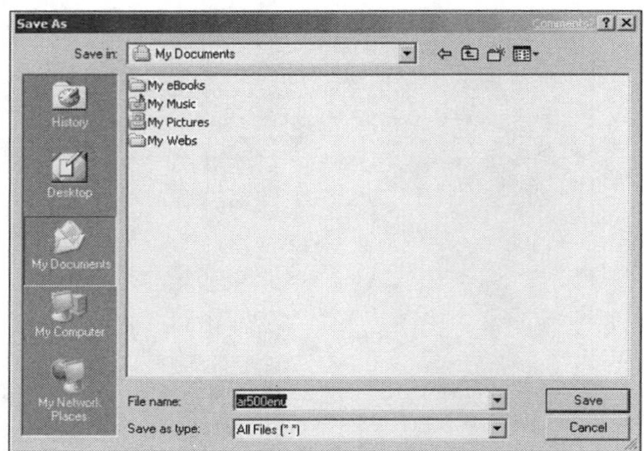

FIGURE 14.5
Step 4: *Choose a location for the file and save it to disk.*

When a link leads to a media file, such as a sound or video clip, you can choose the Open option (rather than Save to disk) when downloading. If you have the right plug-in program to play that type of file, as soon as the file has been downloaded, your browser can play the file automatically.

5. After you deal with any dialog boxes that appear, the download begins, and a status message appears. The status message usually features a Cancel button, so you can quit the download before it finishes if you want to (see Figure 14.6).

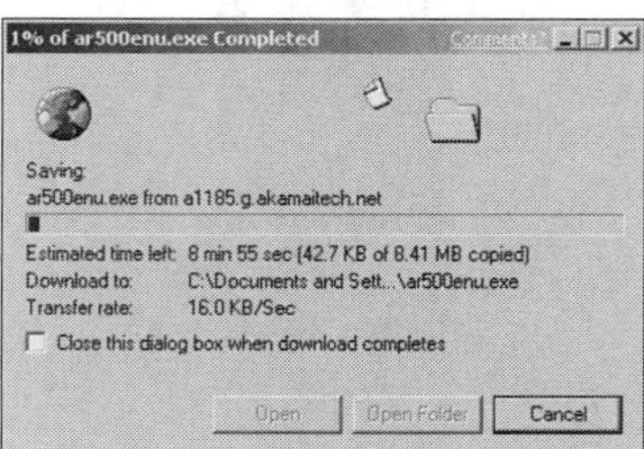

FIGURE 14.6
Step 5: *The status message appears.*

When the download is complete, the status message disappears. You can continue browsing or go use the file you just downloaded, which you can find in the folder you selected in the dialog box described in step 4.

In the download status message, some browsers also display an estimate of how much longer the download will take to finish. Although that estimate can be handy, it's just a guess, and should not be taken as an exact prediction of how long the download will take.

Choosing Files You Can Use

You can download any type of computer file. But not every file or program you find online works on every type of computer.

"Duh!" you might think. But you'd be surprised how often people forget this. Web browsing enables different kinds of computers to all look at the same online content, so after a while people tend to forget that on the Web, PCs, Macs, and other types of computers each use different kinds of files and programs.

When you search for files and programs, you must make sure that the ones you choose are compatible with your computer type, and often also with your operating system (Windows 95/98/Me/NT/2000/XP; DOS; Mac OS9 or OS X; UNIX flavor; and so on).

The Two File Types: Program and Data

Although there are dozens of different types of files, they all generally fall into either of two groups:

- **Program files.** A program file contains a program—a game, a word processor, a plug-in, a utility, and so on. Program files are almost always designed to run on only one type of computer and operating system. For example, a program file designed for a Mac typically will not run in Windows. However, many programs are available in similar but separate versions, one for each system type.
- **Data files.** A data file contains information that can be displayed, or used in some other way, by a program. For example, a word processing document is a data file, to be displayed by a word processing program. Like program files, some data files can be used only by a particular program running on a particular computer type. But most data file types can be used on a variety of systems.

Popular files are usually available from multiple servers, spread across the continent or globe. Often, a downloading page will refer to the servers as *mirror sites* because they all offer an identical copy of the file, a "mirror image."

Common Data File Types on the Net

When you encounter a link to a file, you'll usually have no trouble telling what system the file is made for.

Often, before arriving at the link, you will have navigated through a series of links or form selections in which you specified your system type, so when you finally see links to files, they all point to files that can run on your system. In other cases, the link itself—or text near the link—will tell you the system requirements for the file.

System requirements. The computer type, operating system, and (for a data file) program required to use a particular file. Some files you'll encounter have special hardware requirements as well, such as a particular amount of memory.

Even when the link doesn't fill you in, you can often tell a file's system requirements by its filename extension, the final part of the filename that follows the period. (For example, in the filename `MONTY.DOC`, the extension is `DOC`.) Table 14.1 shows many of the most common file types online.

Data files can often be converted and used by programs other than those in which they were created. For example, nearly all full-featured word processing programs can convert Microsoft Word (`.doc`) files so you can read or edit them. Most spreadsheet programs can handle an Excel or Lotus 1-2-3 file.

If you lack the required program for using a particular kind of data file, check out any similar program you already own to see whether it can convert a file of that type.

TABLE 14.1 Common File Types You'll Find Online for Downloading

Extension	*Type of File*	*Requirements*
`.exe`, `.com`	Program file (a game, utility,	Runs on one (and only one) type of system. Always read any text near the link to be sure that a

TABLE 14.1 continued

Extension	*Type of File*	*Requirements*
	application, and so on)	particular `.exe` or `.com` file will run on your computer.
`.doc`	Word document	Can be opened and edited in either the Windows or Mac version of Word, or Windows' WordPad program.
`.pdf`	Adobe Acrobat document	Can be opened in the Adobe Acrobat Reader program (available for a variety of systems) or in a browser equipped with an Adobe Acrobat plug-in. Can also be converted and displayed by some word processing programs.
`.xls`	Excel spreadsheet	Can be opened and edited in either the Windows or Mac version of Excel.
`.txt`, `.asc`	Plain text file	Can be opened in any word processor or text editor (such as Windows' Notepad) on any system, and displayed by any browser.
`.wri`	Windows Write document	Can be displayed by Windows Write (in Windows 3.1) or WordPad (in Windows 95/98/NT/XP).
`.avi`, `.mp3`, `.mov`, `.qt`, `.mpg`, `.au`, `.mid`, `.snd`	Various types of media files	Can be run by various player programs, or by your browser if it is equipped for them.
`.zip`	Archive, containing one or more compressed files	Must be decompressed (*unzipped*) before the files it contains can be used; see "Working with Zip Files" later in this Hour.

Very few program files are designed to run on both Macs and PCs. However, if you use a PC, you should know that some programs work in multiple PC operating systems. For example, there are programs written to run in both Windows 3.1 and Windows 95/98/Me, and sometimes DOS, as well.

By and large, programs written just for DOS or Windows 3.1 will also run in Windows 95 or NT, although the reverse is never true. And most Windows 95 programs will run in Windows 98/Me or NT (or later versions of Windows), but some NT programs will not run in Windows 95. A very few specialized utility programs written for Windows 98/Me/2000/XP will not run in Windows 95.

If you use a PowerPC-based Mac, you know that you can run some Windows programs on your Mac using a Windows "emulator." You probably also know that those programs do not run as well there as native Mac programs do.

A program always runs best on the system for which it was written, so favor choices that match what you have. And even if you have a PowerPC-based Mac, always favor true Mac files over PC versions.

Finding Sites That Help You Find Files

Where you begin looking for a file depends on the manner in which that file is offered on the Web, or rather, in what way that file is licensed for use by those other than its creator. Most software falls into one of the following four groups:

- **Commercial.** The programs you can buy in a box at the software store. Many software companies have Web sites where you can learn about their products and often download them as well. Typically, you fill in an online form to pay for the software, and then download it.
- **Demo.** Demo software is commercial software that has some features disabled, or automatically stops working—*expires*—after you use it for a set number of days. Demo software is distributed free on commercial and shareware sites and provides a free preview of the real thing.
- **Shareware.** Shareware is software you're allowed to try out for free, but for which you are supposed to pay. After the trial period (usually 30 days), you either pay the programmer or stop using the program. Some shareware expires or has features disabled, like demo software, so you can't continue using it without paying.
- **Freeware.** Freeware is free software you can use all you want, as long as you want, for free.

Appendix A, "Fun Web Sites to Visit," shows the URLs of a great selection of sites for getting shareware, freeware, and commercial software.

All-Purpose Shareware Sites

Sites for downloading shareware appear all over the Web. Many popular shareware programs have their very own Web sites, and links to shareware products can be found on thousands of pages, such as Yahoo!'s shareware directory at

`www.yahoo.com/Computers_and_Internet/Software/Shareware/`

But when you're looking for a shareware, freeware, or demo program to do a particular job, you'll have better luck if you visit a Web site designed to provide access to a wide range of products, sites such as

- **Shareware.com,** whose easy-to-remember URL is `shareware.com` (see Figure 14.7).
- **Download.com.** (Can you guess the URL?)

These sites are much like the search tools you used in Hour 13, providing search term boxes, directories, and other tools for finding files. But the hits they produce are always either links to files that match your search, or links to other Web pages from which those files can be downloaded.

Shareware.com and Download.com are good places to find all sorts of software, including Internet client software, such as a new browser, FTP client (see Appendix B), or Web authoring tool (see Hour 19, "Creating Web Pages and Multimedia Messages").

But a more efficient way to find and download Internet client software is to go to the Tucows directory at `www.tucows.com`, which is a special directory of Internet client software.

The key to using Shareware.com, Download.com, and similar file-finders is to make sure that your search specifies both of the following:

- **The kind of file or program you seek**. Email, word processing, game, paint program—whatever you want.
- **Your computer type and operating system**. Windows 95/98/Me/XP, Mac OS8/OS9/OS X, and so on.

If you include this information in your search, the hit list will show only files and programs of the kind you want, and only those that run on your particular system.

Sites like Shareware.com don't actually store on their own servers the thousands of files to which they offer links. Rather, they find and show you links that lead to files stored on other servers and mirror sites for those other servers (see Figure 14.7).

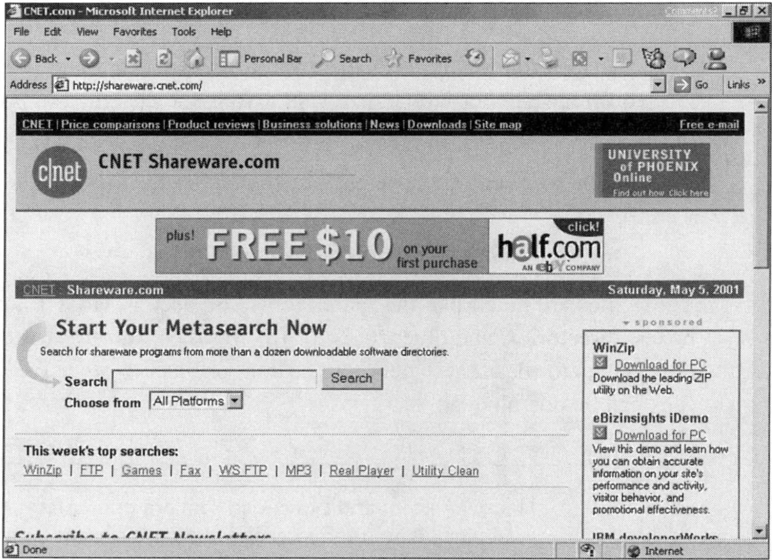

FIGURE 14.7
Shareware.com, a directory for finding shareware, freeware, and demo software.

If it's mainstream, commercial software you want to buy—you know, the stuff you buy in a box at the software store—check out one of the online software shops, such as Beyond.com (`beyond.com`) or MicroWarehouse (`warehouse.com`).

For practice, try finding a solitaire game for your system at Shareware.com, in the following To Do.

To Do: Find a Program on Shareware.com

1. Go to Shareware.com at `www.shareware.com`, type **`solitaire`** in the box labeled Search For, choose your system type from the By Platform list, and then click the Search button (see Figure 14.8).

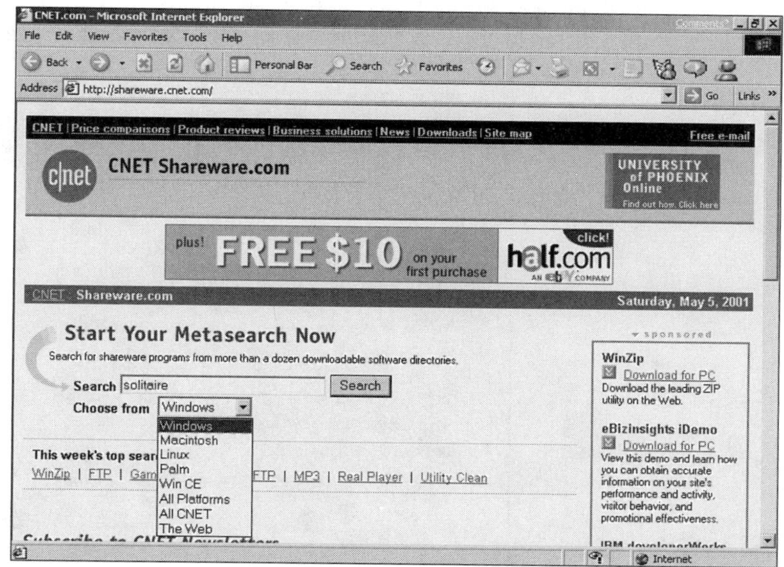

FIGURE 14.8
Step 1: Type in **`solitaire`** *at Shareware.com and choose an operating system.*

2. Read the descriptions of the solitaire programs for your system type, choose a program that you'd like to have, and click its filename (see Figure 14.9).

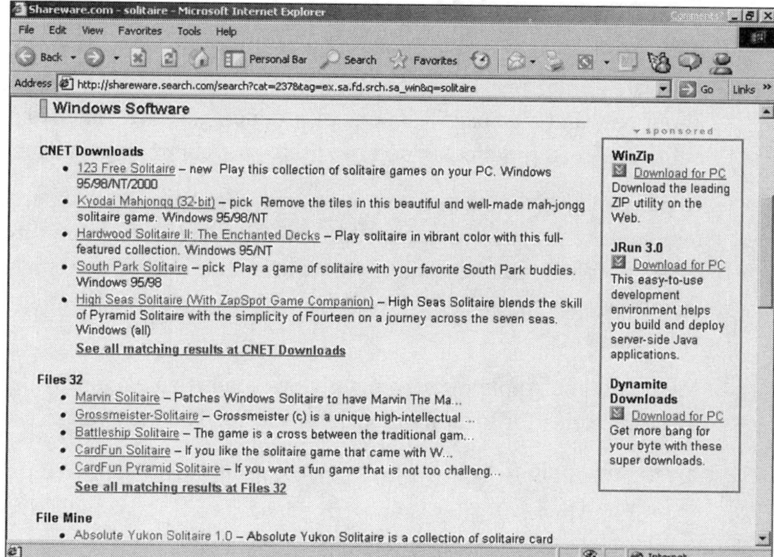

FIGURE 14.9
Step 2: Choose a program that looks interesting and click on it.

3. A page appears with a description of the program. Click on the Download Now link, and a new list of links appears, each link pointing to the identical file stored on a different server. Click one to start the download (see Figure 14.10).

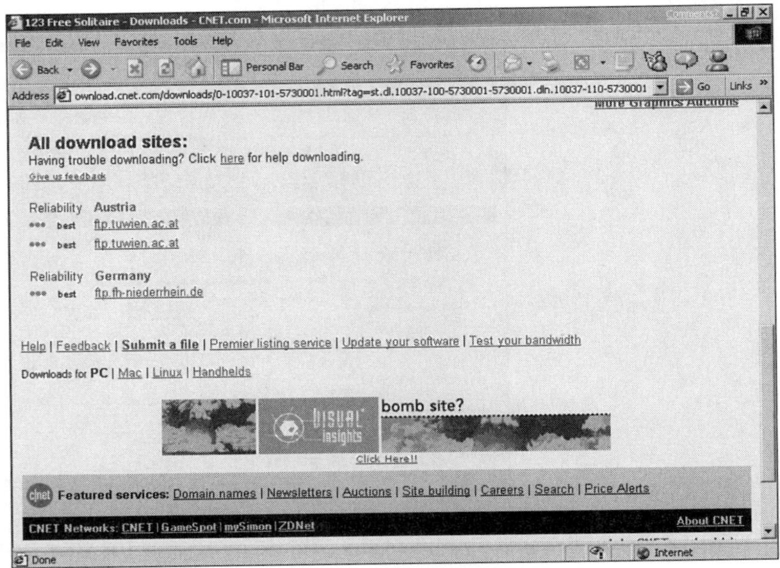

FIGURE 14.10
Step 3: Choose a site from which to download the program.

Commercial Software Sites

As a Web user, you have a lot to gain by frequenting the Web sites of any commercial software companies whose products you use regularly. There, you can not only learn about new and enhanced versions of products you use, but also pick up tips, free enhancements, product support, and fixes for common problems.

In particular, it's important to know about the Web site of the maker of the operating system you use on your computer: Microsoft's site (for Windows users) and Apple's (for Mac OS folks). On these sites, you can find all sorts of free updates and utilities for your operating system, fixes for problems, and news about upcoming new releases and enhancements.

Microsoft and Apple offer so many downloads that each provides its own search tools and directories for locating the file you need. The best places to start

- For Apple files is `www.apple.com/support/` (see Figure 14.11).
- For Microsoft files is `www.microsoft.com/downloads/` (see Figure 14.12).

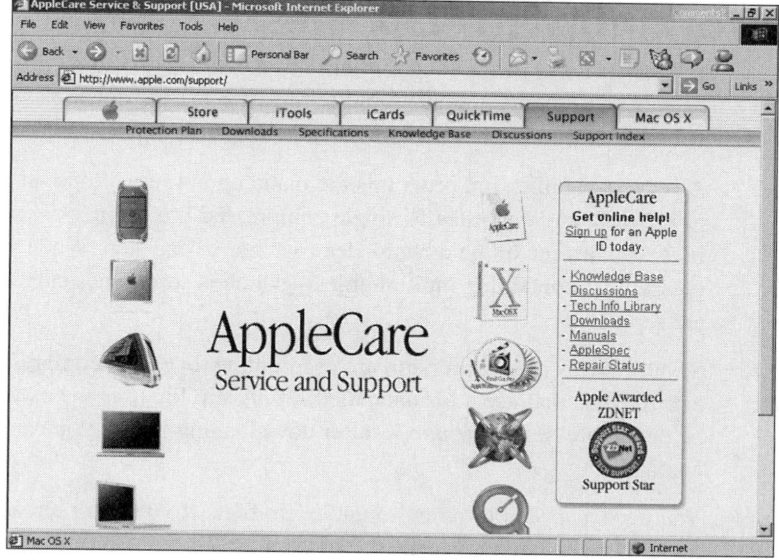

FIGURE 14.11
Apple's support site offers a wealth of free files for Mac users.

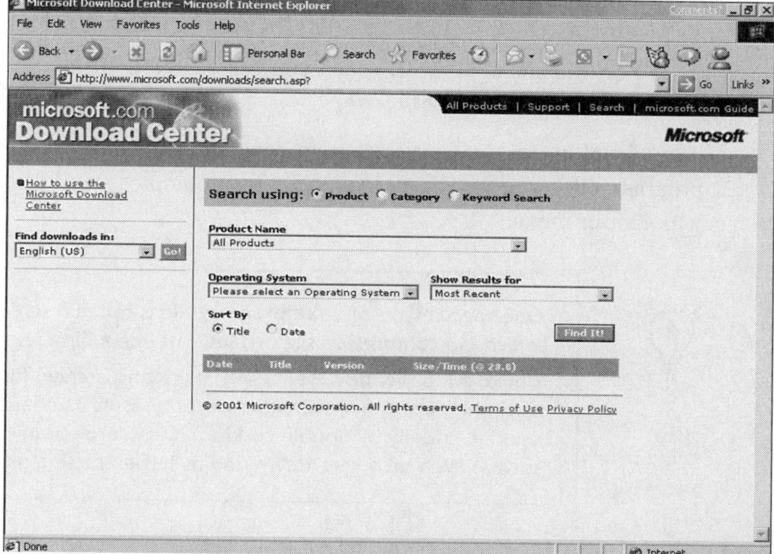

FIGURE 14.12
See Microsoft's free downloads page to pick up all sorts of handy freebies.

Working with Zip Files

The larger a file is, the longer it takes to download. So some files online are *compressed*—converted into smaller files—to cut the download time. After downloading, you must decompress a compressed file to restore it to its original size and use it.

Also, most application programs are made up not just of one fat file, but of a collection of program and data files. A single compressed file can pack together many separate files, so they can all be downloaded together in one step. When you decompress a compressed file containing multiple files—which is sometimes called an *archive*—the files are separated.

Several forms of compression are used online, but most compression programs create archive files that use a format called Zip. A Zip file uses the extension `.zip`, and it must be decompressed—*unzipped*—after downloading before you can use the file or files it contains.

You need a special program to unzip Zip files. If you don't already have one, the most popular shareware unzippers

- For Windows are WinZip, which you can download from `www.winzip.com`, or PKZip, which you can get from PKWare at `www.pkware.com`.
- For Macintosh is ZipIt, which you can download from `http://www.maczipit.com/`.

After installing an unzipping program, you can decompress any Zip file by opening the program, choosing the Zip file you want to decompress, and then choosing Extract from a toolbar or menu.

One special type of `.exe` program file is called a *self-extracting archive,* which is a compressed file or files, just like a Zip file.

Unlike a Zip file, however, a self-extracting archive file does not require an unzipping program. Instead, it decompresses itself automatically when you open it (usually by double-clicking). Most large applications offered online, such as Web browsers, download as self-extracting archives.

Watching Out for Viruses

A few years back, in the movie *Independence Day*, Jeff Goldblum stopped an intergalactic invasion by uploading a computer virus into the aliens' mothership and thereby scrambling the alien system.

NEW TERM **Computer virus.** Program code secretly added to, or attached to, a file or email message that makes mischief when the file or message is opened. Often, the virus is designed to reproduce and spread itself from the file it travels in—its host file—to other files.

Computer viruses are created by immature, sick people, who get a thrill out of cheap little tricks—viruses that display silly messages on your screen—or major attacks—viruses that crash whole computer systems.

If you saw *Independence Day*, you might have wondered, "If Jeff Goldblum puts a virus on the Internet, and I happen to download a file containing that virus, what might happen to my computer? Would I still be able to conquer Earth? Can I get Jeff to come over and fix it?"

Viruses are a significant threat to anyone who spends time online, uses email, and downloads files. It's just plain silly to work on the Internet and not arm yourself with some protection.

You can catch a virus from files you download, *and* from email messages (and files attached to email messages).The key rule when it comes to email is to never open any message or open any file from someone you don't know.

To play it safe, try to limit your downloading choices to commercial sites or reliable shareware sources (such as Shareware.com). Big suppliers regularly scan files for viruses. In addition to exercising caution about where you download files from, you should also install and use a virus scanning program, such as Norton AntiVirus, which can find viruses in files and, in some cases, kill the virus while saving the file. And, make sure to keep your antivirus software current by regularly downloading the updates to it from the manufacturer.

If you intend to scan for viruses, DO NOT open or run a file you have downloaded until AFTER you have used your antivirus software to check it for viruses.

Remember: A virus in a file does no harm until you open the file (or run the program, if the file is a program). So you can download anything safely, and then scan it with the virus program before you ever open or run it. If the virus program detects a bug it cannot remove, just delete the file to delete the virus.

Downloading Files in AOL

Members of America Online have a special advantage in the area of downloads: AOL's Download Center. After signing on to AOL, you can access it by opening the AOL Services menu and selecting Download Center (see Figure 14.13).

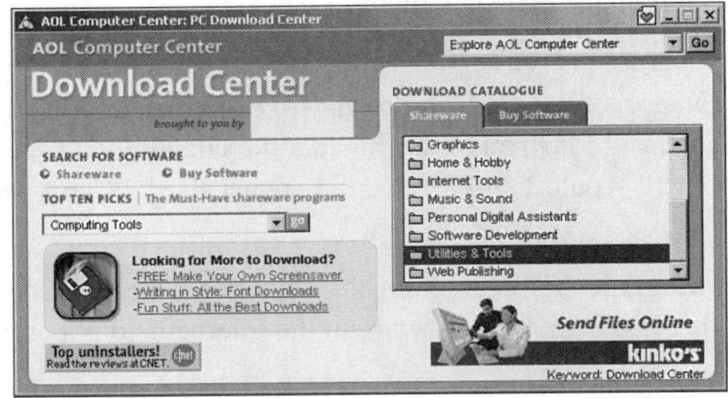

FIGURE 14.13
AOL's Download Center offers links to all sorts of files and programs.

The right window offers two tabs: Shareware and Buy Software. The Buy Software tab connects you to commercial software, whereas the Shareware tab links to, well, shareware.

Both tabs are organized into catalogues that are full of software you can download. After you've chosen the type of file that you want, you'll find a list of files that will fit your needs.

America Online also offers a feature that's great for people who don't want to take the time to download a file during their online session. You can schedule a download for later by selecting the file(s) you want and clicking the Download Later button. Then, you can schedule the download for the middle of the night, when you're (perhaps) asleep.

Summary

Finding the files you need begins with starting at the right site: a commercial software site, a shareware search site, and so on. When you start in the right place, and understand the simple steps required to select, download, and (sometimes) unzip files, getting any files you want is a snap.

Q&A

Q While a file is downloading, can I do other things on my computer, like browse other pages or run another program?

A Most browsers built for Windows 95/98/Me/XP, or Mac 0S8, OS9, or OS X permit you to continue browsing during a download. When using one of these browsers—which include Internet Explorer and Netscape Navigator—you can explore another page, or even start another download, while one download is in progress. The more memory you have in your computer, the better this works. (Don't even *try* it if your computer has less than 32MB of RAM—it'll act like you're standing on its lungs.)

However, regardless of how much memory you have, I always recommend that you leave your computer alone while downloading. Go get coffee, or play with the kids or something, until the download is complete. Using your computer for any other task—even an offline one—slows down both the download and whatever else you're doing, and raises the likelihood that the download might fail partway through, forcing you to start the download over again.

Hour 15

Finding People

Using mainly the search techniques you've picked up in the preceding hours, you can find people on the Internet—or rather, the email addresses, mailing addresses, or telephone numbers through which particular people can be reached.

This people-finding power is one of the Internet's most valuable and controversial capabilities. Applied properly, it can aid research, locate missing persons, track down deadbeats delinquent in their child support payments, reunite old friends, and even help adult adoptees find their birth parents, if they so desire. When abused, this capability aids stalkers and overaggressive direct marketers. Unfortunately, as is always the case with freedom of information, there's no practical way to preserve the benefit of this capability without also enabling its abuse.

At the end of the hour, you'll be able to answer the following questions:

- Where on the Web are search tools I can use to find the addresses, phone numbers, or email addresses of folks I want to contact?
- How do I use a people-finding search tool on the Web?

- How do I use the people-finder that's built in to Internet Explorer?
- How can I also use a people-finding search tool from within my email program?

Throughout this book, I show screen images to illustrate an activity. But in this hour, although I show you how to perform people searches, I never show the *results* of a people search. Some of the "found" people might not appreciate their information published in a book!

Finding the People-Finding Sites

As with all types of search tools, every people-finder on the Web draws from a different database of names and contact information. Note that these tools don't find only people who have Internet accounts; they search public telephone directories, and thus can show you addresses and telephone numbers of people who wouldn't know the Internet if it snuck up and bit 'em.

In this hour, we'll cover people-finding methods and sites that are free on the Internet. There are a number of people finders that charge a fee. These can be useful for finding long-lost relatives or classmates, but they aren't necessarily better than the searching you do yourself. Do some research before paying for such a people-finding service.

For any particular name, a search using one tool may turn up no hits, while a search with a different tool may hit pay dirt. It's important to know where several different search tools are, so that if one tool fails, you can try another. Figure 15.1 shows a typical people-finder page.

If there's a possibility the person you seek has his or her own home page on the Web, using a special people-finding tool may not be necessary. It's usually a good idea to first perform an ordinary search with a tool like AltaVista or Excite, using the person's name (plus maybe the city or town they live in, to help narrow the search) as your search term.

Such a search will likely turn up that person's home page, if they have one (along with any references to other folks who have the same name, of course). If you visit the home page, you'll likely find contact information on it.

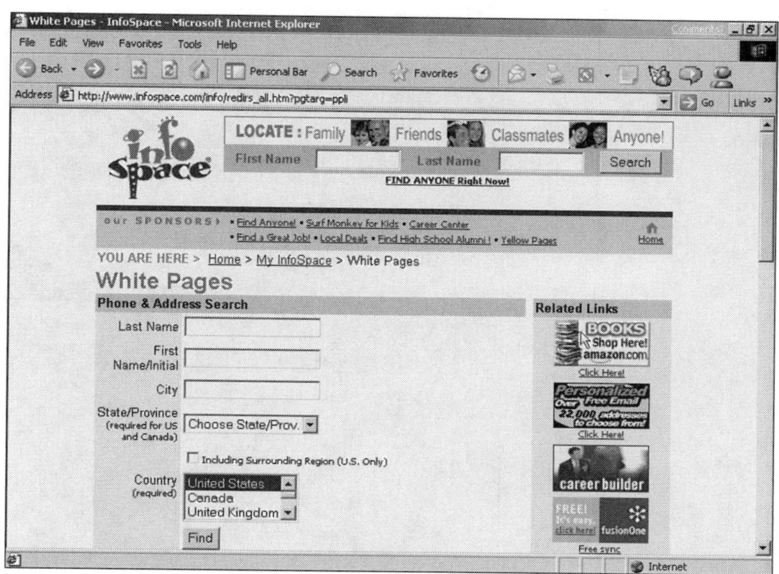

FIGURE 15.1
InfoSpace is one of several handy people-finders on the Web.

You use these tools like any other search tool: Enter as much as you know about the person—name, city, and so on—and the tool finds matches in its database. But that database contains only contact information, so your search won't turn up all sorts of references that have nothing to do with contacting someone.

Some of the better people-finders include the following:

- Yahoo!'s People Search, at `people.yahoo.com`
- Excite's Email Lookup (for email addresses), at `www.excite.com/reference/email_lookup/email`
- Bigfoot, at `www.Bigfoot.com`
- InfoSpace, at `www.infospace.com`

> Depending on the people-finder you use and the options you choose, you may find a person's mailing address, phone number, or email address (or all three). There's also a chance, of course, that you'll find no matches.

To Do: Find Yourself in Yahoo!'s People Search

Because you're probably already familiar with Yahoo!, Yahoo!'s People Search is a great first place to try finding someone.

1. Go to Yahoo!'s People Search at `people.yahoo.com` (see Figure 15.2).

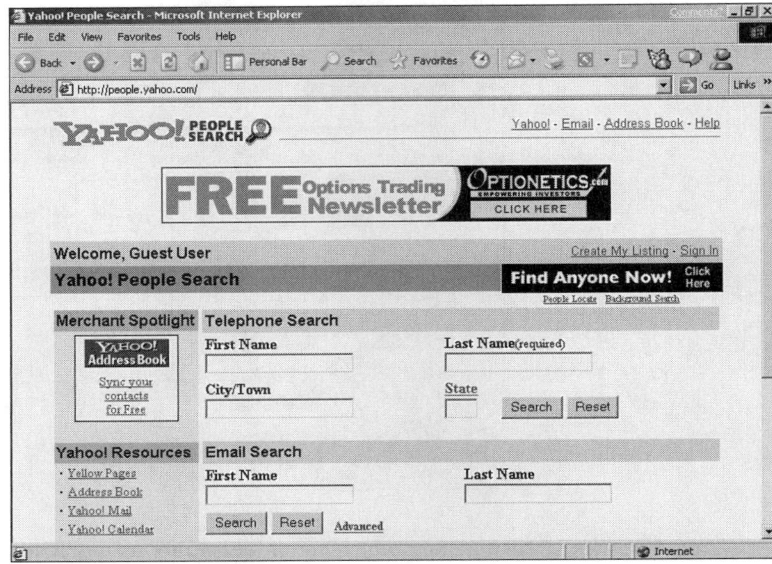

FIGURE 15.2
Step 1: *Go to Yahoo!'s People Search site.*

2. Fill in the boxes in the Telephone Search form: First Name, Last Name, City, and so on, and then click the button labeled Search (see Figure 15.3).

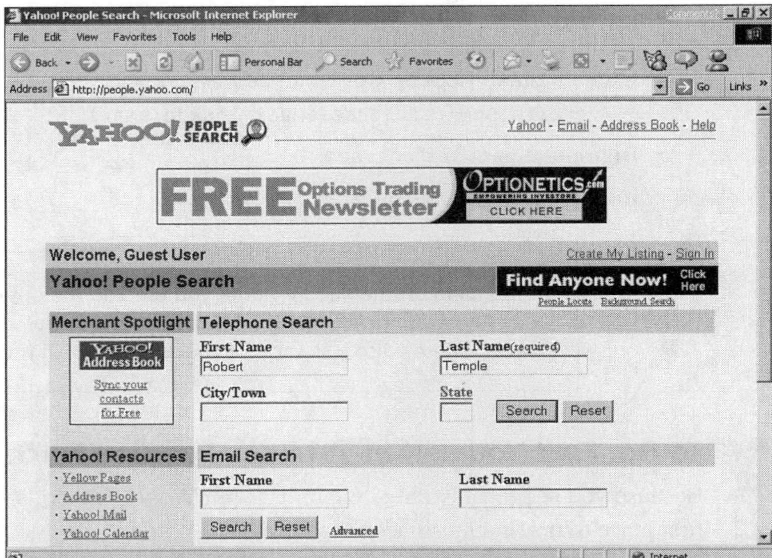

FIGURE 15.3
Step 2: *Fill in the Telephone Search form and click Search.*

3. On the list of matching names (not shown), click Back to return to the People Search page.
4. Now fill in the boxes under Email Search, and click the Search button (see Figure 15.4).

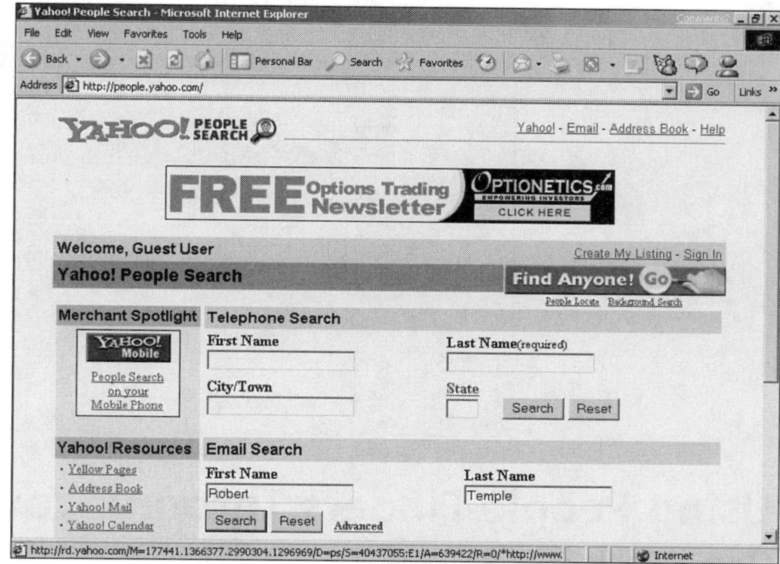

FIGURE 15.4
***Step 4:** Fill in the Email Search form and click Search.*

5. Just for fun, click Back to try another Email Search, but this time, leave some boxes empty, to see how these tools will show you more names to choose from when you don't have complete information about a person (see Figure 15.5).

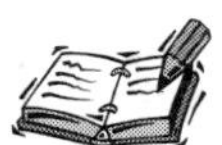

If you found yourself in your Yahoo! searches, you may be wondering, "How did my phone number, email address, or other information get on the Web?"

Most of the information in the search tool databases—including names, addresses, and phone numbers—comes from public telephone records. By agreeing to have your name, address, and phone number listed in the phone book, you've agreed to make it public, so there's nothing to prevent it from winding up in a Web database. Some databases may also obtain records from other online databases (such as your ISP's user directory), or even from online forms you've submitted from Web pages.

So even if you have an unlisted telephone number (which phone companies call "unpublished"), a record about you may find its way into a database from another source. That's just one reason you must be careful about how and when you enter information about yourself in an online form.

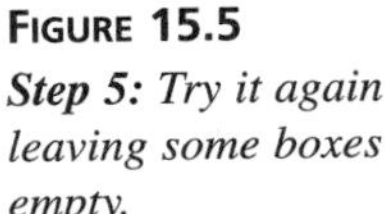

FIGURE 15.5
Step 5: *Try it again leaving some boxes empty.*

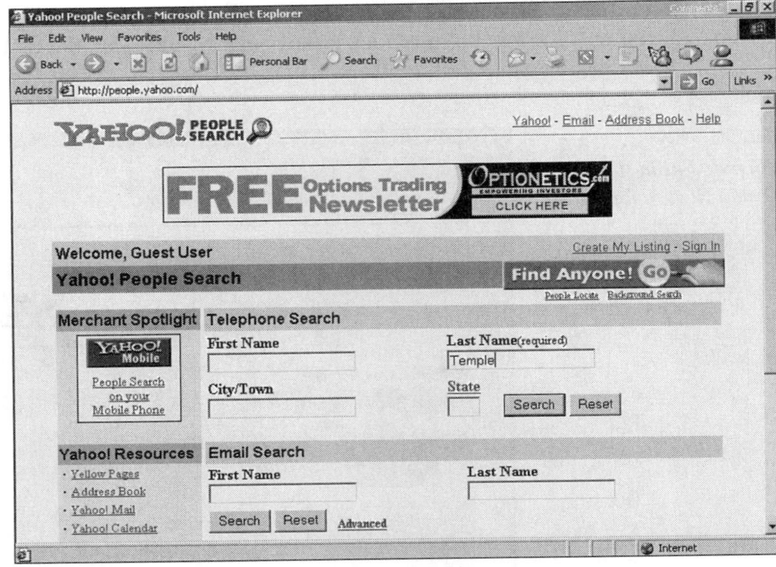

Using People-Finders Through Your Email Program

There is a family of people-finding directories, known collectively as *LDAP directories*, that are specifically and solely for finding email addresses, both in North America and worldwide.

NEW TERM **LDAP.** *Lightweight Directory Access Protocol*, a standard followed by some people-finders so that a single dialog box in an email program can be used to search LDAP directories.

Some LDAP directories, such as the aforementioned Bigfoot (`www.Bigfoot.com`) are accessible through a Web page. But these and several other LDAPs may also be accessed from within some email programs. This enables you to search for an email address from within your email program—which is, after all, the place you need email addresses.

The two email programs included in the big two Internet suites both support LDAP searches, from within their *address book*, a utility that helps you keep track of email addresses.

15

Searching an LDAP directory from within your email program is just like using a people-finder on the Web: You fill in a name and other information in a form. The only difference is in getting to that form. Instead of opening a Web page, you go online, open your email program, and navigate to the LDAP search form.

For example, in Outlook Express, click the Find button and choose People (see Figure 15.6). A search dialog opens. Use the top list in the dialog to choose the LDAP directory to search, fill in the other boxes in the dialog, and then click Find Now.

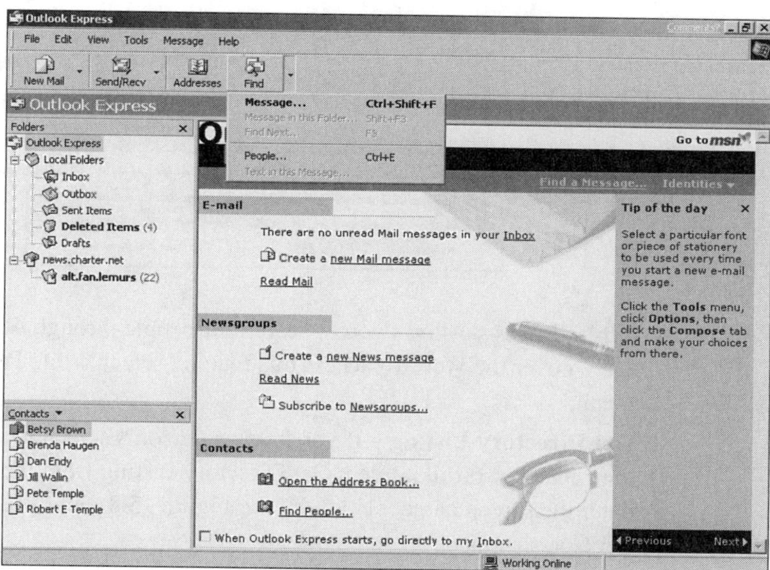

FIGURE 15.6
Searching an LDAP directory from within Outlook Express's Address Book.

Finding People in America Online

America Online members have an advantage when looking for others on the service—because America Online controls the database, it's easy to search.

However, the individual members are the ones who fill out their member profiles in AOL. So, the likelihood of your finding the person you're looking for depends directly on how well that particular member filled out their profile. Many people fill their profiles with jokes, making a serious attempt to find them unlikely to be successful (perhaps that's the point of the jokes!).

Another problem, of course, is the possibility that the person is not a member of AOL at all. If that's the case, you're just as well off to search using an LDAP directory over the Web.

There several different ways to find people through (and on) America Online. In addition, there are ways you can learn about people if you know their screen name but nothing else. Here are the options:

- **People Directory**—This allows you to search the AOL member directory through either a Quick Search or an Advanced Search (see Figure 15.7). You can search for specific things in a person's profile, such as a city of residence, or you can search by name. To access this feature, open the People menu and select People Directory.

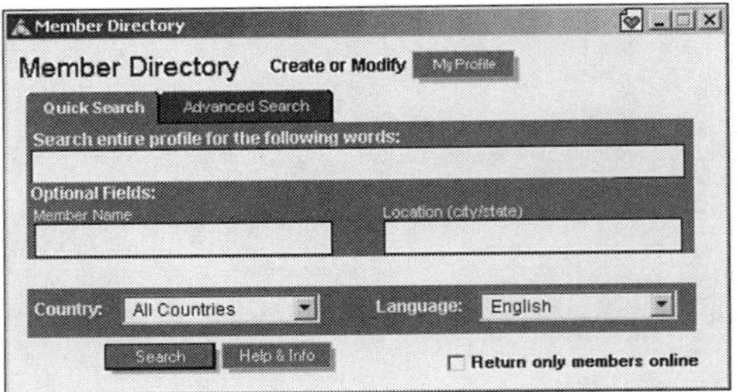

FIGURE 15.7 *Searching AOL's Member Directory can help you find another AOL member.*

- **White Pages**—Allows you to search for people through AOL. This is similar to a search over the Web. To access this feature, select White Pages from the People menu.
- **Get Directory Listing**—If you know a person's screen name and want to read their member profile, select Get Directory Listing from the People menu. Then, enter the screen name, click OK (see Figure 15.8), and you'll see the person's directory listing.

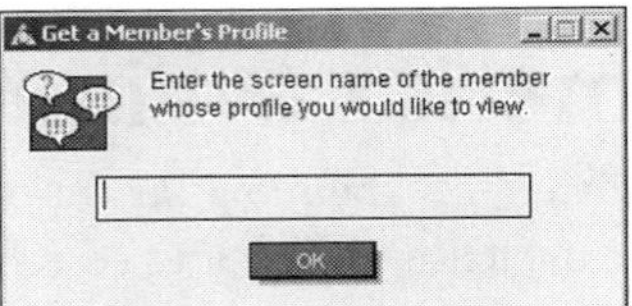

FIGURE 15.8 *If you know a person's screen name, you can enter it to get their member profile.*

- **Locate Member Online**—By selecting this option from the People menu, you can find out whether a given member is online at the present time. If you know the person's screen name, you enter it, and AOL will tell you what they are doing on the service at the moment.

Other Folk-Finding Tips

The all-around easiest ways to find people online are those I've already described. But if those don't pay off for you, try the following methods.

Try an Advanced Search

People-finders are designed first and foremost to be easy to use. For that reason, many do not display their most advanced tools at first. They present an easy-to-use, quick form for general-purpose people-searching, but also supply an optional, advanced form for more sophisticated searches. The advanced form comes in handy when the basic form doesn't dig up the person you want.

For example, on Yahoo!'s people-finder page, you'll see a link labeled Advanced, which brings up the Advanced search page shown in Figure 15.9.

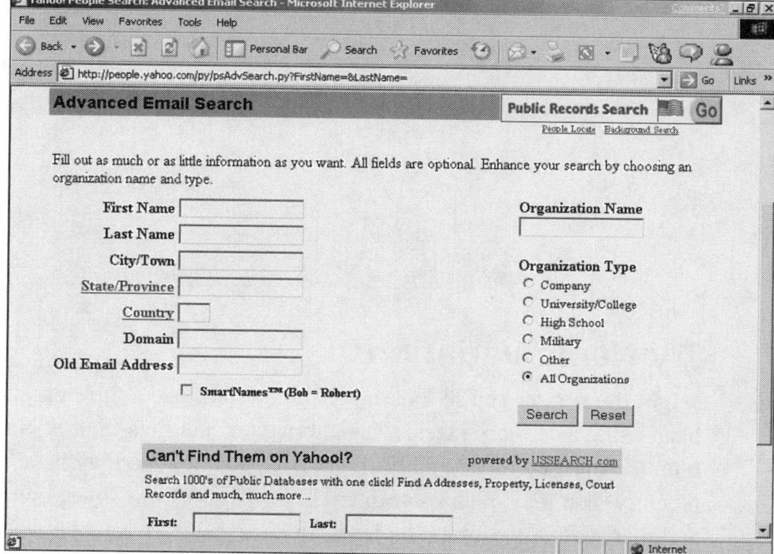

FIGURE 15.9
In addition to their basic, easy-to-use form, some people-finding tools also offer an advanced form for more sophisticated searches.

Besides providing you with more options for more narrowly identifying the person you're looking for, the Advanced search provides a check box for "SmartNames." When this check box is checked, Yahoo! searches not only for the exact name you supplied, but also for common variations of that name. If you entered "Edward," the search might match records for "Edward," "Ed," and "Eddy," too. This feature increases the chances of finding the right person when you're not sure which name form the person uses.

Use a Company or School Directory

Do you know the name of the company the person works for, or a school he or she attends? Many companies, colleges, and universities have their own Web sites, and those Web sites often contain employee and student directories you can browse or search (see Figure 15.10). Just search for and go to the Web site, then browse for a directory.

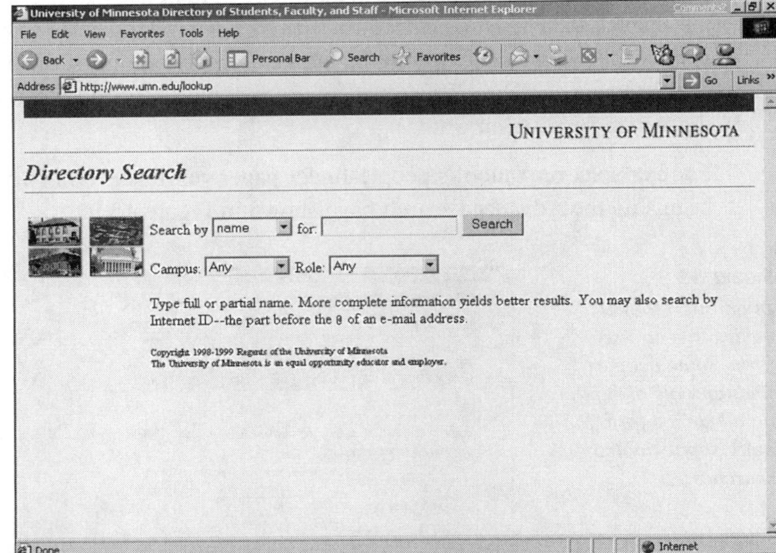

FIGURE 15.10
Like many companies and schools, the University of Minnesota offers on its Web site a searchable directory of students and faculty.

Try Name Variations

Might the person you're looking for sometimes use a different name than the one you've been using as a search term? Try alternative spellings (Sandy, Sandi) or nicknames. Try both the married name and birth name of people who may have married or divorced recently. You may even want to try a compound name made out of both the birth name and married name (for example, Jacqueline Bouvier Kennedy). I know both men and women who use compound or hyphenated married names.

Use Old Communications to Start the New Ones

Do you know either the mailing address or phone number of the person, and just want his or her email address? Don't be shy: Call or write, and just ask for the person's email address so you can conduct future communication online. Life's too short.

Summary

You know from earlier hours that you can find all sorts of information and files online. But until this hour, you may not have realized how easy it is to use the Internet to find an old friend or other contact you need. Most often, finding someone on the Web is a simple matter of opening a people-finding search tool and typing a name.

And, if your search turns up an email address, you have a very powerful way of getting in touch with that person.

Q&A

Q When my people searches turn up email addresses, those addresses appear to be links: They're underlined, and shown in the same color as other links. What are they links to?

A These links are called *email links* or *mailto* links, and they contain an email address. Some browsers are equipped to automatically open your email program when you click a mailto link in a Web page. If your browser is so equipped, you can click a mailto link and immediately begin composing a message addressed to that person.

Q I was looking for Carla Jones, and I found three people with that name. How do I figure out which Carla Jones is the one I want?

A Well, first you should try new searches, supplying as much information as you reliably know about the person. For example, include the state where the person lives; doing so may exclude the other choices. Try running your searches on different tools; another tool may display more detailed information, enabling you to choose the right Carla.

If you still have several choices, send a polite letter or email message (never phone) to all of the Carlas, identifying yourself and the context in which you know Carla, and requesting that the right Carla reply. The wrong Carlas will ignore your message, and the right Carla will contact you (if she wants to).

In your note, say as little as possible, and be tactful. For example, if Carla is an old flame, consider the possible effect of your note on the boyfriends or husbands of the *wrong* Carlas when describing your relationship.

HOUR 16

Working Smarter by Working Offline

"Are you *still* online? I need the *phone!!!*" Sound familiar?

There's no law that says you have to do anything at all offline—stay online all you want, see if I care. These days most of us have unlimited Internet accounts, so it costs us nothing extra to stay online as long as we need to. Still, many of us have only one phone line, and often it's hard to do what you want to do online while still keeping the phone line free for other uses. This hour shows you how you can spend less time online while doing more.

Personally, I find there's a psychological benefit to working offline. When I write email offline, I take my time and express myself more effectively. I often open messages waiting in my Outbox to make final fixes and other edits before sending them. Similarly, when I'm offline I read Web pages and newsgroup messages more carefully and thoughtfully. Something about being online makes me feel like the sand is running out of the hourglass, and I hurry too much. You too may find that the more you do offline, the better your overall Internet experience is.

At the end of this hour, you'll be able to answer the following questions:

- How can I conveniently round up the latest online info and store it on my computer so I can view it offline?
- How can I make composing email offline more convenient?
- How can I download entire newsgroups so I can read their messages offline?

If you use a broadband Internet connection (cable Internet or DSL), you might think that the stuff in this hour is irrelevant to you because your connection is always active, always online.

But some of what you'll read here applies to you, such as keeping newsgroups updated automatically. If you apply these techniques on a broadband connection, your message lists will be up-to-the-minute and ready to go whenever you sit down to read them. You'll save little download time because broadband connections receive information so quickly. But you'll save the steps you'd take to retrieve messages manually.

In addition to the offline techniques you pick up here, you may have heard of two others: Channels and Netcasting. These are two different approaches to a technology called *push*, wherein info is "pushed" from the Net to you. Channels were introduced in Internet Explorer 4 and included in Windows 98, and Netcasting was supported by an optional component of Communicator 4 called Netcaster.

You will see traces of these technologies, especially if you have an outdated browser. Online, you may see buttons here and there labeled "Add Active Channel," which are leftovers from the Channel days. But in practice, these technologies are orphans. IE6 still supports channels but offers no tools for dealing with them, and Netcaster has disappeared altogether in Netscape Communicator.

So although it remains possible to do some offline work through Channels and Netcasting using old tools, I do not recommend it. You will find that the offline browsing techniques you learn in this hour work for virtually all Web pages, newsgroups, and email (unlike Channels and Netcasting), are easy to use, and are not already on the closeout shelf of Internet innovations.

Reading Web Pages Offline, Anytime

Printing or saving Web pages for use offline is great in a pinch or for information you find online that will never change, such as the text of the Declaration of Independence.

But pretty quickly, most saved or printed Web pages fall out of date—the real page that's online changes, but your saved or printed version can't. To take advantage of up-to-date content while still working offline, you need a convenient way to quickly download the current versions of sites you like to keep up with. You can then go offline and peruse them at your leisure.

Exactly how you do this depends upon what browser you use. Over the next several pages, you'll learn how to do this in Internet Explorer (the easiest browser to use for offline work).

Making Web Sites Available Offline in Internet Explorer

If you want to get into offline work, Internet Explorer is the easiest and most effective tool for doing so, as of this writing. Not only does it make it easy to capture Web sites for offline use, but it also makes working with offline email and newsgroups a snap (see the sections on offline email and newsgroups later in this hour).

The following To Do shows how to set up a page for offline browsing.

To Do

To Do: Select a Page for Offline Browsing in Internet Explorer

1. Online in Explorer (5.5 or 6.0), go to the page you want to browse offline (see Figure 16.1).

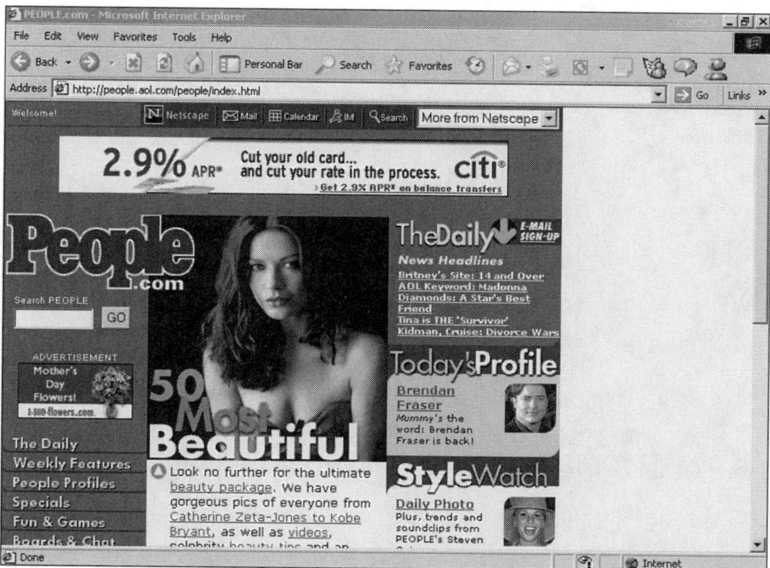

FIGURE 16.1
Step 1: Go to your target page in Internet Explorer.

2. Choose Favorites, Add to Favorites, just as you would for any new favorite you wanted to create (see Figure 16.2).

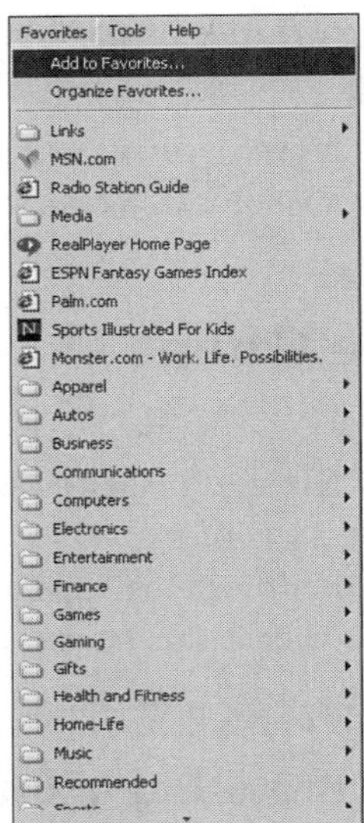

FIGURE 16.2
Step 2: *Choose Favorites, Add to Favorites.*

3. In the Add Favorite dialog box, check the check box labeled Make Available Offline, and then click OK (see Figure 16.3).

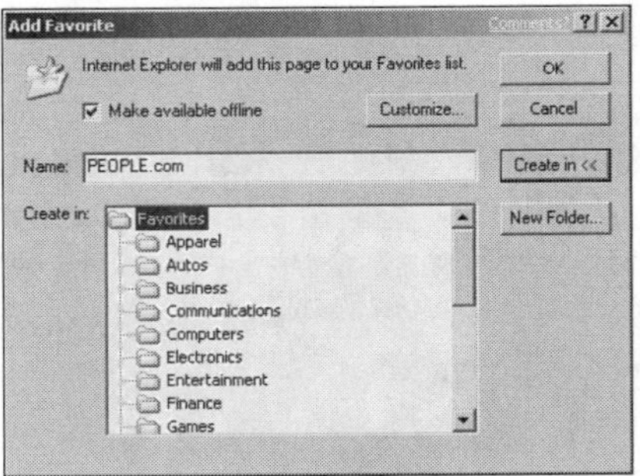

FIGURE 16.3
Step 3: *Check Make Available Offline, and then click OK.*

4. Explorer immediately informs you that it is *synchronizing*—downloading the page to your computer for offline use. (To learn more about synchronizing, see "Updating Offline Pages" later in this hour.)

After synchronization finishes, you can disconnect and then read the pages offline, as described in the next section.

Reading Pages Offline

To read a page offline, you must first shift Internet Explorer into its offline mode:

- If you're not online already, open Explorer and then click Cancel in your connection dialog (or Work Offline) so you don't connect to the Internet. Click the Work Offline button that appears.
- If you're online, don't close Explorer. Close your Internet connection and then, in Explorer, choose File, Work Offline.

After you're in offline mode, just open your Favorites menu. Only the pages available to be read offline appear in the list. To show the others, click the double arrow at the bottom of the menu.

Depending on your version of Windows and your version of Explorer, the appearance of the Favorites menu can differ.

In some versions and combinations, all Favorites always appear on the menu, but those unavailable for offline viewing appear dimmer than the rest—they are grayed out. In others, only the pages available for offline viewing appear on the menu at first; to see the full list, you click the small arrow at the bottom of the menu.

Some favorites may appear in the list even though you did not check the Make Available Offline check box for them. These are sites you've visited recently enough that copies of them are still stored by Explorer to speed up the display of pages you visit often.

Only the most recently visited pages are in the cache file, so you can't count on it to always hold the pages you want to see offline. Be sure to check the Make Available Offline check box, making the page available no matter how long it's been since you last visited it online.

Choose any favorite in bold and read away. You can even click the links on the page. If you click a link that leads to a page that's not available offline, a dialog asks whether you want to connect to the Internet to see that page.

When you're finished working offline, return Explorer to online mode by choosing File, Work Offline again.

Updating Offline Pages

From time to time, you'll want to update the offline pages stored on your computer so that their contents match the latest versions that are online. To do that, you must *synchronize*.

NEW TERM **Synchronize.** To download the latest online content (Web pages, email, or newsgroup messages) so that the offline version on your computer matches the current version online—the two versions are in sync. This term is used the same way in Explorer, Outlook Express, and Communicator.

How often you must synchronize depends on how frequently you expect the online content to change. But synchronizing is so easy that you can simply sync up all your offline content as often as you want, all in one step. You can also set up schedules by which Explorer will automatically synchronize for you.

To synchronize, go online and then choose Tools, Synchronize. The Items to Synchronize dialog appears, as shown in Figure 16.4. Click the Synchronize button. Explorer contacts every page in the list, one by one, and saves the latest version of each on your computer. When the synchronization is finished, you can go offline and take your time reading the updated content.

FIGURE 16.4
Choose Tools, Synchronize to open this dialog, from which you can synchronize or change your sync settings.

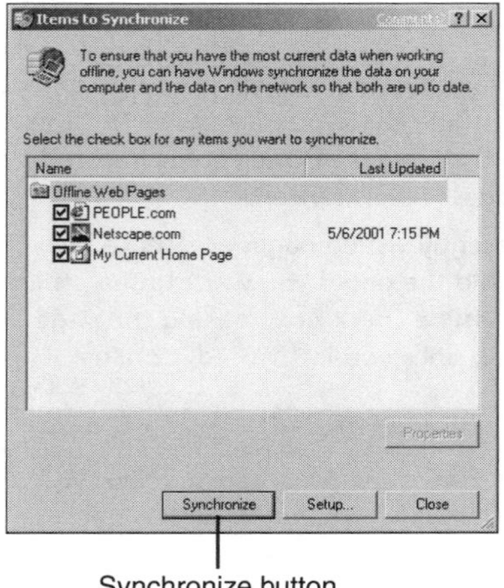

In Figure 16.4, note that a check mark appears next to each page. If you want to skip synchronization for any page, remove its check mark before clicking the Synchronize button.

In Figure 16.4, observe that there are some other buttons you can use to customize your synchronizations:

- Click the Setup button to open a dialog box where you can choose from general options for synchronization, such as configuring Explorer to sync automatically every day, week, or month.
- Click a page in the list to select it and then click the Properties button. This opens a dialog box where you can choose from options for that page alone, such as a daily, weekly, or monthly automatic sync.

One handy feature of the dialog for changing the sync properties of individual pages is on the Download tab, shown in Figure 16.5. By default, when you sync a page you get only the content on *that* page, and not the content on any of the *other* pages to which that page may link. By increasing the number in the blank following the words "Download pages," you can sync not only the page, but also others it links to.

For example, if you put a 2 in that box, synchronization would download the specified page *plus* all the pages it linked to. A 3 would download the page, all pages it linked to, and all pages *those* pages linked to. (Although this option expands your ability to work offline, use it sparingly because it can dramatically increase the time required for synchronization.)

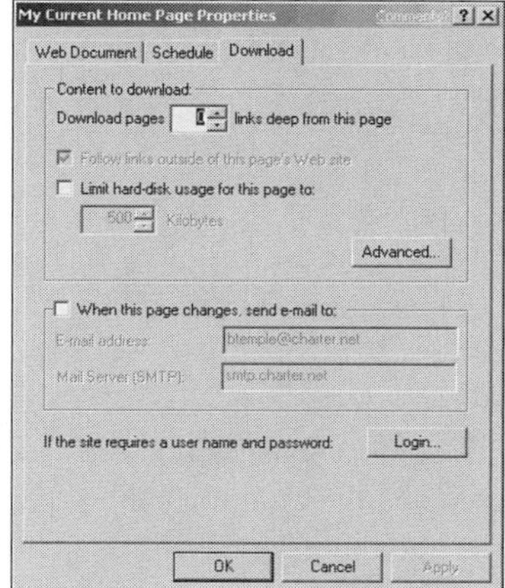

FIGURE 16.5
You can customize properties for each page you designate for offline viewing.

Offline Email and Newsgroups

The Web has no monopoly on letting you work offline. In some ways, you may have even more to gain from doing email and newsgroup tasks offline. Both Explorer and Netscape Communicator feature great tools for making the most of offline mail and news, as you'll learn in the next few pages.

Setting Up Offline Email in Outlook Express

To make Outlook Express a better offline email program, all you need to do is change a few settings…

First, you need to tell Outlook Express to save new messages you write in the Outbox folder until you decide to send them. In Outlook Express, choose Tools, Options, and then click the Send tab (see Figure 16.6). Clear the check box labeled Send Messages Immediately. This prevents the program from trying to connect to the Internet each time you send a message. Instead, you can do all your composing offline and click the Send button on each message when you finish writing it. The messages wait in the Outbox until you click the Send/Recv button. Then Outlook Express connects to the Internet, sends all the messages waiting in the Outbox, and retrieves all new email for you, all in one shot.

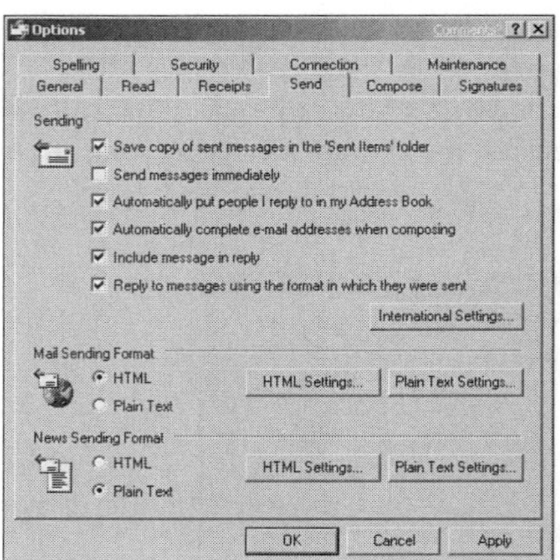

FIGURE 16.6
Clear the Send Messages Immediately check box to make Outlook Express save messages in the Outbox folder to be sent later.

Another change that makes offline work more convenient for some folks is telling Outlook Express to disconnect as soon as it finishes sending and receiving messages. This enables you to click Send/Recv and then forget about the rest. Outlook Express connects (if necessary), sends all Outbox messages, retrieves any new messages, and then disconnects, all without any further input from you (if you haven't saved your login password, you will still have to enter that, however). If you routinely go online just to check email and then get right off again instead of moving on to Web browsing or another activity, this change is for you.

Choose Tools, Options, and then click the Connection tab (see Figure 16.7). Check the check box labeled Hang Up After Sending and Receiving.

16

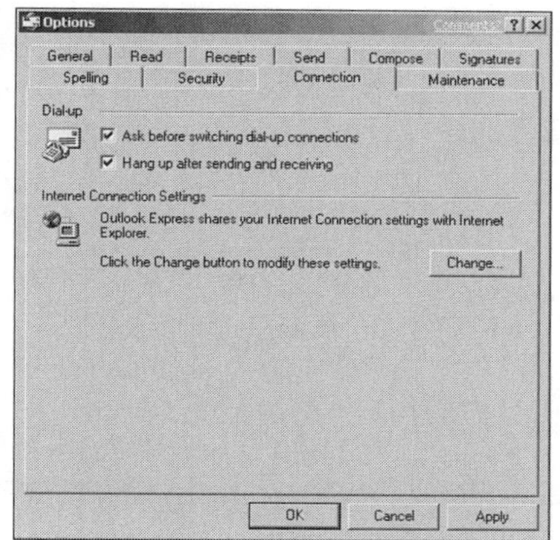

FIGURE 16.7
Check the Hang Up After Sending and Receiving check box to make Outlook Express disconnect automatically after sending all waiting messages and receiving any new ones.

Synchronizing News in Outlook Express

If you use newsgroups regularly, you may find that offline news browsing is the most valuable of all offline techniques.

Ordinarily, when you open a newsgroup online, only the messages' headers are copied to your computer to appear in the message list. No actual message is copied to your computer until you open it online. But by synchronizing newsgroups in Outlook Express, you can download entire newsgroups—messages and all—to your computer. Then you can disconnect and browse them offline at your leisure. This will take up a lot of hard drive space if you subscribe to many newsgroups, however.

To set up offline newsgroups, first be sure you have already subscribed to any newsgroup you'll want to use offline (see Hour 7, "Participating in Newsgroups and Mailing Lists"). Then follow the steps in the following To Do.

To Do: Set Up Newsgroups for Offline Browsing in Outlook Express

1. Click the name of a subscribed newsgroup you will want to browse offline. Then click the Settings button (see Figure 16.8).

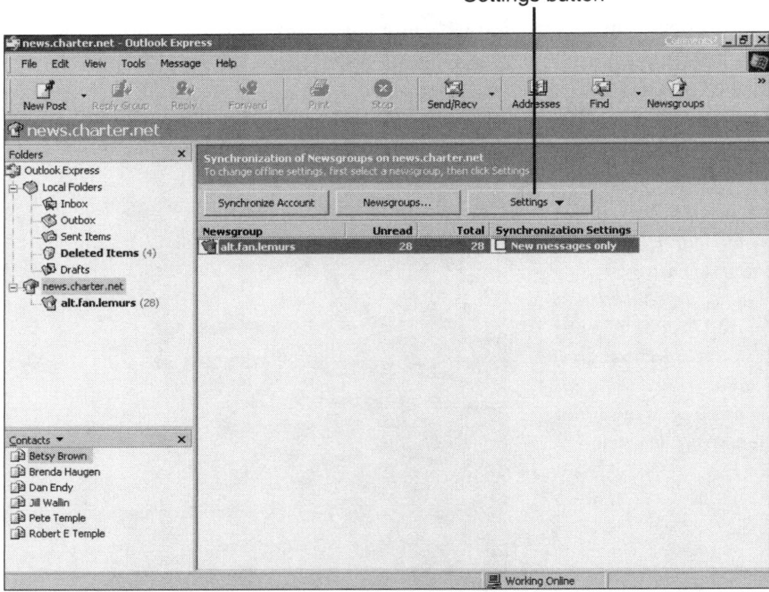

FIGURE 16.8
Step 1: Select a newsgroup and then click Settings.

2. Choose the sync settings for this newsgroup (see Figure 16.9):

   All Messages. Synchronization will download all messages in the newsgroup to your computer for offline browsing.

   New Messages Only. Synchronization will download only the new messages (those posted since the last time you synchronized) to your computer. This is the recommended choice because it gets you up-to-date the quickest.

FIGURE 16.9
Step 2: Choose the synchronization settings for the newsgroup.

3. Repeat steps 1 and 2 for all newsgroups you want to use offline. When you're ready to synchronize, click the Synchronize Account button (see Figure 16.10). After synchronization is complete, you can disconnect from the Internet and read your newsgroups offline.

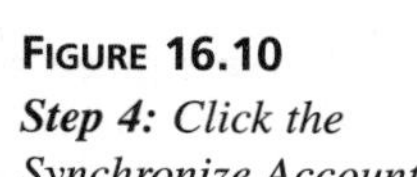

FIGURE 16.10
Step 4: *Click the Synchronize Account button.*

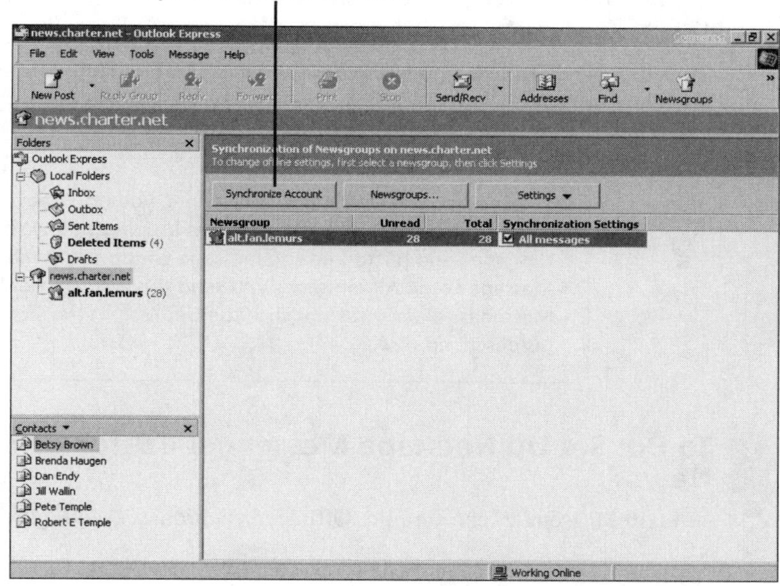

The next time you synchronize, all you have to do is step 4. Steps 1 through 3 are necessary only when you want to change the synchronization settings.

Here are a few handy tips for offline newsgroups:

- If you've set up Outlook Express so that it saves new messages in your Outbox folder (as described earlier in this hour), any newsgroup replies or new postings you send also go to the Outbox, so you can continue working offline.
- Choosing Tools, Synchronize All does three things: 1) Sends any messages waiting in Outbox; 2) Retrieves any new messages; and 3) Synchronizes newsgroups. One-step sync!
- If you find that your newsgroup sync takes too long, sync fewer newsgroups. Or reduce the number of messages downloaded for each group by choosing Tools, Options, clicking the Read tab, and then lowering the number shown in the box in the tab's News section.

Synchronizing Mail and News in Netscape Messenger

In Netscape Messenger, you set up your mail and news synchronization all in one place. Isn't that nice? To learn how, see the following To Do. Before you begin, be sure you have already subscribed to any newsgroups you'll want to use offline.

> To compose email offline in Messenger, you don't have to reconfigure anything. Just compose your message as usual, offline. When you're done, don't click the Send button on the message window. Instead, choose File, Send Message Later. All messages you send this way are held in the Unsent Messages folder until you click the Get Msg button, or until you synchronize (as described next).

To Do: Set Up Netscape Messenger 4.7 for Offline Mail and News

1. In Messenger, choose File, Offline, Synchronize (see Figure 16.11).

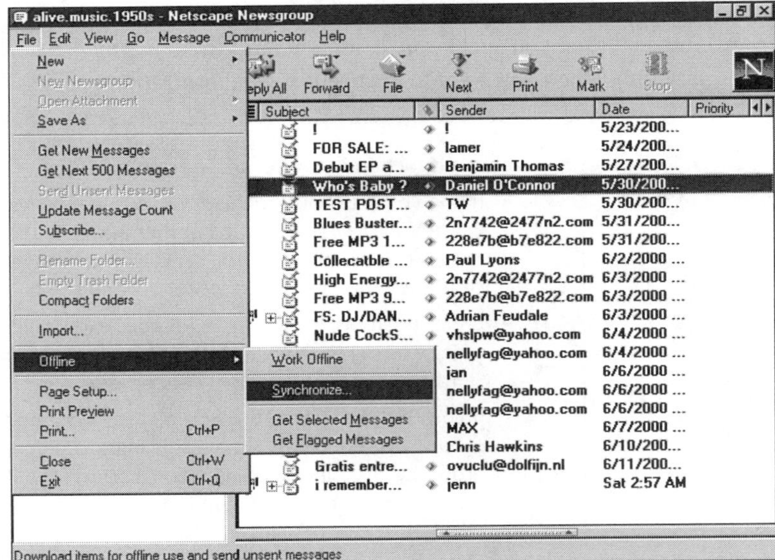

FIGURE 16.11
Step 1: Choose File, Offline, Synchronize.

2. Click the Select Items button (see Figure 16.12).
3. Select a newsgroup or mail folder you want to include in synchronization (see Figure 16.13).

4. Press and hold the Ctrl key, and then select any *other* mail folders or newsgroups you want to include. Then click OK (see Figure 16.14).

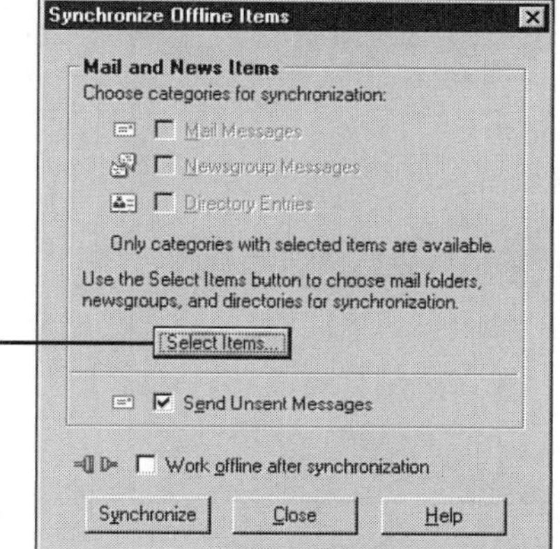

FIGURE 16.12
Step 2: *Click Select Items.*

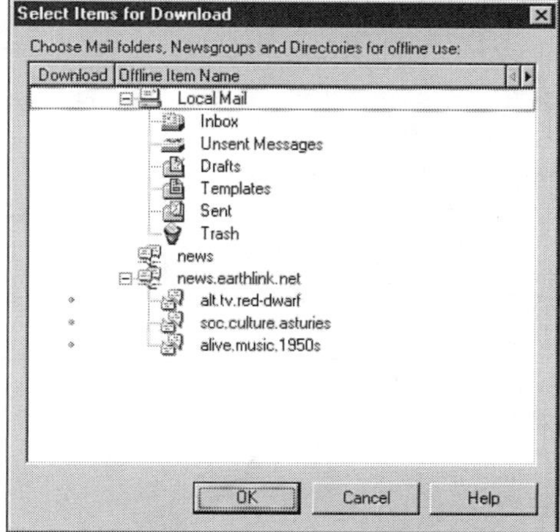

FIGURE 16.13
Step 3: *Select folders to synchronize.*

5. Next, choose options. Check the Send Unsent Messages check box to send any messages waiting in the Unsent Messages folder whenever you synchronize. Check Work Offline after synchronization to instruct Messenger to disconnect automatically as soon as synchronization is complete (see Figure 16.15).
6. Click the Synchronize button (see Figure 16.16).

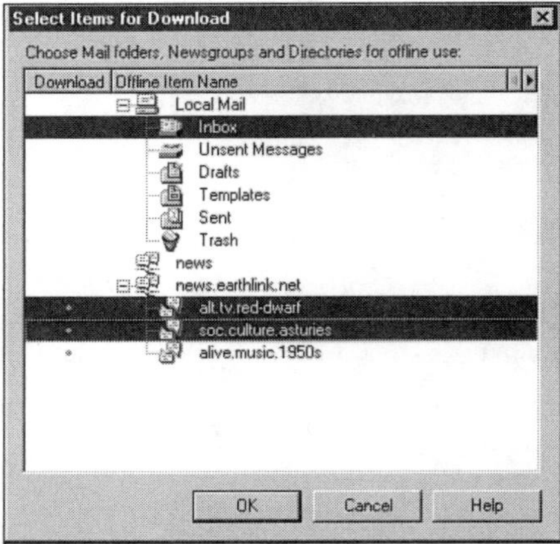

FIGURE 16.14
Step 4: *Click OK.*

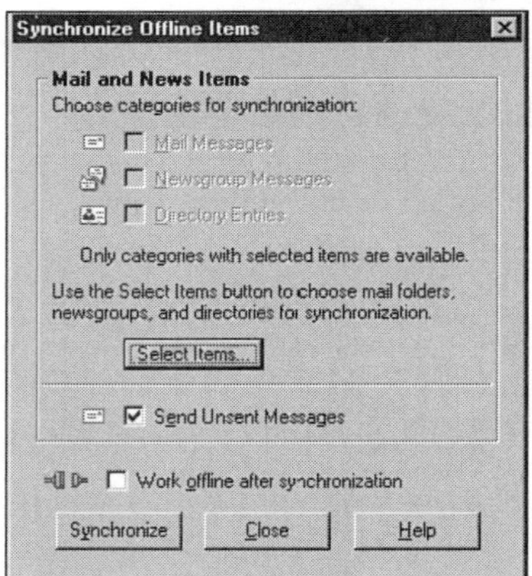

FIGURE 16.15
Step 5: *Choose options.*

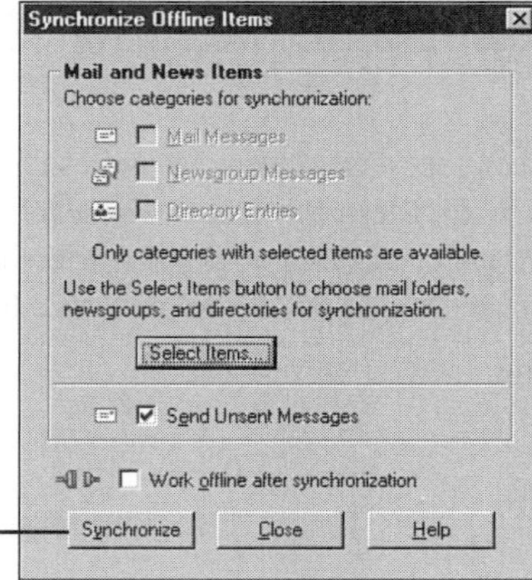

FIGURE 16.16
Step 6: *Click the Synchronize button.*

The next time you want to synchronize, you only need to perform step 1 and step 6 unless you want to change your settings.

Summary

Working offline is relatively unknown to newer Internet users, and a surprising number of them do not use—or even really know about—the offline features in their Internet programs. Why? In the old days, when most ISPs charged by the hour used, it was more important to manage your online time. The availability of faster, cheaper connections, two-phone-line homes, and content that can't be used offline (such as live stock tickers or streaming audio and video) is inclining lots of folks to spend *more* time online, not less. But everybody's needs are different, and when you know how to work offline, the Internet does not control your schedule—*you* do.

Q&A

Q I try to use offline techniques, but I'm still tying up my phone line. Is there anything else I can try, short of putting in a second phone line?

A Have you checked out whether you can receive cable Internet or DSL Internet service in your neighborhood? Although more expensive than a regular dial-up account, these connections let you use your phone while online, and they're much faster than a dial-up account, to boot.

Q I don't mind tying up my phone line, except that people can't leave me messages on my answering machine while I'm online. What can I do?

A Chuck the answering machine and get voice mail from your phone company or another reliable provider. Make sure the company you choose understands that when your line is busy, you want callers to be directed straight to voice mail instead of hearing a busy signal. If you use call waiting, you may have to have your voice mail configured so that it rings once or twice first (so you'll know you have a call if you're talking on the phone) and then jumps to voice mail (in case you're online). Get into the habit of checking for voice messages as soon as you go offline.

Note that many voice mail systems indicate that you have messages by making the dial tone on your phone line stutter a little. In some cases, especially when using an older modem, that stuttering causes modems to think there's no dial tone, so they refuse to connect. If you do get voice mail, you may find that if you have messages waiting, you can't go online until you've listened to the messages so the dial tone can revert to normal.

PART V

Making the Web Part of Your Life

Hour

HOUR 17

Enjoying Safe Family Fun and Games

Is cyberspace a family place? If you have kids, you might be wondering. One day the media touts the Net as the greatest thing since Gutenberg, and the next it's the harbinger of the Apocalypse, an instrument of pornographers, pedophiles, and disgruntled loners.

Actually, it's neither. It's a tool, and like any tool, it can be put to good uses or bad. A hammer can build shelter or bash a finger. I think an adult has a right to use the Internet any way he or she wants to—within the law and without bothering anybody. But if you have kids who will use the Net (and they should!), you need to know how to insulate them from the Net's racier regions.

More importantly, there have been cases of pedophiles and other such creeps starting online relationships with kids (and gullible grownups!) that eventually lead to face-to-face meetings, and then to tragedy. In this hour, you learn commonsense rules for creep-proofing your kids.

At the end of the hour, you'll be able to answer the following questions:

- How can I get my family's surfing off to a fun, safe start?
- What steps can I take and teach to my kids to keep them safe online?
- How can I use a utility or Internet Explorer's built-in censor to block out the smutty stuff?
- How do I use AOL's Parental Controls?

Choosing a Family Starting Point

A good first step for family Web surfing is to choose a good starting point, a "family home page" of sorts. A good general-purpose family page provides a jumping-off point in which all the links are family-friendly. Kids starting out should be taught to begin at that page, use only the links on that page, and use the Back button to return to that page after visiting any of its links. (If you make that page your home page, they can click the Home button to return to it anytime.) These habits corral a kid's surfing to a limited, appropriate range of sites.

One way to safeguard your Internet experience is to choose an Internet provider that censors content for you. These ISPs specialize in providing Internet service to families. Check out:

- `www.cleanfamily.com`
- `family.net`
- `ratedg.com`

For most folks who want their Internet service controlled for the kids but free for the adults, these services are an extreme. But if the principal surfers in your home are the kids, you might want to see whether one of these services has a local access number for you.

You'll probably want to browse and search for a family page that best fits your family. Some good choices appear in Appendix A, "Fun Web Sites to Visit," but here are a few more suggestions:

- **Yahooligans!** at `www.yahooligans.com`. A kid's offshoot of the Yahoo! search tool with links and a search engine that both lead only to good kid stuff (see Figure 17.1).
- **4Kids Treehouse** at `www.4kids.com`. A colorful site with great links and activities for kids, plus resources for parents.

- **Family.com** at `www.family.com`. An online family magazine.
- **Ask Jeeves for Kids** at `www.ajkids.com`.
- **The American Library Association's Cool Sites for Kids** page at `www.ala.org/alsc/children_links.html`.

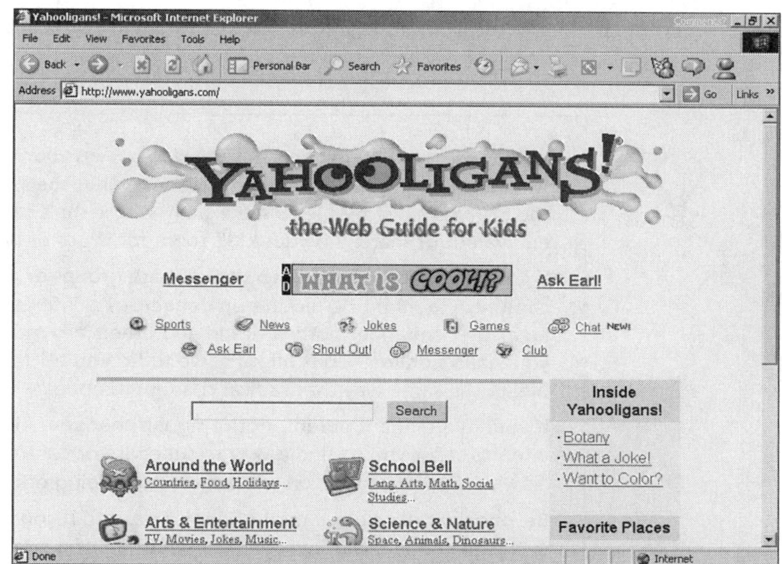

FIGURE 17.1
Yahooligans! makes a good starting point for family Web surfing.

> After you've learned how to create Web pages (see Hour 19, "Creating Web Pages and Multimedia Messages"), you can create your own family home page and fill it with links you would like your kids to have easy access to.

Important Family Safety Steps

Everybody's different, and so is every family. It's not my place to say what's best for you or your kids, but if you want some guidance about keeping your kids safe online, permit me to offer a few suggestions here. Then follow your own judgment.

Supervise!

This one's so obvious, and yet so difficult. As a parent, I know that it simply isn't practical to supervise our kids every second of the day. And if you're a tired parent of a preteen, the idea of the kid going off to his room for an hour to surf the Net is appealing.

You must make your own choice about when to cut the cord, based not on what's convenient but on your kid. Some kids are mature enough to surf responsibly at seven, but others can't be trusted at 17. Only you know your kids well enough to decide.

If you're not sure whether your kid is ready to go solo but you don't have time to supervise, keep him offline until either you are sure that he's ready or you have the time. The Internet has lots to offer a kid, but your kid can live without it until the time is right for both of you.

I know some experts say it's not good to spy on your kids. But if your kid surfs unsupervised and you want to know what she's been up to, open the browser's history file to see exactly where she's been. It's the cyber-equivalent of searching your kid's room for drugs or weapons.

If your kid is visiting the Web sites of hate groups or providers of unsavory content, she might be picking up dangerous reinforcement of feelings or ideas that endanger both your kid and others around her. At the very least, your child's online habits might serve to tip you off that your kid is in trouble, in the same way that radical changes in appearance or mood might.

If you, as a diligent parent, notice signals that your kid might be at risk, it's important for you to find a way to supervise or control that kid's online activities, OR keep tabs on what she's been doing online, OR pull the plug.

Beyond that, though, it might be important to recognize that if your kid is in trouble online, that's probably a symptom of a larger problem that has nothing to do with the Internet. In such cases, controlling what your kid does online is only Step 1. After that, you need to identify and address the *real* problem, and maybe find some help for your child.

Don't Defeat Passwords

Your Internet connection, email account, and a few other activities require you to enter a username and password to prevent unauthorized access. Some software, particularly Internet connection software, enables you to enter the password in a dialog box once so that you never have to type it again. That's a convenient feature, but it enables anyone who can flip a switch to get online using your computer.

My advice is that you leave your computer configured so that a password is required for both connecting to the Internet and retrieving email. Never tell your kids the passwords, and never log on or retrieve email in their sight.

This will ensure that you always know when your kids are online, and that they cannot receive email from anyone without your knowledge.

Be Extra Careful with Broadband

If you use a broadband Internet connection, your connection can be always online, always ready to go. This condition makes it awfully easy for a child to sit down at your computer and go where he or she maybe shouldn't.

Make sure you do not check any "remember password" boxes when setting up and using your broadband connection. This will help ensure that no one uses the Internet without your permission and supervision.

> In Windows, you can set up a password-protected screen saver, so that when you leave your computer, after a few minutes of inactivity, a nifty animated picture or other display covers your screen. No one can clear that picture and do anything on your computer without entering the password. This is a great way to keep your computer—and your kids—safe, particularly if you use a broadband connection.
>
> To set up a screen saver, point to an empty area of your Windows desktop, right-click, choose Properties from the menu that appears, and then choose Screen Saver on the dialog box that appears. Be sure to check the check box marked "Password Protected."

Resist Chat

It's a shame to recommend resisting chat because there's plenty of good clean fun to be had in chat rooms. It must be said: Chat rooms are the most dangerous places on the Internet. This is not because of all the sex-related chat rooms, although it's related to those.

On the Web, the worst thing that can happen to a kid is that he or she will be exposed to *ideas*—words and pictures—that you don't approve of. In chat, your kids can easily meet up with *people* who may hurt them. People are much more dangerous than ideas.

It works like this: A pedophile or some other dangerous character—often posing as a kid—frequents chat rooms where kids hang out and establishes friendships, especially with lonely kids who are easy prey. As the friendship grows, the creep manipulates the kid into dropping the anonymous chat nicknames and exchanging email addresses for private correspondence. Eventually, a private, face-to-face meeting is arranged.

There already have been numerous cases of kids abused this way. And the initial contact is almost always made in a chat room.

> Most chat clients (including Microsoft Chat) include a dialog box in which you can not only create your chat nickname, but also enter personal information such as your name or email address. (I pointed this out in Hour 6, "Chatting and Instant Messenger," but it bears repeating.)
>
> Because this information is accessible to others online with whom you chat, I strongly recommend entering nothing on such dialog boxes except your nickname.
>
> It's also a good idea to change your nickname from time to time, to keep chat friendships from getting too close.

Obviously, I recommend never allowing a child to use chat unsupervised, even if that child is trusted to surf the Web unsupervised. Even supervised chatting is risky—by teaching a child how to chat, you increase the chances that the child might sneak into a chat session unsupervised.

In fact, if you don't use chat yourself, I would recommend simply not installing a chat client on your computer. Remember that many Web sites offer chat areas that anyone can access directly from his or her browser, without a chat client installed.

Online Rules for Kids

I know, I know, my kids hate rules, too. But these rules are pretty easy, and it's essential that you teach them to your kids even if you can't always be sure they will be followed. In particular, if you have older kids who you permit to use the Net unsupervised, it's important that they know the rules for safe surfing. (Some folks suggest writing these rules up, having the kids sign them as a contract, and then posting the contract on the wall behind the computer.)

Tell your kids the following:

- Never reveal to anyone online your real name, email address, phone number, mailing address, school name, or username/password without a parent's involvement and consent. Any other personal information, such as birthday or Social Security number, is also best kept secret. And never, ever, ever send anyone a picture of yourself.
- Never reveal anything about your parents, siblings, teachers, or friends. Any such information can help a creep find you, and it exposes family and friends to risks, too.

- Never arrange to meet in person any online friend unless a parent consents before the meeting is arranged, the parent will be present at that meeting, and that meeting will take place in a public setting, such as a restaurant or mall.
- Anytime you come across anything online that makes you uneasy, go elsewhere or get offline. There's too much good stuff online to waste time looking at the bad.
- Never download or upload a file, or install any software on the computer, without a parent's consent.

Resources for Parents

Want to know more about protecting your kids online, teaching them to use the Net smartly, finding great family sites, or just plain old parenting advice? You'll find all of this and more at the following sites:

- **Parent Soup** at `www.parentsoup.com` (see Figure 17.2).
- **The Parents Place** at `www.parentsplace.com`.
- **Kids Health** at `www.kidshealth.org`.
- ***All About Kids*** magazine at `www.aak.com`.

FIGURE 17.2
Parent Soup is one of the best online resources for moms and dads.

Censoring Web Content

You've probably heard that there are programs that can control what your kids see online. So why didn't I just mention them in the first place and save you all this "online rules" crud?

Well, it's debatable how effective these programs are. First, most are really focused on the Web and aren't much protection elsewhere, such as in chat or email. And most censoring programs—erring properly on the cautious side, I suppose—inevitably censor out totally benign stuff that you or your kids might find valuable. (You'll see an example of this later, with Content Advisor.)

Also, these programs might filter out sexual content, depictions of violence, and profanity, but what about ugly ideas? For example, these programs generally do not block out racist, sexist, or nationalist hate-mongering as long as those views are expressed without the use of profanity or epithets.

So even though these self-censoring tools are available, they're no replacement for adult supervision and safe-surfing practices. And if you really do supervise your kids, you probably don't *need* a censoring program. Still, you might find one or more of these programs useful, and they are getting better.

Getting a Safe-Surfing Program

Microsoft Internet Explorer has its own censoring program, which you'll learn about next. So does AOL, which you'll also learn about in a minute or two. But you might also want to check out the Web pages of other popular self-censoring utilities.

From these pages, you can learn more about each product and, in most cases, download a copy for your system:

- **Net Nanny:** `www.netnanny.com`
- **SurfWatch:** `www.surfwatch.com`
- **Cybersitter:** `www.cybersitter.com`
- **The Internet Filter:** `turnercom.com/if`
- **Cyber Patrol:** `www.cyberpatrol.com`

If you use WebTV as your Internet window, note that it supplies its own censoring system that you can apply to restrict what your kids can see.

Using Internet Explorer's Built-In Content Advisor

Internet Explorer, versions 3 and newer, has its own built-in system called Content Advisor for controlling access to Web sites. Content Advisor works very much like the other safe-surfing programs, except it's a little harder to use than some, and it possesses many of the same strengths and drawbacks.

Understanding Content Advisor

Content Advisor relies on a rating system from the Recreational Software Advisory Council (RSAC), which also rates entertainment software and video games.

The RSAC ratings system assigns a score (0 to 4) to a Web site for each of four criteria: Language, Nudity, Sex, and Violence. The higher the score in each category, the more intense the content that page contains.

For example, if a site has a score of 0 in the Language category, it contains nothing worse than "inoffensive slang." A Language score of 4, however, indicates "explicit or crude language" on the site. After a Web site has been rated, the rating is built into the site so that Content Advisor can read the site's score before displaying anything.

Using the Content tab, you choose your own limit in each RSAC category. For example, suppose you are okay with violence up to level 3 but want to screen out all sexual content above a 2. After you set your limits and enable Content Advisor, Internet Explorer refuses to show you any page whose RSAC rating exceeds your limits in any category, unless you type in a password which you create. So, for example, if you screen out all nudity, then try to go to Playboy's Web site, you'll be blocked (see Figure 17.3).

There's one problem: Only a tiny portion of sites online have been rated. Enabling Content Advisor therefore blocks not only rated pages you might find offensive, but also *all* pages—offensive or not—that have not been rated, which includes most of the Web.

As you might guess, blocking unrated pages severely cramps your surfing and has little to do with protecting you from offensive content. As you'll see in the upcoming To Do, you can choose an optional setting to allow unrated pages, but doing so defeats the purpose of Content Advisor because those pages will be permitted regardless of their content. You can also create a special list of pages that are always accessible (or never accessible) regardless of the Content Advisor's settings, but obviously that list would be pretty short relative to the wealth of sites available online.

FIGURE 17.3
After you've enabled it, Content Advisor blocks Internet Explorer from displaying Web pages whose RSAC ratings exceed your limits.

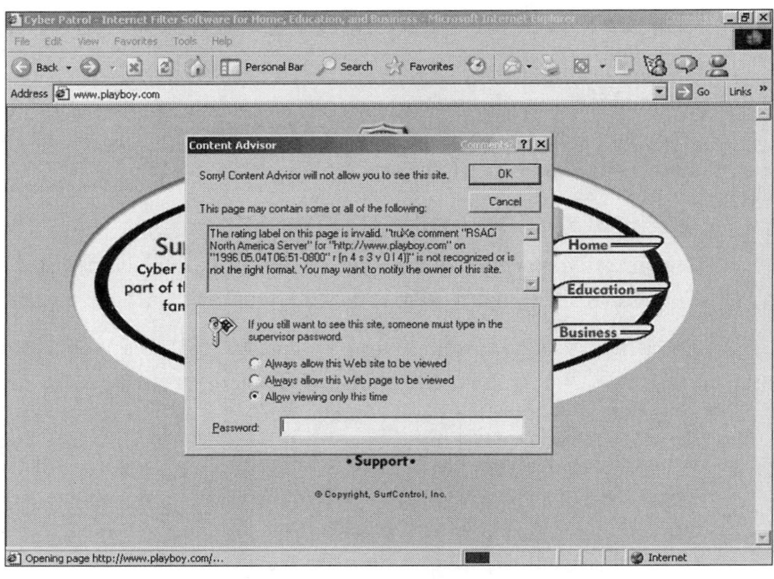

Content Advisor works for both Web browsing and Microsoft's Chat program (see Hour 6), blocking entrance to unsavory or unrated chat rooms.

To use Content Advisor for Chat, replace Step 1 of the following To Do by opening Chat and choosing View, Options, and then choosing the Settings tab. Proceed with the remaining steps of the To Do.

However, note that although Content Advisor might keep kids out of X-rated chats, it does nothing to protect them from the pervs who wander into G-rated chats. My advice, no matter what censorship tools you might deploy: Kids don't belong in chat. Period.

To Do: Enable and Configure Content Advisor

1. In Internet Explorer, open the Internet Options dialog box (choose Tools, Internet Options) and then choose the Content tab (see Figure 17.4).
2. Click the Enable button to display the Content Advisor (see Figure 17.5).
3. The Rating scale appears, showing the current setting for Language.

   Point to the slider control, click and hold, and drag the slider along the scale (see Figure 17.6). As the slider reaches each marker on the scale, a description appears below the scale with the type of language that setting permits. The farther to the right you pull the slider, the more lenient the setting. (Think of 0 as a G rating, 1 as PG, 2 as PG-13, 3 as R, and 4 as X.) After you've found the rating level you want, release the slider.

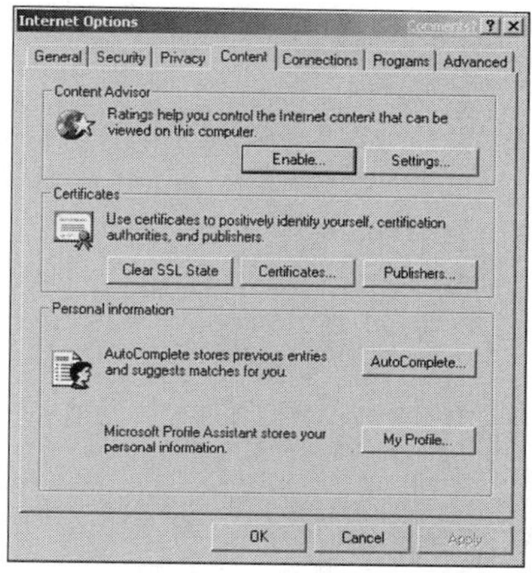

FIGURE 17.4
Step 1: *Open Internet Options and then choose the Content tab.*

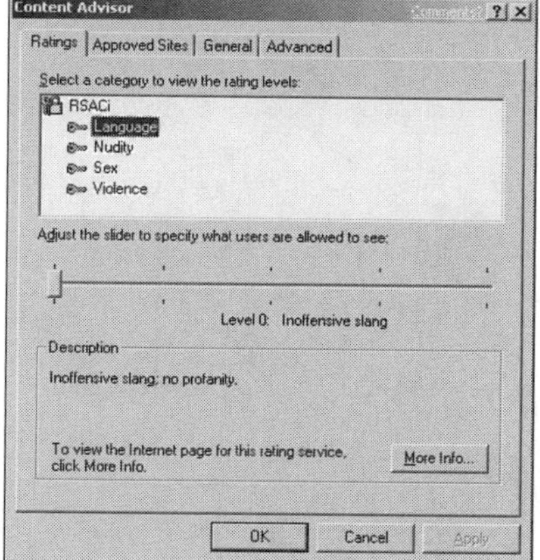

FIGURE 17.5
Step 2: *Click the Enable button to display Content Advisor.*

4. Click on Nudity and choose your rating for that category. Do Sex and Violence, too (see Figure 17.7).
5. When you have finished choosing ratings, click the General tab and check either (or neither, or both) of the following options (see Figure 17.8):

   Users can see sites that have no rating. Check this check box to allow the display of unrated pages. Content Advisor will continue to block rated pages that exceed your settings, but will permit unrated pages regardless of their content.

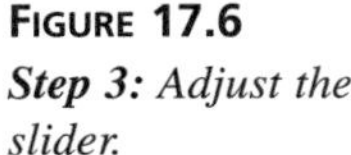

FIGURE 17.6
***Step 3:** Adjust the slider.*

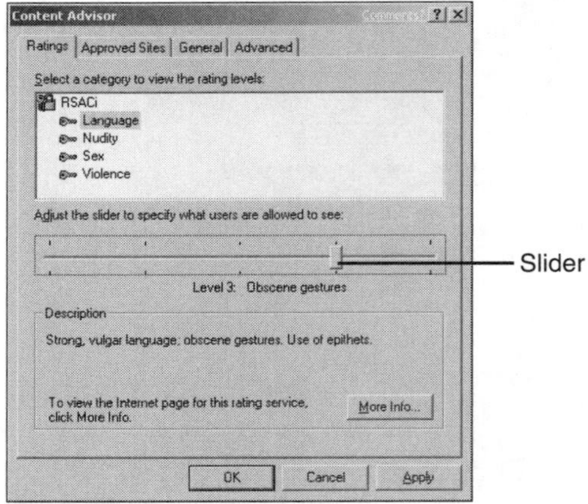

FIGURE 17.7
***Step 4:** Do the same for Nudity, Sex, and Violence.*

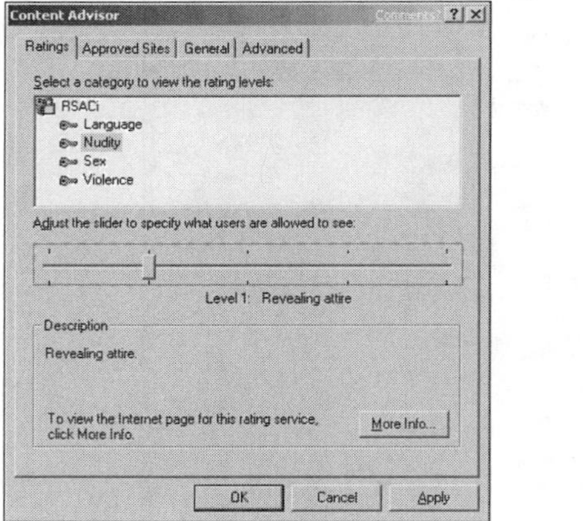

Depending on whether this is the first time you've accessed Content Advisor and the exact order of steps you follow, you will be asked at some point to choose the supervisor password. Once it's entered, no one can change any Content Advisor settings without entering it.

Supervisor can type a password to allow users to see restricted content. When this check box is checked, a dialog box pops up prompting for the Supervisor password whenever someone tries to open a page that Content Advisor would block. If the password is typed, the page appears. With this useful option, your kids can appeal to you for a temporary censorship waiver for a particular Web site.

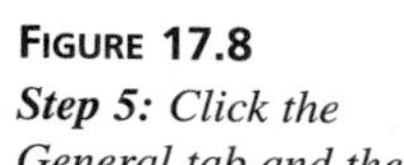

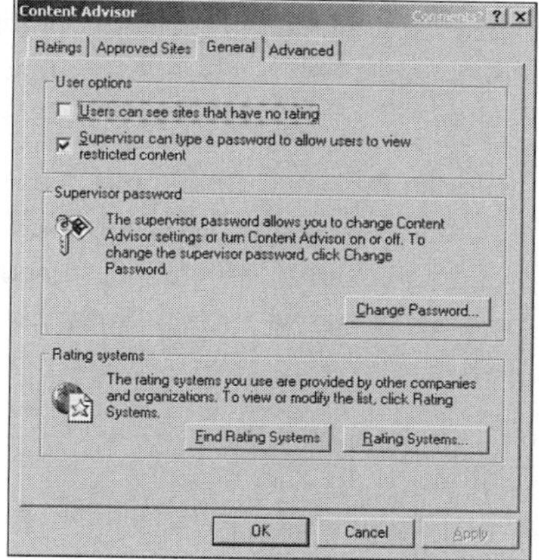

FIGURE 17.8
Step 5: *Click the General tab and then select User options.*

6. Click the Approved Sites tab. Type the address of any Web site you want to be handled in a special way, and then click Always (to make this site always accessible, regardless of any other Content Advisor settings) or Never (to make this site inaccessible). Continue typing addresses and clicking Always or Never until the list shows all the sites for which you want special handling (see Figure 17.9). The approved sites show up with a green check mark next to them, while the disapproved sites have a red minus sign.

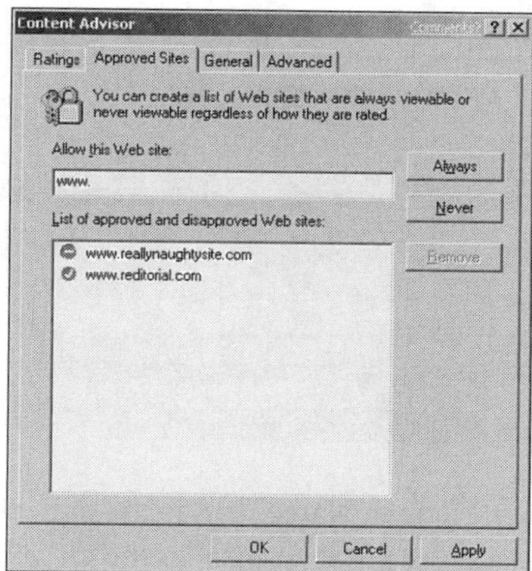

FIGURE 17.9
Step 6: *At the Approved Sites tab, enter lists of approved and disapproved Web sites.*

7. Click OK on any tab, and then click OK on the Internet Options dialog box. Your settings are now in effect, and they will stay in effect until you change them or click the Disable button on the Content tab. (The Supervisor password is required for disabling Content Advisor or changing the settings.)

Using AOL's Parental Controls

America Online has always touted itself as a family-friendly online service. As such, it's been at the forefront of developing technologies that allow parents to have control over what their children see and do online.

AOL's Parental Controls is a leader in this area, although it does suffer from some of the same drawbacks as some of the other Web-censoring programs. For example, if you choose the tightest security level ("Kids Only," which is designed for elementary-aged kids), it blocks such sites as the official sites of Britney Spears and the Backstreet Boys, which your kids may want to see.

At the core of Parental Controls are the screen names. You can have up to seven screen names per AOL account. This allows families to pay one monthly fee, yet allow all of its members (unless it's a particularly *large* family) to have their own screen name.

Each screen name can also have its own settings, or level of access. Because of this, parents can let their teenagers see more content than their preschoolers are allowed access to. And, as long as you make sure each child only knows his or her own password, you can be relatively certain they're only seeing what you think is appropriate for them.

Parental Controls are available from the Settings tab within AOL. Click on Parental Controls, then click the Set Parental Controls link. You'll then be viewing the Parental Controls screen at which you can change settings (see Figure 17.10).

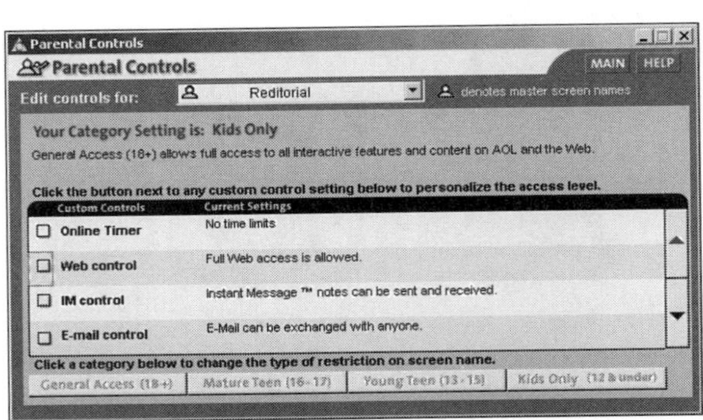

FIGURE 17.10
AOL's Parental Controls allows different settings for different family members.

Each AOL account has a Master Screen Name; this is the only person who is allowed to change the Parental Controls settings for the others in the clan. You choose the screen name for which you would like to set Parental Controls in the box at the top of the window. Then, you're allowed to make the following choices for that person:

- **Online timer**—Allows you to set time limits for the user to be online.
- **Web control**—You can choose from four settings: Kids Only (12 and under), Young Teen (13-15), Mature Teen (16-17), and General Access (18 and older). Kids Only allows only access to AOL's Kids Only Channel, whereas General Access allows full, unrestricted movement on the Web.
- **IM control**—Allows you to set whether Instant Messages can be sent and retrieved.
- **E-mail control**—Allows you to customize whether email can be sent and retrieved, and from whom.
- **Chat control**—Allows you to block certain types of chat areas from access, or all chat within AOL.
- **Additional Master**—Allows you to make another screen name a Master, so you can have more than one person setting controls.
- **Download control**—You can determine what types of downloads (if any) you allow.
- **Newsgroup**—You can set the types of newsgroups you'll allow each screen name to access.
- **Premium Services**—Determine whether access to extra AOL services (for which you are charged extra) is allowed.

Summary

As you can see, there's no sure-fire way to protect unsupervised kids online. But there's no reason to worry, either. A few smart choices, along with your supervision and guidance, will enable your family to enjoy the Internet's benefits while steering clear of its troubles.

I know I mentioned a lot of scary stuff here, but I do want you to relax and enjoy the Net. Look at it this way: People get hit by cars every day. Now, does that mean you should never leave the house, or lay awake worrying? No. It just means that you should look both ways and hold your kid's hand when crossing.

Q&A

Q I thought I heard they passed a law against online porn. If they did, why is it still there?

A The highly controversial Communications Decency Act (CDA) sought to impose penalties against anyone who made available online anything that was "harmful" to minors.

As everyone expected, the U.S. Supreme Court ruled the CDA unconstitutional in June 1997, declaring that protecting freedom of speech includes protecting unpopular forms of expression.

So for the time being, the Internet is a protected free-speech zone, which is probably best. But new censorship initiatives continue to erupt, as do campaigns to counter them. To learn more about the controversy, check out the Electronic Frontier Foundation (a free speech online advocacy group) at `www.eff.org`.

HOUR 18

Buying and Selling on the Net

Only a few years ago, there was a huge hullabaloo about doing business online and the exploding interest in what we now call *e-commerce* (electronic commerce). But it was all talk—despite noises to the contrary, little real business was happening on the Web. Most business Web pages were mere e-advertising, not points of sale.

But today, you can buy or sell just about anything online. Companies are beginning to approach the Web not just as an intriguing place to experiment, but as a market they mustn't miss.

In this hour, you'll get a taste of e-commerce from both sides of the e-counter. First, we'll learn how to shop and invest online safely. Next, you'll learn the ways you can do business online, and learn how to get started.

At the end of the hour, you'll be able to answer the following questions:

- How do I find and purchase products online?
- Can I buy stocks and other financial stuff on the Web?

- How do I find all the places online where the thing I want might be available, in one step?
- How do I buy or sell stuff through an online auction?

Shopping 'Til You Drop

Whattaya wanna buy? Whatever it is, you can probably buy it from a Web page that sells products, also known as a *virtual storefront* (see Figure 18.1).

NEW TERM **Virtual storefront.** This is just a fancy, highfalutin' buzzword for a Web page from which you can buy stuff. In coming years, you'll see the word "virtual" tacked onto all sorts of online activities to make them sound cooler: virtual jobs, virtual travel, virtual dentistry…

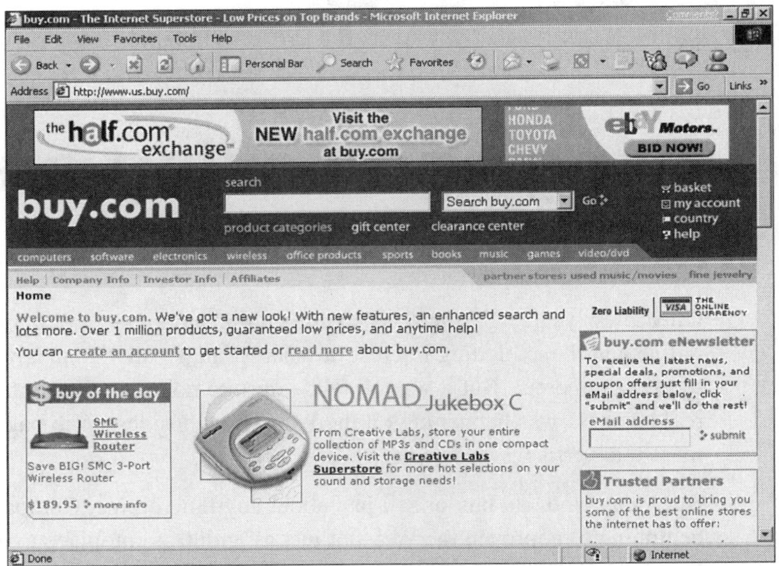

FIGURE 18.1
Virtual storefronts are the hip way to buy online, 24 hours a day, with no snotty clerks standing over you to make sure you're not shoplifting.

Using only the Web-surfing skills you already possess, you can enjoy the benefits of online shopping:

- **24-hour, 365-day shopping.** Except for rare moments when the server is down for maintenance and repair, online stores are always open.
- **Access to product photos and specifications.** While you're browsing an online catalog, you often can click links to display product photos, lists of options, and even detailed measurements or other specifications. Such stuff can help you make an informed buying decision.

- **Search tools.** Pages with extensive product listings often include a search tool for finding any product available from the merchant.
- **Web specials.** Some merchants offer discounts or other deals that are available only to those ordering online and not to phone, mail order, or in-person customers.
- **Custom ordering.** Some stores feature forms that let you specify exactly what you want (see Figure 18.2). For example, PC sellers that are online, such as Dell or Gateway, let you choose your PC's specifications—processor, hard disk size, CD-ROM speed, and so on—from lists in a form. When you finish, the price for your system appears, along with a link for placing the order. At an online clothing shop, you can specify exact measurements, color, monogramming, and other custom specifications.
- **Mailing lists.** Many online merchants offer a form for subscribing to a mailing list with updates about new products and specials.

You know this already, but it bears repeating: Making an online purchase usually requires typing your credit card number and other sensitive information in a form. That's something you should never do on a site that's not secure.

Explore virtual storefronts to your heart's content, comparing prices and other terms to make the best buy. But when you arrive at the actual page where you fill in your order form or open an account with the merchant, confirm that the page is secure. In most browsers, a secure site is indicated by either a locked golden padlock or a solid (unbroken) gold key near the bottom of the window. If you see a broken key, an unlocked padlock, or no icon at all, buy elsewhere.

Caveat emptor—buyer beware—online as anywhere else. As an online consumer, it behooves you to be an informed one. You can find reviews of products and merchants all over the Web. One good way to find reviews is to use the product name along with the word "review" as a search term.

You might also want to check out the Web pages of consumer advocates who alert us to schemes, scams, and duds:

Consumer's Union (publishers of *Consumer Reports* magazine): `www.ConsumerReports.org`

Consumer World: `www.consumerworld.org`

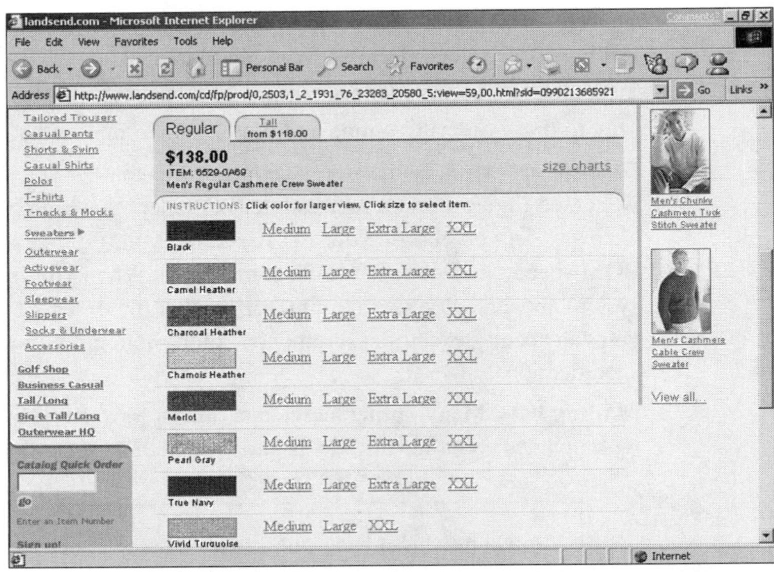

FIGURE 18.2
Forms on virtual storefronts can help you configure a custom order or get a price quote on one.

Using Accounts and Shopping Baskets

You already know how to fill out a form, and usually that's all there is to shopping. But many merchants equip their storefronts with either or both of the following to make shopping there more convenient:

- **Accounts.** When you set up an account with an online merchant, you give that merchant a record of your name and shipping address, and often your credit card information, too. After entering this information once, you can shop and buy there at any time without having to enter it again. All you have to do is enter an account username and password, and the site knows who you are, how you pay, and where to ship your stuff.
- **Shopping baskets (a.k.a. shopping carts).** A shopping basket lets you conveniently choose multiple products and then place the order for all of it, instead of having to order each item as you select it. Shopping baskets also provide you with a chance to look over your list of selections and the total price so you can change or delete items before committing to the order.

Often, accounts and shopping baskets require the use of *cookies* on your computer. If you have configured your browser to reject cookies and you try to set up an account or make a purchase, you might get a message from the site informing you that you must accept cookies in order to shop there.

In the following To Do, you can get a feel for accounts, shopping baskets, and virtual storefronts by finding and ordering music CDs from CD Universe, a popular source for CDs, tapes, and videos. Note that you don't actually have to make a purchase; I'll show you how to cancel before committing.

> If music is what you want to buy, note that there's no need to buy a CD. Often, you can get exactly the tunes you want in near-CD quality MP3 files online, either free or for a fee that's lower than the cost of a CD. You can play your MP3 tunes on your PC, or on a handheld MP3 player. See Hour 12, "Plug-in and Add-on Programs."

To Do: Find Some CDs and Put Them in a Basket

1. Go to CD Universe at `www.cduniverse.com` (see Figure 18.3).

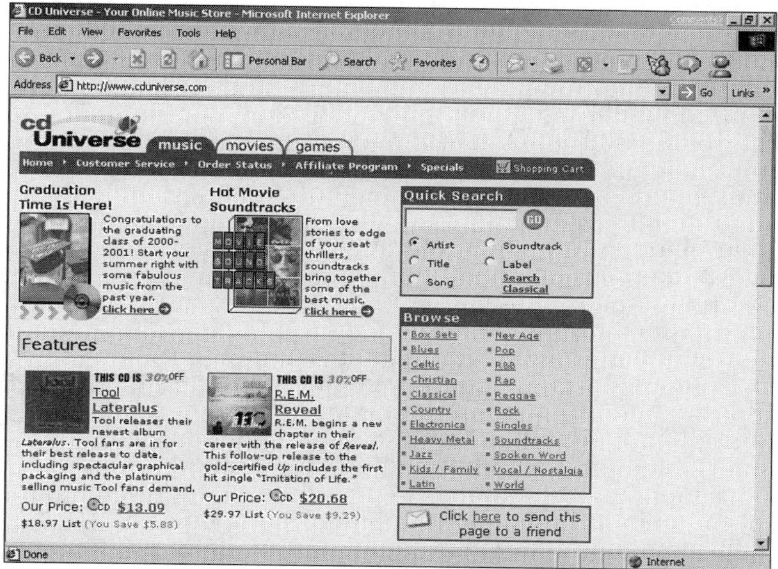

FIGURE 18.3
Step 1: Go to CD Universe.

2. In the Quick Search form at the top of the page, type the name of a recording artist in the box to the right of the Artist box, and then click Go (see Figure 18.4).

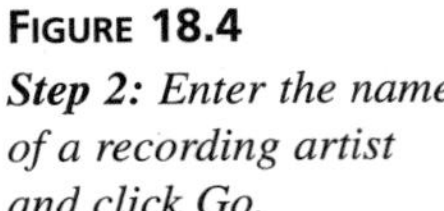

FIGURE 18.4
Step 2: Enter the name of a recording artist and click Go.

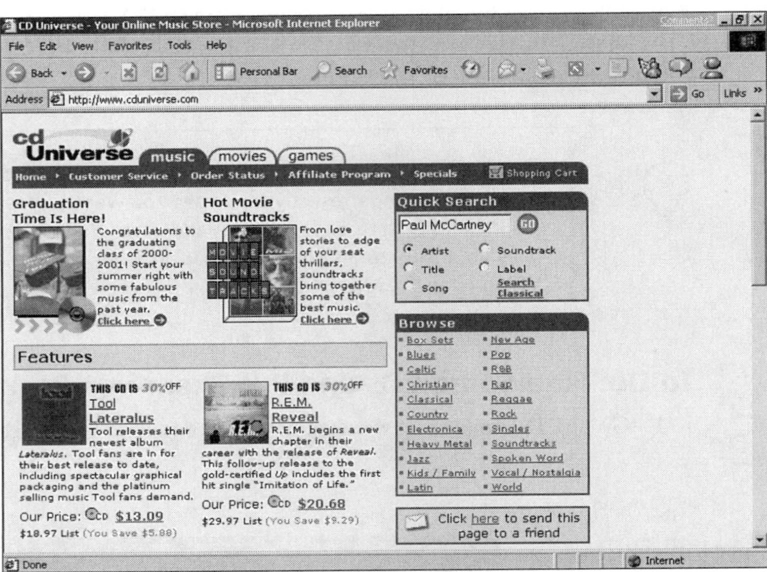

3. After a few moments, a list appears with titles available from that artist (see Figure 18.5). If CD Universe isn't sure which artist you want, a list of artists matching your search term appears first. Choose one to display the list of titles.

FIGURE 18.5
Step 3: Review the list of albums.

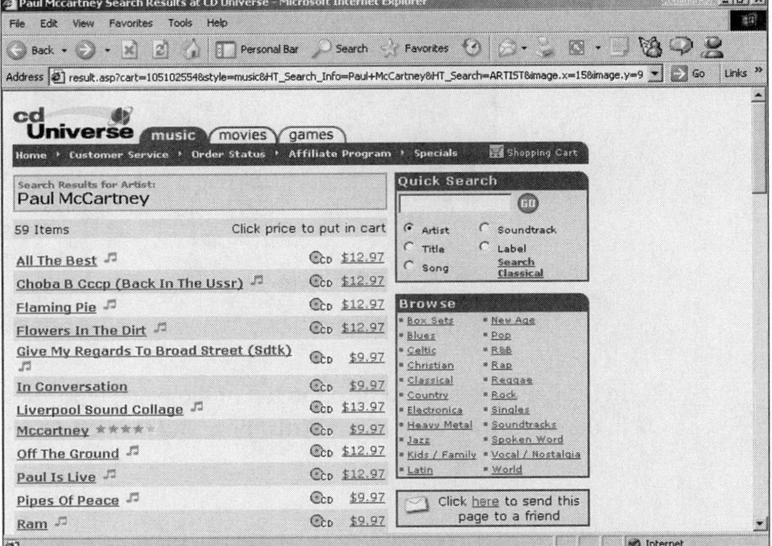

4. Choose a CD or tape by clicking its price (see Figure 18.6). If you're not sure which CD you want, click the title of the CD to learn more about it, including a list of songs.

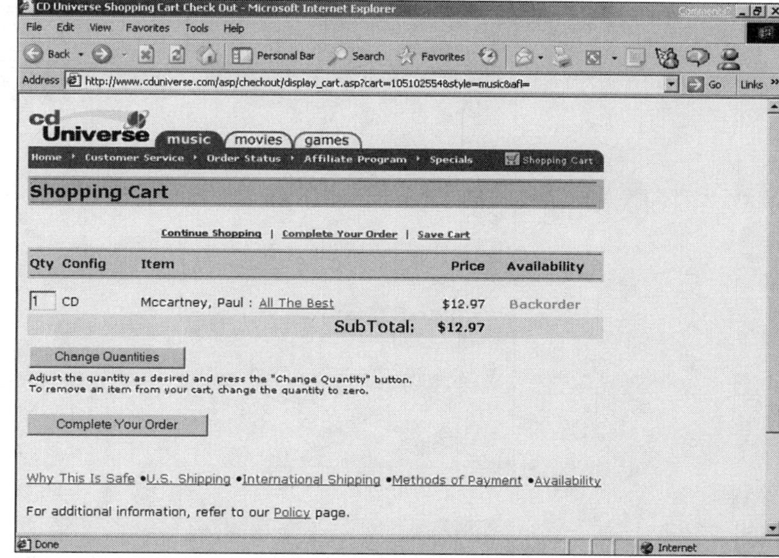

FIGURE 18.6
Step 4: *Choose a CD or tape by clicking its price.*

5. Review the info on the Shopping Cart screen, and then click Continue Shopping. Choose another title by clicking its price, and you will again see your Shopping Cart, now with two CDs listed (see Figure 18.7).
6. Click Complete Your Order to start the purchasing process. You will see the Account Entry screen (see Figure 18.8). To quit without purchasing anything, just leave the site now. To order your selections, click New Account, complete the form that appears, and follow any prompts.

18

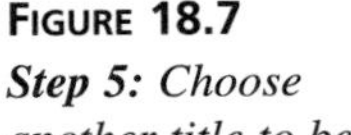

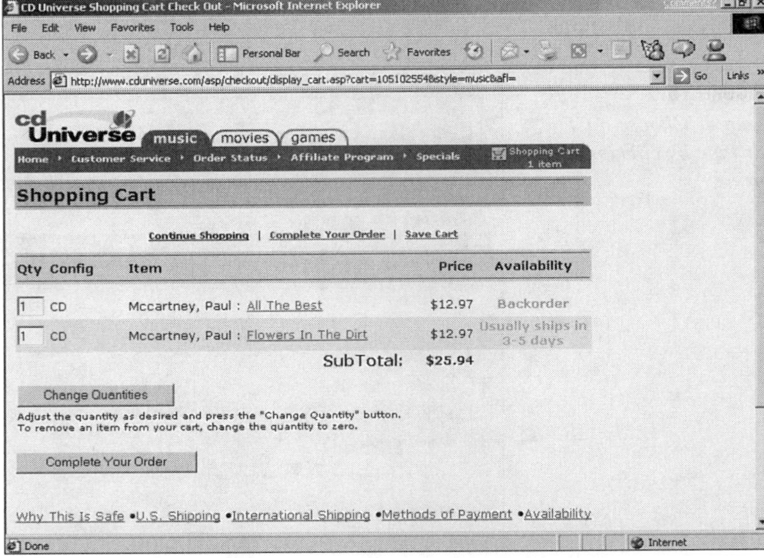

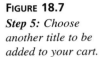

FIGURE 18.7
Step 5: Choose another title to be added to your cart.

Checkout - Microsoft Internet Explorer
File Edit View Favorites Tools Help
Address https://www.cduniverse.com/asp/checkout/checkout.asp?cart=105102554&style=music&afl=
cd Universe music movies games
Home · Customer Service · Order Status · Affiliate Program · Specials Shopping Cart 2 items
Account Entry
If you already have a CD Universe or Video Universe account, enter your name and password in "Enter Existing Account". To create a new account, click the New Account link.
Existing Account
First Name
Last Name
Password
Enter
New Account
Click here for a New Account
Your account information is strictly confidential, and is used solely to fill your order. If you have forgotten your password Click Here
Internet

FIGURE 18.8
Step 6: Either cancel your order now or fill out the New Account form to order your selections.

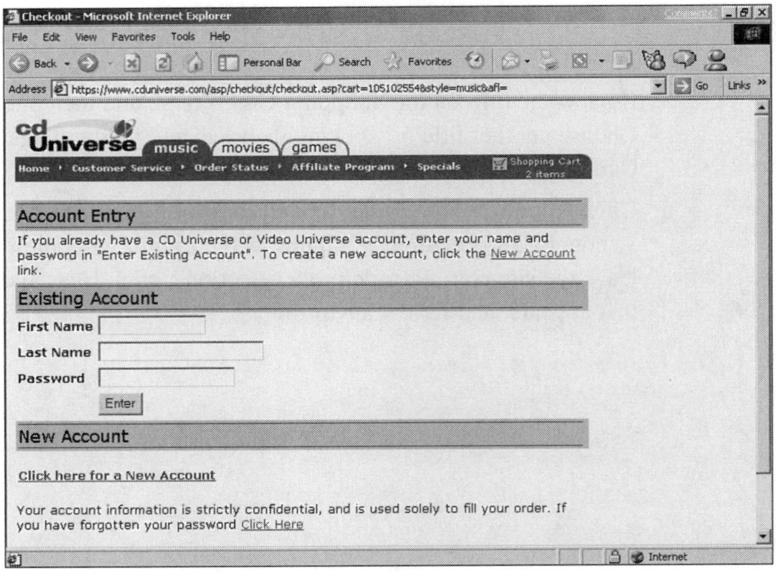

Immediately after you place an order from an online store, some sort of confirmation of your order should appear in your Web browser. Many stores also email you a confirmation of your order.

Make a note of any information that appears in the confirmation—especially anything called an *order number*—and save any email message you receive. You'll need this information to query the merchant if your merchandise doesn't arrive within the time promised, or if it isn't what you ordered. If your order confirmation doesn't appear right away, find a shopping cart button to click to see your order.

Buying Stocks and Such

The Web is a great place to sell intangible goods, such as stocks or securities. After all, if the product is intangible, why shouldn't the transaction be?

Obviously, such purchases carry the greatest risk of all online shopping activities. They generally involve moving around large amounts of money and putting it at risk in investments. But if that's your thing, you should know that trading online can be substantially cheaper than using a traditional broker, and in many cases your transactions are executed much more quickly—usually within minutes.

The steps for online investing are roughly the same as those for buying anything else online. Typically, you set up an account with an online brokerage, after which you may buy and sell at will.

However, note that opening an account with an online broker typically requires disclosing detailed information about yourself. You'll have to disclose your bank account numbers, Social Security number, and other private, sensitive information you don't have to reveal when making other kinds of purchases online.

Investment Starting Points

To learn more about investing online, or to take the plunge and buy those 1,000 shares of PepsiCo, consult the following sites.

For Financial Information and Advice

To learn more about online investing, read company profiles, and explore other money matters, check out the following sites:

- **Stockpoint:** `www.stockpoint.com`
- **CNN's Financial News Network:** `cnnfn.com`
- **Wall Street Journal:** `www.wsj.com`

- **Dow Jones Business Information Services:** `bis.dowjones.com`
- **MoneyAdvisor:** `www.moneyadvisor.com`
- ***Success* Magazine:** `www.successmagazine.com`
- **Yahoo! Finance:** `quote.yahoo.com`
- **The Motley Fool:** `www.fool.com`
- **NASDAQ:** `www.nasdaq.com`

For Making Investments

If you're ready to go ahead and put your money on the line (online!), visit these online brokers:

- **Mr. Stock:** `www.mrstock.com`
- **American Express Financial Services Direct:** `www.americanexpress.com/direct`
- **E*Trade:** `www.etrade.com`
- **Charles Schwab:** `www.eschwab.com`
- **Datek:** `www.datek.com`

Finding All the Sites Online That Sell What You Want

Instead of surfing blindly to various retailers and auction houses to find a particular item, you can call upon any of several services that search the shopping sites for a particular item and provide a list of links to sites that offer it. The price or current bid is included for each site (see Figure 18.9). These sites are sometimes called "shopping agents."

> New shopping agents are coming online all the time. If you want to try one, it's a good idea to use a search engine to search for "shopping agents" and find the most recent sites.

Agents aren't foolproof—they can't find absolutely every site that might offer what you want. They'll only search the most popular shopping sites, or sites that have made a special business arrangement with them. But they might help you ensure that you get the best price (or best source) for that special item. And they often feature product information, reviews, and comparisons that can help you choose which product to buy. Check out:

- `www.mysimon.com`
- `DealTime.com`
- `shop.Lycos.com`
- `ValueFind.com`

FIGURE 18.9
Sites like MySimon search multiple shopping/auction sites to help you find out who has the product you want for the best price.

Buying and Selling Through Online Auctions

Lately, auction houses have joined the ranks of the hottest places to pick up bargains or unusual items on the Net. Not only are online auction houses great places to pick up new and used merchandise—and especially hard-to-find collectibles—but the bidding process can be a lot of fun, too. eBay, at `www.ebay.com` (see Figure 18.10), might be the most popular online auction house now, but there others, including the following:

- **Yahoo! Auctions:** `auctions.yahoo.com`
- **Amazon.com Auctions:** `auctions.amazon.com`
- **Auctions.com:** `auctions.com`
- **Butterfield & Butterfield:** `www.butterfields.com`

Also, you'll often see links to auctions on retail sites. You can bid on an item you might otherwise buy outright, and maybe save a bundle.

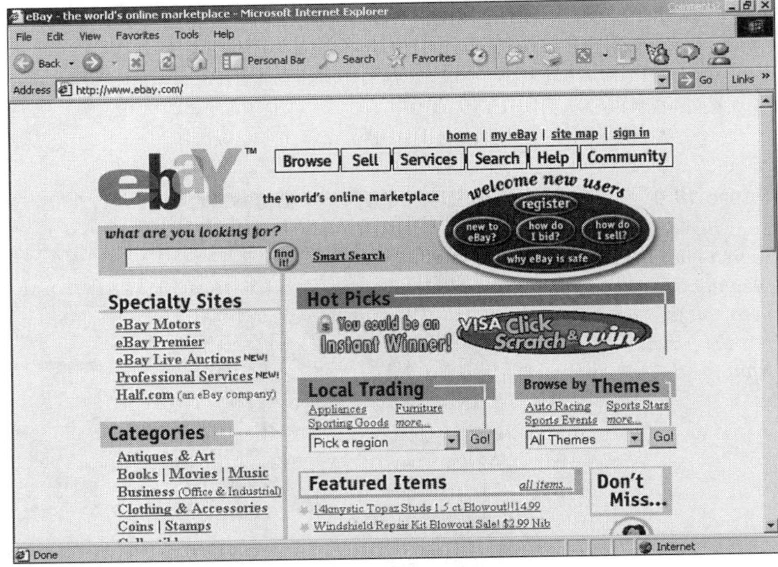

FIGURE 18.10
eBay, a popular online auction house.

How Online Auction Houses Work

Although you can usually view the items up for auction without registering, you typically must register with the auction house—a quick process of filling in an online form—to bid on items or to sell an item. Once registered, you can use the search tools or categories on the auction house's page to browse for items to bid on. Note that most auctions go on for several days, and some go on for a week, so it's not necessary to sit in front of your computer for hours to join in the fun.

The auction house usually has no role in the actual financial transaction between seller and buyer, so a secure page is not really necessary. Typically, if you win an auction, the auction house emails both you and the seller to notify you about the win and to give you each other's contact info. After that, you and the seller have a set period of time in which to contact each other to arrange payment and shipping. Many sellers who use these auction houses are commercial merchants who can accept payment by credit card via email or telephone. Some individual sellers might require that you pay by money order or personal check.

eBay features a Feedback forum (see Figure 18.11) where buyers and sellers can post positive and negative comments about their experiences with each other. Before buying, you can always check out the comments others have made about the seller to determine whether that seller is a safe person to do business with.

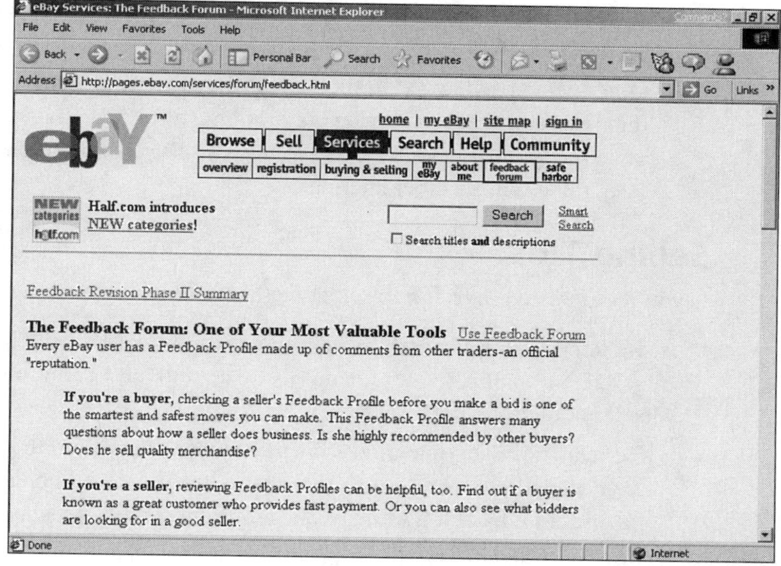

FIGURE 18.11
Some auction houses have feedback forums so you can see what others have to say about a person before you do business with that person.

To minimize the risk on bigger-ticket items, auction houses offer links to *escrow services* that make purchasing a little safer for buyer and seller (for a fee, of course).

The buyer pays the escrow service, not the seller. The seller does not ship anything until he knows that the escrow service has the buyer's money. When the buyer informs the escrow service that the item has arrived, the escrow service pays the seller.

Bidding Tips

If you want to try online auctions, here are a few important tips:

- Always check out the feedback about a seller before bidding to make sure the seller is reliable.
- Before you bid on an item, always search the Web or other sources to see whether the same item is for sale elsewhere and for how much. That way you can be sure not to bid more than you would pay for the same item elsewhere. (Try a shopping agent for this.)
- Check out any payment terms in the listing. If no terms are listed, use the links provided to email the seller and ask what forms of payment the seller accepts (check, money order, and so on). You might want to think twice (or use an escrow

service) before dealing with a seller who accepts only money orders, which is the second riskiest way to pay by mail after cash.

- Don't get carried away. In the heat of the auction, it's easy to get caught in a bidding war and wind up paying way too much for that Elvis candleholder you think you simply *must* have. Decide the most you're willing to pay and stick to it. If you lose, there will be other auctions.

Selling Tips

If you're interested in trying to sell something online, here are a few quick tips:

- Be honest. Don't overstate the importance or worth of the item you're trying to sell. Don't call it an antique unless it is one. Don't call it one-of-a-kind and then sell another one next week.
- Be realistic. Everyone thinks his or her own stuff is worth more than it is. If you have something that's worth more to you than it would be to anyone else, that's a keepsake. Why sell it? Keep your minimum pricing reasonable.
- Provide a picture. Descriptions are great, but most people want to see the real piece. A high-resolution photo will help drive your price up.
- Send it quickly. As soon as you receive payment, send the item you sold. It'll ease anxiety for the buyer, and help drive up your rating on the auction service.
- Check other means of selling. Sometimes, the newspaper or online classifieds are still the best way to sell an item.

Using a Payment Service

Online payment services like PayPal (`www.paypal.com`) and Billpoint (`www.billpoint.com`) offer secure transactions that can allow you to send or receive a payment instantly. All you have to do is set up an account at one of the services, and you can start using it to buy and sell.

The payments are processed rapidly, and the security of the transaction allows the merchandise to change hands more quickly.

Summary

By now you're ready to begin spending money online, making money online, or both. I hope you've seen that actually buying or selling on the Web is pretty easy, but doing either one *well*—taking into account all of the risks and issues surrounding these activities—takes preparation, care, and practice.

Q&A

Q You say to buy only from shops I trust. I'm not sure who I can trust in my *family*. How am I supposed to know who to trust online?

A Well, you aren't. You can't trust *any* company until you've had some experience with it. But there are a few steps you can take to decrease your chances of getting stung.

When possible, deal with online companies you've already dealt with offline, such as mail order companies whose print catalogs you've used or retailers whose stores you've visited. If the company was reliable on the phone or at the store, it probably will be okay online. If an online company is new to you, see whether it offers a toll-free number for phone orders. Try placing a phone order first. If that works out well, order online next time. If you can't test the company that way, make your first order small and cheap and place a second order only if the first one goes well.

Finally, always make purchases with credit cards. I know that sounds funny, given my warnings about sending credit card numbers to insecure sites. But when the site is secure, using a credit card is safest. If a merchant lets you down, you can call the credit card company and dispute the charge.

When you're using an online auction, always check out the seller's feedback, if available. And when you're purchasing a big-ticket item you've won at auction, consider using one of the escrow services the auction houses offer.

HOUR 19

Creating Web Pages and Multimedia Messages

Got something to say, or to sell? Want to offer your experiences or expertise to the world? There's no better way to do that today than by creating and publishing your own Web page.

Building a Web page is easier than you might think—if you know how to surf the Web and to use any word processing program, you already possess the prerequisite skills for Web authoring. This hour takes you the rest of the way, showing you several ways to create attractive Web pages. The basic skills you'll learn here will form a foundation upon which you can build later, on your own, to add scripts, multimedia, and other advanced techniques to your skill set. You'll also learn how to create fancy, formatted email and newsgroup messages in this hour.

At the end of the hour, you'll be able to answer the following questions:

- What exactly is a Web page, and what does it take to create one?
- How can I use a wizard or template to produce a simple page very quickly?

- How can I compose and edit Web pages in a Web page–editing program?
- How do I publish my pages on a Web server?
- How can I apply my Web authoring skills to create email and newsgroup messages adorned with fonts and pictures?

Understanding Web Authoring

Before you can dive into creating a Web page, you need to pick up a more intimate understanding of how a Web page works than you'll get simply by surfing the Web.

What's in a Web Page?

A Web page is actually a file in a format called HTML, which stands for Hypertext Markup Language. An HTML file contains nothing but text—the actual text you'll see online, and instructions for how that text is to appear (see Figure 19.1).

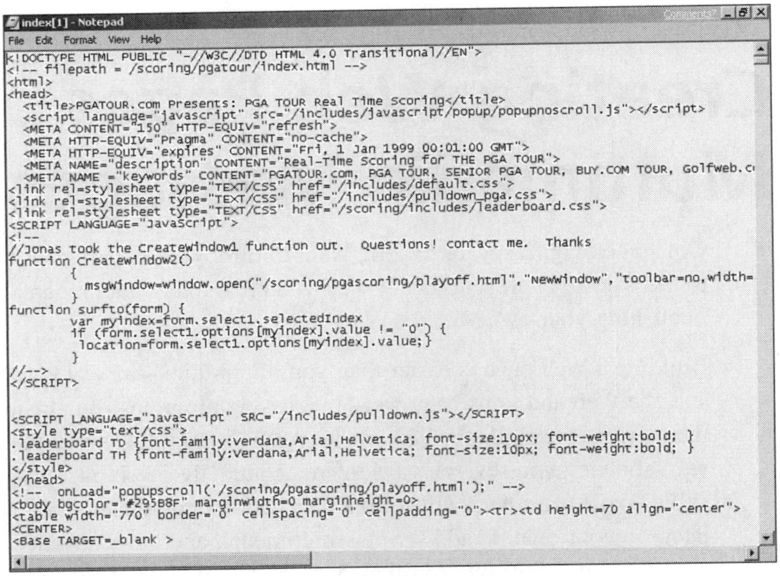

```
index[1] - Notepad
File Edit Format View Help
<!DOCTYPE HTML PUBLIC "-//W3C//DTD HTML 4.0 Transitional//EN">
<!-- filepath = /scoring/pgatour/index.html -->
<html>
<head>
  <title>PGATOUR.com Presents: PGA TOUR Real Time Scoring</title>
  <script language="javascript" src="/includes/javascript/popup/popupnoscroll.js"></script>
  <META CONTENT="150" HTTP-EQUIV="refresh">
  <META HTTP-EQUIV="Pragma" CONTENT="no-cache">
  <META HTTP-EQUIV="expires" CONTENT="Fri, 1 Jan 1999 00:01:00 GMT">
  <META NAME="description" CONTENT="Real-Time Scoring for THE PGA TOUR">
  <META NAME ="keywords" CONTENT="PGATOUR.com, PGA TOUR, SENIOR PGA TOUR, BUY.COM TOUR, Golfweb.c
<link rel=stylesheet type="TEXT/CSS" href="/includes/default.css">
<link rel=stylesheet type="TEXT/CSS" href="/includes/pulldown_pga.css">
<link rel=stylesheet type="TEXT/CSS" href="/scoring/includes/leaderboard.css">
<SCRIPT LANGUAGE="JavaScript">
<!--
//Jonas took the CreateWindow1 function out.  Questions! contact me.  Thanks
function CreateWindow2()
        {
          msgWindow=window.open("/scoring/pgascoring/playoff.html","NewWindow","toolbar=no,width=
        }
function surfto(form) {
        var myindex=form.select1.selectedIndex
        if (form.select1.options[myindex].value != "0") {
         location=form.select1.options[myindex].value;}
        }
//-->
</SCRIPT>


<SCRIPT LANGUAGE="JavaScript" SRC="/includes/pulldown.js"></SCRIPT>
<style type="text/css">
.leaderboard TD {font-family:Verdana,Arial,Helvetica; font-size:10px; font-weight:bold; }
.leaderboard TH {font-family:Verdana,Arial,Helvetica; font-size:10px; font-weight:bold; }
</style>
</head>
<!--  onLoad="popupscroll('/scoring/pgascoring/playoff.html');" -->
<body bgcolor="#295B8F" marginwidth=0 marginheight=0>
<table width="770" border="0" cellspacing="0" cellpadding="0"><tr><td height=70 align="center">
<CENTER>
<Base TARGET=_blank >
```

FIGURE 19.1
The actual text of an HTML file.

The text in an HTML file also includes the URLs of any links on the page, as well as the filenames, locations, and page positions of any pictures or other multimedia files, which are stored in their own separate files.

When an HTML file is viewed through a browser, the browser formats the text onscreen as ordered, locates the picture files, and displays them in their specified positions. The browser also reads the URLs that the links point to, so it knows where to take a visitor who clicks a link. Figure 19.2 shows the very same file as Figure 19.1, but in Figure 19.2, it is interpreted by a Web browser.

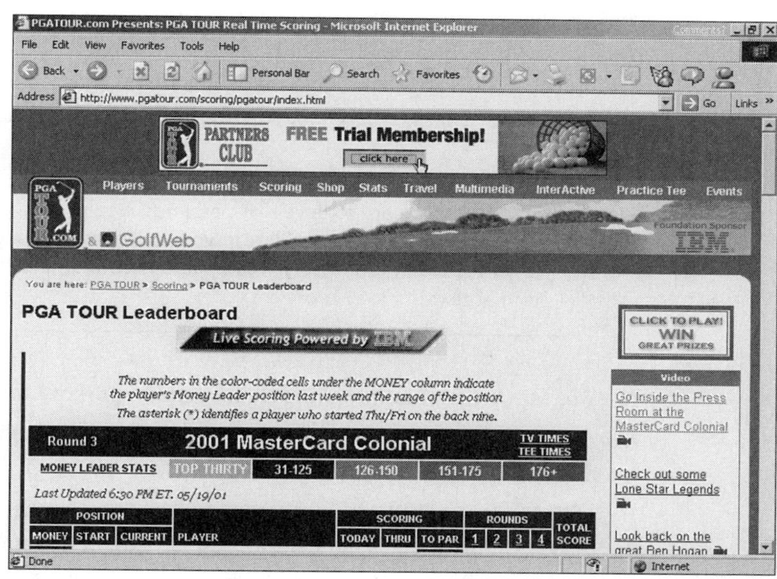

FIGURE 19.2
The same file as Figure 19.1, now interpreted by a browser.

In general, the formatting instructions contained in an HTML file do not precisely control how the page will appear. Rather, the file provides a general idea of how the page is to appear, and each browser realizes those instructions slightly differently. That's why the very same Web page often looks different in two different browsers.

For example, the HTML file might specify that a particular line of text is to be displayed as a heading. One browser might follow that instruction by making the text big and bold, whereas another might follow it by underlining the text. This idea is often difficult to get used to for new authors accustomed to word processors that enable precise formatting control.

There are new, advanced Web authoring techniques that give you greater control, but the formatting applied by those techniques is not visible through all browsers. So it's still generally true that formatting a Web page is not about controlling *exactly* how the page will look, but rather about designating the role each element plays in the page: a heading, a normal paragraph, and so on.

A Web page can be made up of many different parts, but most Web pages contain most or all of the following core elements:

- A *title*, which browsers typically display in the title bar of the window in which the page appears. Note that the actual title does not appear within the layout of the page, although many authors repeat the title in a big heading near the top of the page layout.
- *Headings*, which browsers typically display in large, bold, or otherwise emphasized type. A Web page can have many headings, and headings can be *nested* up to six levels deep. That is, there can be subheadings, sub-subheadings, and so on.

In HTML, there are six levels of headings, beginning with Heading 1 (the biggest and boldest, usually reserved for creating a page's title) and going down to Heading 6 (a very small, minor heading, indistinguishable from normal text in many browsers).

- *Normal text*, which makes up the basic, general-purpose text of the page.
- *Horizontal lines* (sometimes called *rules*) that dress up the page and separate it into logical sections.
- *Hyperlinks* (or simply *links*) to many different things: other Web pages; multimedia files (external images, animation, sound, video); document files; email addresses; and files or programs on other types of servers (such as Telnet, FTP, and Gopher). Links might also lead to specific spots within the current page.
- *Lists*, bulleted (like this one) or numbered.
- *Inline images*, pictures that are incorporated into the layout of the page to jazz it up or make it more informative.
- A *background*, an inline image that, unlike a regular image, covers the entire background of the page so that text and other images can be seen on top of it. Instead of an image, you can use a solid background color.
- *Tables*, text and inline images organized in neat rows and columns.

What Tools Can I Use to Write a Page?

If you were skilled in HTML code, you could write a Web page simply by typing the correct code in a text file, using any word processor or text editing program (such as Windows Notepad). Some folks do it that way, but doing so makes it hard to see what you're creating; you have to jump from the editor to a browser every time you want to see how the page will look online.

A better choice is a WYSIWYG Web authoring program (see Figure 19.3). This shows you the page as it will look online, while you're working on it.

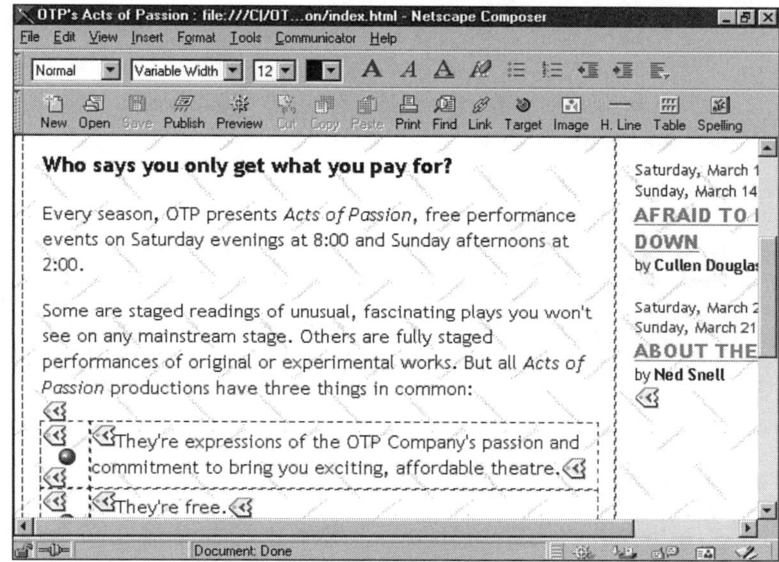

FIGURE 19.3
A WYSIWYG Web authoring program such as Netscape Composer, shown here, lets you use familiar word processing techniques to create a Web page.

NEW TERM **WYSIWYG (What You See Is What You Get).** A program that shows you, as you create something, exactly how it will look in its finished form, on paper or onscreen. For Windows and the Mac, most word processors, presentation programs, desktop publishers, and Web authoring programs are WYSIWYG.

19

If you're careful to select and install the complete suite, you get a WYSIWYG editor with either of the Big Two browsers:

- The full Netscape Communicator suite includes Composer, which you open from within Netscape Navigator by choosing Communicator, Composer.
- The full Microsoft Internet Explorer suite includes FrontPage Express (not to be confused with the more sophisticated program FrontPage described in the following section), which you open from the same menu where you can open the browser. In Windows, choose Programs, Internet Explorer, FrontPage Express.

If your copy of Internet Explorer does not include FrontPage Express, you can get it through Windows Update. In Windows 98/NT/Me/XP, click the Start button, choose Windows Update, and then follow the prompts. In the list of programs and files that appears, check the check box for FrontPage Express.

Other commercial (not free) Web authoring packages include Microsoft's FrontPage (included in some editions of the Office program suite) and Adobe's PageMill. These more sophisticated programs are worth looking into if you're ambitious about authoring. But most beginners will find that the free programs included in the browser suites more than meet their needs.

You can learn about and download other Web authoring programs from the Tucows Internet software directory at `www.tucows.com`.

Even when you're using a WYSIWYG editor, pages you create might look different when seen through different browsers. WYS is not always WYG.

And it's always a good idea to display the document in a browser now and then to check its appearance. Netscape Composer and FrontPage Express each include a button for viewing the page you're editing in Netscape Navigator and Internet Explorer, respectively.

Where Do I Get the Pictures?

The pictures you'll use on your Web pages can come from anywhere. You can draw them in a paint program such as CorelDraw! or Windows 95/98's Paint accessory, scan them from your own photos, or even use images captured by a digital camera.

What matters isn't the source of the pictures, but rather the image file format in which they're stored. The pictures you include on a Web page, either as inline images or as background images, must be in either the GIF (`.GIF`) or JPEG (`.JPG`) file format. (GIF is usually preferable because it is supported by all graphical browsers, although JPEG is also supported by most browsers and often produces better-looking results with photographs.) If the program you use to create images won't save in GIF or JPEG format, many paint programs (and some Web authoring programs) can convert your files to GIF or JPEG.

If you want to use pictures but don't want to create them, you can find libraries of commercial, shareware, and free clip art files in GIF and JPEG format both online and at your local software store.

See Appendix A, "Fun Web Sites to Visit," for the URLs of great places to pick up clip art, animations, and other cool content for your Web pages.

Making Quick Pages with a Wizard

The quickest way to build a page is by running a *page wizard*. Both Netscape Composer and FrontPage Express have one of these wizards, which leads you through a few quick dialog boxes where you fill in blanks and choose some options. When you finish, the wizard spits out a finished Web page, ready for publishing.

A wizard doesn't give you as much control as composing the page in a Web authoring program does, but it is faster. And if the results aren't exactly what you want, you can always open your wizard-built page in your Web authoring program and change it.

Netscape Composer's wizard, which is unusual because you must use it while online, also allows you to build pages that are hosted on Netscape's servers, for free.

To Do: Create a Page Fast with Netscape Composer's Wizard

1. Open Netscape Navigator (not Composer) and connect to the Internet (see Figure 19.4).

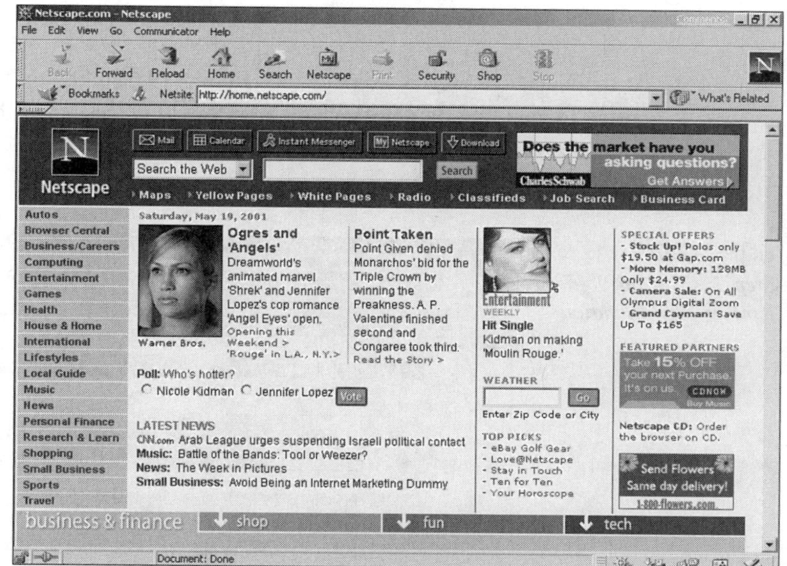

FIGURE 19.4
Step 1: Open Netscape Navigator.

2. In Navigator, choose File, New, Page From Wizard (see Figure 19.5).

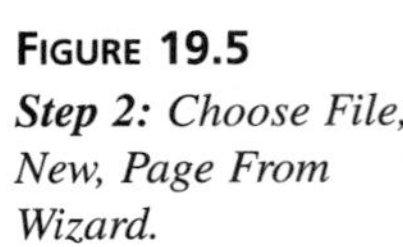

FIGURE 19.5
Step 2: *Choose File, New, Page From Wizard.*

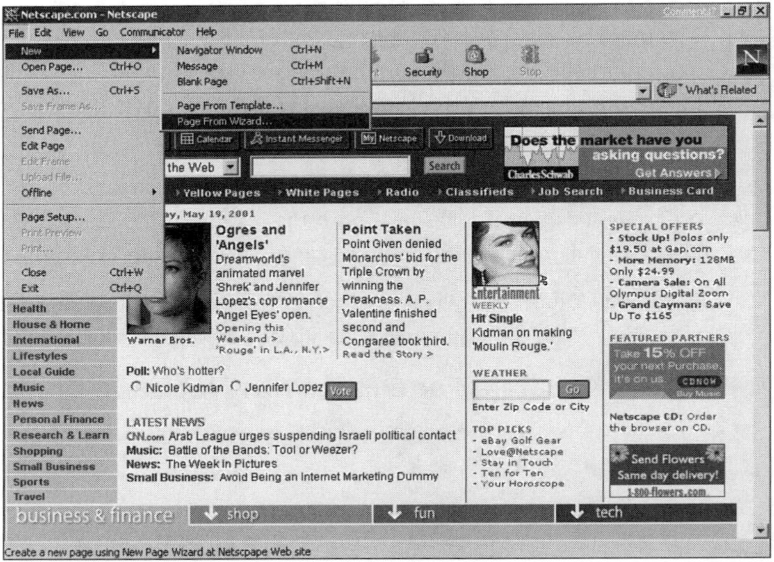

3. At the Netscape Web Sites page (see Figure 19.6), click on the Join Now or Sign In button, depending on whether you are already signed up with Netscape for some other service (such as Instant Messenger). If you haven't joined, you can go ahead and do it; it's free.

FIGURE 19.6
Step 3: *Click the Join Now or Sign In button.*

4. You will go to the Site Tools page (see Figure 19.7), where you can launch a Quick Start program to create your pages. Click the Quick Start button.

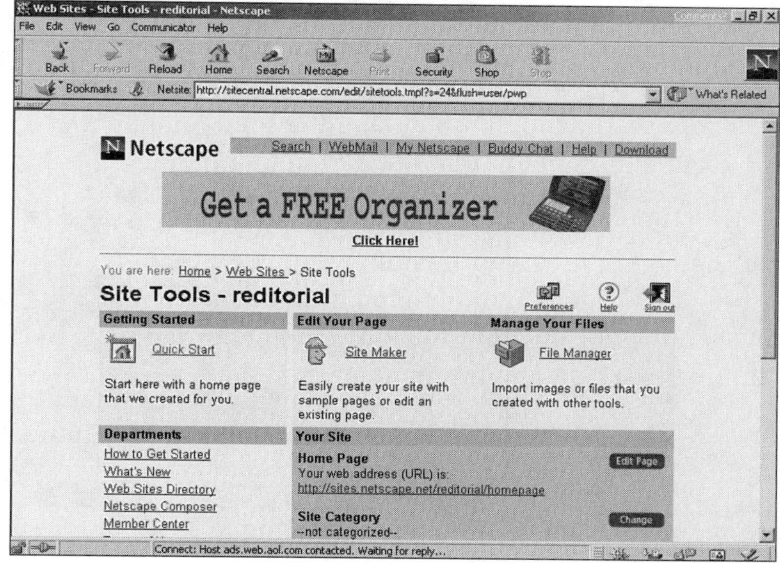

FIGURE 19.7
Step 4: Click the Quick Start button.

5. You are now in the Edit area (see Figure 19.8). Here, you can change text, background color, add elements, and more. Have fun playing with your page! When you're done, the page can be published to the URL that Netscape provides for you.

FIGURE 19.8
Step 5: Edit your page.

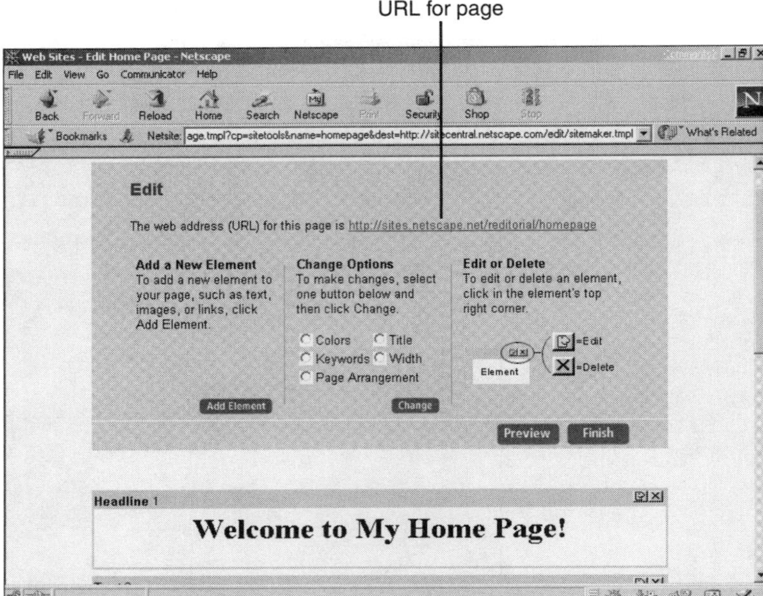

Composing a Page in a WYSIWYG Editor

Composing a Web page in a WYSIWYG editor is very much like composing and formatting a document in any word processor. You type your text and then format it by selecting it with your mouse and applying formatting—such as bold, fonts, and so on—from toolbar buttons or menu items. If you look at the toolbars in Composer (see Figure 19.9) or FrontPage Express, you'll probably recognize many of the tools, such as a drop-down list for choosing a font or a big "B" for applying boldface.

Although the Web authoring programs present you with lots of formatting tools, it bears repeating here that precise formatting you apply—such as font selections—might not be supported by all browsers. The formatting that matters most is the application of *styles*, which you choose from a drop-down list on the toolbar in both Composer and FrontPage Express. It's the style that really tells browsers how to handle a block of text.

Besides using a Web authoring program or a wizard, there's one more way to create a page: your word processor. The latest versions of both Microsoft Word and WordPerfect can save files in HTML format.

A word processor is not as good for authoring as a real authoring program, but it will do in a pinch. More importantly, these programs make it easy to convert existing documents into Web page files. For example, you can open your resume in Word and then save it as an HTML file. Now it's ready for the Web.

You do have to be careful to use standard fonts like Times New Roman or Arial. If you use other fonts, they may not appear properly on a user's computer if the user doesn't have that particular font installed.

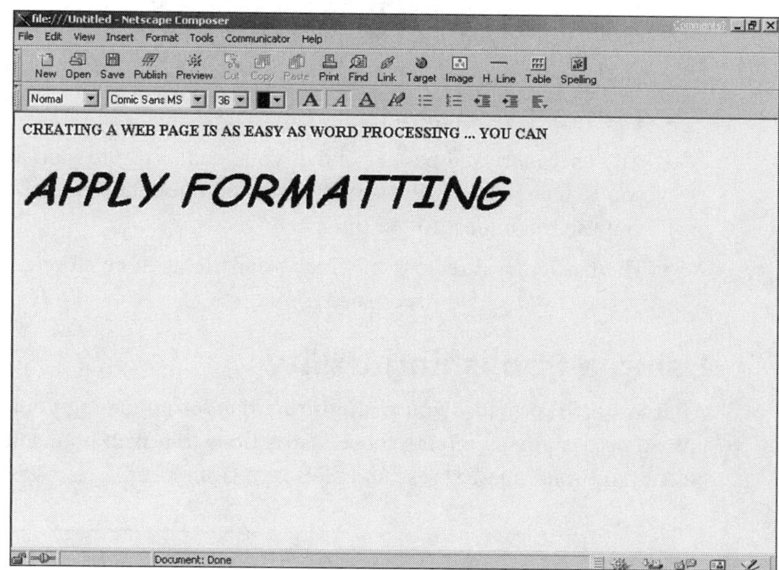

FIGURE 19.9
Using a WYSIWYG Web authoring program is very much like using any Windows or Mac word processor.

19

Publishing Your Web Page

After your Web page is finished, you must upload it to a Web server so that others on the Internet can see it. So first you need space on somebody's Web server—enough to hold all the files that make up your page (the HTML file plus picture files). A typical Web page with a picture or two usually requires less than 100KB of space on a server. The larger and more picture-laden your page, the more server space you'll need.

Preparing to Publish

If your page is related to your job, you might be able to get permission to publish it on your company's server. Talk to your company's network administrator or Webmaster.

Most colleges and universities also have Web servers and often allow students and faculty to publish on them.

If you don't have permission to publish your Web page on your company or school's server and don't plan to create your own server (which is prohibitively expensive and technical for beginners), you need to acquire space on somebody else's Web server, usually your ISP's.

After you know whose server will hold your Web page files, you must upload the files from your PC to the server. The exact procedures for doing this differ from one ISP to the next. You must get complete uploading instructions directly from the company whose server you will use. In particular, you need to know the following:

- The server's address, such as `http://www.server.com` or `ftp.server.com`.
- The *uploading protocol* used by the server (such as FTP).
- Any username and password that you need to use to gain access to the server. (If you're using your ISP's server, these might be the same username and password you use to connect to the Internet.)
- The particular directory in which your files will be stored, such as `http://www.server.com/ned/`.

Using a Publishing Utility

After your ISP provides you with instructions for uploading your files, you can make uploading easy by supplying those instructions to a Web publishing program like those built in to FrontPage Express and Netscape Composer.

Most servers allow you to upload Web page files through an FTP client program. Although the publishing programs included in some authoring programs might make publishing simpler, they're not always any easier than simply doing a good old-fashioned FTP upload. See Appendix B, "Tools for the Serious User: FTP and Telnet," to learn more about FTP.

To use either of these utilities, first open your Web editor and open the page you want to publish. Then do the following:

- **In Netscape Composer,** click the Publish button and follow the prompts.
- **In FrontPage Express,** choose File, Save As to open the Save dialog box. In Page Location, type the complete URL the page will have on the Web. Click OK and follow the prompts.

> The first time you use one of these publishing utilities, you need to spend a few minutes supplying information about the Web server you'll use. After you've done that, your uploads from then on will be very quick and easy. These utilities remember all your server information, so after you enter the information once, you don't need to fiddle with it again. Just start the publishing procedure as before, and most of the steps happen automatically.

Using AOL Hometown

America Online offers a page-building technology called 1-2-3 Publish, which uses templates to build simple pages that are hosted within AOL Hometown. But here's the best part—you don't have to be an AOL member in order to access this free service.

All you have to do is go to AOL Hometown at `hometown.aol.com` (see Figure 19.10), and click on the Beginners Start Here link on the right side of the page. You can literally have your own page published within minutes!

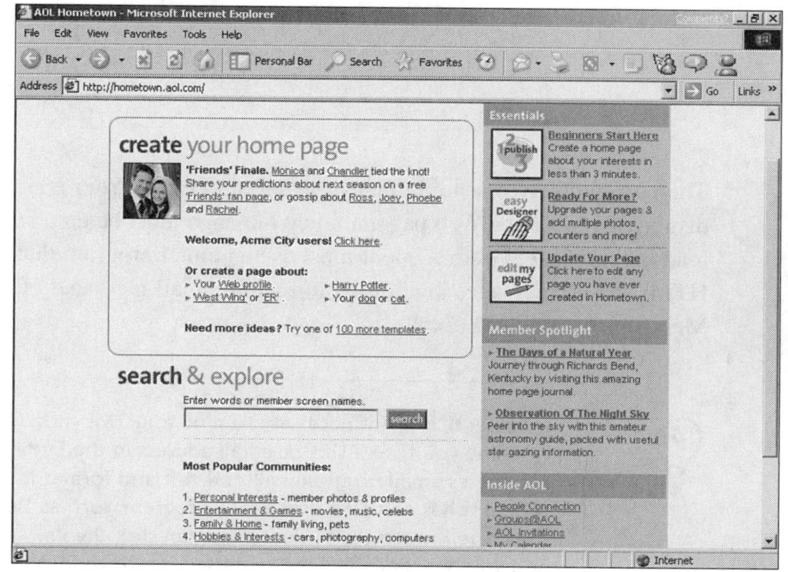

FIGURE 19.10
AOL Hometown allows you to build your own page within minutes.

Creating Formatted Email and Newsgroup Messages

In Hour 5, you created email messages—wonderful, simple email messages containing nothing but text. What you might not know is that email can contain the same kinds of content and formatting you use in a Web page (see Figure 19.11). You can send messages containing all kinds of fonts, colors, pictures, and links. If it can be put in a Web page, it can go in a message.

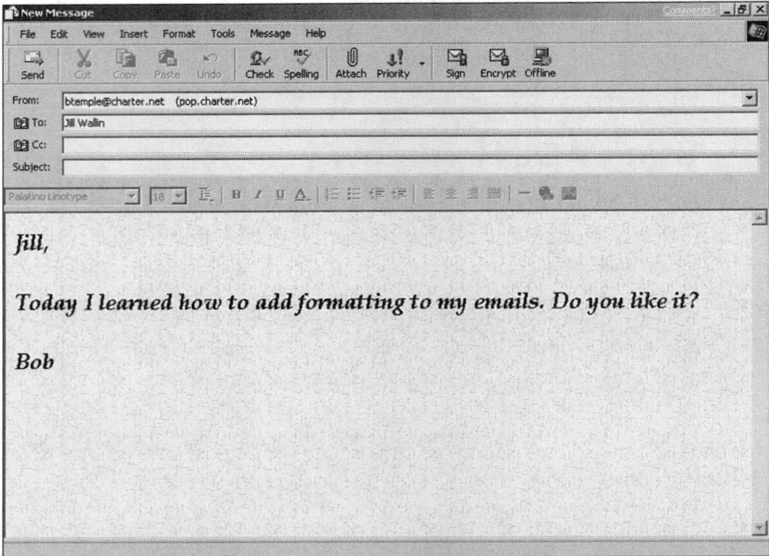

FIGURE 19.11
In HTML-supporting messaging programs, you can create and display email and newsgroup messages with all the pizzazz of Web pages.

There's one hitch to sending fancy messages like this: Your recipient might not be able to display them. Like a Web page, a fancy message must be created in HTML format. To read the message, your recipient must use an email program that's capable of displaying HTML-based messages in addition to regular email messages, such as Netscape Messenger or Outlook Express.

In general, it is not necessary to send an HTML message—you just send links. Anytime you type a URL or email address in the body of a message, the recipient's email program will detect it and format it as a link (that is, if the recipient has an up-to-date email program, such as Outlook Express or Netscape Messenger. The recipient can click the link to go where it leads, and you can click the links in messages received from others.

Many people using Internet email today either cannot receive HTML messages or choose not to. So unless you happen to know that your intended recipient has an email program showing HTML messages, it's best to stick with plain text messages.

When you're composing an HTML message in either program, you'll notice that the toolbar and menu bar show most of the tools and options available in the suite's Web authoring program. You compose and format an HTML message in Outlook Express exactly as you do a Web page in FrontPage Express, and you compose and format an HTML message in Netscape Messenger exactly as you do a Web page in Netscape Composer.

Starting a New HTML Message

To create an HTML message, do the following:

- **In Outlook Express,** open a new message window as you usually would. From the message window's menu bar, choose Format, Rich Text (HTML).
- **In Netscape Messenger,** you must change the Preferences to send HTML messages. Choose Edit, Preferences, and then choose the Formatting subcategory under the Mail & Newsgroups category. Check the check box near the top called Use the HTML editor to compose messages.

By default, most programs that can send HTML messages automatically send replies in the same format in which the message was received. In other words, if someone sends you an HTML message (which means the sender's email program can display HTML) and you click Reply to respond to it, the message you create is automatically in HTML format.

Using Stationery (Yes, Stationery!)

In Outlook Express, you have a fast and easy way to create really cool-looking HTML messages: Stationery, or predefined HTML message templates into which you can plug your message.

To use Stationery, just choose Message, New Message Using from Outlook Express's menu bar. You'll see a selection of different stationery styles you can use (see Figure 19.12).

When the stationery appears (see Figure 19.13), you can then compose your message and edit its appearance in any way you want. Have fun!

The Format menu offers lots of options for upgrading your outgoing emails. By selecting Background, you can choose a picture for the background of an email. If you select Stationery/More Stationery, you can even design your own stationery to use.

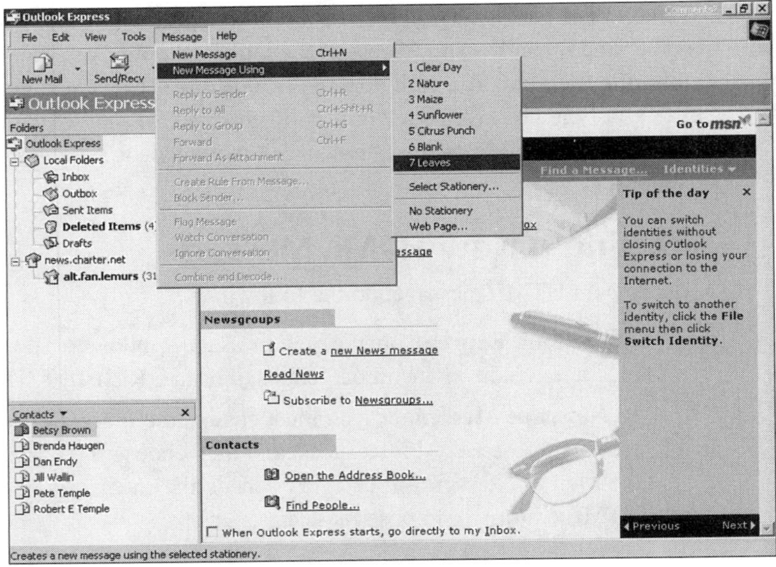

FIGURE 19.12
Choose a stationery to start a cool HTML message in Outlook Express.

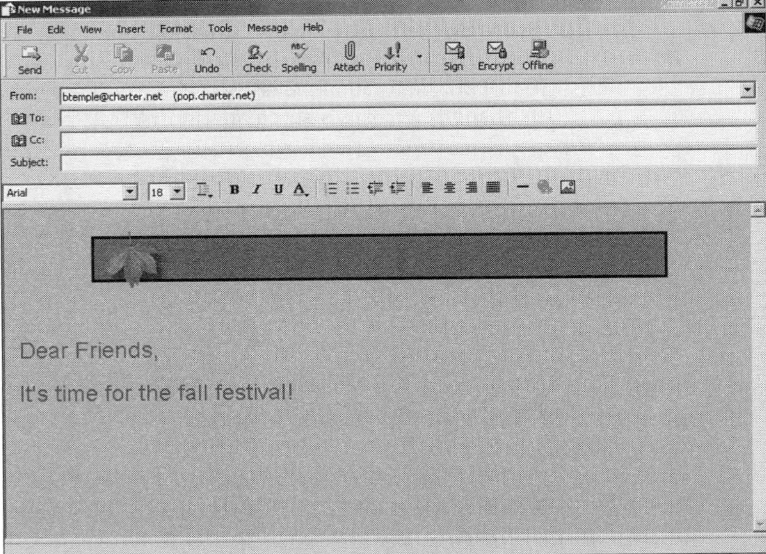

FIGURE 19.13
Stationery gives you an attractively designed template into which you can plug your own messages.

Just click the Create New button, and you can pick from a number of different options, or use your own art to jazz up emails. Go crazy!

Summary

You don't have to create your own Web page—it's not like there's a shortage. But if you really do have something to say, you'll find creating and publishing a page pretty easy, especially if you rely on the tools in an Internet suite.

Q&A

Q What about Java? What about video clips, and sound, and forms, and frames? I want to be a Web *auteur*!

A Well, Web authoring is a very big topic. You've learned a huge part of it in just one hour, but there are thousand-page books devoted to the subject, and even 1,000 pages doesn't cover everything about authoring.

Besides practicing and sharpening the skills you've already learned, your next step (other than learning frames, perhaps) should be to learn more about online multimedia, specifically how to do more with pictures and how to add sound, video, and animation to your pages. There are many good books about this. Also, carefully study the design and layout of pages that impress you. Learn from what others are doing. Flash is an extremely popular program for the Web right now, as many sites are offering pages that include elaborate Flash presentations.

After multimedia, the next hurdle is writing Java applets and JavaScript or CGI scripts, all of which can be used to enable special interactive capabilities that aren't part of plain HTML. There are many good books about these, too, but many folks, upon learning about these topics, suddenly decide that they already know enough about Web authoring. Just about anybody can learn to create Web pages and add multimedia to them. But learning Java, JavaScript, or CGI takes thinking like a programmer, and that's a specialized talent.

HOUR 20

Going Wireless

This is a dangerous chapter to write, for a couple of reasons. First, wireless technology is the fastest-evolving technology related to the Internet today. So, because things are changing so quickly, there's a very real chance that the stuff you read about in this hour won't be the latest and greatest technologies any more.

Also, there are a lot of different options for how you access the Internet wirelessly. Web-ready cell phones, personal digital assistants (PDAs), laptops equipped with wireless technology, Pocket PCs, pagers, wireless email devices—the list goes on and on.

Within each of the above types, too, there is a wide variety of options from which to choose.

So this hour serves as an overview for how to benefit from the boom in wireless technology and gives you a few ideas of how it might fit into your life. If you're serious about investing in some wireless technology, you may want to look at a more detailed reference on the subject, such as a book devoted to it.

By the end of this hour, you will be able to answer the following questions:

- What is wireless Internet/email, and why should I consider it?
- What kind of equipment do I need to use wireless Internet technology?
- Do I need a service provider for wireless?
- What is the difference between real-time and synchronized connections?
- What are some of the different technologies available, and how can they benefit me?

What Is Wireless Internet/Email?

Up to this point, we've covered Internet connections and going through Web sites and newsgroups and email and so on. All of those possibilities involve your computer communicating with other computers in other parts of the world through the help of your Internet service provider.

Whether it's a dial-up or broadband connection, whether it's at work or at home, all that data we've been sending back and forth has been traveling through wires and cables.

You plug that phone line into your modem, and the data travels through that wire, out to a bunch of different wires. You hook up your Ethernet card to your DSL modem, and the data travels through those (albeit bigger) wires. At work, when you plug into your network, that network most likely connects to the Internet through—you guessed it—wires.

Now, imagine the world without wires. Imagine that as you're riding in the passenger seat on the way to the big sales presentation that you can use your laptop to receive an email with the latest PowerPoint sales presentation. Imagine that right after your broker calls you with a tip on a hot stock, you can end the call and check the stock's current price on the same cell phone you just used for the call. Imagine that you can synchronize your Palm handheld with your computer right before boarding a plane, and read your email and check out your favorite Web sites on the flight, without breaking the no-cell-phone rule.

It's all real. Wireless communication allows your piece of hardware—be it a PDA, cell phone, laptop, whatever—to receive information from the Internet over the air. Generally speaking, the data is transmitted from a service provider to some type of antenna that is connected to the hardware device you are using.

There's also another type of wireless Internet/email, like in the preceding airplane example, in which you synchronize your device with a computer that has a wire connection, download the Internet data, then view it later. We'll get more in-depth on both types of wireless in a minute.

Regardless of which type of wireless Internet you use, and regardless of which type of device you use, wireless Internet is what its name implies—access to the Internet, without wires.

Real-time Versus Synched

With real-time wireless access, you are connected to the Internet wirelessly, live. That is, if you compose an email on the device you're using and send it, it goes, immediately. New emails pop until your Inbox all the time. When you check the baseball scores, they are up-to-date.

Synchronized connectivity is what many people do with their handheld PDAs. Palm devices, Handspring Visors, and Pocket PCs all allow this type of connecting. Using a provider such as AvantGo (a free service), you determine which sites you want to check in on when you connect. Then, when you synchronize your PDA with your computer, it will pull down the latest data from the Internet and load it into the PDA.

Then, you can check that data (including email) at a later time. If you reply to emails or compose new ones, they won't be sent until you synchronize again. Web sites aren't updated until you synchronize again.

It's a great way to use wireless without having to spend anything for a real-time connection. If your needs don't include having all-the-time access to the Internet live, this might be the way for you to go. AvantGo (see Figure 20.1) has a directory of Web sites you can choose to have the service update. Depending on the type of device you have, you either get a scaled-down version of the site, or the full site.

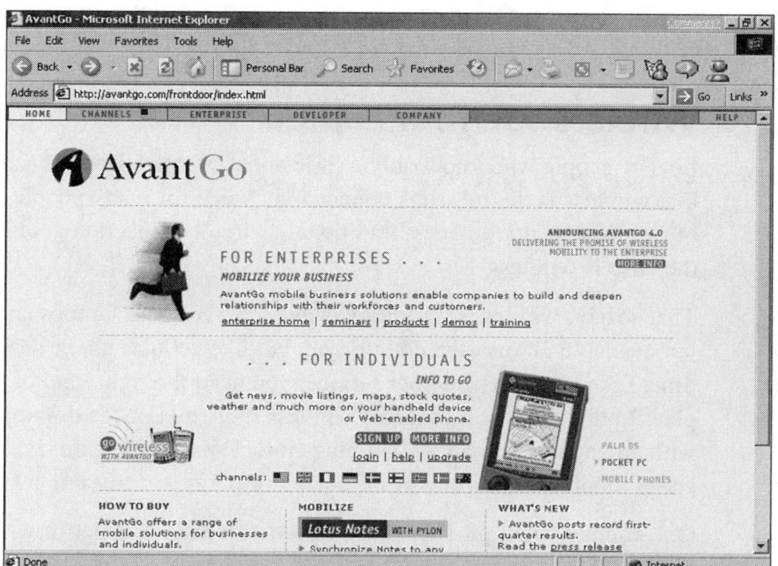

FIGURE 20.1
AvantGo allows you to synchronize with the Internet.

AvantGo also offers a paid service you can use if you choose live or real-time wireless Internet access.

Hardware to Get You Going

We've mentioned a few different types of hardware devices that you can use to access the Internet or email wirelessly. The varieties range widely; your choice should be made based on your personal situation.

For example, if you're constantly traveling for business within a specific region and use your laptop regularly during those travels, wireless connectivity for your laptop might be wise. If you don't need to have the whole laptop with you all the time but really need email availability and ease, a Web-enabled cell phone or wireless PDA might work for you.

Read through the following descriptions to help you decide what might be best for you.

Cost is always going to be a factor, unless you're Bill Gates. (And if you are, Hi, Bill! Give me a call sometime!) Before investing in any of these technologies, examine not only the cost of the hardware, but also the cost of the service package you must buy to access the Internet wirelessly.

Wireless for Your Laptop

Lots of people who know only a little about wireless Internet might be surprised to find that wireless is the full-time connection choice for many people. That is, there are a lot of people who don't have a traditional "wired" connection at all; the only connection they use is wireless.

That's right, wireless technology is available for both laptops and desktop computers. It's not available all over the country yet, but like cellular phone service, it's only a matter of time. Like any other Internet service, you need the right kind of modem and a service plan. In this case, you'll need a wireless modem. For the desktop, the modem is external, with an antenna and a line that plugs into a special PC card. For a laptop, the modem either mounts to the back of the screen or plugs directly into a PC card slot in the side.

One company that provides this service is called Ricochet (`www.ricochet.com`; see Figure 20.2).

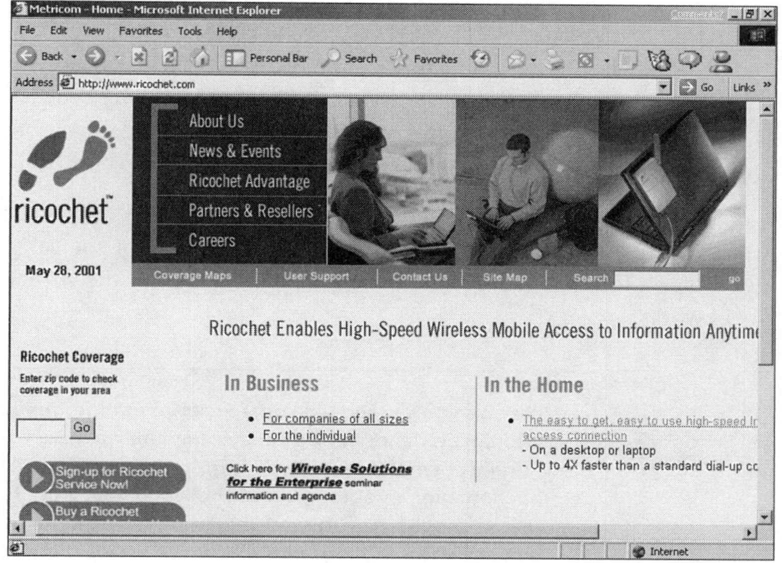

FIGURE 20.2
Wireless access for your regular computer is available through companies like Ricochet.

This type of service is great for the mobile professional. Individual packages start at around $80/month, and corporate discounts are typically available on multiple accounts. It allows your sales staff, for example, to keep in contact with the service department while on the road without ever having to plug in to a network connection or phone outlet.

> Another type of wireless service is satellite Internet. It uses a pizza-sized dish similar to the satellite television dishes (sometimes the same dish!), and gives you Internet access from satellite communications. Although this is wireless, of course, it's not really the type of wireless communications we're covering in this hour. We're examining wireless connectivity that you can use on the go, and for satellite service, you need to stay close to the dish.

This is a radio-frequency-based transmission system. Depending on the provider you use, the service might have antennas mounted on local water towers or other tall structures, such as buildings or radio towers. Some providers rely on a line-of-sight method of transmission—that is, your antenna must be able to "see" the antenna it communicates with. Others use a broader transmission method more similar to those used by radio stations.

Regardless, you pay for the convenience of being mobile; there are typically much larger up-front and ongoing costs associated with this type of account than with a traditional dial-up plan.

Internet/Email into Your Cell Phone or Pager

Although it's only been around for a few years, this is actually one of the "oldest" of the wireless technologies. Cell phones and pagers have long been able to receive text messages, scores from stadiums around the country, stock quotes, and so on. It's been a pretty one-way service, however, and it's been costly.

Now, cell phones and pagers can receive longer messages than before, and you can even use them to respond, to a degree. It's a little clumsy, of course, to use a cell phone to type a message—to get an "o" for example, you press the "6" button three times. But it works.

Perhaps you've seen the commercial where the trendy Gen Xers are crowded into a loud dance bar, and they communicate back and forth to each other using this type of text messaging. Sometimes called *"texting,"* it's a growing phenomenon in other parts of the world, and will soon be huge here in the U.S. It's a quick way to send very brief messages to a cell phone, and it can be done without having to talk, which makes it great for situations in which there is too much noise (such as in the aforementioned commercial) or where noise isn't appreciated (such as a library).

Many cell phone service providers allow you to use them for email if you want. Sometimes this carries a per-message fee, sometimes a flat monthly fee, and sometimes it's included free in a package deal. The way it works is this: To send you an email, the sender uses your phone number (including area code) as the name, followed by "@" and the domain of the service provider. An example of this might be `6125551212@verizon.com`.

This is useful as an email forwarding tool. For example, if your ISP allows your email to be forwarded to another account for free, have them forwarded to your cell phone number (if that's free, too). Then, when you're on the road, you can check your emails. And they'll still be waiting for you on your regular computer, too.

Now, you can get the Web, or at least some of it, on your cell phone, too. The type of service varies greatly. Some providers create their own content (which they get from Web partners) and have it all ready for you at your fingertips when you want it. This can include stock quotes, news headlines, scores, weather, flight data, and so on (see Figure 20.3). Others use a "web clipping" feature that allows you to view scaled-down sites from other providers.

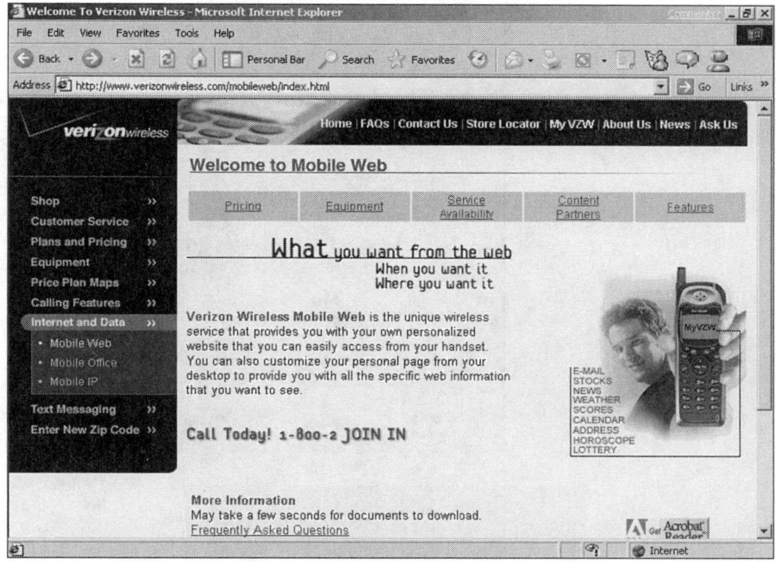

FIGURE 20.3
Verizon Wireless offers a service that pushes info into your cell phone from the Web.

Newer Web frameworks allow sites to sense the type of device that is accessing it by detecting the type of browser being used. This allows the server to deliver the type of content that best suits that browser, and thus the device. In other words, down the road a bit you're likely to find more sites that "know" you are using a cell phone, and thus display the right kind of pages for you.

No industry standard has been developed for a cell phone–based browser, making it difficult for developers to accommodate them all. As the industry evolves, however, this technology will become more widespread.

Handheld Computers

These are the fellas that force you to choose between synchronized and real-time Internet connectivity. There are lots of choices here, but they fall into two main categories: those that use the Palm operating system, and those that use Pocket PC technology, which is a Microsoft product.

On the Palm side, there are the Palm organizers themselves, some of which have built-in antennas for wireless access. Those that don't can add a wireless modem so you can access the Web and email. The primary competitor is the Handspring line of PDAs (see Figure 20.4).

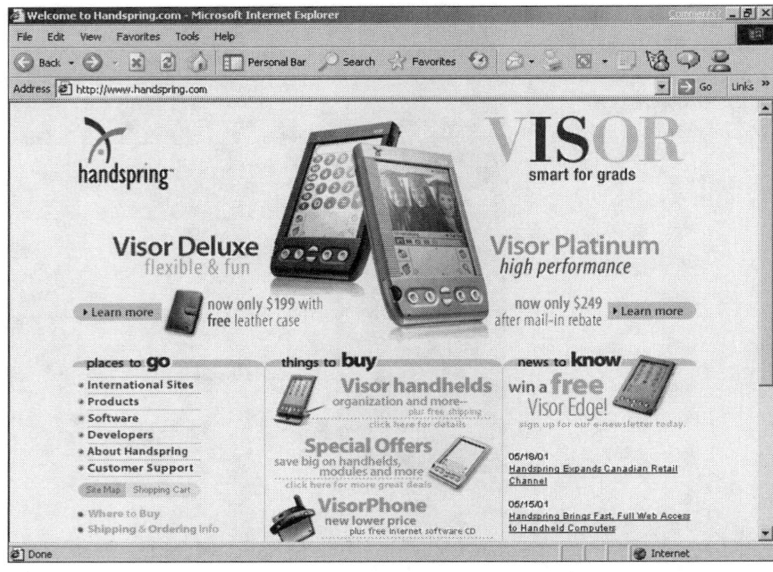

FIGURE 20.4
Handspring produces PDAs and modems that allow wireless access.

On the Pocket PC side, there are several competitors for the hardware dollar. These include Compaq's iPaq line (see Figure 20.5) of handheld computers and Hewlett-Packard's Jornada.

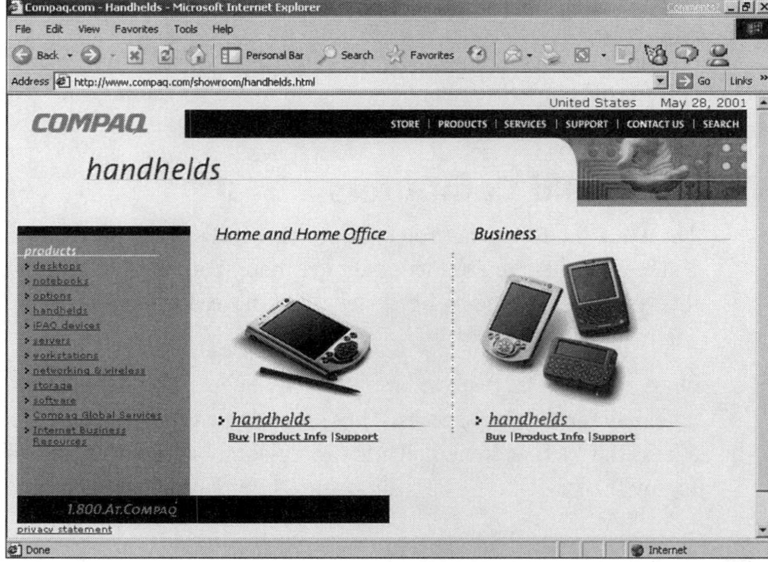

FIGURE 20.5
Compaq produces a line of handheld computers through which you can access the Web wirelessly.

> This is not the book to discuss the relative merits of the different types of handheld computers. At this writing, the Palm/Pocket PC war is being fought tooth and nail. They both have great features and some limitations, all of which could easily make up another 400-page book.

These are probably the most popular way to access the Internet wirelessly (be it real time or synched). They are big enough to allow you to compose an email without too much difficulty, yet small enough to be truly portable.

Service packages for wireless connections for these types of devices vary widely and depend on what features you expect to get (email, Web, or both). These offer a great middle ground between a cell phone, which is very limited in size and capabilities, and a laptop, which is bulky.

Wireless Email Devices

Wireless email devices fall somewhere between a PDA and a pager. A little like a pager on steroids, maybe.

The Blackberry models from RIM (see Figure 20.6) offer a small screen like a PDA, but with a tiny, built-in keyboard for composing messages. These are widely used in business (in part because of aggressive pricing for multiple-unit purchases). They allow you to stay connected to your email wherever you may be.

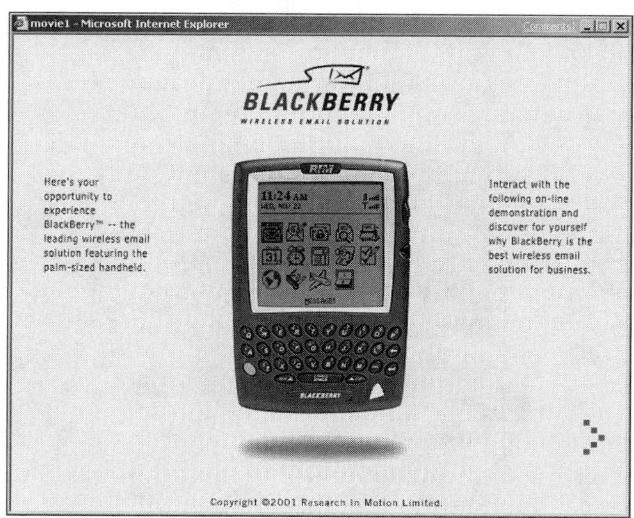

FIGURE 20.6
The Blackberry email unit includes a built-in, tiny keyboard.

20

In addition to sending and receiving email, you can keep an address book and calendar, use the built-in calculator, take notes, keep a task list, and more, all similar to what you can do on the Palm or Pocket PC. Two different models (the other is closer to pager-sized) are available.

Phone/PDA Combination

Ask any techie and he'll tell you: The future of wireless communication, and perhaps the Web in general, is in your cell phone. The cell phone has become such a staple of everyone's life—not just business people—that it only seems natural that its ability to communicate wirelessly would be used to the advantage of Web developers.

Although the cell phone is a staple, the PDA is the hottest form of technology. For business, for students—for anyone, really—PDAs are selling faster than any other device. It seemed only natural to try to combine the two technologies together in some way.

There are two ways to do this: Take the PDA and add a phone to it, or take a phone and add a PDA to it. Great news: They both work.

Kyocera (see Figure 20.7), among other cell phone manufacturers, is now building "smart phones" that include an internal screen and the Palm-based software. This eliminates the need to carry both types of devices, but the result is a somewhat clunky piece of machinery—all of the advances in size reduction over the years are lost.

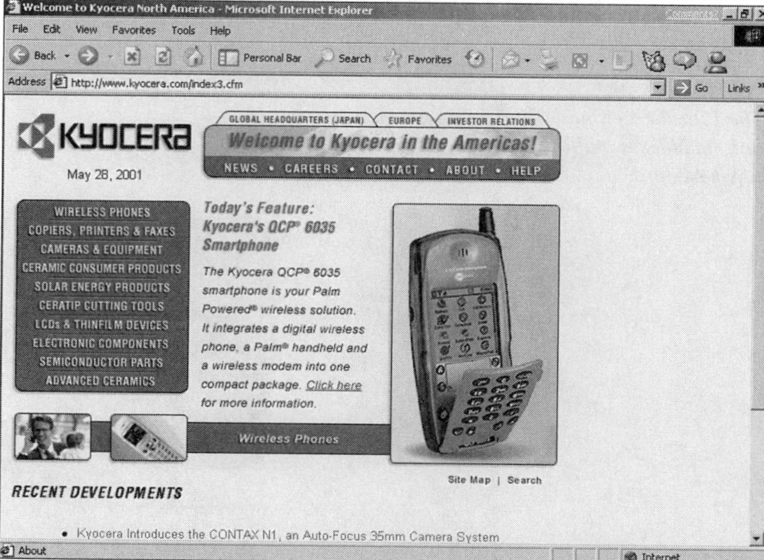

FIGURE 20.7
Kyocera and other phone makers are now building phones with built-in PDAs.

Still, it's better than carrying both pieces. The other obstacle is cost; these units are still in the $400–500 range.

The other way involves adding a phone to your PDA. Handspring offers a product called the VisorPhone (see Figure 20.8) that allows you to literally insert a phone module into the PDA's expansion slot, and it allows the PDA to act as a phone. This option will also run $400–500 by the time you add in the cost of the phone module.

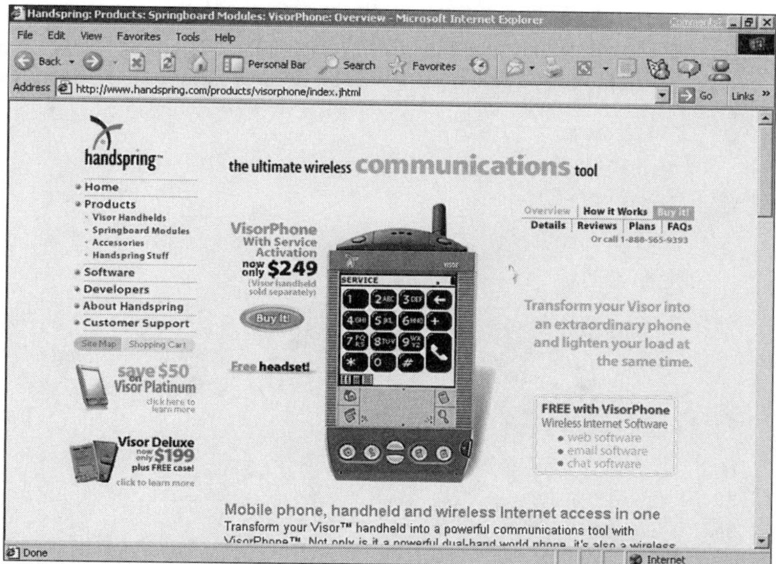

FIGURE 20.8
VisorPhone turns your Handspring PDA into a cell phone.

People might think you're a little strange if they see you talking into your PDA, but they'll get over it.

Summary

20

Wireless technology is evolving at a furious pace, and various technologies like PDAs and cell phones are being merged together for the good of all mankind. Well, okay, maybe not for the good of all mankind.

It's only a matter of time before the entirety of the Internet can be surfed from the palm of your hand for a price that is affordable to the common person.

Q&A

Q Why is the transition of Web to PDA so difficult?

A There are a number of reasons. Those Web pages take up a lot of RAM, and the small PDAs don't have much to spare. Also, most Web pages are set to be viewed at 800×600 pixels; in other words, the PDA screen is way too small.

Forward-thinking Web developers have created technologies that take any page on their site and automatically convert the data to smaller size (both in screen and in memory used), so they're PDA-ready. The sites that do the best job of making their data ready for wireless will be the ones that have the longest lives.

PART VI

Integrating the Web Into Your Life

Hour

Hour 21

Ten Ways the Web Can Change Your Business Life

Prior to 2000, there were a lot of people whose business lives were changed profoundly by the Internet—they left their "traditional" jobs and went to dot-com companies for work. Some made millions, some lost their shirts.

In 2000, the downturn in the dot-com industry caused more people's business lives to be changed for the worse. Thousands of dot-commers were laid off, fired, or simply left to stand by while their companies, starved for revenue and at the end of their venture capital, died.

But that's not the kind of "change" we're going to talk about in this hour. Whether you left your brick-and-mortar firm for a dot-com company or not, the Internet can and does have a profound impact on your daily work life. It doesn't matter whether you're a corporate attorney sitting in the corner office atop the skyscraper or a lowly author sitting in his basement office pecking out another chapter (hey, that one hit a little too close to home), the Internet can change your business life.

And for the better.

By the end of this hour, you'll be able to answer the following questions, among others:

- How can I use the Internet to find a new job?
- How can I use the Internet to help with my taxes?
- How can I use the Internet to attract customers?
- Can I form a corporation or get business advice online?
- How can I use email to effectively communicate with clients?

1. Form a Corporation

First, some Mike Brady–like words of advice: Starting a corporation is serious business (pardon the pun). It's not to be taken lightly or done on the spur of the moment. It requires market research, a sound business plan, legal advice, and so on.

True, there's lots to consider when you're ready to start your own business. But if you're ready to go, you can actually form your corporation online, using forms available through a company called American Incorporators Ltd. Its Web site at www.ailcorp.com (see Figure 21.1) allows you to fill out a simple online form to begin the incorporation process. There's also lots of helpful advice on the fees and procedures for incorporating in various states.

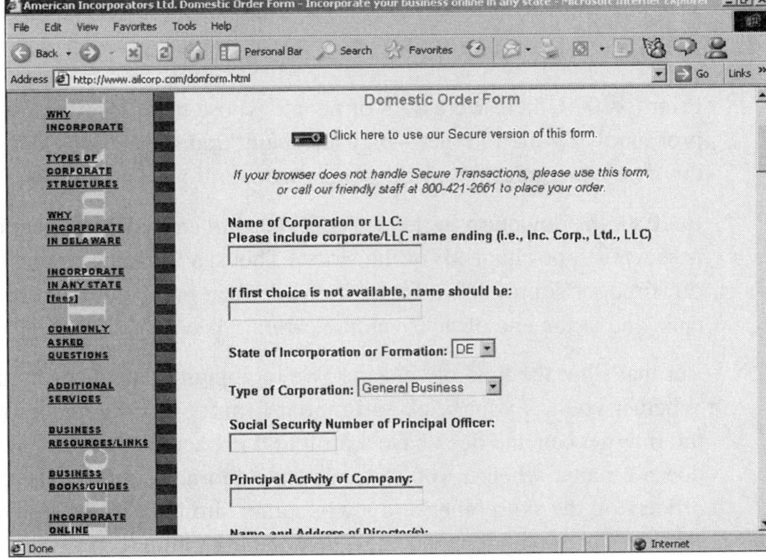

FIGURE 21.1
From the American Incorporators Ltd. Web site, you can form a corporation online.

However, if you're serious about forming a corporation, you don't have to do it online in order to benefit from the Internet. You can also use the Internet to do some of the due diligence required before launching that business.

A great place to start is the Small Business Administration's Web site at `www.sba.gov` (see Figure 21.2). There, you can find information about starting a business, getting financing (including SBA loans), and many other services, some of which you may not have realized you needed!

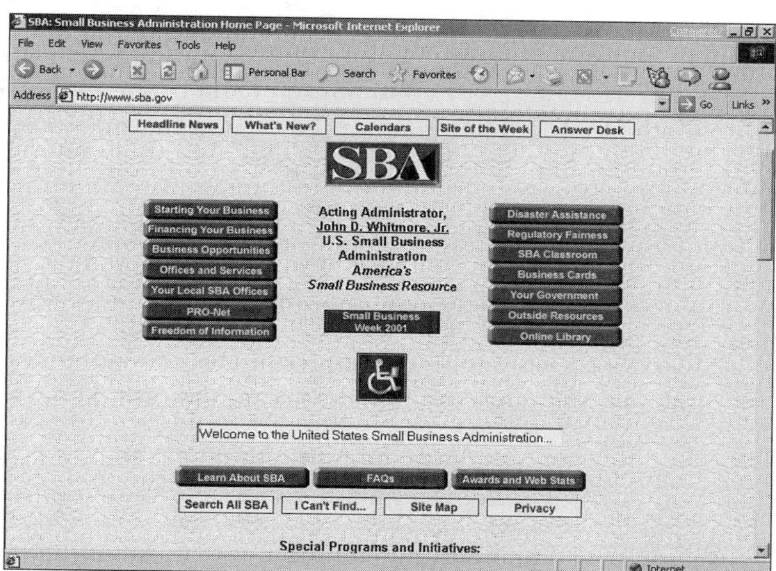

FIGURE 21.2
The Small Business Administration offers help for entrepreneurs.

2. Find a New Job or Career

More and more companies and government organizations are finding their new employees online. They post their want ads on the Internet, use Internet-based recruiting agencies, read resumes posted online, and more.

If you know of a particular company you would like to work for, the best place to start is on that company's Web site; many companies feature a Job Openings page. (To find a company's Web site, go to any search site and use the company's name as a search term.)

If you're not sure where you want to work, check out one of the general-purpose careers pages, such as Monster.com (`www.monster.com`; see Figure 21.3).

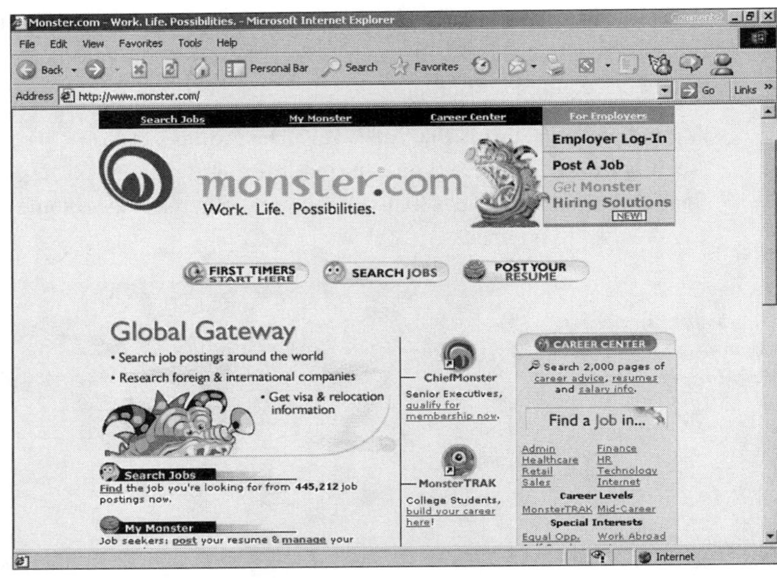

FIGURE 21.3
Monster.com offers career opportunities in thousands of companies.

Note that big job sites like Monster.com not only list job openings, but also can help you with your resume, choosing a career that matches your skills, and much more.

Some "career" sites on the Web help fill up their databases with job openings by copying them from other sources. Sounds like a valuable resource, but it can cause problems. If an employer posts an ad on one site, it typically has an expiration date; a date on which the ad no longer appears. However, if it gets copied to another site, it may not expire on that site.

The result can be that you go to a site, see a posting that appears to be right up your alley and apply for it, only to find that it was filled months ago. Frustrating, to say the least.

There are lots of job-search sites on the Web. One way to better target your search is to use the site of your local daily newspaper. Most major dailies have excellent classified sections online that are searchable. In some cases, you can even post your resume on the site for viewing by prospective employers. The Minneapolis-based *Star Tribune* is one such newspaper. It's job-search area is called Work Avenue (see Figure 21.4).

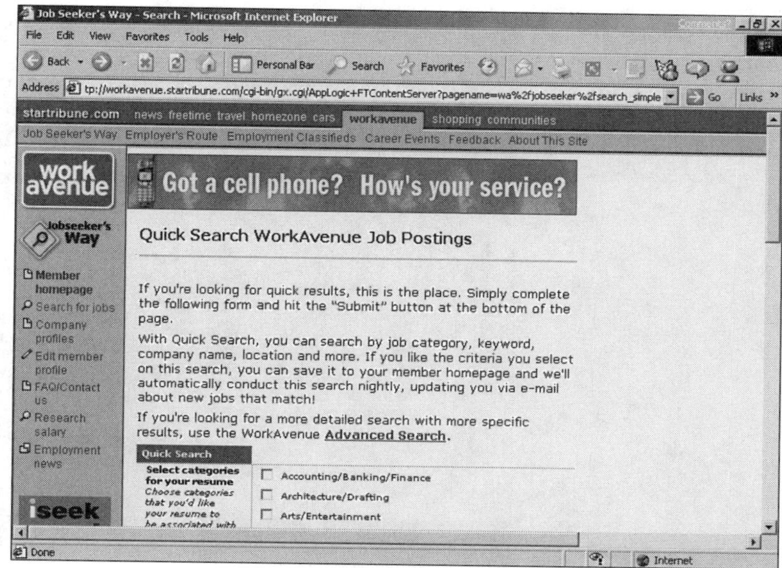

FIGURE 21.4
Most major daily newspapers offer good job-search areas on their sites.

The better job-search sites also allow you to set up a "saved search." With this service, you fill out a form with the type of job you're looking for, and the site automatically conducts a search of its database for you daily or weekly. Typically, you are notified by email of new postings that match your search criteria. It's a great way to conduct a job search round the clock, by only entering the data once.

3. Get a Degree or Professional Training

Yes, you can get a fully accredited college degree online—in many cases, from the same major colleges and universities that offer the regular kind of degree. In addition to degrees, you can get many other kinds of training online, such as training for various kinds of non-degree certificates. Figure 21.5 shows Barrington University, a school in Canada that offers a wide range of fully accredited degree programs online.

NEW TERM **Distance learning**. The name for a range of different methods for educating people dispersed across distances instead of grouped together in a classroom. The term includes training delivered by television, but also two kinds of Internet-delivered training: *asynchronous* and *synchronous*. In asynchronous distance learning (the most common type), you study online whenever it's convenient for you—even at 3:00 a.m., if that's when you have the time. In synchronous distance learning, you must be online at scheduled class times, and you can interact "live" with your instructor and other classmates.

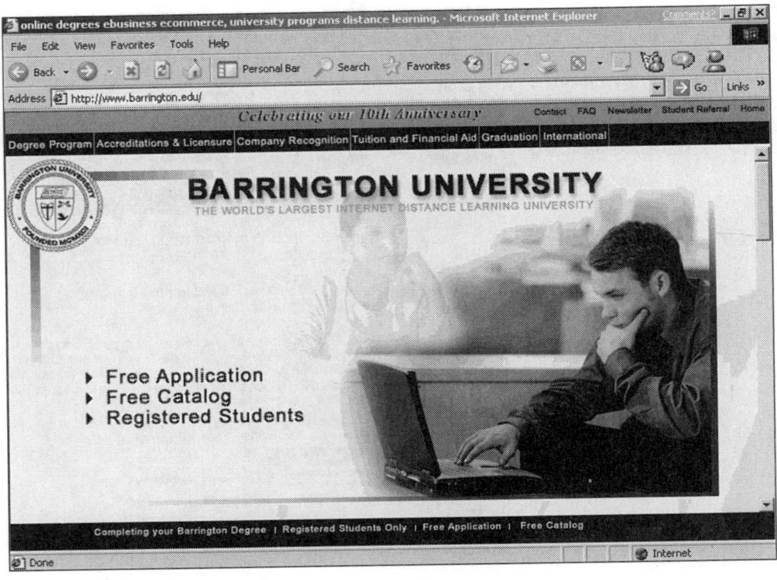

FIGURE 21.5
Barrington University is one of a growing list of colleges, universities, and other schools offering education online.

Some programs are entirely online, but, in most cases, you'll be required to visit a nearby test center a time or two to take tests in person. This approach still enables you to do most of your studying online, whenever it's convenient for you, but also ensures the validity of the degree by making it impossible for cheaters to pay someone to complete a degree in their name.

> Some of the schools that offer degrees online might also carry with them a stigma of being, shall we say, less-than-credible. Do some research on any school that grants a degree online, to make sure that the degree will truly mean something when you attempt to use it to get a job.
>
> Another option is to take classes from a "traditional" university online; many major colleges offer such programs. You may not be able to earn your degree this way, but you can make progress toward it.

The best way to start looking for training is to check out the Web sites of schools near you, to see whether they offer any courses or programs online. Doing so ensures that getting to the test locations will be convenient for you.

If you can't find the program you want offered online by a nearby school, search on the term "distance learning," followed by what you want to study.

4. Ship Packages

Sent a package by UPS, FedEx, the U.S. Postal Service, or another carrier? Or are you waiting for a package from someone else? Did you know that you can track those packages online, finding out exactly where they are en route and when they will arrive at their destination?

All you need is the tracking number of each package. You get that on your slips and receipts when you send; if you're the receiver, you can ask the sender to tell you the tracking number. (Many online stores automatically send you the tracking number in an email message when confirming your order.)

Go to the Web site of the carrier: UPS is at `www.ups.com`; FedEx is at `www.fedex.com` (see Figure 21.6); the U.S. Postal Service is at `www.usps.gov`. Find a link for "tracking" or "track shipments," click it, and then type the tracking number in the form provided and click the button near the form that submits the form.

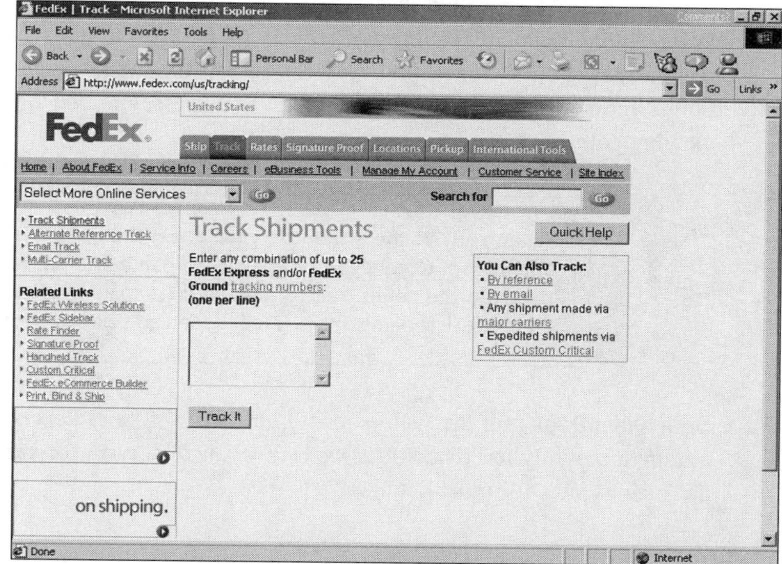

FIGURE 21.6
Federal Express (shown here), and many other carriers let you track packages online, if you know the tracking number.

A summary report might appear at first, giving only a little information. But on the UPS site, a tiny button appears next to each package in the report. Click it, and you'll see a report of where the package has been, and when it will arrive.

You can even use the more advanced sites to ship packages by ordering a pickup and filling in a form for who the package is going to and so on. On some sites, you're even allowed to input the addresses of companies you regularly ship to, and they're saved for you for easy access later.

You can also use these sites to determine the cost of shipping packages before you send them.

5. Keep Your Company's Books

Once you've set up that new business venture, you're going to need to keep track of your finances. The two leading providers of small-business accounting software—Peachtree and QuickBooks, from Intuit— both offer an online accounting method, along with their regular, installed programs.

Why use an online accounting program? Well, there are reasons for and against it, of course. The primary reason for it is that it allows you to have access to your books anywhere you have a connection to the Internet. That's beneficial, especially if you're paying an accountant to help you.

For example, let's say keeping the books isn't your strong point, and you hire a part-time bookkeeper to enter transactions and the like. Using the Internet, that person could keep things up to date from his home or place of business, and you would have access to viewing your books any time you want.

When you use these services, your books are online, but they aren't viewable by just anyone. You create a username and password that must be used to get to the pages that contain your company's data. These pages are kept on a secure server, so the average Joe can't get to them.

Both QuickBooks for the Web (shown in Figure 21.7) and Peachtree's Web Accounting require a monthly fee. They offer varying levels of service for varying rates—check out the various sites for more details.

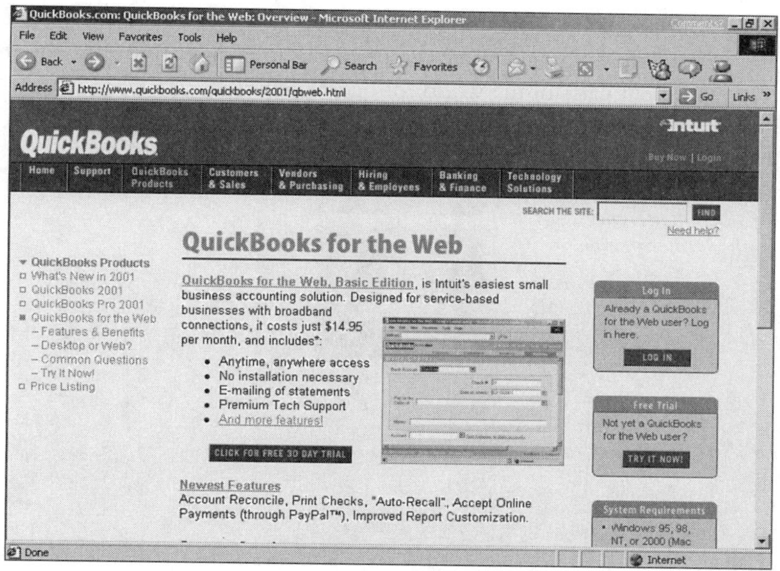

FIGURE 21.7
QuickBooks for the Web (shown here) and Peachtree Web Accounting both allow you to keep up with your books from any computer with an Internet connection.

6. Conduct a Video Conference

Another technology that has developed rapidly is video conferencing. There are many different ways to do it, and it's becoming a staple of the office environment because of its ease and low cost.

There are several different types of video conferences you can conduct. Microsoft's NetMeeting (see Figure 21.8), which is included in the full versions of Internet Explorer, allows a one-on-one video conference for anyone with the right equipment (a fast connection, sound card, microphone, computer video camera).

It's also pretty easy to configure; as usual, Microsoft walks you effectively through the process.

> Besides not always looking too good, especially on slower connections, video conferencing often degrades the audio quality of the call. You and your conferencing partner may decide it's better to shut off the video so you can hear each other more clearly.

For bigger conferences, CUseeMe is the way to go. Available at the Web site `www.cuseeme.com`, the CUseeMe Conference Server program allows you to see up to four people in separate video windows at any one time. This makes it feel a little more like a meeting, and allows you to bring in people from a number of different offices in different parts of the world for one meeting.

FIGURE 21.8
NetMeeting allows you to video conference with another person.

7. Handle Your Business Taxes Electronically

More and more, your old friend the IRS has gone electronic in its handling of forms and payments. On the personal side, millions of people have taken advantage of e-filing their Form 1040s, getting their refunds back more quickly as a benefit.

Businesses can benefit from the Internet as well. The IRS's Electronic Federal Tax Payment System (EFTPS) is currently available as an option to businesses, but it's only a matter of time before it's a mandate. Not only can you download any form you need to fill out, print it, and send it back, but now you can also file more of the forms by computer.

Businesses have to file lots of tax forms and make deposits of federal (and state) withholding amounts and social security taxes, and so on. Small-business owners that may be handling these forms themselves and accounting departments of larger firms can save lots of time and energy by filing these forms electronically.

The IRS offers a Windows-based program free of charge that allows employers to e-file their various IRS forms and make tax deposits, all with a few clicks of the button. To learn about the IRS's many services for small businesses, go to the IRS Web site (`www.irs.gov`—see Figure 21.9), and you'll see several links to business-related pages.

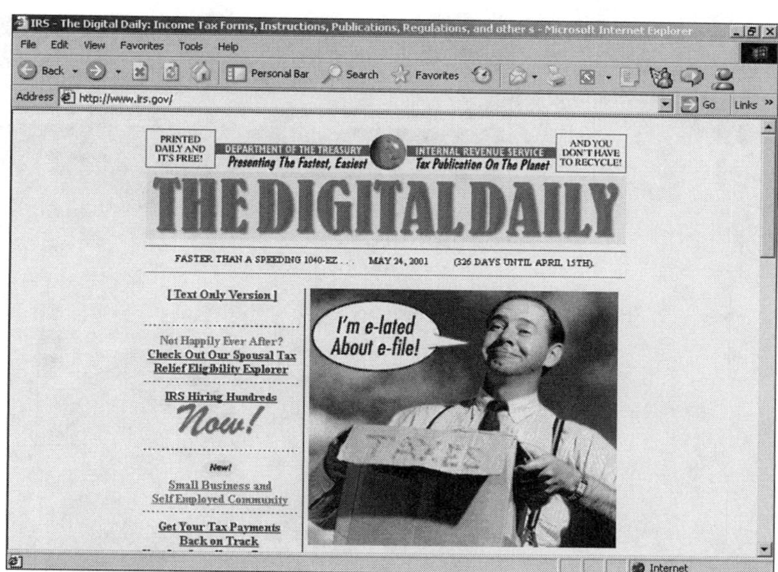

FIGURE 21.9
The IRS Web site offers e-filing of business forms and electronic payment of business taxes.

8. Attract New Customers with Your Web Site

Back in Hour 19, you learned the basics of how to build a Web site. We're in the twenty-first century now, kids, and the Web is an integral part of doing business. More and more, when you contact a business by phone, you'll hear, "That information is available on our Web site. "

Business Web sites are a 24-hour-a-day marketing brochure for a company. As such, you need to commit the kind of time and money that you would put into a high-quality sales brochure.

After the sales call has ended, or perhaps even before your business makes contact with a potential client, they're going to check you out on the Web. If they don't like what they see, you might lose them. But a helpful, service-oriented Web site will bring in new customers.

The key is to make it easy for them. If you're selling over the Internet, make the buying experience easy. If you're just offering information, make it easy for the average customer to find exactly what they're looking for. Better yet, offer a service they can't get elsewhere. At the Kinko's Web site (`www.kinkos.com`; see Figure 21.10), you can send a file electronically to your local Kinko's for printing, and it'll be ready for you in no time.

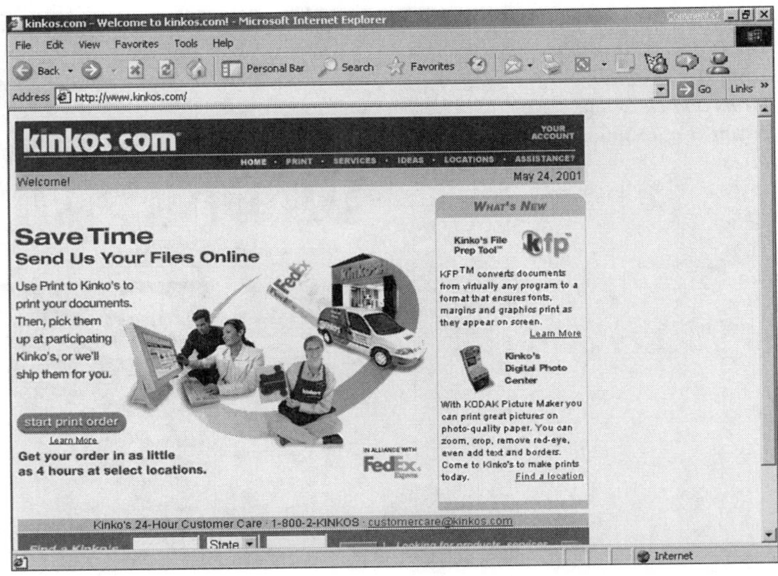

FIGURE 21.10
The Kinko's Web site offers a direct-printing service.

Finally, advertise your site. You've spent a lot of time and money on it, now don't let it go to waste. Put the address on everything you give out—letterhead, business cards, envelopes, billing statements, invoices, purchase orders. Anything that has your company's name or logo on it should have the Web address, too.

9. Network with Clients Using Email

I don't know what line of work you're in, but regardless of what it is, email is your friend. Not only does it allow you to quickly and succinctly get a message out, it also allows you to communicate with all your clients or select groups of them en masse.

Email's great because it allows you to keep a stream of communication going with a potential client without them feeling bugged. Rather than calling on the phone weekly or so to remind them of your company's services, a quick email keeps your business in the forefront of their mind without them feeling like you've *intruded* with a "sales call."

For your existing customers, even the smallest business can quickly set up its email program for group emails. You can use this feature to send an e-newsletter to all your clients or to send a targeted newsletter to seasonal clients, for example.

Both Outlook Express and Netscape Messenger allow you to set up "groups" for sending mass emails. In Outlook Express, just open the Address Book from the Tools menu, then select New, New Group. You can name your group, then click the Select Members button (see Figure 21.11) to add people from your address book to the group. To send a message to that group, all you have to do is type the group name in the To: field of the email, and all the members will get the message.

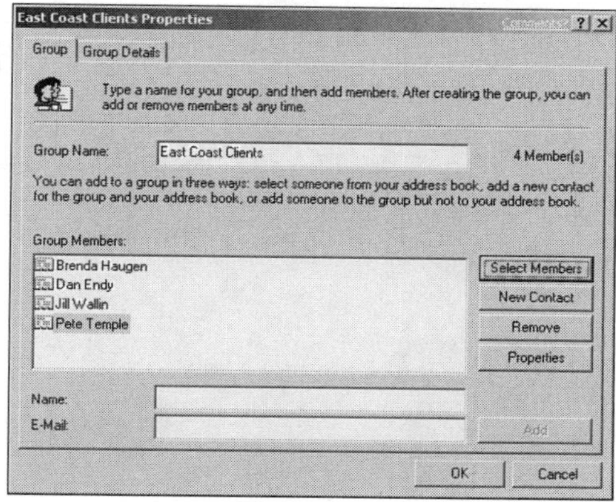

FIGURE 21.11
Creating an email group is easy in Outlook Express.

When sending a group email, I recommend putting your own email address in the To: field, and putting the group name in the Bcc: field. This way, the group members won't see all the other email addresses that received the message, only yours.

In Messenger, they are called Mailing Lists. To create a new list, select Address Book from the Communicator menu, then click the New List button.

10. Track Customer Relationships Online

Contact management and sales cycle management are two aspects of any business that almost always require some form of software to keep everything running smoothly.

There are several sites that allow sales departments and all of their staff to work seamlessly to benefit both the internal organization and its customers. Salesforce.com (`www.salesforce.com`) is one such entity. Using Salesforce.com, you can keep customer information up-to-date, allowing your sales, marketing, and customer service departments to work together more efficiently and effectively (see Figure 21.12).

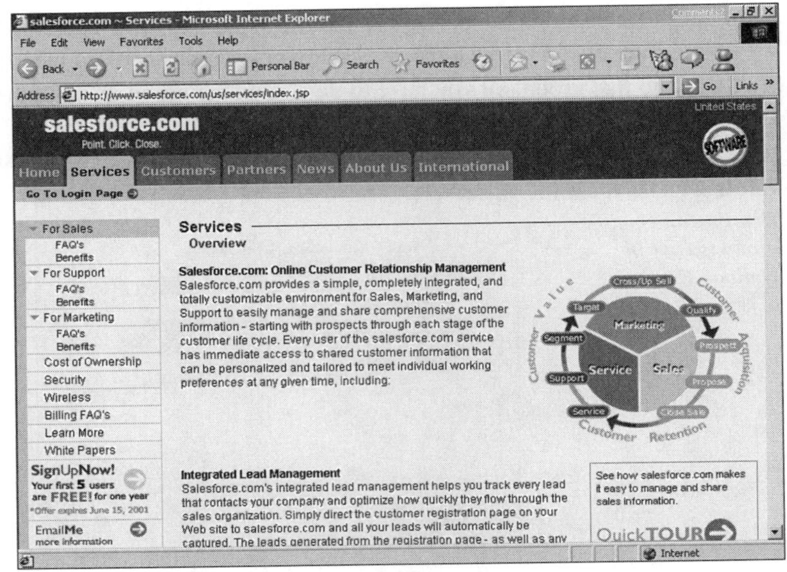

FIGURE 21.12
Salesforce.com tracks customer information to improve sales performance.

The information can then be accessed over the Internet—even wirelessly, if your business is so equipped.

Most of the popular contact management software programs, such as Act!, offer some form of online capability for keeping track of things on the road.

Summary

There are a million ways the Internet can benefit a business or a businessperson, but they limited me to 10, so I had to choose. The 10 I chose are typical examples. After you're online for a while, you'll undoubtedly find some other ways the Internet helps you at work.

Q&A

Q You went through 10 ways and didn't even talk about e-commerce. Wouldn't selling over the Internet be a benefit?

A Lest you think I'm some kind of a ninny, of course e-commerce can help a business. It's not for every business, but if you don't sell directly over the Internet, your business should at least have some sales information online.

E-commerce solutions are available even for very small businesses through companies that provide that service for a fee. Do a search using "e-commerce solutions" as your search term in your favorite search engine, and you'll find some companies that offer it.

Q When the dot-com companies started to crash, did it have an impact on regular businesses' Web operations?

A Yes and no. Many brick-and-mortar businesses also downsized their Web operations, cut back on staff, and so on. But their Web sites needed to stay up in order to support their traditional operations.

Here's the key difference: Web-based companies crashed because they didn't have enough revenue to keep going. Traditional businesses are using the Web to enhance their already-existing revenue streams, or to increase them through e-sales. So, if they bit off more than they could chew in going online, they may have scaled back. But if they're still in business, their Web sites are generally still needed, too.

HOUR 22

Ten Ways the Web Can Change Your Family Life

In the last hour, you learned 10 of the many ways the Internet can be used to benefit your life at work. This and the following two hours are more catered to your home life, divided into different segments.

In this hour, we'll take a look at how the Internet can improve your family life, even if you are a family of one.

By the end of this hour, you'll be able to answer the following questions, among others:

- How can I keep track of my family's schedule online?
- Can I use the Internet to look for a new house?
- How can I find medical advice online?
- Can I shop online for groceries?
- How can I use the Internet to plan a vacation?
- How can I use the Internet to participate in community- or church-related activities?
- How can a family Web site benefit us?

1. Keep Your Family Calendar

I don't know what your family's calendar looks like, but ours is a little messy. Soccer games and practices, dance classes, doctor's appointments, parties, and more get scrawled on there. Then the dates get changed, things get crossed off, and, well, the whole thing starts looking like the dog got a hold of it.

Plus, you don't have access to it while you're at work. So when the boss asks whether you can stay late Thursday night, you're not sure whether that means missing out on a family event.

There are many ways to fix that problem, of course. Putting your family's calendar into a program like Microsoft Outlook and syncing it with your PDA is one way. But you can also put your calendar on the Internet and have access to it any time you're online.

Netscape Calendar, a free service brought to you by Netscape/AOL, makes it simple.

You don't have to be using Netscape Navigator to use Netscape Calendar. It's accessed from the Netscape home page (`home.netscape.com`), so you can get to it any time you're online, regardless of what browser or Internet connection you use.

At the top of the Netscape home page at `home.netscape.com`, there's a button called Calendar. Click it to get started using Calendar. If you're an AOL member or have already registered with Netscape (for example, for the purpose of using Instant Messenger), you can just sign in using that screen name and password. If not, you'll need to sign up (there's no cost).

After you're in, you can enter appointments, schedule events, and even use the service to notify friends of various events or find out when your favorite sports teams are playing. Then, your calendar is available to you any time you sign in (see Figure 22.1).

FIGURE 22.1
Netscape Calendar allows you to check your family's schedule from any computer with an Internet connection.

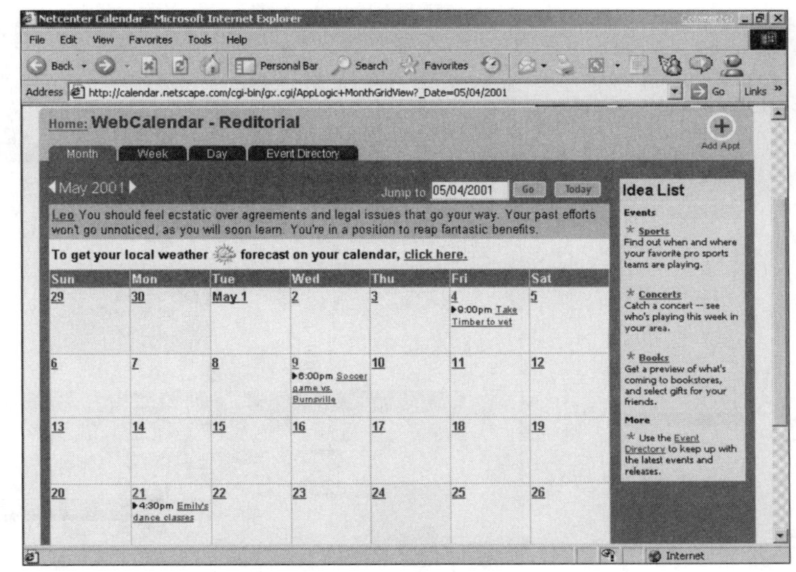

2. Find a New Place to Live

Every few years, I get antsy and move. I dunno why. But if you're at all like me, you're always on the lookout for a new city or town to call home.

Using search techniques you already know, you can learn a lot about any community you're considering. But another way is to visit a site like Moving Center (`www.movingcenter.com`). Moving Center is a thorough directory of links that lead to information and services that not only help you plan a move, but also help you decide *where* to move (see Figure 22.2).

For example, you can click the link to Community Info (it's on the Getting Started page) to look up all sorts of useful information about hundreds of cities and towns: schools, cost of living, jobs, crime statistics, and much more. After you choose a city, Moving Center's links can help you find realtors and rentals, calculate mortgage payments or moving costs, find a local Internet provider, and so on.

If you're just looking for a new home in the community in which you currently live, there are many great ways to search. One is to choose a local real estate company's Web site and do a search of listings there.

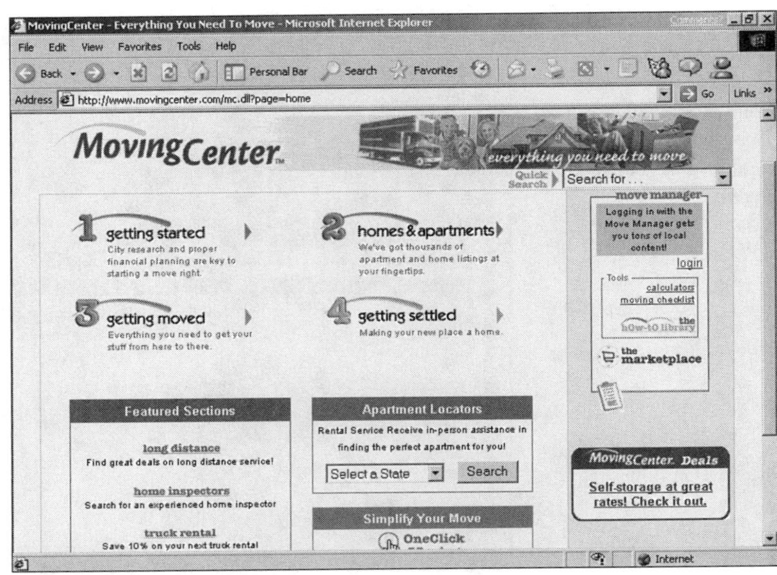

FIGURE 22.2
Moving Center is a great first stop when you're trying to decide where to live.

3. Get Medical Advice

Where does it hurt? Really? Well, here's what you should do: Get off the silly Internet and go see the doctor!

Still, as long as you're not using it as an excuse to avoid the doctor when you really need one, the Internet is a great place to learn more about what ails you and/or those you love. One great starting point is DrKoop.com (yes, *that* Dr. Koop, the former U.S. Surgeon General), a one-stop shop for authoritative medical info (see Figure 22.3). You'll find it at `www.drkoop.com`.

You can also find lots of great medical info at WebMD, located at `www.webmd.com`.

You can benefit from other types of medical information on the Web, too. For example, there are newsgroups that act as support groups for people with various diseases or ailments. You can find newsgroups in which people share information about everything from allergies to epilepsy to diabetes and more.

22

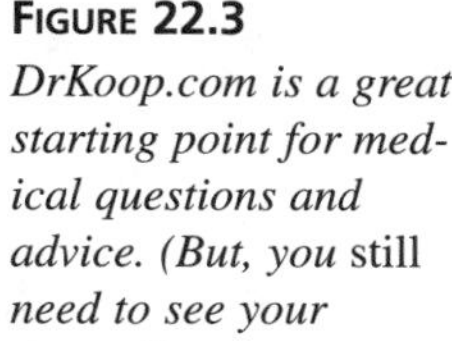

FIGURE 22.3
DrKoop.com is a great starting point for medical questions and advice. (But, you still *need to see your doctor!)*

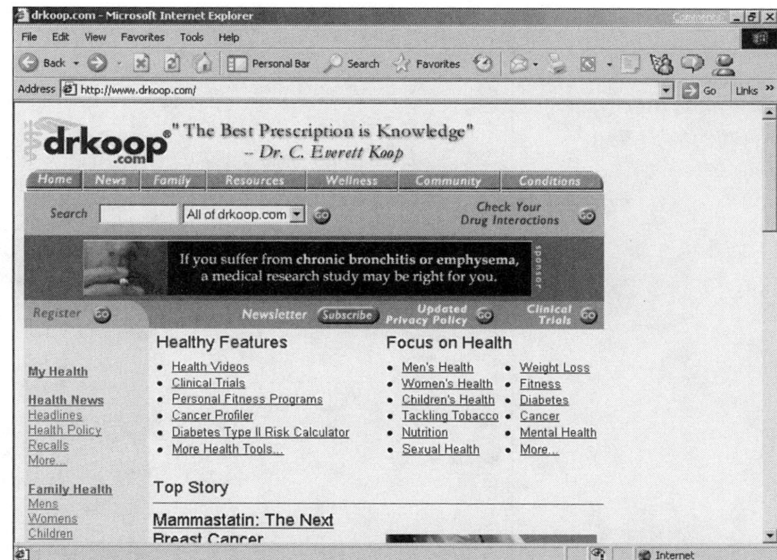

4. Sign up for Sports or Other Programs

When the kids hit a certain age, we as parents become tied to our community organization, be they sports-related or otherwise. In our family at least, it seems we're constantly registering for soccer leagues, basketball camp, dance classes, band lessons, and the like.

It might seem unlikely that the non-profit organizations that run many of these programs would have Web sites, but many do. In the long run, there's a significant cost savings for these groups to use the Web to promote their programs and sign-ups, because they save on paper and printing costs for the fliers they've traditionally used.

Some programs can allow you to sign up online, some don't. But most, at the very least, use their sites to announce sign-up dates. Some allow you to download the registration form, which you can then print out, fill out, and return the old-fashioned way.

For example, the Minnesota Youth Soccer Association, which oversees amateur soccer in the state (see Figure 22.4), offers a Web site that includes a variety of forms, from parental consent to medical release forms. You can also download (or read online) the association's bylaws, its policies and rules manual, and even find directions to virtually every soccer field in the state.

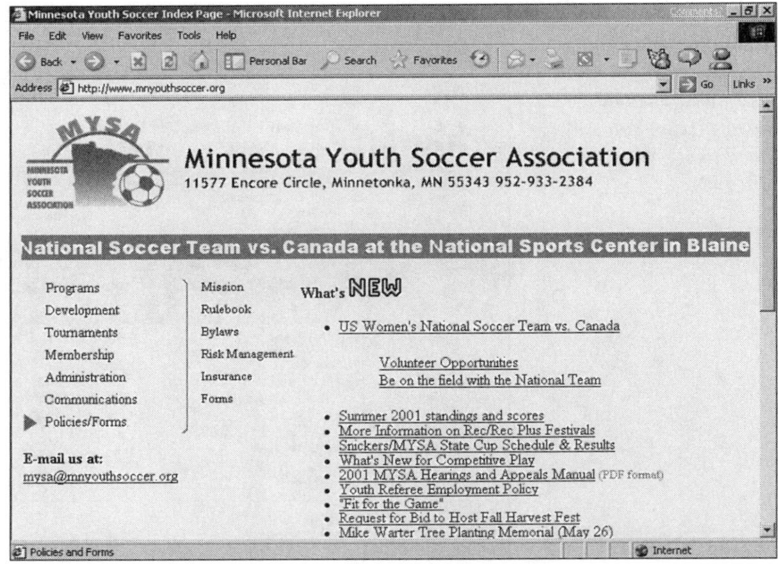

FIGURE 22.4
Many youth sport organizations offer Web sites that include downloadable forms.

But even local organizations, like your city's recreation department, are likely to have Web sites that offer helpful information, and sometimes even include online registration forms.

5. Find Family-Oriented Recreation Opportunities

Folks tend to think of the Internet as a tool for finding out what's happening far away. But it's also handy for finding out what's going on in your community: special events, theater, community meetings and local politics, school lunch menus, and much more.

Most cities and towns have one or more community Web sites with links to such information. If you don't have the addresses of those sites, another way to go is to check out the Yahoo! page for your community.

Begin by going to Yahoo! at `www.yahoo.com`. Scroll to the bottom of that page, where you'll see a heading called "More Yahoo!s." Under that, you'll see the word "Local:" followed by a number of links. Click on the link called "Events." Enter your ZIP code in the box provided (see Figure 22.5), click Search Listings, and Yahoo! will offer you links to events that are happening in communities near that ZIP code.

FIGURE 22.5
Enter your ZIP code on the Local Events page and you'll find events happening in your community.

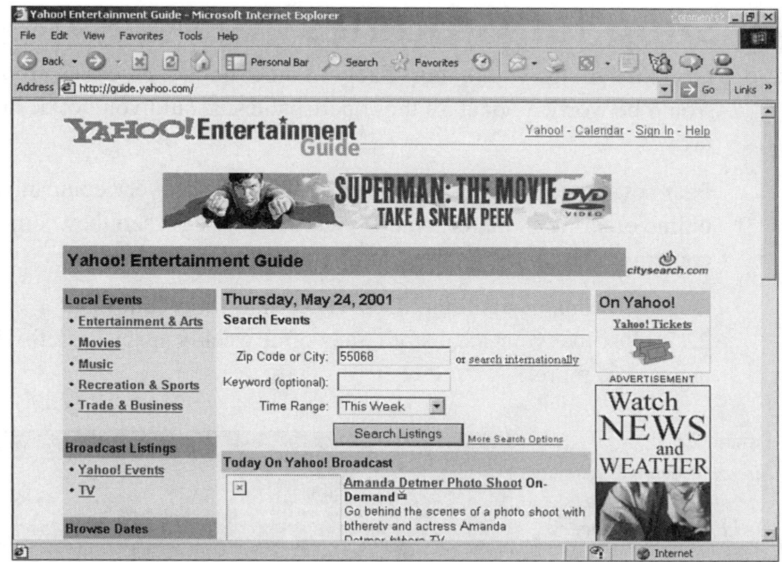

If you'd like to get specific to your city, or find information about the city itself, just do a search on the city's name (including state) on your favorite search page. Or, on Yahoo!, you can go through the directory by choosing Regional, then U.S. States, then your state, then your city (there may be additional steps in between, depending on how big your state is). This leads you to a "Local Web Directory" that includes links to sites in the community (see Figure 22.6).

FIGURE 22.6
Yahoo! offers a Local Web Directory for just about every city in the U.S.

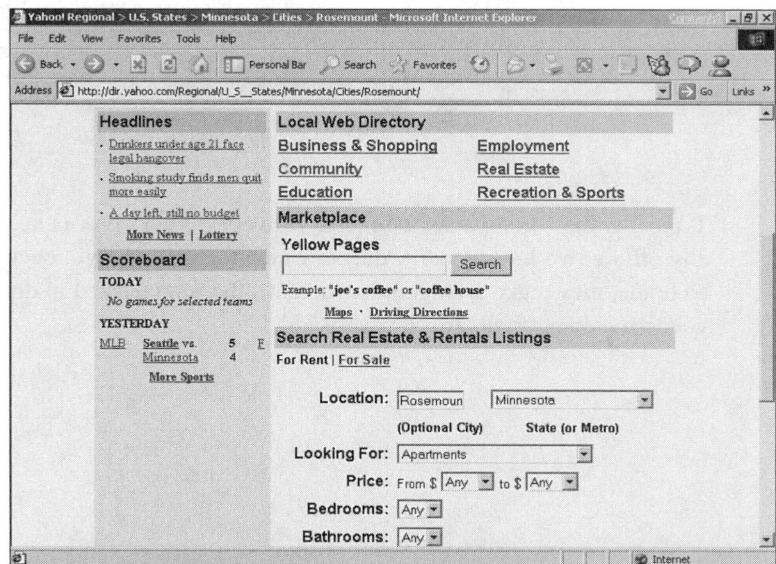

6. Shop for Groceries

Of all the things you're most likely to order online, groceries probably aren't at the top. You'd be worried about all those perishables, should you not be home when the delivery arrives.

Fear not. There's a growing number of grocery-delivery companies that offer regional online ordering of goods. And if you're not home when they come, they leave the stuff in coolers that keep things fresh until you arrive.

One such company is SimonDelivers.com, a Twin Cities–based company (see Figure 22.7). Just like your local store, they offer weekly specials, deli selections, cut-to-order meats, and more.

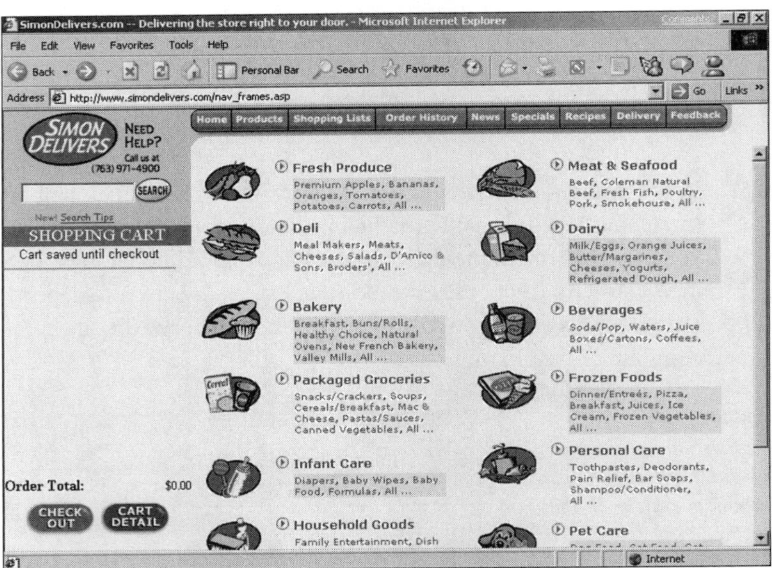

FIGURE 22.7
SimonDelivers is just one of many companies that offers grocery delivery following an Internet order.

Typically, these companies offer free delivery if your order is large enough, and generally offer a two-hour window during which the delivery will occur. If you're not going to be home, they make arrangements to leave the food packed in dry ice so it all—yes, even your ice cream—stays fresh.

7. Plan a Vacation

One of the first industries to truly embrace and benefit from the Internet was the travel industry. After all, allowing people to find out all kinds of information about faraway lands and being able to book tickets right there online makes it all very easy. So, whether you're Clark Griswold planning to drive the "family truckster" across country to WallyWorld or you're planning some other kind of trip, you can do it all online.

Travelocity.com (see Figure 22.8) is one of many sites that allows you to book all aspects of a trip in one location. You can book your flights, make car reservations, book your hotels, and more. You can even plan a cruise or take advantage of a pre-arranged vacation package there.

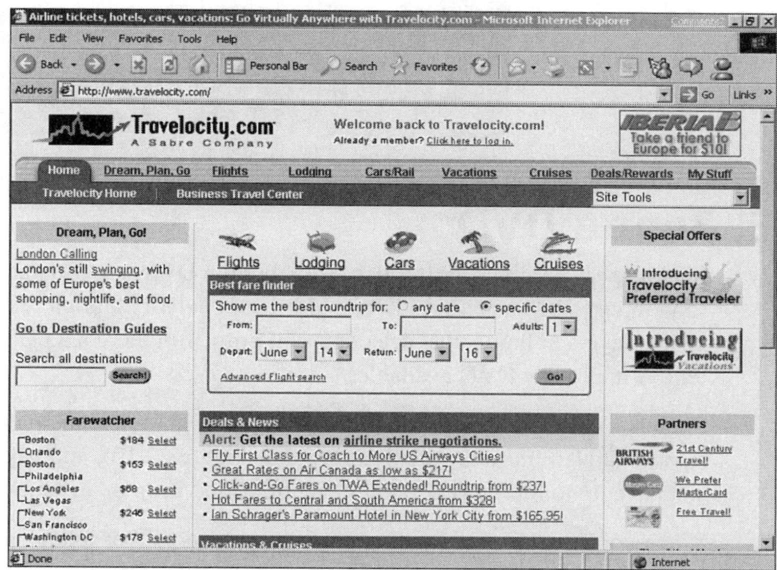

FIGURE 22.8
Travelocity.com allows you to make all the reservations necessary for your family vacation.

Every major airline allows online booking, and most of them will help you make your hotel and car arrangements, too, through partnerships they have with various other entities.

If your destination is a major vacation hot spot, such as Walt Disney World, you can go to that organization's Web site and handle your reservations there. For example, the Disney Web site (`disney.go.com`; see Figure 22.9) includes a link to Vacations, through which you can buy theme park tickets or plan an entire Disney experience.

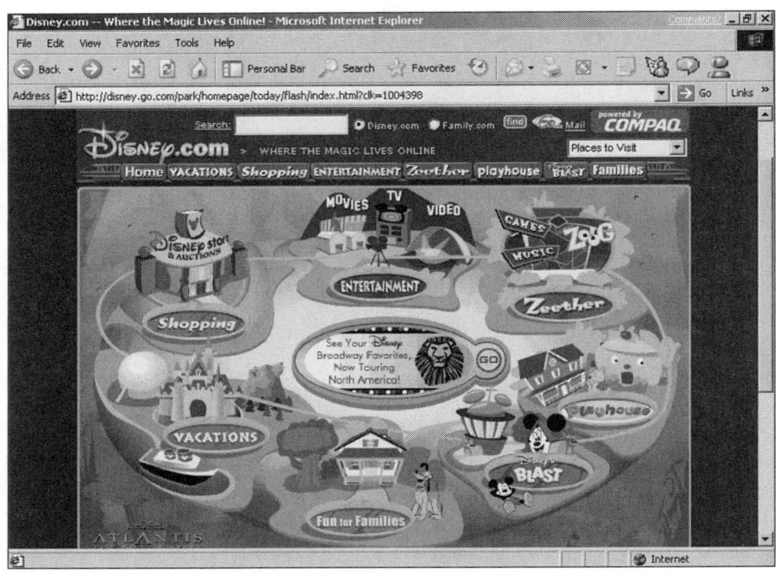

FIGURE 22.9
Many destinations, like Walt Disney World, offer Web sites that allow you to book your entire vacation.

8. Rent a DVD

I can't speak for your local video store, but the DVD selection at mine leaves a little something to be desired. As DVDs grow in popularity and more and more people get DVD players at home, that selection will grow. But there's a place online where you can rent virtually any DVD available.

Sounds like a pain in the rear, getting DVDs by mail. But the process is very simple. You sign up at NetFlix (`www.netflix.com`; see Figure 22.10), and pay a flat monthly fee. You can have up to three DVDs at any one time, and keep them as long as you want.

When you're done, you return them in a postage-paid envelope, and your next selection will arrive shortly. With their expanded content, DVDs are meant to be used differently than videos. The tapes are typically watched once and returned, whereas DVDs allow you to interact more with them. Having them for an unlimited amount of time seems like a pretty good idea.

22

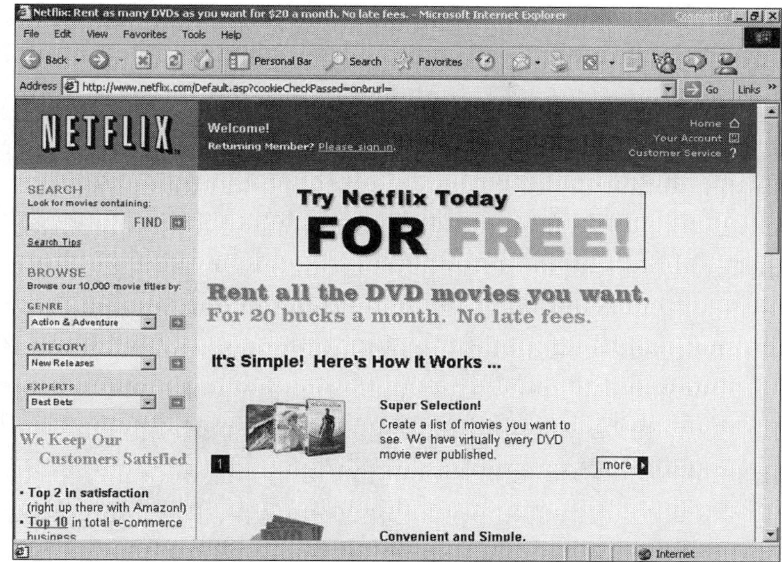

FIGURE 22.10
NetFlix allows you to rent from a huge selection of DVDs for a flat monthly fee.

9. Create a Family Web Site

Back in Hour 19, you learned about creating Web pages. Lots of families around the world have created Web pages and you can, too.

Why? Well, they serve multiple purposes. You needn't be a famous family to get benefit from having a family Web page. And although it certainly would be a way to keep far-flung family members abreast of the latest news, you don't need to be spread out, either.

Some families create them just for fun (see Figure 22.11). They enjoy planning the pages together, give each of the kids their own page(s) to express themselves, and so on. It's kind of a big family art project.

But many families do it to preserve their family history. You'll find a lot of genealogy links on family pages on the Web. If someone in the family has gone to great pains to keep the family history, why keep it hidden? Publish it on the Web!

If researching your family's genealogy is of interest to you, check out Hour 24, "Ten Ways the Internet Can Change Your Personal Life." Researching genealogy is covered there.

FIGURE 22.11
This family's Web site includes fun pages and a genealogy page.

10. Participate in Religious Activities

Just like you can participate in your community organizations online, you can also participate in church and church-related activities. Many churches, synagogues, and other houses of worship now offer Web sites for their members (both current and potential).

Almost all of them offer a worship schedule, so you'll know when you can attend (see Figure 22.12). Some allow you to read the church bulletin online, or even sign up to volunteer at an event. Most offer some information on upcoming events for the various ministries the church carries out. They typically offer lots of information about the church for potential members, and many offer links to other related organizations.

Good examples of church Web sites are all over the Web. If you're looking for a church to join, go to your favorite search site and use a search term that includes the religion, city, and state of your choice (as in "Lutheran Minneapolis Minnesota"). You'll get links to lots of churches in your area.

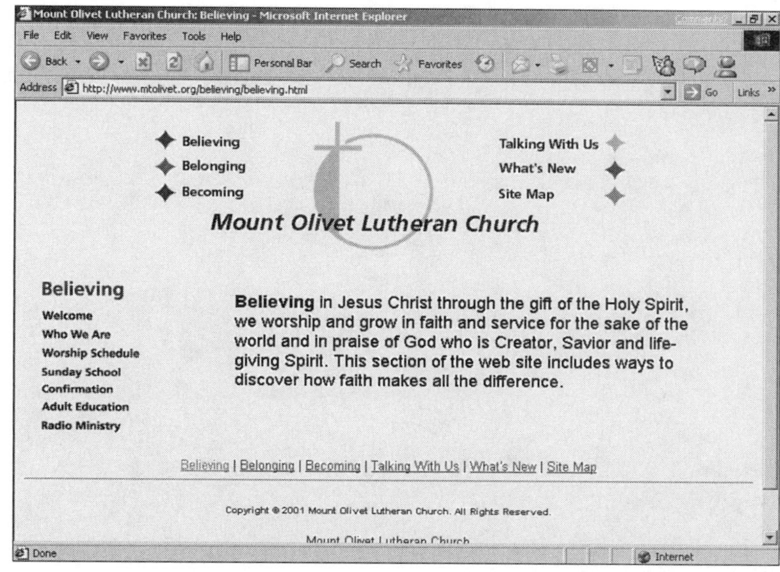

FIGURE 22.12
Mount Olivet Church in Minneapolis offers a Web site for members and potential members.

Summary

One of the things people complain about in today's world is that with the fast-paced society in which we live, there's not enough family time. The Internet can help in a number of ways. First, by giving you fast access to information, you can use it to quickly plan a family outing, vacation, social event, and so on. You can also use it to enjoy a family project, like building a Web site together.

Q&A

Q We love to go out to eat as a family. Does the Web offer resources to help us?

A Yes. There are any number of "local guides" you can use to find entertainment and dining options. RealCities (`www.realcities.com`) and Digital City (`www.digitalcity.com`) are just two. These sites typically offer links to local restaurants.

Q I would like to take the kids to a drive-in movie. Where can I find listings?

A Simple. Just go to Moviefone at `www.movielistings.com`. You can enter a particular theater or the name of a particular film and a ZIP code, and find what you're looking for. There are other ways to search this site, too, and there's more on this in Hour 24.

Hour 23

Ten Ways the Web Can Change Your School Life

Ah, school days. Or were those school daze? It's all a little foggy. Years later, though, here I am again, going through school—only this time through my children's eyes.

Man, are things ever different. For one thing, my daughter is learning things in sixth grade math that I was taught in ninth grade. But that's beside the point, really. Learning today isn't done the way it was *when I was a boy* (a phrase I promised myself back then that I would never use).

Kids today have access to computers and the marvelous software programs that make their lives easier. A spell-checker would have been a dream come true for me in high school and college; now *not* having the benefit of a spell-check system seems somehow prehistoric. Whether it's first grade or graduate school, the Internet has helped to change the educational landscape. Today, college students can often watch lectures over the Internet or download the professor's notes from physics class.

Some classes have used the Internet to perform some amazing, far-off tasks, like conducting a videoconference with a classroom in China, or communicating with Space Shuttle astronauts over the Internet.

That's all wonderful, amazing technology. In this hour, however, we're going to look at some ways the Internet can change your school life in more basic ways. Of course, different age levels will use the Internet in different ways, but I've tried to supply a sampling of all age levels.

By the end of this hour, you should be able to answer the following questions:

- How can the Internet help me choose a college?
- How can I use the Internet for research purposes?
- How can I keep up with everything at school using the Internet?
- Can I register for classes online?
- How do I use the Internet to apply for a student loan?
- How can email help me as a student?

1. Choose a College

One of the biggest decisions any college-bound student has to make is also the first—which college am I going to attend? There are lots of ways that the Internet can help with this decision.

Many high school students already have a few schools in mind that they might like to attend—whether it's the local university, a parent's alma mater, or someplace their guidance counselor recommended.

To check out those schools, just go to the school's Web site (if the school you're thinking about attending doesn't have a Web site, I wouldn't go there). Yahoo! has a good list of colleges and universities in its database. Just go to the main Yahoo! page (`www.yahoo.com`) and click on "Colleges and Universities" under the Education header. Then, you'll be able to navigate through the list to drill down to a state or city level, and eventually get a list of schools in the area.

CollegeNet is another resource that allows you to conduct a search of schools based on criteria you decide. Just go to the main CollegeNet page at `www.collegenet.com` and click on the College Search button (see Figure 23.1). You can then determine how broad or narrow a search you would like to conduct. Among the criteria you can choose from are type of institution (four-year, community college, graduate-level, and so on), states and regions, types of majors offered, and public or private. You can even exclude schools that cost too much money.

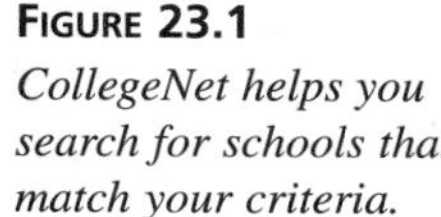

FIGURE 23.1
CollegeNet helps you search for schools that match your criteria.

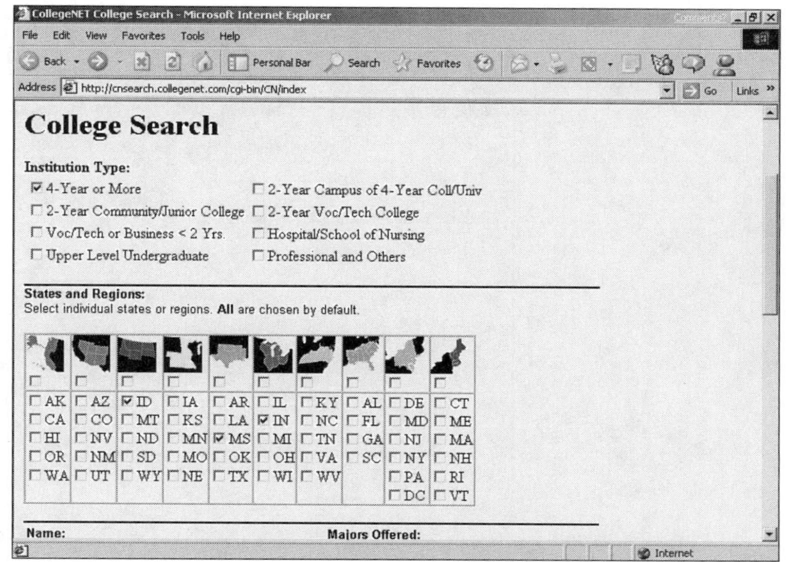

After the search is completed, you get a list of schools that includes tuition for in-state and out-of-state students, plus information on campus life, activities, admissions, and financial aid. It's a great place to start, and you might find out about some schools that you had never thought about but that might be perfect for you!

After you've chosen the university, you can use CollegeNet's link to the undergrad application that school offers, and your application will be on its way in no time.

2. Register for the ACT or SAT Test

Another important step in getting ready for college is to take either the ACT assessment test or the SAT exam (or both). There aren't many colleges that will allow you to be admitted and enroll in classes without taking one or both of these tests.

Thankfully, the Internet offers help with these tests in a couple of different ways. Both ACT and SAT maintain Web sites that can help you find test dates and times, locate and buy resources that will help you prepare for the exams, and even register to take the test.

The SAT site is located at `www.collegeboard.com`. Registering there for the test is very easy. Just click on the SAT Registration link and you're on your way (see Figure 23.2).

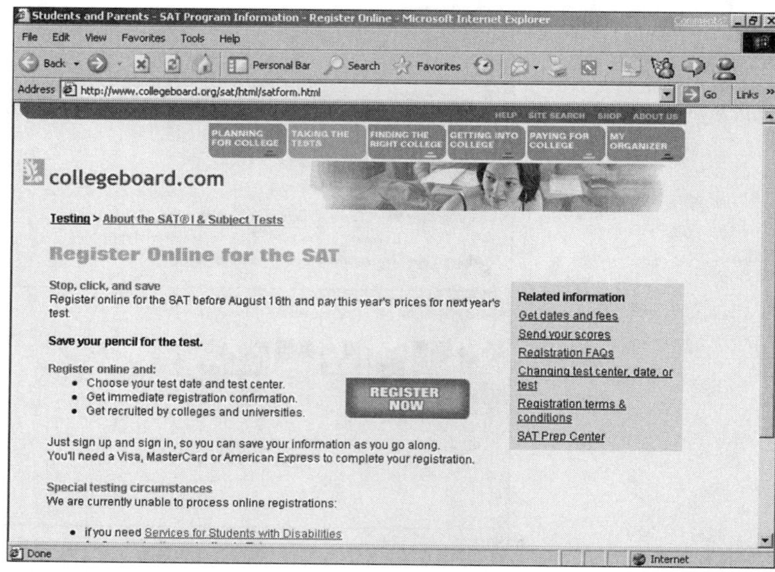

FIGURE 23.2
Collegeboard.com allows you to register for the SAT.

The sites for both of the exams also offer various study aids (including software you can buy) and practice tests you can take to help you get ready.

3. Order Your College Transcript

Applying for a new job, and need a copy of your college transcript in a hurry? Find the Web site of your alma mater (just use the school's name as a search term), and then explore the site to find out how to order transcripts. For those of you who happened to graduate from Indiana University Northwest (anyone…? anyone…?), Figure 23.3 shows the page on that school's Web site where you learn all the ways to get your transcript.

> The Web sites of some colleges and universities are sometimes huge and very difficult to find your way around in. However, most have built-in search tools. If you can get to the site and then locate a link to the search tools, you can simply enter "transcripts" as a search term to locate the page where transcripts are covered.

A few schools have online order forms on which you can fill in your name, address, payment info (credit card number—make sure the site is secure!), and other information so that the school can mail your transcript to you right away. (You have to get it in the mail, on paper—schools do not yet issue "official" transcripts in electronic form, although they will one day.) On other sites, you can open and print a fax form you fill in and fax to the school to place your order.

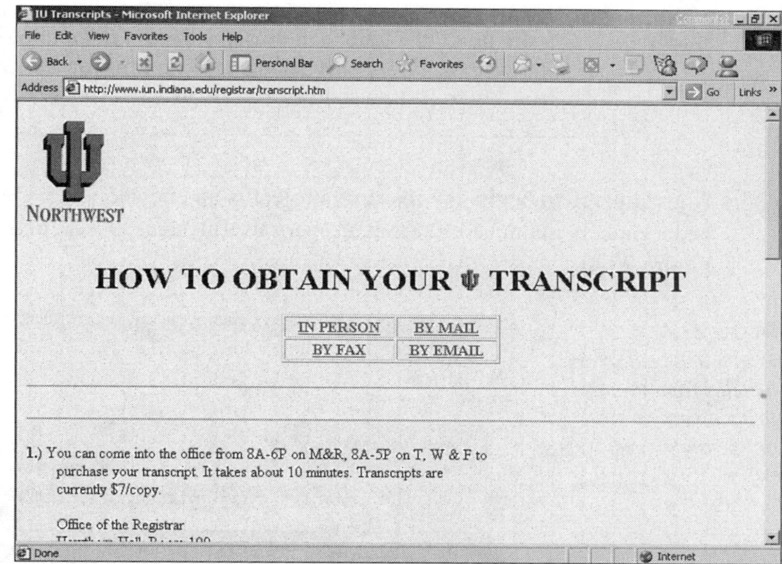

FIGURE 23.3
If you need your college transcript, you might be able to order it straight from your alma mater's Web site.

4. Conduct Research

Probably more valuable than any other resource the Internet offers to students is the ability to conduct research any time of day or night. Libraries are still key to any student's school experience, but the Internet allows access to that data and much more.

Many university programs have built huge databases of information, either from lectures or from scholarly papers written by faculty that can be accessed by students working on a research project.

But what if your project is simpler? What if you're a fourth grader working on a paper on Abraham Lincoln?

The key portion of the word "research" is "search." Any research project—using the Internet or not—requires that you search for information. That could be in card catalog at the library or using your favorite search page on the Web.

A search on the term "Abraham Lincoln" will reveal everything from biography pages to Web sites maintained by museums and historic sites related to the man.

You should be careful in any research you do, be it online or offline, to try to make sure the source of the material is a reputable one. Anyone can put a site up on the Web, and thus anyone can claim to be the "official" site of this or that. Often, professional-looking sites contain data that is simply not true. Try to stick to sources that are likely to contain truthful information.

A great place to begin any research project is an encyclopedia. On the Internet, encyclopedia-makers maintain sites that are very useful, such as `www.britannica.com` (see Figure 23.4).

FIGURE 23.4
Britannica.com offers articles from the printed version to online audiences.

Here, you can find articles right from the printed version of the encyclopedia, plus links to more information about the topics your uncover. For example, doing a search on the term "Abraham Lincoln" at `www.britannica.com` yields links to other sites on the Web with good information, links to information within the Encyclopedia Britannica site, and links to current events related to the topic (see Figure 23.5). At this writing, much of this data is free, but look for at least some of it to become subscription-based in the near future.

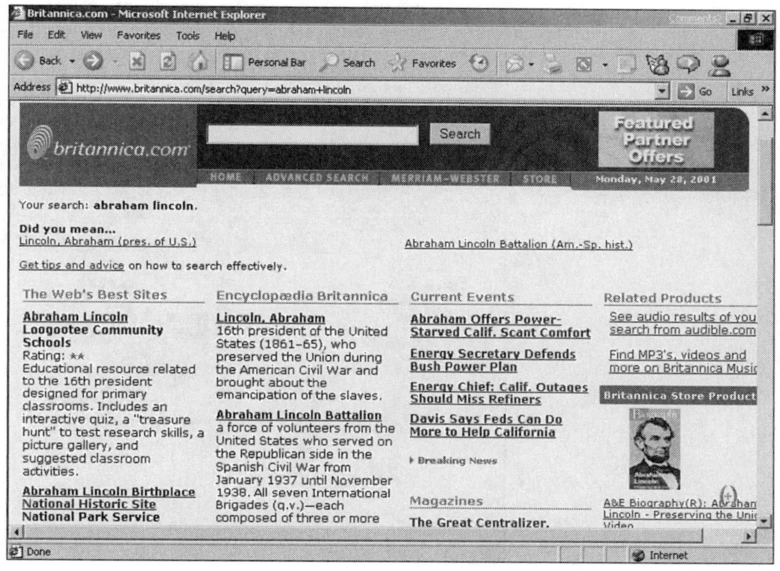

FIGURE 23.5
Searching for Abraham Lincoln on Britannica.com yields this result.

As you've no doubt noted by now, Internet searches often yield less-than-ideal results. As you can see from Figure 23.5, the Current Events section brought in results that had nothing to do with Abraham Lincoln. That's because there isn't a lot of "current" information about Honest Abe. So the matches are recent articles that contain information about something having to do with "Abraham" or "Lincoln."

5. Apply for a Student Loan

College is expensive. No doubt about it. Thousands of student loans are granted every year to help students pay for undergrad, graduate school, law school, and the like. They get to go to school now, and a few years down the road, they get the pleasure of making the payments!

Most major banks allow customers to apply for loans of all types, including student loans, to help get Junior through school. There are lots of different types of loans, of course, but if it's a federal student loan you're looking for, you're going to have to fill out the Free Application for Federal Student Aid (FAFSA) form, to see whether you qualify. It's available at the U.S. Department of Education's FAFSA site at `www.fafsa.ed.gov` (see Figure 23.6).

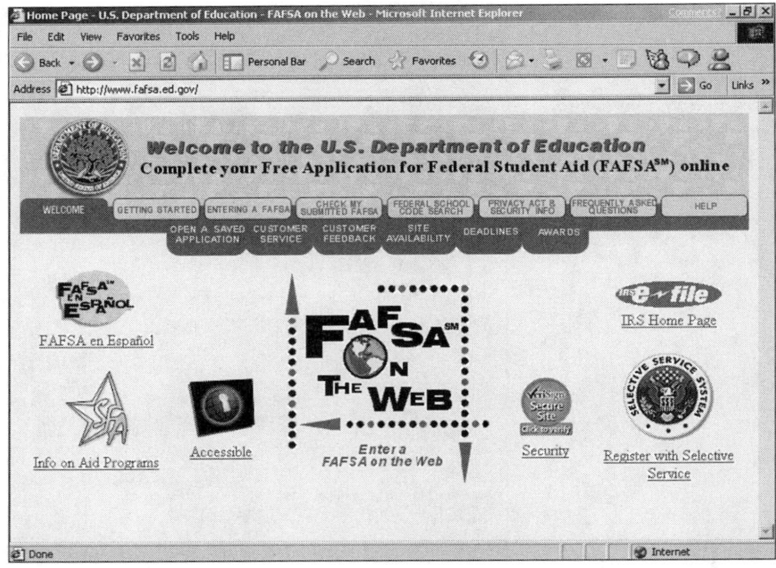

FIGURE 23.6
The FAFSA Web site allows you to fill out the application for federal student loans, to see whether you qualify.

The FAFSA determines how much the federal government believes your family should contribute to the cost of your child's education—that is, the government's opinion of your ability to pay. After you know how much, if any, federal aid you might be able to receive, you'll know if you need to apply for another type of loan to pay for school.

6. Find Scholarship Money

Paying for college becomes more difficult every year. Parents begin to fret about it at their child's birth (sometimes before), and still struggle to put enough money away to help their children down the line. You can sacrifice everything to make your child the next Tiger Woods or Albert Einstein, but you're bucking the odds there, too.

When the kid's getting close to his or her high school graduation, there are still some things you can do to help them. Literally millions of dollars of college scholarships go unused every year.

Why? Because people don't know they exist, or don't think they are qualified, or both. It can't hurt to find out, especially if it brings the chance that any scholarship is attainable. Every little bit helps, right?

There are lots of "scholarship search" sites available on the Web. Just use your favorite search site to search for the term "scholarships," and you see a bunch. A good place to start is Scholarships.com (see Figure 23.7).

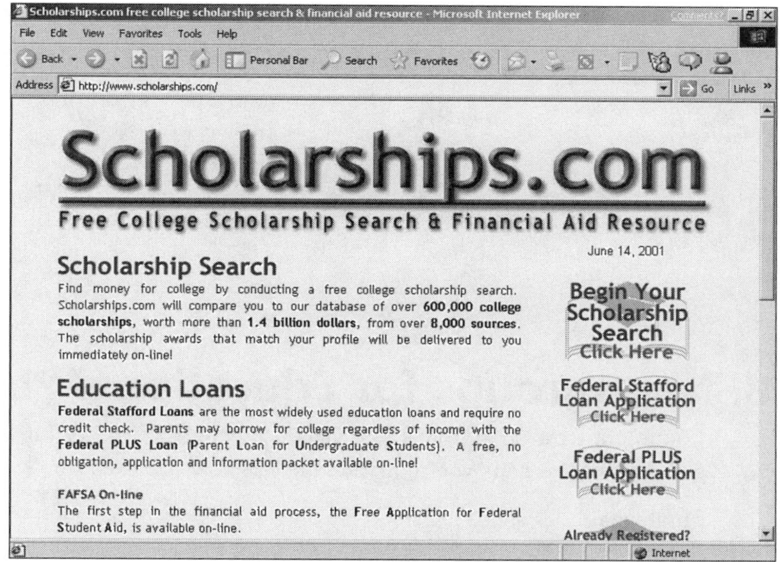

FIGURE 23.7
Scholarships.com gives students a chance to find scholarship money they might otherwise have missed.

Scholarships.com solves the problem of whether you are qualified for a particular scholarship for you. It maintains a database of scholarships and their requirements. You input your bio information, and are "matched" to scholarships that you are likely to qualify for.

7. Ask a Teacher

America Online members have a great resource available to them called Ask a Teacher. It's part of the Kids Only channel in AOL, which includes an area called Homework Help.

Within Homework Help you'll find lots of helpful areas, including an encyclopedia, dictionary, thesaurus, and calculator, plus special study areas groups by subject (English, math, science, social studies). One area on the Homework Help page is called Ask a Teacher (see Figure 23.8).

It acts like a bulletin board. You choose a subject area and post a question, and a real-life teacher will post an answer. It's not immediate, so you need to allow a little time.

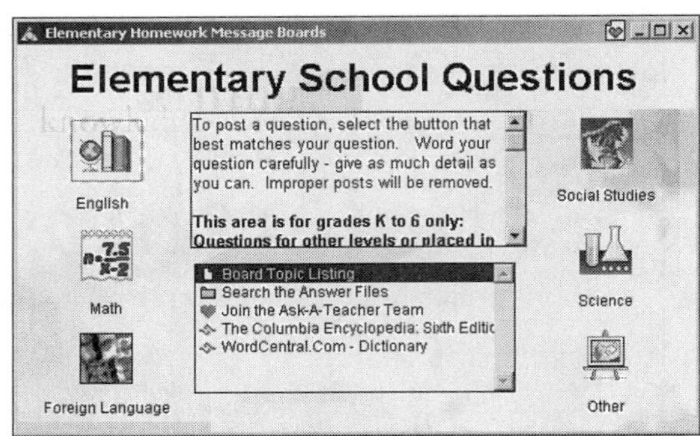

FIGURE 23.8
America Online's Ask a Teacher allows you to get homework help from real teachers.

8. Newsgroups for Educational Purposes

You might view newsgroups as a place for people to use for fun, entertainment, hobbies, and the like. Perhaps you think newsgroups can't be used for serious pursuits.

Think again.

Newsgroups have all kinds of wonderful uses, and helping students is one of them. There are newsgroups available on all kinds of topics, including very scholarly ones.

For example, let's say you're studying microbiology. Using your newsreader (if you need a refresher on newsgroups, refer to Hour 7) search for newsgroups pertaining to biology. There are several newsgroups for biology, including one called "`bionet.microbiology`" (see Figure 23.9).

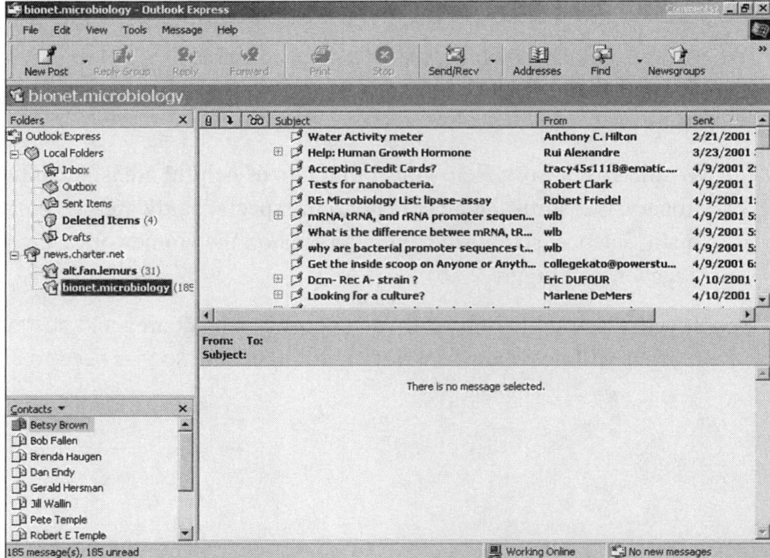

FIGURE 23.9
Newsgroups can be found on a variety of subject matters.

After you're there, you can read the postings for general information, or post a question if there's something specific you would like to know. Newsgroups of this type are much more likely to stay on-topic than a chat room of a similar nature.

9. Check In with Teachers and Keep Up with Homework

It happens all the time around my house: A child comes home and can't remember exactly which pages she has to read for homework, or when a particular assignment is due.

Many schools in the U.S. have help for kids who have questions about homework assignments. Each teacher might have a page on the school's Web site in which they keep an up-to-date list of homework and when it is due.

Some schools also offer study aids right on their Web sites. As you see in Figure 23.10, a local high school's English department has created pages for the current subject of classroom work, John Steinbeck. These pages include everything from background information to items related directly to classroom work, such as reading guide questions, vocabulary, and more.

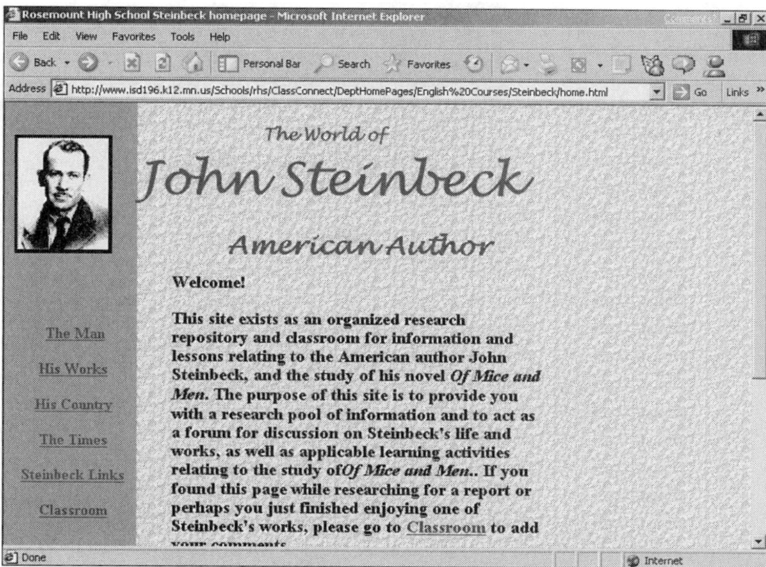

FIGURE 23.10
Some schools offer study aids for their students.

Most schools' and school districts' Web sites also offer email addresses for teachers, so that parents and students can keep the flow of information going.

10. Email Your Assignments

One growing trend in colleges and universities around the globe is the ability of on-campus students to email in their assignments. Distance learners have been doing this all along, of course, but more and more, traditional on-campus students are being allowed to do it.

It's up to the individual teacher or professor, of course, but if they give it the go-ahead, it can be very convenient for the students. First, you don't have to worry about printing out the paper. Plus, you can work right up to the deadline, because you don't have to allow time to print and deliver the paper to the professor's office or classroom!

(Now, that's not an excuse to procrastinate!)

It's a simple email (see Figure 23.11) to send off. Just make sure you've followed the professor's guidelines for the type of document (Word, text-only, and so on) and for how he or she would like it delivered (as an attachment or in the body of the email).

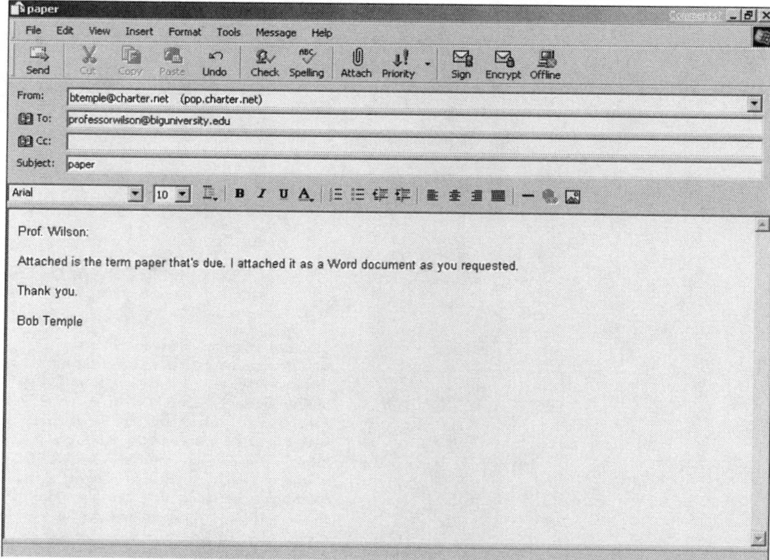

FIGURE 23.11
Sending assignments in by email can make things easier for students.

Summary

There are as many ways for students to benefit from the Internet as there are students willing to try. Whether you're looking for help with homework, help finding or enrolling in a school or university, or whatever, the Internet is there for you (and your kids).

Q&A

Q I've heard a lot about students buying research papers on the Internet. How big a problem is that?

A Irresponsible students have been buying test questions, lecture notes, papers, and more from other students long before the Internet came to be. There's a million ways for students to cheat throughout their educational careers if they really want to. It's unfortunate that the Internet gets used for some of the things it does, when there are so many great uses for it.

Students need to realize that eventually, even at big universities, professors are going to start seeing the same papers appearing over and over.

What's particularly funny is that the Internet makes it so easy to find information on virtually any subject, that for the time and effort a student puts in to buying a paper from some place, they could just as easily create their own.

HOUR 24

Ten Ways the Web Can Change Your Personal Life

Let's get personal.

Okay, maybe not too personal. I wouldn't want to invade your privacy or anything. I just want to talk a little bit about how the Internet can change your personal life.

Now, before your imagination gets the best of you, this isn't just about your sex life. There's a lot more to a person's personal life than just "relationships," you know. So we're going to spend this hour talking about other parts of your personal life.

In the previous three hours, we've covered business, family, and school uses for the Internet. There are also lots of ways you can use the Internet for yourself, whether it's to further a hobby, for entertainment, to buy something, to keep track of your finances, or whatever the case may be.

By the end of this hour, you should be able to answer the following questions:

- How can I use the Internet to help me at tax time?
- How can I keep up with the latest news online?
- Can I use the Internet to help with my finances?
- Can the Internet help me with TV or movie listings?
- How can the Internet help me track my ancestry?
- How can the Internet shorten my commute?

1. Get Tax Forms or File Your Tax Returns

I don't know about you, but whenever I need a particular IRS publication, it's never available from the stacks at my library or bank. You can get nearly any Federal tax form, instructions booklet, or other publication straight from the Internal Revenue Web site. In most cases, you can download the publication and print it right from your computer.

To reach the IRS Web site, start at `www.irs.gov`, and follow the links you see.

Where you get state tax forms and information depends, of course, on your state. In most states they are available from the Department of Revenue, or whatever agency you pay your taxes to. Start at your state government's Web site, and follow links until you find it.

The latest trend in tax filing is e-filing—that is, filing the forms over the Internet. There are a number of ways to do this, but you have to be careful which company you use. You can buy an over-the-counter tax software program and use its e-file option. Or, you can even completely fill out your tax form online, using an IRS-approved vendor, and file them directly from that Web site.

The IRS keeps a list of the partners it allows to provide this service. The list can be found on the IRS Web site at `www.irs.gov/elec_svs/partners.html`. These partners, such as TaxACT (see Figure 24.1), allow you to e-file your return.

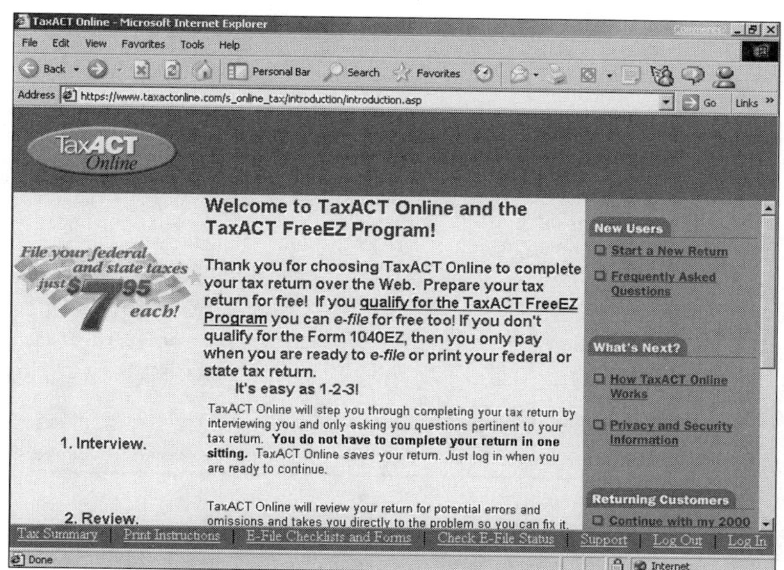

FIGURE 24.1
IRS-approved partners like TaxACT allow you to file your returns online.

2. Read Your Local Newspaper

Yes, you can pay to have the daily paper delivered, or—in a growing number of cities—you can read the same paper online, for free, and reduce the size of your recycling pile. Me, I prefer to hold a paper paper, but to each his own. (My job is to tell you what you *can* do, and let you make up your own mind.)

Figure 24.2 shows the online version of *The Washington Post*. The online version includes the complete text of the day's paper, including such handy items as classified ads and job listings.

You can usually find any paper's Web site address listed somewhere within the printed version. You can also try to guess its address by simply sticking "www" in front of the paper's name, and ".com" on the end (as in `www.washingtonpost.com`), and you might hit it right. Failing that, use the paper's name as a search term.

Table 24.1 shows the Web addresses of some of the nation's most popular online newspapers.

TABLE 24.1 U.S. Newspaper Web Sites

Newspaper	*Online address*
USA Today	`www.usatoday.com`
New York Times	`www.nytimes.com`
Los Angeles Times	`www.latimes.com`
Washington Post	`www.washingtonpost.com`
Wall Street Journal	`www.wsj.com`
Miami Herald	`www.miami.com/herald/`
Chicago Tribune	`www.chicagotribune.com`
Boston Globe	`www.boston.com/globe/`
Dallas Morning News	`www.dallasnews.com`
San Jose Mercury News	`www0.mercurycenter.com`

How come the paper's free online but costs 50 cents a day in print? A newspaper makes most of its money from ads, not the cover price. The cover price doesn't even cover the cost of the printing and distribution. Because ads appear on the online version, and there are no printing costs, the ads alone pay for the online paper.

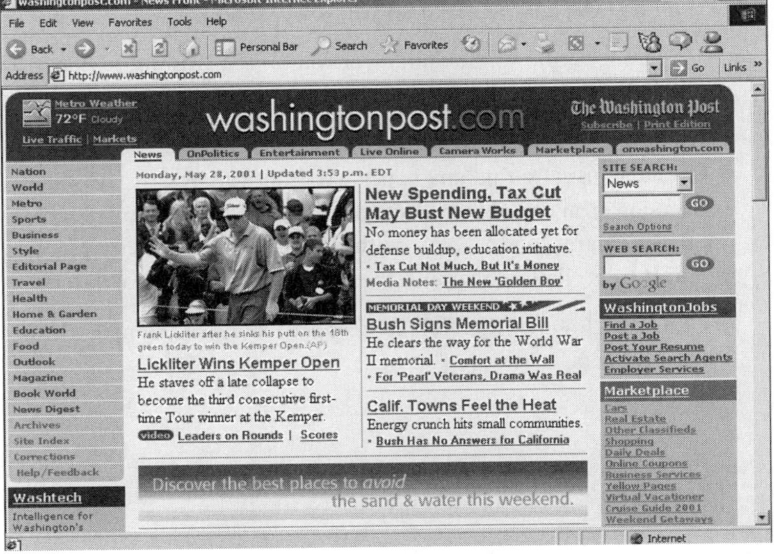

FIGURE 24.2
More and more major daily newspapers offer an online version that features the complete text of the printed version.

You usually cannot read today's online newspaper tomorrow, as you can with a printed paper. Each day, the current day's online newspaper displaces yesterday's. Some newspapers do keep archived articles, but you often have to pay a small fee to read them.

If you're looking for a particular newspaper's online version and can't find it, check out the American Journalism Review's Web site at `ajr.newslink.org`. There, you'll find links to all kinds of newspapers, large and small, daily and weekly, across the U.S.

3. Order Your Credit Report

A good credit history is important, and an accurate credit history is, too. There are three major national credit bureaus that might have files on you, assuming you've ever applied for credit. You can see what's in those files for just a few bucks.

In some cases, you have a right to request a free copy of your credit history from these agencies. If you've been turned down for credit, for example, you are entitled to a free copy of your reports. For more information about the Fair Credit Reporting Act, see the Federal Trade Commission's Web site at `www.ftc.gov/bcp/conline/pubs/credit/fcra.htm`.

A good starting place is CreditReport-Net.com, which you'll find at (do I really need to say?) `www.creditreport-net.com`. As Figure 24.3 shows, you can get your report from all three major credit bureaus, online, in 30 seconds, for eight bucks.

In case you need to contact one of the credit bureaus directly, here are their addresses:

- **Experian**: `www.experian.com`
- **Equifax**: `www.equifax.com`
- **Trans Union**: `www.transunion.com`

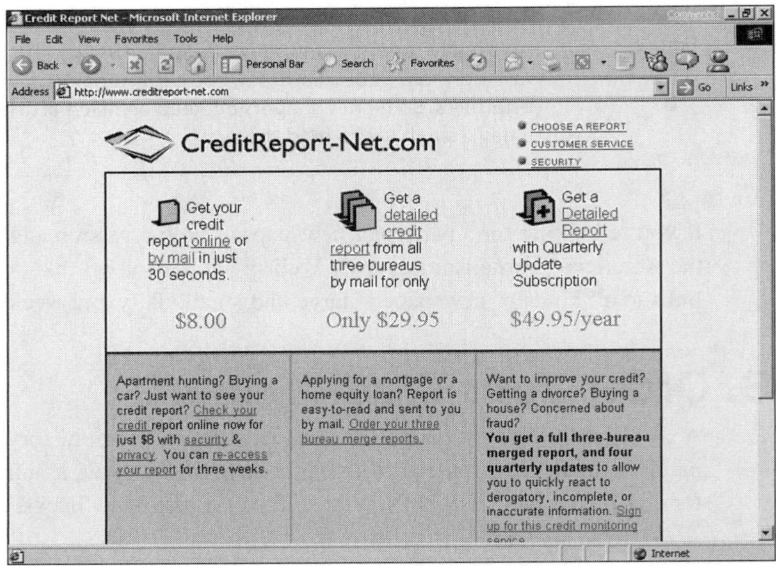

FIGURE 24.3
CreditReport-Net.com offers easy access to your credit history.

4. Play Games

There are tons of interactive games on the Web. Some you play against a computer, like video games. Others you can play "live" against other players that are online at the same time as you.

A good starting point for linking to online games is the Games You Can Play on the WWW directory, at `www.grouper.com/play.html` (see Figure 24.4).

Web-based games are made possible through a wide variety of different technologies. Some games are very simple, and can be played through any browser. But many of the newer, cooler games require browsers capable of processing Java programs, and others require special plug-ins or player programs to be added to your browser.

When you click a link in the Games You Can Play on the WWW directory, the page you go to tells you about any special technical requirements for playing the game, and will probably also offer links for downloading any programs required for play.

Because interactive games might have these special requirements, if you intend to play a lot of games, it's important that you keep up with the latest release of your browser, and use a well-equipped, fast computer and fast Internet connection, preferably broadband.

FIGURE 24.4
The Games You Can Play on the WWW page provides links to dozens of Interactive games.

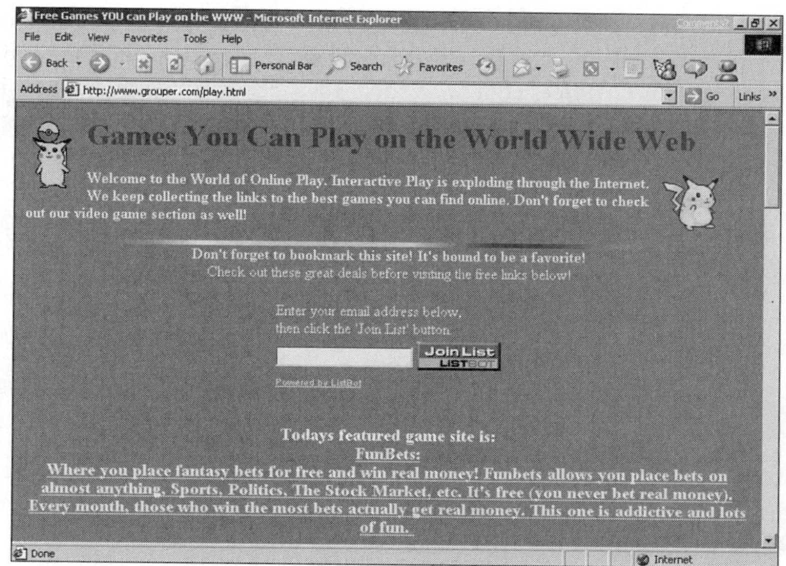

5. Buy a Car

You can, in fact, really buy a car online. You can research features, prices, and reviews; calculate loan payments; find out the fair trade-in value of your old car; apply for a car loan; get prices for the car you want from actual dealers; find out what rebates are currently in effect; negotiate a final price; and finally *buy*—all online. All you have to do offline is sign some papers when you take delivery.

But as I'm sure you know, nothing online substitutes for a real, in-person test-drive. And most of the so-called "online" buying services do little more than forward your name, contact information, and desired model to one of your local dealers, who then contacts you with a price—that's hardly a huge advantage over going to see the dealer yourself. And in a recent report, *Consumer Reports* determined that there are advantages to car shopping online, but that you should not expect to wind up with a better price than you would get offline.

What you can get online is *information*. For example, after you've decided which car you want to buy (both from reading online information and from taking test-drives), you can easily learn online the exact invoice price for the car you want (or retail value, for a used car), and the amount of the dealer's "holdback" (the phantom payback dealers get above invoice). This information enables you to walk into a dealer knowing what the dealer paid, and what a reasonable profit might be. That's powerful negotiating information.

There are plenty of good starting points for car shopping, including the sites of the carmakers themselves (`www.ford.com`, `www.honda.com`, and so on). But a better place to start is CarPrices.com (`www.carprices.com`; see Figure 24.5), which features links to reviews, invoice and sticker prices, manufacturer's Web sites, payment calculators, online buying services, and much more.

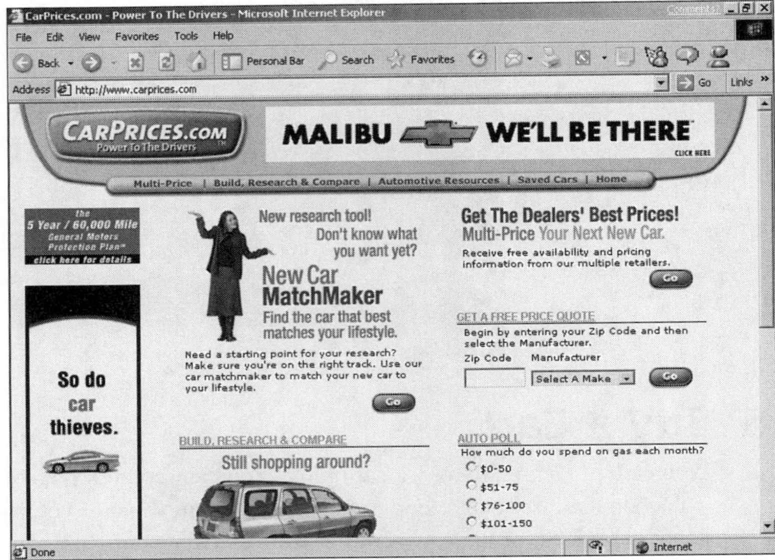

FIGURE 24.5
CarPrices.com is a great first stop when you're thinking about new wheels.

Another good place to find car prices is Edmunds.com at `www.edmunds.com`. If you're working on a trade-in or buying or selling a used car, you can get the "blue book" value straight from the source, the Kelley Blue Book, at `www.kbb.com`.

6. Sample CDs Before You Buy

The Web is awash with sound clips presented as samples of CDs. When considering purchasing a CD, you can listen to the samples online, to try before you buy.

If you use any of the major online CD-buying sources (`www.cdnow.com`, `www.cduniverse.com`, `www.amazon.com`) and display a description of a particular CD's contents, you'll often find links on that same page that download or play sound clips from the CD. You'll find similar links on the Web sites of all the major record companies (see Figure 26.6).

Exactly how you play the clips depends upon what file format they're presented in, and what kind of player programs you have on your computer.

Most clips are provided in .WAV or .MP3 formats, which you download and then play in a player program, online or off. Some clips are provided in RealAudio format, for which you must have the RealPlayer, and which must be played online.

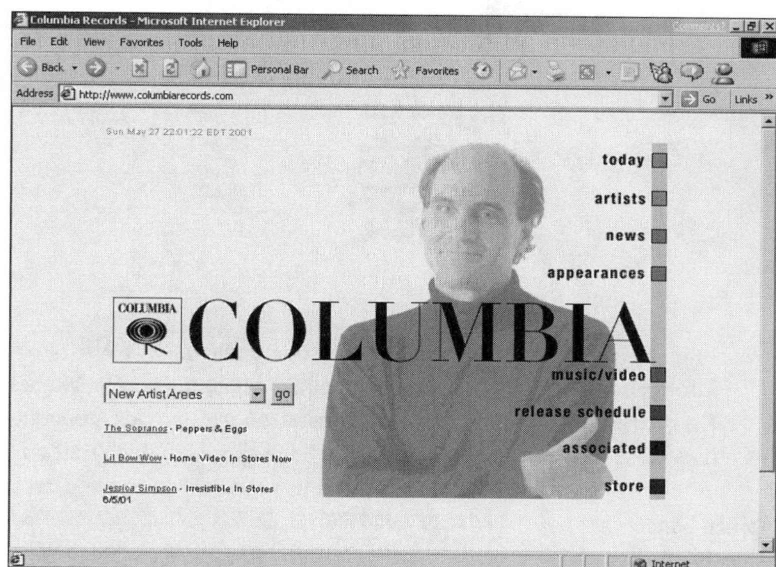

FIGURE 24.6
Online CD stores and record companies (like Columbia Records, shown here) often offer online sound clips to give you a taste of a CD before you buy it.

24

7. Avoid Traffic Jams

Taking a driving trip, and want to know which route to take in order to avoid construction delays? Check out Rand McNally's road construction Web site, by going to `www.randmcnally.com`. Under the Road Trip Guide header, click on Up-to-Date Road Construction (see Figure 24.7).

That's great for planning long-distance trips, because it can save you a lot of time working through construction. But what about your everyday commute? Most people who have a commute of more than a few miles have several options for roads they can take to get to or from work.

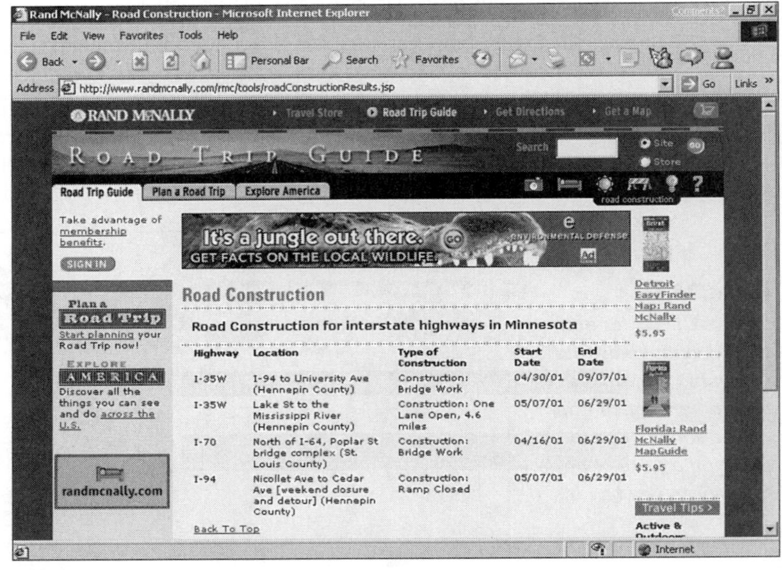

FIGURE 24.7
On Rand McNally's construction site, you can learn where the roadwork is—so you can plan another route.

In many states, the transportation department maintains a Web site that includes current traffic information—where it's moving smoothly, where it's not. In Minnesota, for example, the Department of Transportation has cameras on major roads around the metro area. Based on the data these cameras provide, you can tell the speed at which traffic is moving (see Figure 24.8).

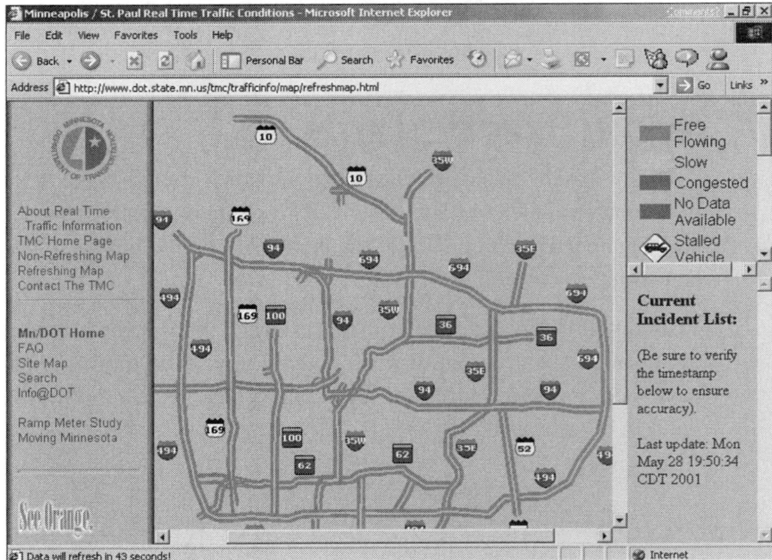

FIGURE 24.8
Many states, like Minnesota, maintain online traffic flow reports you can check before heading out on your commute.

If you're looking for directions from one location to another, a great resource is Mapquest (`www.mapquest.com`). Simply input the two addresses, and you get complete written directions plus a map to refer to. You can even download the directions to a PDA or other device, if you have the right software.

8. Consult *TV Guide*

TV Guide is online, and free (see Figure 24.9). Just go to `www.tvguide.com`, and click the link for TV listings. (You might be prompted for your ZIP code, so that the guide can show your local programming and list times for your time zone.) Programs appear in an onscreen grid; you can click on a show's name in the grid to learn more about it.

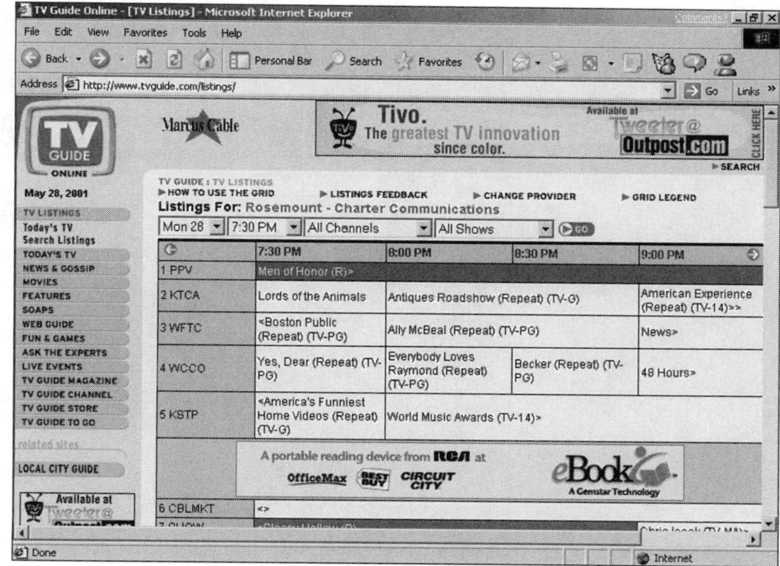

FIGURE 24.9
What's on tonight? TV Guide online can tell you.

If you have one of those pizza-size satellite dishes, you can also see a complete program guide on the Web sites of the companies that provide your programming. Check out `www.directv.com`. (That site's programming grid shows both DirecTV and USSB programs.)

9. Play the Stock Market

Thousands, perhaps millions, of people have become their very own stockbroker since the Internet has come into the mainstream. Buying and selling of stocks and other securities online is big business.

Of course, one must do so at one's own risk. Being an educated investor is essential to having success. As Kenny Rogers once said, you gotta know when to hold 'em, know when to fold 'em, know when to walk away, and know when to run.

The Web sites of major investment firms like Merrill Lynch or Salomon Smith Barney offer users the ability to invest online. There are also online-only companies, like Datek (`www.datek.com`) and Etrade (`www.etrade.com`; see Figure 24.10) that allow you to do it.

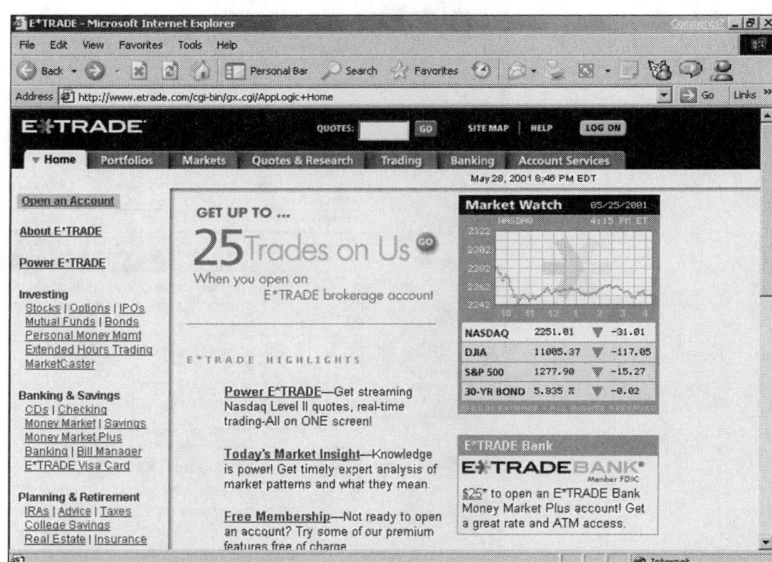

FIGURE 24.10
Etrade and others allow you the ability to make online trades.

10. Trace Your Family's History

No organization has gone to greater lengths to preserve family histories than the Mormon church, which maintains a Web site especially designed to help people find their ancestors.

If you're serious about tracing your family's history, this site (`www.familysearch.com`; see Figure 24.11) is a great place to get going. Just click on the Search tab, and you'll be able to enter the name of an ancestor to find out more information. If you have detailed information on the person, such as his or her parents' names, you can narrow your search very quickly.

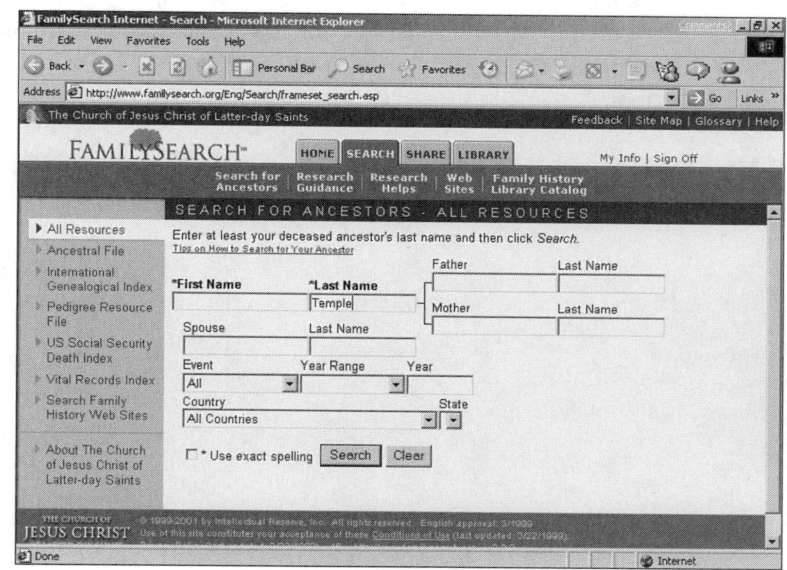

FIGURE 24.11
FamilySearch allows you to track down information about your ancestors.

Or, you can enter only a last name, and get all sorts of matches that you can sift through.

24

Summary

In this hour, we talked about "personal" things you can do online, without getting too personal about it. There is, of course, another level to one's personal life, but what you do with that is, well, personal.

In these last four hours, you've seen a total of 40 ways the Internet can play a role in your daily life. There are thousands more ways. In fact, for most of life's endeavors, there's a way the Internet can play a role in one way or another.

Q&A

Q What about my hobbies? Isn't there a way the Internet can play a role there?

A Of course. Whether your hobbies are fantasy sports leagues, kayaking, or model railroad building, there are Web sites that can support you. Use your favorite search site to do a search on the hobbies that interest you.

Q In the last four hours, you've talked about a lot of different things we can do on the Internet. What's the best thing?

A Don't be silly. There isn't one single *best* thing you can use the Internet for. It can be used to educate, entertain, enlighten, and a whole lot of other words that start with "e." As long as you use it for good, and not for evil, the Internet is a valuable tool.

PART VII
Appendixes

APPENDIX A

Fun Web Sites to Visit

Browsers and Other Client Programs

> Addresses for the two most popular Internet software suites—Internet Explorer and Netscape Communicator—are included in the following list.
>
> Note that in your Web travels, however, on all sorts of pages, you will encounter little buttons with the Netscape Navigator or Internet Explorer logo on them, usually accompanied by the words "Download Now." Clicking one of these buttons takes you directly to the download page for the product.

- Microsoft Internet Explorer
  `www.microsoft.com/ie`
- NeoPlanet
  `www.neoplanet.com`

- Netscape Communicator (Navigator)
  www.netscape.com or home.netscape.com
- Opera
  www.opera.com

Plug-Ins, Helpers, and Other Browser Accessories

- Adobe Acrobat Reader
  www.adobe.com/products/acrobat/readermain.html
- Macromedia Shockwave/Flash Players
  www.macromedia.com/shockwave
- Microsoft Free Downloads
  www.microsoft.com/msdownload
- Netscape Plug-ins Directory
  home.netscape.com/plugins
- Plug-In Plaza
  browserwatch.internet.com/plug-in.html
- RealAudio/RealVideo
  www.real.com

General-Purpose Software Download Sites

- Tucows Directory
  www.tucows.com
- Download.com
  download.cnet.com
- Handango
  www.handango.com
- Kitty-Kat Software (Mac Stuff)
  www.newc.com/kks

- Shareware. com
  `shareware.cnet.com`
- Shareware Junkies
  `www.sharewarejunkies.com`
- Softword Technology
  `www.pc-shareware.com`

Search Engines

- Alta Vista
  `www.altavista.com`
- Ask Jeeves
  `www.askjeeves.com`
- Excite
  `www.excite.com`
- Go
  `www.go.com`
- Google
  `www.google.com`
- Lycos
  `www.lycos.com`
- NBCi
  `www.nbci.com`
- WebCrawler
  `www.webcrawler.com`
- Yahoo!
  `www.yahoo.com`

Web Authoring Resources

Clip Art and Templates

- Free Graphics
  `www.jgpublish.com/free.htm`

- Clip Art Universe
  www.nzwwa.com/mirror/clipart/
- Yahoo!'s Clip Art Directory
  dir.yahoo.com/Computers
- Multimedia/Clip Art Directory
  www.clipart.com/

General Web Authoring

- Netscape Developer's Edge
  developer.netscape.com/library/documentation/jsframe.html
- Yahoo!'s WWW Listings
  dir.yahoo.com/Computers_and_Internet/Software/Reviews/Titles/Internet/Web_Authoring_Tools/
- The Virtual Library
  WWW.Stars.com/
- The Web Toolbox
  www.rtis.com/nat/user/toolbox/
- The HTTP Specification
  www.w3.org/pub/WWW/Protocols/

Arts, Culture, and Society

- #1 Online Greeting Cards
  www.1onlinegreetingcards.com
- American Council for the Arts
  www.artsusa.org
- ArtsNet
  www.artsnet.org
- ArtSource
  www.ilpi.com/artsource/welcome.html
- Association of African American Museums
  www.artnoir.com/aaam.html

- Classical Music Online
  www.scapecast.com/onworld/CMO
- Florida Museum of Hispanic and Latin American Art
  www.latinoweb.com/museo
- Internet Underground Music Archive
  www.iuma.com
- Jazz Online
  www.jazzonln.com
- The Louvre
  www.paris.org/Musees/Louvre
- Museum of Modern Art (MOMA)
  www.moma.org
- Museum of Natural History
  www.mnh.si.edu
- National Air and Space Museum
  www.nasm.edu
- On-Line Books
  digital.library.upenn.edu/books/
- Smithsonian Institution
  www.si.edu
- Virgin Records
  www.virginrecords.com
- Ultimate Band List
  ubl.artistdirect.com

Business

- BizWeb
  www.bizweb.com
- CD Rate Scanner
  bankcd.com

- CNNfn (Cable News Network Financial Network)
  www.cnnfn.com
- CommerceNet
  www.commerce.net
- Dow Jones Interactive
  bis.dowjones.com
- The Economist
  www.economist.com
- inc.com
  www.inc.com
- MSN MoneyCentral Investor
  moneycentral.msn.com/investor/home.asp
- Small Business Administration
  www.sba.gov
- Wall Street Research Net
  www.wsrn.com

Government

- FedWorld
  www.fedworld.gov
- Library of Congress
  lcweb.loc.gov
- The U.S. Senate
  www.senate.gov
- The U.S. House of Representatives
  www.house.gov
- The White House
  www.whitehouse.gov

Education

- 100 Most Popular College & University Sites
  www.100hot.com/directory/education/college.html
- College Board Online
  www.collegeboard.org
- The Homeschool Zone
  www.homeschoolzone.com
- Online Educational Resources
  quest.arc.nasa.gov/OER
- United Negro College Fund
  www.uncf.org
- U.S. Department of Education
  www.ed.gov

Entertainment/Media

- Absolute Trivia
  www.absolutetrivia.com
- DirecTV (Digital Satellite)
  www.directv.com
- Roger Ebert
  www.suntimes.com/ebert/ebert.html
- E Online
  www.eonline.com
- Film.com
  www.film.com
- Internet Movie Database
  www.imdb.com
- Monty Python Online
  www.pythonline.com

- NetFlix
  `www.netflix.com`
- *New York Times* Crossword Puzzles
  `www.nytimes.com/diversions/`
- Mr. Showbiz
  `mrshowbiz.go.com`
- *TV Guide*
  `www.tvguide.com`

TV Networks

- ABC
  `abc.go.com`
- American Movie Classics
  `www.amctv.com`
- CBS
  `www.cbs.com`
- NBC
  `home.nbci.com`
- PBS
  `www.pbs.org`
- Fox
  `www.fox.com`
- Cinemax
  `www.cinemax.com`
- HBO
  `www.hbo.com`
- MTV
  `www.mtv.com`
- The Disney Channel
  `disney.go.com/disneychannel`
- ESPN
  `espn.go.com`

Movie Studios

- Universal Studios
  www.mca.com
- MGM
  www.mgmua.com
- Paramount Pictures
  www.paramount.com
- Sony Pictures Entertainment
  www.spe.sony.com/movies/index.html
- Fox Home Entertainment
  www.tofhe.com
- Walt Disney Pictures
  disney.go.com/DisneyPictures
- Warner Bros.
  www2.warnerbros.com/web/movies/index.jsp

Health

- Alcoholics Anonymous
  www.alcoholics-anonymous.org
- HealthWorld Online
  www.healthy.net
- National Breast Cancer Coalition
  www.natlbcc.org
- The Hunger Site
  www.thehungersite.com
- World Health Organization
  www.who.int

Kid Stuff

- Children's Storybooks Online
  www.magickeys.com/books/links.html

- Clubs for Boys
  www.worldkids.net/clubs/boys.htm
- Crayola
  www.crayola.com
- DC Comics Online
  www.dccomics.com
- A Girl's World.com
  www.agirlsworld.com
- Children's Museum of Indianapolis
  www.childrensmuseum.org
- Kid's Corner
  kids.ot.com
- Postopia
  www.postopia.com
- Roald Dahl
  www.roalddahl.com
- Sports Illustrated for Kids
  www.sikids.com
- Yahooligans! News for Kids
  www.yahooligans.com/content/news/
- The Children's Literature Web Guide
  www.ucalgary.ca/~dkbrown

Shopping Malls

- CyberMall.com
  cybermall.com
- Internet Shopping Outlet
  www.shoplet.com
- Malls.com
  malls.com/awesome

- A Shopper's Utopia
  `shop-utopia.com`
- 21st Century Plaza
  `www.21stcenturyplaza.com`

Sports

- Yahoo! Sports Events
  `www.broadcast.com/Sports_Events/`
- CNNsi (*Sports Illustrated*)
  `cnnsi.com`
- Golf. com
  `www.golf.com`
- Major League Baseball
  `www.mlb.com`
- Major League Soccer
  `www.mls.com`
- NASCAR
  `www.nascar.com`
- National Basketball Association
  `www.nba.com`
- National Football League
  `www.nfl.com`
- National Hockey League
  `www.nhl.com`

Travel

- American Automobile Association
  `www.aaa.com`
- American Express Travel
  `www.americanexpress.com/travel`

- Fodor's Travel Guides
  www.fodors.com
- Frugal Flyer
  www.frugalflyer.com
- TravelNow.com
  www.travelnow.com
- Travelocity
  www.travelocity.com

Computer-Related Sites

Computer Systems

- Apple Computer
  www.apple.com
- Compaq
  www.compaq.com
- Dell
  www.dell.com
- Gateway
  www.gateway.com
- IBM
  www.ibm.com
- Sun Microsystems, Inc.
  www.sun.com
- Toshiba
  www.toshiba.com

Printers

- Brother
  www.brother.com
- Canon
  www.canon.com

- Epson

  www.epson.com

- Hewlett-Packard

  www.hp.com

Modems

- US Robotics

  www.usr.com

- Zoom

  www.zoom.com

Major Commercial Software Companies

- Adobe Systems Incorporated

  www.adobe.com

- Apple Computer

  www.apple.com

- Claris

  www.claris.com

- Corel Corp.

  www.corel.com

- Electronic Arts

  www.ea.com

- IBM

  www.ibm.com

- Intuit

  www.intuit.com

- Microsoft

  www.microsoft.com

- Netscape Communications

  www.netscape.com or home.netscape.com

- Novell
  `www.novell.com`
- Symantec
  `www.symantec.com`

APPENDIX B

Tools for the Serious User: FTP and Telnet

People surfed the Internet for over a decade before there was a World Wide Web. During those years, the principal tools for using the Net—other than email and newsgroups—were good old Telnet, FTP, and, in the final pre-Web years, Gopher. After you get the hang of them, these tools aren't really any more difficult to use than the Web or email. But because they take you beyond the familiar confines of the more popular Internet tools, you might lump FTP, Telnet, and Gopher together as "serious" tools—after all, you won't use them unless you're serious enough about what you're doing to go beyond the Web.

There's so much available on the Web these days that most newcomers to the Net never bother with FTP, Gopher, or Telnet. Much of what used to be accessible only through these tools now resides on Web pages. But not *everything* in the serious tools' domain has made it to the Web yet, so these tools remain an important part of your Net toolset. To use *all* of the Internet, you must be familiar with these powerful tools, which are easier to use than you might expect. (You don't have to be all *that* serious!)

Downloading Files with FTP

You already know how to download files from the Web. But some files you might want are stored not on Web servers, but on *FTP servers*.

FTP stands for *File Transfer Protocol*, but you really don't need to know that. Everybody uses just the abbreviation, like NBC or VCR. Still, the name says it all: FTP is used for transferring files between computers. The files stored on FTP servers are waiting to be downloaded by an *FTP client*, a program on your computer that communicates with FTP servers through the Internet.

Many FTP servers are *password-protected* to limit access to only authorized users. When you try to access a password-protected FTP server, you're prompted to enter a username and password. If you don't have a correct username and password for using that particular server, you're locked out.

However, many FTP servers are called *anonymous* FTP servers because they require no username and password at all, or they display instructions that allow you to enter a "guest" username (often "anonymous") and password (usually your email address) to use the server. When you access an anonymous FTP server through your Web browser, you often do not have to log on (even with a guest password) because your browser automatically completes the logon with your email address if required.

> The kinds of files you can download from FTP servers are the same as those you download from Web pages (`.exe`, `.doc`, `.zip`, and so on) and are subject to the same issues and considerations (such as whether a particular file can run on your type of computer). For more information about these concerns, review Hour 14, "Downloading Programs and Files."

Understanding FTP Addresses

As with any server, you access an FTP server by entering its address into the address box in your browser. FTP server addresses are made up of sections separated by periods, just like Web addresses, and often—but not always—begin with `ftp`. For example, the following is an FTP server addresses:

```
ftp.microsoft.com
```

Files for downloading are stored in particular directories on FTP servers, just as Web page files are stored in particular Web server directories (see Figure B.1). The FTP address can point directly to a file or directory. For example, the address

```
ftp.microsoft.com/products/windows/windowsce/007logo.jpg
```

points directly to a file called 007logo.jpg in a directory called products/windows/windowsce on a server called `ftp.microsoft.com`.

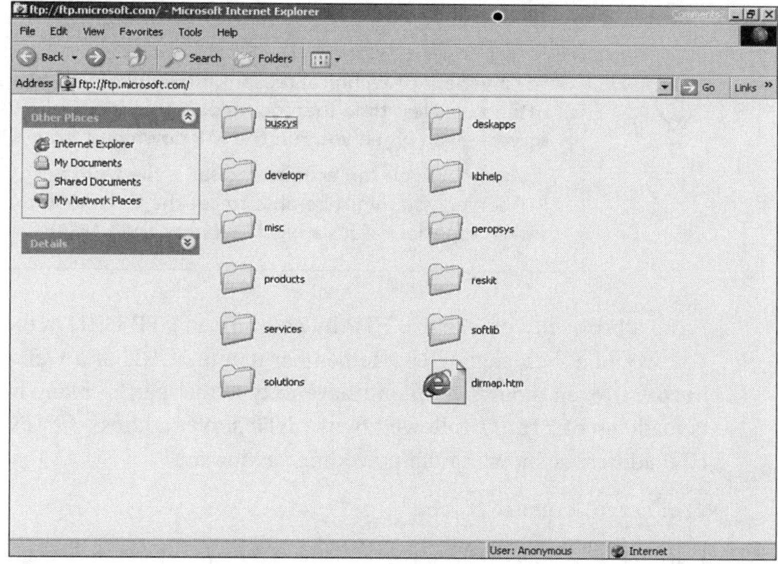

FIGURE B.1
FTP servers organize files into directories.

When you view an FTP directory through some Web browsers, some links in the directory might be preceded by folder icons, indicating that they lead to further listings (*subdirectories*), whereas other links show icons that represent the types of files found there (such as a printed page for a document file).

B

When you look at an FTP directory through Internet Explorer in Windows (see Figure B.1), it looks exactly like an ordinary folder on your PC. The browser window looks like a folder window, files appear as icons, and FTP subdirectories appear as folders. You can open and close FTP folders and files in this window exactly as you would if the folders and files were on your hard disk, by double-clicking on them.

Downloading an FTP File with Your Web Browser

As I pointed out earlier in this book, many Web browsers are multipurpose clients. At the very least, any Web browser can act as a Web client and communicate with Web servers. But many Web clients—including all versions of Netscape Navigator and

Internet Explorer—can double as FTP clients (and triple as Gopher clients—but more about that later). If you have such a browser, you don't need a separate FTP client for downloading files from FTP servers.

For a variety of technical reasons, downloading a file from an FTP server often takes less time than downloading a file of the same size from a Web server—even when you run the FTP download from a Web browser.

If you know you can acquire the same file from both a Web server and an FTP server, you might be able to cut the download time by choosing the FTP server, especially if it's a big file (larger than 1MB).

From a browser, you can use FTP by entering an FTP URL in the address box, just as you would a Web page URL. Remember that the URL of a Web page begins with `http://` (even though you don't have to type that part in many browsers). An FTP URL is made up of `ftp://` followed by the FTP server address. For example, the URLs for the FTP addresses shown in the preceding section are

```
ftp://ftp.microsoft.com
```

```
ftp://ftp.microsoft.com/products/windows/windowsce/007logo.jpg
```

If your Web browser allows you to omit the `http://` prefix when entering a Web page URL, it probably also lets you omit the `ftp://` prefix in an FTP URL.

However, this feature does not work as reliably with FTP URLs as it does with Web URLs. When you're entering an FTP URL in any Web browser, always include the complete `ftp://` prefix.

You can download a file by entering either the complete FTP address of the file or the address of the FTP server, and then browsing through its directories to locate and select the file. When you view FTP directories through a browser, every directory name is a link. Click a directory name and the contents of that directory appear.

Whichever way you get to an FTP file, after you select it, the download proceeds exactly like a regular Web download.

Because most Web browsers do FTP, you'll often come across links in Web pages that are *FTP links*—they point either to an FTP server or directory or to a specific file on the server. In particular, the hits turned up by file searches often include links to files that reside on FTP servers.

If the link points to a file, clicking the link starts the download, just like any other download. You might not even know you're doing an FTP download unless you look closely at the download status message.

If the link points to an FTP server or directory, you'll need to browse through the directory listings to find and select a file. That's when knowing FTP comes in handy.

Using an FTP Client

For most people, the FTP capabilities of a Web browser are all the FTP power they need. But you should know that FTP can do more than download a file. Using FTP, you can send (or *upload*) files to an FTP server so others can download them, and you can control your uploading and downloading to a very fine degree—such as downloading a whole family of files in one operation. Such advanced FTPing typically requires a real FTP client, not a Web browser posing as one.

Why would you ever upload a file? Well, one common case is if you're publishing a Web page. After you create a Web page on your computer, you must upload it to a Web server to make it accessible to others. See Hour 19, "Creating Web Pages and Multimedia Messages."

Windows (95 and newer) and the Macintosh have their own built-in FTP clients, but they're rather old-fashioned, requiring you to learn and use a family of FTP commands. Most casual Net users don't use FTP often enough to justify learning to use these utilitarian FTP clients.

A better choice is an easy-to-use FTP client that combines the simplicity of a Web browser with the full power of FTP. You can find many such clients online by searching or by looking in the Tucows Internet software directory at `www.tucows.com`.

A popular choice for Windows is WS_FTP, which you can get from `www.ipswitch.com`. Another similar program is FTP Commander, a freeware program you can download from `www.vista.ru`. Like most easy FTP clients, these programs display the directory of the FTP site you've accessed on the right side of the window and your PC's hard disk directory on the left. To download a file, you simply move it from one side to the other. In FTP Commander, you do this by highlighting the files you want to transfer and then clicking the Copy button that points to the other side of the window. In a graphical FTP client like WS_FTP, you can do it the same way, or you can actually drag files from one side to the other (see Figure B.2).

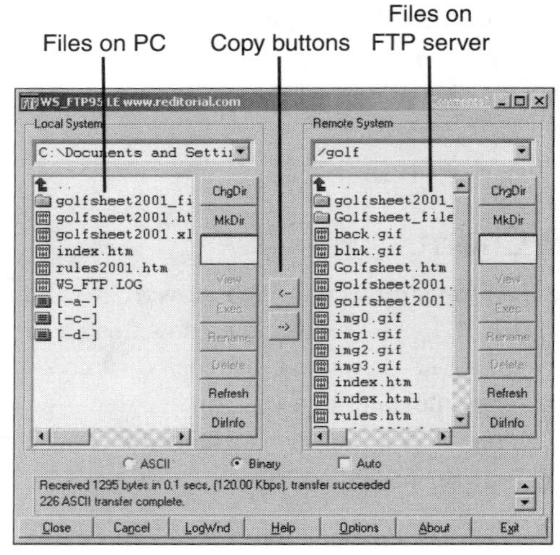

FIGURE B.2
In easier-to-use FTP clients, such as WS_FTP, you transfer files by moving them from one side of the screen to the other.

Remember that URLs are used only in Web browsers. When you're accessing an FTP server through a real FTP client, you do not enter an FTP URL—such as `ftp://ftp.microsoft.com`—but only the FTP address itself—such as `ftp.microsoft.com`.

Burrowing Through the Net with Gopher

Gopher was the first real attempt to make the Net easier to use, and it worked—but not as well as the Web, which was developed hot on Gopher's heels.

Gopher introduced the idea that you can explore online information by navigating through an organized index of menu items—*links*, in effect (see Figure B.3). You can explore all of the information stored on Gopher servers the world over (most of which are in colleges and universities) by clicking your way through the menus and links in Gopherspace.

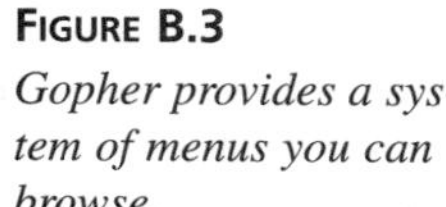

FIGURE B.3
Gopher provides a system of menus you can browse.

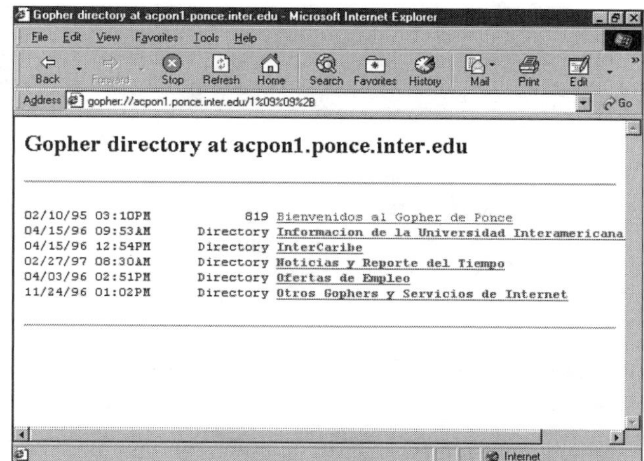

NEW TERM **Gopherspace.** Describes all of the Gopher servers in the world and the information they contain. All of the Gopher servers are interconnected, so clicking a menu item on a menu displayed by one Gopher server might display a new menu or file that's stored on another Gopher server.

As on an FTP server, all of the online information accessible through Gopher is organized like a table of contents or index. You generally begin at a high-level directory. When you click an item in that directory, a more specific subdirectory of choices appears. You continue clicking down through the menu structure until you reach your goal—usually a document that shows you the information to which your choices have led.

Also like FTP, when each item in a Gopher menu is viewed through a Web browser (or graphical Gopher client), it's preceded by an icon that indicates what the link leads to. Items flagged by folder icons lead to other Gopher menus, items flagged by page icons lead to documents, and so on.

Browsing Gopherspace Through a Web Browser

Just as most Web browsers can act as FTP clients, most of them—including, yet again, all versions of Netscape Navigator and Internet Explorer—can also be used as Gopher clients. So you probably already have your Gopher client, ready to go.

In case you hadn't already guessed, you access Gopherspace through a Web browser by entering a Gopher URL in the address box. A Gopher URL begins with the prefix `gopher://` followed by a server address. (This URL stuff gets pretty obvious after a while, doesn't it?)

Unlike a real FTP client, a real Gopher client offers no advantage over using your Web browser for Gopher. But just in case you use a browser that doesn't do Gopher, note that there are Gopher client programs available for just about any system.

Your ISP can probably set you up with a Gopher client from among the programs it offers to subscribers. You can also find a Gopher client by conducting a Web search or by looking in the Tucows Internet software directory at `www.tucows.com`.

Gopher was developed at the University of Minnesota. In fact, Gopher borrows its name from its mascot, although the name also implies that you use it to "burrow" or "go for" information. The University of Minnesota Gopher—sometimes referred to as the "Mother Gopher"— is a great place to begin exploring. You can find it at `gopher.tc.umn.edu`.

Using Remote Computers Through Telnet

Using one Web server is like using any other. The same goes for FTP servers, news servers, and Gopher servers. Telnet, however, is the exception to the rule. Using Telnet, you access another computer out there on the Internet—known to Telnet as a *remote computer*—and use that computer as if you were using a terminal that was connected directly to that computer (see Figure B.4).

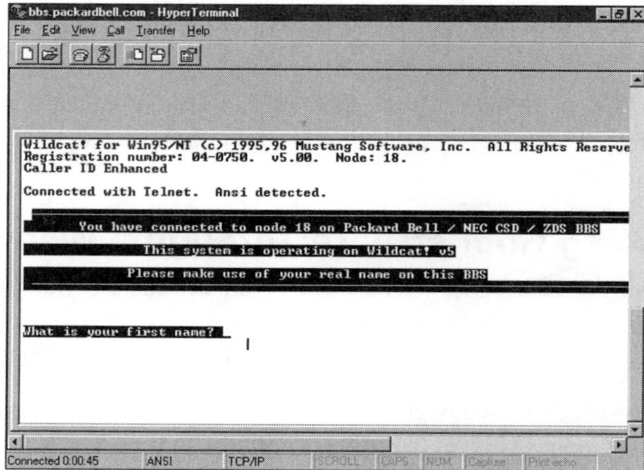

FIGURE B.4
Telnet lets you access a remote computer and use it as if you were there.

Understanding Telnet

As more and more Web sites become dynamic—meaning they pull data from a database as you request it—Telnet is becoming less popular.

> Telnet systems don't support your mouse, trackball, or any other pointing device. You do everything in a Telnet session with your keyboard.

The trick with Telnet is that all the computers you're accessing work differently. Each has its own procedures for logging on, navigating menus, and more. In fact, accessing a remote computer through Telnet is the easy part. Getting logged on to that computer, and then figuring out how to operate it is the challenge.

When you start a Telnet session from a Web link, you'll often find instructions on the same page the link is on that describe how to log on after you click the link. Some helpful Telnet systems actually tell you the guest username and password when you arrive. Some Web pages even serve as handy directories to computers accessible through Telnet.

Getting a Telnet Client

Now, I know what you're expecting. You're expecting me to tell you that your Web browser doubles as a Telnet client. You lose. (*Psych!*) You can use Telnet only through a real Telnet client.

Fortunately, Windows (95 and newer) and the Macintosh have built-in Telnet clients. Even more fortunately, most Windows and Mac Web browsers know how to open the Telnet client automatically, as a helper program, when you click a link leading to a Telnet server. So although you must operate the remote computer through your Telnet client, you can navigate to the server and begin your Telnet session from within your browser.

> Many Gopher links lead to Telnet sessions. A link that leads to Telnet is preceded by an icon that looks like a computer terminal. If you're browsing Gopher from within your Web browser, clicking this link generally opens the Telnet client that your Web browser is configured to open.

To begin a Telnet session, simply open your Start menu, select Run, type the word "telnet" in the Open field, and press Enter. The Microsoft Telnet client will open, as you see in Figure B.5.

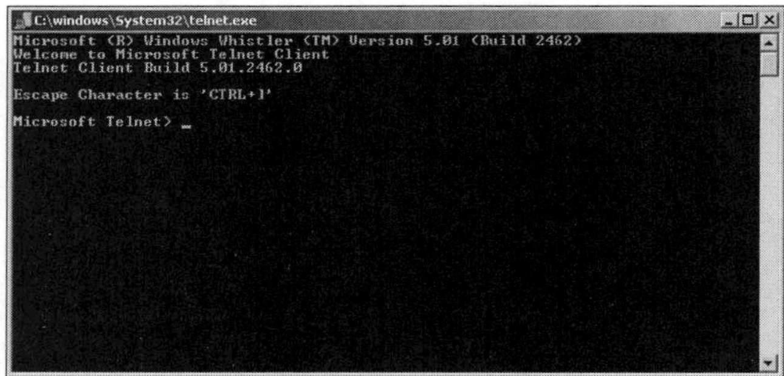

FIGURE B.5
Windows' built-in telnet client allows you to access sites remotely.

Remember, Telnet is all keyboard based, so there's nothing to click with your mouse. You'll need to learn a few easy commands, which can be found by typing "?/help" at the prompt in the telnet client. For example, the command to open a telnet site is the letter "o" followed by a space and the address of the site. So, if you have a telnet address handy, give it a try!

APPENDIX C

Protecting Your Privacy (and Other Security Stuff)

You may hear a lot on the news about what a dangerous place the Internet can be. Because you're reading this, you're brave enough to go online anyhow, even if you're a little concerned. (I like that about you.)

Although there are a few online pitfalls to watch out for, most of the stuff you hear about danger online is hype, and the few real risks are easily avoidable.

Smart Surfing

Forms are the one part of Web browsing where you really need to be careful about your privacy. When you finish making all of your entries and selections in a form, you send it to the server. A button always appears near the form, usually labeled Submit, Send, or Done. (I'll just call it the Submit button from here on, as long as you remember that it's not always labeled that way.) When you click the Submit button, your form entries are sent to the server.

Nothing you do in a form goes to the server until you click the Submit button. You can fill in all or part of a form and, as long as you don't click that button, you can jump to another page or go offline, and you will not have sent a word to the server.

Before you click the submit button, you can also go back and change any entries you made in the form.

Why Are Forms Risky Sometimes?

In general, when you visit a Web site, you retrieve information from the server, but you don't *send* anything about yourself to the server. You can browse all you like, and you're basically anonymous.

When you fill in a form, however, you send to the server the information you supplied in the form. Most of the time, that's perfectly safe because the information you're sending isn't anything private. For example, you perform most Internet searches by typing a search term, a word or two related to what you're looking for, in a simple form. A search term really doesn't reveal much about you.

However, some forms want more from you, including such potentially sensitive information as

- Your name
- Your email address
- Your mailing address or telephone number
- Your credit card number
- Your Social Security number

Most often, a form collects this information when you're making a purchase. If you join some sort of online organization or club, you may also be prompted to supply detailed information about yourself.

And some sites prompt you to "join" the site to use it; to join, you must supply a little information about yourself, which the owner of the site typically uses for market research purposes or sells to other companies.

Important Safety Questions

To make the most of the Web, you can't remain totally private; sooner or later, you're probably going to fill in a form with information about yourself. But before filling in any form, ask yourself four very important questions:

- **Is the information requested by the form really necessary?** Some forms collect more information from you than is really required. Don't feel like you must fill in every blank. Include only as much information as you're comfortable sharing. If you find that the form requires you to fill in blanks you don't want to, consider whether the benefits of the form are worth the risks.

On many online forms, each required field is marked with an asterisk (*) or in some other manner, meaning you can skip the rest. My advice? Never fill in any unrequired field (why reveal more than you have to?), and again, if there's anything in the required fields that you would rather not reveal, skip the form altogether. Nothing offered through that form is worth exposing yourself in any way with which you're not fully comfortable.

- **Do I trust the owners of this site with the information I'm providing?** Is the site operated by a known company, one you trust, or is it a company you've never heard of? Just as you would over the telephone, think twice about whom you're dealing with before revealing anything about yourself. Of course, the more sensitive the information you're sending, the more you must trust the site. You can be much more casual about sharing your email address than about revealing your credit card number.
- **Is the site secure?** Sending information to a secure site does nothing to protect you if the site owner is unscrupulous. But it does protect you against someone other than the site owner seeing the information you send.
- **What is the site's privacy policy?** Many sites provide a link that leads to a page outlining the site's *privacy policy*—the particular set of rules that site promises to follow regarding what it can and cannot do with information you enter on forms there. Checking out the privacy policy may help you decide whether to send information—just remember that there's really no way to know whether a site honestly follows the policy it promises.

Identifying Secure Sites

To use the security systems built in to secure sites, your browser must be compatible with the security systems used. Both Internet Explorer and Netscape Navigator are compatible with the systems used by secure sites today.

When you send information to an unsecure site, it's possible (although difficult) for a criminal to "harvest" that information on its way. For example, if you send your name and credit card info, a crook could intercept that information en route between you and the server and later use it to make a purchase or perpetrate some other kind of fraud.

Using a security-compatible browser to send information to a secure Web site makes harvesting impossible; the information you send will be seen only by the owner of the site to which you send it. Of course, if the site owner is a crook, you still have a problem—he or she can use your information, so you still need to be careful. But secure sites do protect you from intrusion by a third party.

It's also necessary, of course, that the provider's servers are secure, because that's where your data will be sitting after it crosses over the Internet. But it's just like any other credit-card purchase. We worry about the "carbons" on the old-fashioned credit card machines, about what the waiter's doing with your card between the table and the kitchen, and so on. Just watch your statements carefully for purchases you didn't make.

Most browsers show you whether a page you're viewing is on a secure site or not:

- Internet Explorer versions 4 and higher display a locked yellow padlock at the bottom of the window (near the center) when you're communicating with a secure site. The lock does not appear at all when you're on an unsecure site.
- In Netscape (versions 4 and higher), a tiny padlock appears in the lower-left corner of the browser window. When the padlock appears to be unlocked, you are not connected to a secure site. When the padlock is locked and yellow, the site is secure.

In security dialog boxes and warnings in Netscape Navigator, secure sites are often described as *encrypted*. This means the information you send to the site is encrypted, and thus secure.

In addition to little locks and keys, most browsers also have a failsafe: They display a warning message to you before you send information to an unsecure site, so you have a chance to cancel (if you want) before actually sending anything. When you are about to exit a secure site, another warning appears to tell you that, so you can resume exercising the caution you apply when you're on unsecure sites.

Depending upon how they're configured, Internet Explorer and Netscape Navigator display such a warning before you send anything to any site, secure *or* unsecure. The dialog box always informs you whether you're sending to a secure or unsecure site, and gives you a chance to cancel. You can click Yes to go ahead and send the information, or No to abort the transmission.

Knowing Whom You're Dealing With: *Certificates*

Now and then you'll come across a certificate on the Web (see Figure C.1). When you first see one, it seems like a big deal, but it's not. You won't see certificates often, and when you do, you can deal with them in just a click or two.

NEW TERM **Certificate.** A *certificate* is a dialog box that appears when you enter some Web sites to certify the identity of the site and its owner. They provide assurance that you're actually communicating with the company you think you are. They appear most often when a site is sending some sort of program code, such as Java or a plug-in to your browser; the certificate identifies the company so you can decide whether you trust that company enough to let it run a program in your browser.

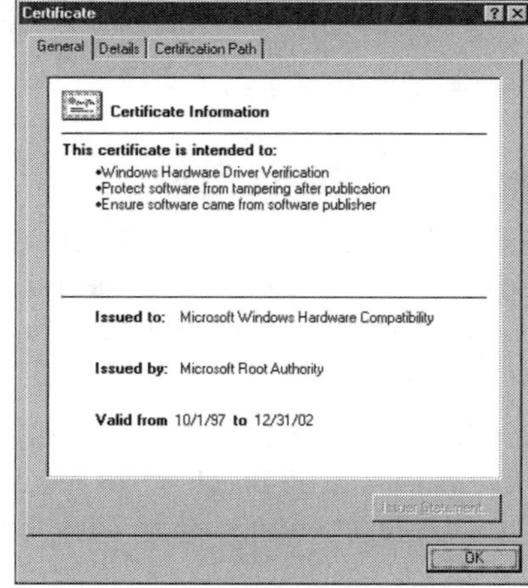

FIGURE C.1
A certificate, which identifies the site to which you're connected.

C

Because a certificate positively identifies the company you're communicating with, you can better decide whether to accept program code, send your credit card or other info, or do anything else that might expose you to risk.

When a certificate appears, your browser usually presents you with a few options for dealing with it: You can accept the certificate (to interact with the site) or reject it. The exact options differ depending on the certificate.

Sometimes, when dealing with the certificate, you'll be prompted to choose whether to accept Java or other *script* code from the site. If you don't trust the site, that gives you the option to reject the certificate to prevent it from sending program code to your computer.

Protecting Yourself with Browser Security

Most browsers let you customize the way they handle security. You can often choose the circumstances under which a browser displays security warnings, choose which sites can run Java or other program code on your computer, and more.

I want to put you in the driver's seat, to give you as much Internet education as is possible in 400 or so pages, so that's why I'm describing the ways you can customize your browser's security settings.

However, I *strongly* caution you to leave your security settings alone until and unless you begin to feel that your browser is applying security that's too lenient or too strict for your particular needs.

The default security settings built in to most browsers strike just the right balance between safety and convenience. So unless you have reason to think they're broke, don't fix 'em.

Customizing Security in Netscape

To open the security area in Netscape Navigator 6, select Privacy and Security from the Tasks menu. You'll see a number of choices for security measures, including a Password Manager and a Form Manager. The Security Manager (see Figure C.2) allows you to set your preferences for when security dialog boxes appear.

Use the check boxes and lists in the various tabs to choose when warnings should appear. (For maximum security, make sure all check boxes on this dialog box are checked.) To learn more about what each setting means, click the dialog box's Help button.

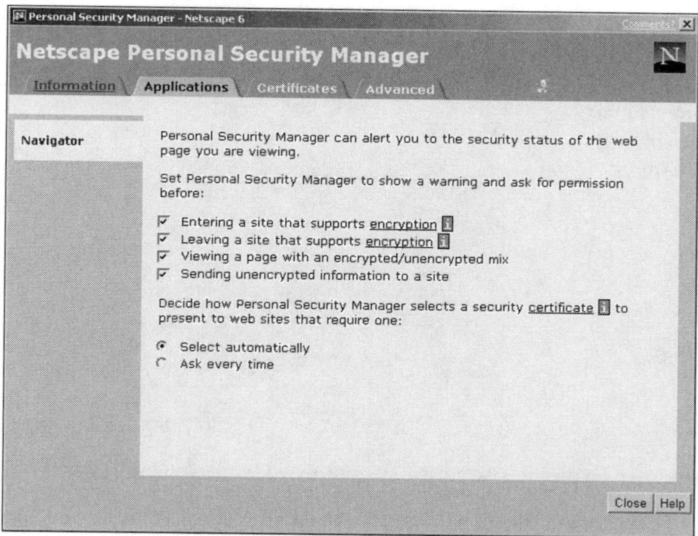

FIGURE C.2
Customizing security settings in Netscape Navigator.

To control whether servers can run Java or JavaScript code on your computer, open Navigator's preferences dialog box (Edit, Preferences) and click Advanced in the list on the left side of the dialog box. A dialog box opens on which you can check or uncheck check boxes to enable or disable Java and JavaScript.

Increasingly, sites assume that your browser can run Java and JavaScript, and are not built to deliver their information effectively to any browser that can't. So in general, it's best to leave these items enabled. However, if you frequently visit particular sites with poor Java or JavaScript programming on them (resulting in a flood of annoying error messages to you) or if a particular activity requires that you shut off Java or JavaScript processing (as some online training sites do), it's handy to know where the "off button" for Java and JavaScript is located.

Customizing Security in Internet Explorer 6

To open Internet Explorer's security settings dialog box (see Figure C.3), choose Tools, Internet Options to open the Internet Properties dialog box, and then click the Security tab.

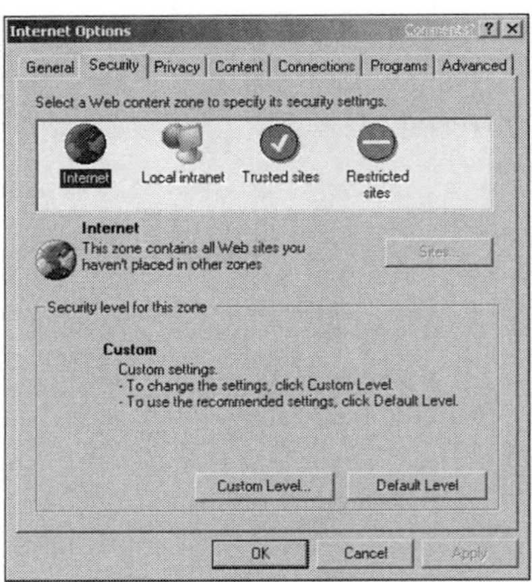

FIGURE C.3
The Internet Properties dialog box's Security tab, where you customize security in Internet Explorer.

Internet Explorer's security system divides all sites into four different security *zones*:

- **Internet zone.** All Internet Web sites that you have not included in your trusted sites zone or your restricted sites zone
- **Local intranet zone.** Includes all pages on your local intranet, if you have one
- **Trusted sites zone.** Includes Web sites you have selected as trusted sites, those for which you may want less strict security than others
- **Restricted sites zone.** Sites you don't particularly trust, generally ones for which you'll want higher security than for other zones

NEW TERM **Intranet.** An intranet is an internal, private network, usually a company network, that looks and acts like the Internet but isn't open to the outside world. If your computer is not part of a company network, you can ignore the local intranet zone.

Using the Security tab, you can add sites to your trusted sites and restricted sites zones and choose security settings for each of the four zones.

Understanding Zone Security Settings

The security settings for a zone determine how aggressive the security system in Internet Explorer will be when communicating with Web sites in that zone. There are four standard security levels: Low, Medium-Low, Medium, and High. For example, you can always view pages on any site, regardless of security settings. (To completely block access to particular sites, use Internet Explorer's Content Advisor.) But within a zone for which high security is in effect, if a server attempts to send a script or other program code that could give your computer a virus or other problem, Internet Explorer prevents the code from reaching your computer.

By default, each of the four zones has a reasonable security setting: high for restricted sites, medium for the intranet and Internet zones, and low for trusted sites.

But if you tire of being prompted every time an Internet page sends some Java to your computer, you might want to change the security level for the Internet zone to low. Conversely, if you've experienced lots of problems with downloaded scripts, you might want to apply high security to the whole Internet zone. And if you trust your co-workers, you might want to change your intranet zone to low security.

I Want a Cookie! I *Don't* Want a Cookie!

Besides scripts, servers can put another thing on your computer you may not know about—cookies. A cookie is a small amount of information a server stores on your computer for later reference. Typically, a server stores an identifying code of some sort on your computer so that it can automatically identify you any time you visit.

Cookies are usually harmless and often useful. For example, an online store from which you've purchased once may put a cookie on your computer that identifies you. Anytime you return to that site to shop, the server automatically knows who you are, and you needn't bother filling in a form to identify yourself.

But your computer is your domain, and you get to decide what someone else can put there. You can customize either of the Big Two browsers to accept or reject cookies. If you reject them all, however, you may not be able to access some online merchants.

In Internet Explorer, open the Tools menu and select Internet Options. On the Security tab, highlight the Internet zone and click Custom Level. Scroll down the list until you see the options for cookies, and make your selections.

In Netscape 6, select Preferences from the Edit menu. Under Advanced, select Cookies, and you'll be able to make your selections for how to handle them.

C

> Internet Explorer's Security Settings dialog box is a valuable but tricky place. After you gain experience, you can use it to customize the browser to a high degree. But before you have experience, making random changes here is likely to change your online life in ways you won't enjoy.
>
> If you inadvertently change something in the dialog box and don't know how to fix it, click the Reset button.

Special Considerations for Broadband Internet Users

If you use a cable Internet connection or DSL line, your computer is considered somewhat more vulnerable to hackers, viruses, and other forms of Internet mischief than computers that hook up through regular dial-up lines. That's true in part because of the "always-on" nature of these connections; when you're online 24 hours a day, you leave yourself open to intrusion at all times. A *firewall* allows you to protect your computer from hackers, who often target the IP address ranges used by broadband providers.

NEW TERM **Firewall.** Firewalls used to be the exclusive province of corporate networks, but concern over broadband security has moved firewalls into the home. You can purchase easy-to-use software packages that set up a firewall for you and also help guard your computer in other ways. Table C.1 lists some of these products, along with the URLs where you can learn more about each.

TABLE C.1 Internet Security Packages Featuring Firewall Protection

Program	*URL for Info*
Norton Internet Security 2001	`www.symantec.com`
McAfee Personal Firewall	`www.mcafee.com`
eSafe	`www.ealaddin.com`
Zone Alarm	`www.zonelabs.com`
BlackIce Agent	`www.networkice.com`

Like all forms of protection, such as preventing cookies, a firewall makes you safer, but may also make using some advanced Internet services, such as online training, difficult or impossible.

If you set up a firewall, check the software's manual to learn how to temporarily disable the firewall or perform other adjustments to enable these services to do their thing.

Watching Out for Spyware

This one might sound a little bit "out there," but it's actually a growing concern in the Internet community. Some of the programs you download may contain a little "extra" that you might not want on your system.

As another means of making money on their software, some developers are selling the rights to advertisers to place banners in their products. That's not a big deal, but they may come with a little piece of tracking software that records your surfing tendencies and reports them back to the mothership.

These companies claim that no "private" data is transmitted, but nonetheless, your habits are being watched and reported. It's a little too Big Brother-like for my liking.

There are software programs you can get that will rid your computer of these "extras." Check out Spychecker at `www.spychecker.com`, and Ad-Aware at `www.lavasoft.de`.

GLOSSARY

ActiveX. A set of rules for sharing information between applications. ActiveX controls make it easier for files to be executed by a **browser.**

address book. A feature in **email** programs that stores your contacts' **email address** and other information for reference and to make addressing an email message easier.

attachment. A computer file (graphics, text, program, or any other type) sent with an email message.

authoring. The process of writing a **Web page**.

BCC (blind carbon copy). When emailing, it is a way to send a copy of an email message without letting the other recipients know you are sending a copy.

Bookmark. **Netscape Navigator**'s method for letting a user create a shortcut back to a Web page the user will want to revisit. See also **Favorite**.

Boolean operators. These operators are designed to put conditions on a search. The most common Boolean operators are `AND`, `OR`, and `NOT`.

broadband. Any of several different types of Internet connections that provide speeds far in excess of typical dial-up connections; see **cable Internet**, see **DSL**.

browse. To wander around a portion of the World Wide Web, screen by screen, looking for items of interest. Also known as *surfing* or *cruising*.

browser. An Internet program used to explore the **World Wide Web**; two examples are **Internet Explorer** and **Netscape**.

cable Internet. A new way to get very fast Internet service (in limited areas) through the same cable through which you get cable television.

CC (carbon copy). A copy of an email message, sent to someone other than the message's principal recipient.

cellular modem. Used most often in portable computers, a **modem** that communicates without connection to a phone line, just as a cellular phone does. Can be used to access the Internet from places where no phone line is available. See also **wireless modem.**

certificate. A file used in secure connections to authenticate the server to a client.

Chat. An Internet resource, sometimes also known as Internet Relay Chat (IRC), that allows two or more Internet users to participate in a live conversation through typing messages.

chat client. The program required for participating in a **chat** session.

client. A software tool for using a particular type of Internet server resource. A client interacts with a **server** on which the resource is located.

Communicator. Also known as Netscape 4.7, it is a suite of Internet tools from Netscape Communications Corp. It includes a Web browser (**Navigator**), email and newsreader (Messenger), and Web authoring (**Composer**).

Composer. The Web authoring component of Netscape Communicator.

compression. The process of making a computer file smaller so that it can be copied more quickly between computers. Compressed files, sometimes called zip files, must be decompressed on the receiving computer before they can be used.

cookie. A collection of information that a Web server can leave on your computer for later access.

cross-posting. A method by which you can post a single article to multiple **newsgroups**.

cyberspace. A broad expression used to describe the activity, communication, and culture happening on the Internet and other computer networks.

dial-up IP account. An Internet account, accessed through a modem and telephone line, that offers complete access to the Internet through TCP/IP communications.

direct connection. A permanent, 24-hour link between a computer and the Internet. A computer with a direct connection can use the Internet at any time.

DNS. (Domain Name System) A method that converts word-based addresses, or *domain names*, into **IP addresses**. This allows users to remember word addresses, like `www.microsoft.com`, instead of the string of numbers that is an IP address.

domain name. See **DNS**.

download. Transferring a file from a host computer to your computer.

DSL. Digital subscriber line, a **broadband** Internet connection that uses your regular phone line.

email. Short for *electronic mail*. A system that enables a person to compose a message on a computer and transmit that message through a computer network, such as the Internet, to another computer user.

email address. The word-based Internet address of a user, typically made up of a username, an `@` sign, and a domain name (`user@domain`).

emoticons. Short for *emotional icons*, these character combinations are a way to express emotion in typed messages, such as email and newsgroup messages. For example, `:)` is a smile.

Explorer. See **Internet Explorer**.

FAQ file. Short for *Frequently Asked Questions file*. A computer file containing the answers to frequently asked questions about a particular topic.

Favorite. **Internet Explorer**'s method for letting a user create a shortcut back to a Web page the user will want to revisit. See also **Bookmark**.

filter. A system for automatically organizing and deleting selected email messages.

flame. Hostile messages, often sent through email or posted in newsgroups, from Internet users in reaction to breaches of **netiquette**.

form. A part of a Web page in which users can type entries or make selections.

frame. A discrete part, or "pane," in a Web page in which the screen area has been divided up into multiple, independent panes, each of which contains a separate document.

freeware. Software available to anyone, free of charge (unlike **shareware**, which requires payment).

FrontPage Express. The WYSIWYG (What-You-See-Is-What-You-Get) HTML (Web page) editor shipped with Internet Explorer.

FTP. Short for *File Transfer Protocol*. The basic method for copying a file from one computer to another through the Internet.

GIF. (Graphic Interchange Format) A form of image file, using the file extension `.gif`, commonly used for **inline images** in Web pages.

Gopher. An Internet service using a system of menus layered on top of existing resources that makes locating information and using services easier. See Appendix B.

helper program. Programs that run or show files that aren't part of a Web page and don't appear as part of the Web browser.

home page. Frequently, this term refers to the cover of a particular Web site. The home page is the main, or first, page displayed for an organization's or person's World Wide Web site. "Home page" also describes the page a Web browser is configured to access first when you go online, or anytime you click the browser's Home button.

HTML. (Hypertext Markup Language) The document formatting language used to create pages on the World Wide Web.

hyperlink. See **link**.

imagemap. In a Web page, a single picture that contains multiple **links,** each leading somewhere different.

inline image. An image that appears within the layout of a Web page.

instant message. A message that appears to its recipient the instant you send it, if the recipient happens to be online at the time.

Internet. A large, loosely organized internetwork connecting public and private computer systems all over the world so that they can exchange messages and share information.

Internet Explorer. A **browser** for the World Wide Web, distributed by Microsoft and available for free download from the Web and in a variety of software packages.

Internet Relay Chat. See **Chat**.

Internet service provider. A company from which you can obtain access to the Internet. This term, or its abbreviation, ISP, is often used to distinguish the many companies that offer Internet access from **online services**, another kind of Internet provider.

intranet. An internal corporate network, usually a local area network, that is based on Internet technologies, such as the use of Web **browsers** to display information.

IP address. The numeric Internet address of a user or computer, made up of four sets of numbers separated by periods; for example, `192.180.77.69`. In practice, Internet users more often encounter word-based addresses (`www.kooky.com`), which are translated into numerical IP addresses by the domain name system (**DNS**).

IRC. See **Chat**.

ISP. See **Internet service provider**.

Java/JavaScript. Two of the programming languages used for enabling some advanced and interactive capabilities in Web pages.

link. In a **Web page**, a block of text, an image, or part of an image that the user can activate (usually by clicking) to make something happen. Clicking on links can jump the user to another Web page, start a program, or **download** a file.

listserv. A program that automatically manages a **mailing list**.

log on. The act of accessing a computer system by typing a required username (or user ID) and password. Also described by other terms, including *sign on/in*, or *log in*.

lurking. Reading a newsgroup without posting to it, to study its culture.

mailing list. An online discussion group in which members share news and information through broadcasted email messages.

MIME. (Multipurpose Internet Mail Extensions) A standard for designating how various types of files are to be treated online.

modem. A device that allows your computer to talk to other computers using your phone line.

MP3. A type of computer audio file, available for **download** from the Internet, that contains near-CD-quality music you can play offline.

multimedia. A description for systems capable of displaying or playing text, pictures, sound, video, and animation, or a way of describing that material.

Navigator. The name of the popular browser from Netscape Communications Corp., available by itself, or within the **Communicator** suite. Navigator is often referred to casually as "Netscape," after its creator. Like Internet Explorer, it may be **downloaded** free from the Internet.

netiquette. The code of proper conduct (etiquette) on the Internet.

NetMeeting. A voice/video conferencing client included in the Internet Explorer suite.

Netscape. The name of the popular browser from Netscape Communications Corp. Like Internet Explorer, it may be **downloaded** free from the Internet.

network. A set of computers interconnected so that they can communicate and share information and resources. Connected networks together form an internetwork.

newsgroup. An Internet resource through which people post and read messages related to a specific topic. See Hour 7.

newsreader. A **client** program for reading and posting messages on **newsgroups**.

offline. The state of being disconnected from a network.

online. The state of being connected to a network.

online service. A company such as America Online or CompuServe that offers its subscribers both Internet access and unique content available only on the service.

outbox. A term used in some **email** programs to describe a folder where outgoing messages are stored temporarily until the user is ready to send them.

pane. See **frame**.

password. A secret code, known only to the user, that allows the user to access a computer that is protected by a security system.

Personal Digital Assistant. A handheld computer device such as a Palm-based or Pocket PC unit, used by people for personal organization. Properly equipped PDAs can access the Internet wirelessly.

plug-in. A program that increases the capabilities of a Web browser.

portal. A Web page that is designed to serve as a popular starting point for Web-surfing sessions. Portals typically include tools for searching the Web; links to news, weather, and sports scores; and other popular links.

PPP. (Point-to-Point Protocol) One kind of communications protocol that enables a **dial-up IP** connection.

search tool. A Web page that provides tools for finding specific information on the Internet.

server. A networked computer that serves a particular type of information to users or performs a particular function.

shareware. Software programs that users are permitted to acquire and evaluate for free. Shareware is different from freeware in that, if a person likes the shareware program and plans to use it on a regular basis, he or she is expected to send a fee to the programmer.

shortcut. See **Favorite** and **Bookmark**.

shorthand. A system of letter abbreviations used to efficiently express certain ideas in email messages, newsgroup postings, and Internet Relay Chat sessions. Examples are IMO (in my opinion) and BTW (by the way).

spam. Mass emailed material meant for promotion, advertisement, or annoyance.

streaming audio/video. The capability of multimedia to begin playback as the file is being downloaded; makes live audio/video broadcasts through the Internet possible.

TCP/IP. (Transmission Control Protocol/Internet Protocol) The fundamental set of inter-networking protocols that makes the Internet work.

Telnet. A service for accessing other computers on the Internet and for using the resources that are there.

thread. A series of newsgroup articles all dealing with the same topic. Someone replies to an article, and then someone else replies to the reply, and so on.

upload. Transferring a file to a host computer from your computer.

URL. Short for *Uniform Resource Locator*. A method of standardizing the addresses of different types of Internet resources so that they can all be accessed easily from within a Web browser.

username. Used with a password to gain access to a computer. A dial-up IP user typically has a username and password for dialing the access provider's Internet server.

Web. See World Wide Web.

Web email. A method of sending and receiving email that is used through a browser rather than an email client program.

Web page. A document stored on a Web server, typically in the file format HTML (.htm or .html). Web pages are retrieved from Web **servers** and displayed by Web **browsers**.

Web site. A collection of World Wide Web documents, usually consisting of a home, or top, page and several related pages.

wireless modem. Used most often in portable computers and handheld devices, a **modem** that communicates without connection to a phone line, using radio communications or another medium. A wireless modem is used the same way as a **cellular modem**, but does not use the cellular telephone networks for its communications.

World Wide Web. (WWW or Web) An Internet service composed of a set of computers that provides an easy-to-use system for finding information and moving among resources.

zip file. See **compression**.

INDEX

Symbols

A

B

D

F

J - K

L

M

N

P

Q - R

T

U - V

X - Y - Z